# TRANSNATIONAL
# INDUSTRIAL RELATIONS

# TRANSNATIONAL INDUSTRIAL RELATIONS

## THE IMPACT OF MULTI-NATIONAL CORPORATIONS AND ECONOMIC REGIONALISM ON INDUSTRIAL RELATIONS

*A Symposium held at Geneva by
the International Institute for Labour Studies*

EDITED BY

## HANS GÜNTER

## PALGRAVE MACMILLAN

© The International Institute for Labour Studies 1972

Softcover reprint of the hardcover 7th edition 1972

All rights reserved. No part of this publication
may be reproduced or transmitted, in any form
or by any means, without permission.

*First published 1972 by*
THE MACMILLAN PRESS LTD
*London and Basingstoke*
*Associated companies in New York Toronto*
*Dublin Melbourne Johannesburg and Madras*

Library of Congress catalog card no. 77–175933

SBN 333 13004 9

ISBN 978-1-349-01293-0     ISBN 978-1-349-01291-6 (eBook)
DOI 10.1007/978-1-349-01291-6

This volume consists mainly of papers
presented to and discussed at the
Symposium on International Collective Bargaining
held at the International Institute for Labour Studies
from 29 April to 2 May 1969
under the chairmanship of
OTTO KAHN-FREUND

# CONTENTS

*Contents*

vi

Contents

vii

# AUTHORS AND PARTICIPANTS

*Chairman*

Otto Kahn-Freund, Professor of Comparative Law, University of Oxford, United Kingdom.

*Director of the Symposium*

Robert W. Cox,* Director, International Institute for Labour Studies, Geneva, Switzerland.

*Rapporteur*

Hans Günter,* Staff Associate, International Institute for Labour Studies, Geneva, Switzerland.

*Participants*

Marcel Biart, Assistant Director, Personnel Department, Solvay et Cie S.A., Brussels, Belgium.

David H. Blake,* Assistant Professor of Political Science, Wayne State University, Detroit, United States.

Roger Blanpain,* Director, Institute for Labour Relations, University of Louvain, Belgium.

Karl Casserini,* Head of the Economics Department, International Metalworkers' Federation, Geneva, Switzerland.

Richard P. Conlon, Chairman and Managing Director, Business International S.A., Geneva, Switzerland.

Michel Despax,* Professor, Faculty of Law and Economics, University of Toulouse, France.

J. E. van Dierendonck,* Head of the Directorate for Social Affairs, Commission of the European Communities, Brussels, Belgium.

Pierre Granjeat, Conseiller référendaire, Cour des Comptes, Paris, France.

Paul Haenni, Honorary Director, International Management Development Institute, Geneva, Switzerland.

Jeffrey Harrod,* Graduate Institute of International Studies, Geneva, Switzerland.

Jacques Houssiaux,* Professeur, Faculty of Law and Economics, University of Paris, France.

* Author.

ix

## Authors and Participants

Marcos Kaplan,[*][1] Professor, Institute of International Studies, University of Chile, Santiago, Chile.

Jack Lee,[*] President, Institute of Personnel Management, London, United Kingdom.

Charles Levinson, General Secretary, International Federation of Chemical and General Workers' Unions, Geneva, Switzerland.

Heribert Maier, Head of the Economic, Social and Political Department, International Confederation of Free Trade Unions, Brussels, Belgium.

Zdeněk Mošna,[*] Dean of the Faculty of Management and Head of the Department of Labour, Economics and Personnel Management, Prague School of Economics, Czechoslovakia.

Joseph S. Nye,[*] Associate Professor of Government and Research Associate, Center for International Affairs, Harvard University, United States.

Clas-Erik Odhner, Head of the Research Department, Swedish Confederation of Trade Unions, Stockholm, Sweden.

M. G. O'Leary, Vice-President, Alcan International Ltd, Montreal, Canada.

Michel Parion, Chief of the Social Division, French National Building Federation, and Secretary-General, International Federation of European Building Employers, Paris, France.

Howard Perlmutter,[*] Professor, Wharton Graduate School of Finance and Commerce, University of Pennsylvania, United States.

B. C. Roberts,[*] Professor of Industrial Relations, London School of Economics and Political Science, United Kingdom.

Johannes Schregle, Chief, Labour Law and Labour Relations Branch, International Labour Office, Geneva, Switzerland.

Norman Scott,[*] Graduate Institute of International Studies, Geneva, Switzerland.

Kenneth F. Walker, Senior Staff Associate, International Institute for Labour Studies, Geneva, Switzerland.

Reinhold Weil, Director, Institute for Applied Labour Science, Cologne, Federal Republic of Germany.

---

[*] Author.
[1] Professor Kaplan was unable to attend the Symposium.

x

# INTRODUCTION

*by*

*Hans Günter*

## I. THE SETTING FOR TRANSNATIONAL INDUSTRIAL RELATIONS

WHILE the main impetus for the studies presented in this volume was provided by the widespread interest in the implications of international collective bargaining, its subject is a rather broader one. It is concerned with the effects, in the field of industrial relations, of developments in world economic organisation. The term 'transnational' is used here to describe processes crossing national boundaries. Industrial relations become transnationalised to the extent that conditions for labour are affected by these processes. International collective bargaining, i.e. bargaining between management and unions setting rules for labour employed in different countries, is one formal procedure by which industrial relations would become transnationalised. However, many other formal or informal processes could operate transnationally on industrial relations, e.g. setting of standard guidelines centrally by multi-national management, co-ordination of bargaining or action programmes between national unions, harmonisation of economic conditions or social legislation, or simply the influence of the demonstration effect. These processes may involve management, labour or both as well as States or international organisations. Some of these processes are more closely examined in later chapters of this book.

Two major contemporary trends which might be conducive to a transnationalisation of industrial relations are the growth of the multi-national corporation and the growth of regional economic integration (economic regionalism).[1] Neither of these is a new phenomenon. What is new about them is, firstly, the acceleration of growth in recent decades. This acceleration becomes evident from increases in turnover

---

[1] 'Regional' is used throughout as referring to an international grouping of contiguous States and not as applying to geographical sub-divisions of a State.

and investments in the case of the multi-national corporations, and, as regards regional economic integration, from the number of inter-governmental organisations created. Secondly, both phenomena have undergone qualitative change. For the multi-national corporation this change is associated with the modern technology and information techniques embodied in its operations, and its resulting control over key industries in many countries. As regards regional economic integration, especially its more structured forms for which the European Common Market is a prototype, qualitative change stems from the fact that economic unification is viewed as a preliminary stage to some sort of regional political integration.

The present-day multi-national corporation has an active controlling interest which goes far beyond the capital investment aspect which may have predominated in earlier periods of 'internationalisation'.[1] The operations and behaviour of multi-national firms have therefore both quantitatively and qualitatively a greater economic and social impact than in the past. Taking these characteristics of modern inter-national business into account, the growth of the multi-national corporation can be defined as the extension of a 'single management decision-making system into a number of countries.[2] This system is characterised by a headquarters, usually found in the country of origin of the corporation, which influences (directs, co-ordinates or guides) decisions or operations in subsidiaries abroad in line with an optimal use of the resources under its control.[3] Commanding resources transnationally under functional considerations, the single management decision-making system may come into conflict with national or regional aspirations.

The classic organisational forms of regional economic integration[4] are free trade areas (absence of international tariffs between members) or customs unions (no internal tariffs, and common external tariff). Their merits and demerits are traditionally discussed in terms of 'trade

---

[1] i.e. formal business organisation on an international scale as to shareholders or operations.

[2] Without regard as to whether the system is ethnocentric, polycentric or geocentric, in Howard V. Perlmutter's terminology (see Chapter 2).

[3] The 'typical' multi-national corporation is probably the worldwide manufacturing firm. Trading companies may be on the borderline. Financial holding companies, less concerned with an optimal allocation of total resources, might not usually fall within the multi-national category. Admittedly, it can be difficult in certain cases to establish whether a single management decision-making system exists, the more so as this may vary as to the types of decision. Careful examination may especially be required to ascertain whether a company is multi-national with regard to specific industrial relations issues.

[4] Commonly judged on measures of economic interchange (transactions of goods, services and factors of production) i.e. criteria for behavioural integration.

creation' or 'trade diversion'.[1] Modern economic integration still uses the two organisational forms mentioned and still is judged on its effects upon world trade,[2] but particularly in the case of the E.E.C. and LAFTA strive ultimately towards broad mobilisation of a region's resources and modernisation of its structures involving policies and central decision-making processes for the whole of the region, i.e. integration, in its full political sense. In speaking of 'international regionalism', Joseph S. Nye[3] thinks particularly of such complex types of economic integration with a spillover to political organisation.

Many economists and politicians look at the multi-national corporation and at regional economic integration as engines of growth.

Interest in them now rivals or takes precedence over a preoccupation with world trade expansion as a means of promoting growth. As regards their growth effect, both phenomena appear to be mutually reinforcing. Regional economic integration in Europe and elsewhere has favoured the operations and spread of multi-national corporations. In turn, multi-national corporations, prominent in high growth industries may enhance the economic performance of the region.

While economic growth generates the resources needed for solving social problems nationally and on a world scale, it is bound to accentuate these problems if accompanied by increasing inequalities. An exclusive concern with growth maximisation by the multi-national corporation might result in policies which aggravate national or sectoral inequalities unless adequately counteracted by welfare re-distribution falling usually within the competence of the State. Economic integration via the creation of a common market develops some automatic tendencies towards a narrowing of national or sectoral economic differentials and in structured forms of integration, such as the E.E.C., inequalities are reduced through explicit measures of economic and social harmonisation.

Problems of inequalities and of control resulting from the growth of the multi-national corporation in the European region are the main concern of Jean-Jacques Servan-Schreiber's *Le défi américain*. [4] The remedy

---

[1] Even the modern theoretical treatment of these issues, e.g. by J. Viner: *The Customs Union Issue* (New York, Carnegie Endowment of International Peace, 1950), barely goes beyond this basic dichotomy.

[2] The trade diversion caused by the functioning of the E.E.C. – especially through its preferential arrangements with associated member countries – conflicts with the basic GATT doctrine, i.e. the achievement of maximum growth benefits from world trade and their optimal distribution.

[3] See Chapter 3.

[4] English edition: *The American Challenge* (New York, Atheneum, 1968).

which he and others advocate against the predominance of the foreign-based (American) corporation is *le pari européen*[1] (the European gamble), i.e. a commitment by European Governments to promote the mobilis-ation and concentration of the resources of the region. Integration on a continental basis in respect of the economic, technological and, hope-fully, some aspects of the political system is expected to countervail the functionally organised world-wide corporation. In some people's opinion, the creation of regional multi-national corporations (promoted by the E.E.C. through the elaboration of a European company legis-lation and suggested for Latin America by Marcos Kaplan[2] in the form of a public multi-national corporation for Latin America) is the most adequate organisational form of regional co-operation. It means that functional regional integration would be opposed to functional world-wide integration for particular lines of economic activity. If this is going to happen, it may be, as Caroline M. Miles suggests,[3] that the formation of regional companies is essential for true integration of regional markets.

This is the general setting in which transnational industrial relations may emerge. The multi-national corporation, either world-wide or regionally organised, an easily identified entity as regards economic resources and decision-making, appears to have the highest potential for conferring on industrial relations transnational features. Except for a few cases,[4] transnational decisions on work rules and related issues of interest to labour emanate, where they have appeared at all, unilaterally from management (usually in the form of general company guidelines for personnel policy). While industrial relations in the national circumstances and also in the regional framework of the E.E.C. are now widely structured on a 'pluralistic' basis, which recognises a social role for organised labour at the different levels, the multi-national firm as a whole is usually a 'unitary' structure.[5] Particularly

[1] Title of a book by Louis Armand and Michel Drancourt (Paris, Librairie Athène, Fayard, 1963).
[2] See Chapter 9.
[3] See Caroline M. Miles: 'The International Corporation', *International Affairs*, Vol. 45, No. 2, April 1969, p. 266.
[4] Such as the international collective bargaining in 1967 between Chrysler and U.A.W. for their workers in the United States and Canada; the co-ordination in 1969 of national bargaining in the subsidiaries of St Gobain by the International Chemical and General Workers' Federation, leading to the acceptance of the demands of national unions; and, possibly, talks between the International Metalworkers' Federation and Philips, Brown–Boveri and other firms of European origin regarding issues in their subsidiaries.
[5] Adapting the terminology of A. Fox in *Industrial Sociology and Industrial Relations* (Royal Commission on Trade Union's and Employers' Association, Research Papers 3, H.M.S.O. London 1966, Part 1, pp. 2–14).

in the case where wages and labour conditions in a firm's subsidiaries are better than those prevailing in comparable local establishments, and local unions are accepted for industrial relations, multi-national management often sees little justification for a protective function of unions relating to the company as a whole. Moreover, as the few precedents show, negotiations with unions at the level of the entire corporation necessarily will exceed the field of work rules proper to embrace aspects considered as 'managerial prerogatives', such as decisions on investments, location of plants, introduction of technological change, redundancy, etc. Such a sharing of decision making is usually viewed by multi-national management as a potential menace to the company's particular competence from which it derives a comparative advantage: the world-wide optimal allocation of resources.

In the circumstances, the development of regularised transnational industrial relations appears to depend foremost both upon managerial policy and upon the reactions of unions to the multi-national corporation. The major issue in the union reaction is their ability to evolve an efficient multi-national counterpart structure to the corporation. Symbiosis (of the multi-national corporation and the unions) seems to be, as Robert W. Cox puts it in the following chapter 'the reaction most likely to lead towards transnational industrial relations'.

## II. PRESENTATION OF MATERIAL AND ACKNOWLEDGEMENTS

The papers presented as chapters of the present volume are grouped under a number of headings which, starting with an outline of the problem area and an evaluation of the underlying trends, distinguish several specific themes which emerged during the discussions at the 1969 Symposium. The account of the discussion is also arranged according to these major headings and thus includes elements of an analysis. It is intended thus to elaborate and develop the ideas presented by the authors in their papers and to highlight new issues and future research needs identified in the discussions.

For analytical reasons an attempt has been made in the groupings of the chapters to separate industrial relations implications of the multi-national corporation from the implications of regional economic integration. In real life situations, however, these trends may be intimately inter-locked as the contributions of David H. Blake and

Jacques Houssiaux tend to demonstrate. Exceptionally, the two case studies of Canada and Jamaica have not been presented as relating to a particular theme, but are placed together firstly because of the similarity in their methodological approach, and secondly in order to contrast the impact of multi-national corporations in two very dissimilar environments. The chapter written by Marcos Kaplan, which at first sight might have been included under the heading of economic integration, has been presented separately because of the originality of its suggestions and the region-specific environment in which they are embedded.

Finally, all chapters relating to different aspects of the E.E.C. experience have been grouped together, although further sub-divisions according to special areas or as to analytical, normative or descriptive material might have been tempting. However, despite certain diversities, they deal with an entity which might be lost if broken up further.

An annotated bibliography on multi-national corporations, focusing on aspects directly relevant to the themes of the present book, is included as an appendix. The bibliography is restricted to recent publications in English and French. Time constraints impeded the compilation of a similar bibliography (over and above the literature referred to in the pertinent chapters) for the subject of regional economic integration. For some additional recent material relating to the E.E.C. and to EFTA, the interested reader might wish to refer to the annotated bibliography *International Integration*, published by the O.E.C.D.

The present book is a co-operative effort. Contributions of various kind have facilitated my editorial task. I am particularly thankful to Robert W. Cox, Director of the International Institute for Labour Studies, for his advice, especially on the conceptual problems of the issues under review – and the patience with which he has followed the various time-consuming stages of editing. I also wish to record my appreciation to the authors of chapters and all participants of the 1969 Symposium. Their co-operation as regards the required editorial modifications and the suggestions which they offered for the summary account of the discussions have been of great value. I am grateful for the comments of Jeffrey Harrod, and the assistance in stylistic editing by Karel Norsky, Staff Associates of the Institute. The annexed bibliography has grown out of a document prepared for the 1969 Symposium and has been prepared in the library of the Institute under the direction of the Librarian, Mr Oldrich Cerny. My thanks also go to the secretarial staff of the Institute for typing and retyping the manuscripts; they had the kindness of leaving the editor the illusion that they were enthusiastic about it. May I add that, in spite of the great amount of help which I received, the errors and the conclusions in the parts written by myself are naturally exclusively mine.

# THE THEME AND ITS SETTING

In the following chapter, Robert W. Cox, Director of the International Institute of Labour Studies, sketches a framework for the study of transnational tendencies in industrial relations and highlights some of the main issues involved. He assumes that industrial relations systems are subordinate to other systems—economic, political and technological—and will therefore reflect changes occurring in those fields as a result of two major contemporary trends in world economic structure: the growth of functionally organised multinational corporations, and the growth of regionally organised economic integration.

To the extent that these trends lead to transnational decision-making about major work rules and earnings, industrial relations would tend to become themselves transnational. On the other hand, the strategies adopted by the parties in industrial relations in response to such developments might affect the future of world economic organisation. In this way, Robert W. Cox outlines the major theme and setting of the book.

Chapter 1

# BASIC TRENDS AFFECTING THE LOCATION OF DECISION-MAKING POWERS IN INDUSTRIAL RELATIONS

*by*

*Robert W. Cox*

THE purpose of this symposium[1] is to examine the prospects for transnational industrial relations – that is, the prospect that the processes for making decisions about work rules, incomes and the other subject matter of industrial relations will increasingly flow across national boundaries and will therefore overflow the national institutions which have been dealing with them until they become restructured internationally.

It seems doubtful if such a change would come about through the development of industrial relations systems in and of themselves. There is no dynamic native to industrial relations systems which tends to transform them from their national base into international systems. This at any rate is an initial assumption, that industrial relations are subordinate to other systems – economic, political and technological systems – which determine their character. A change towards making industrial relations transnational would come about, then, as a result of changes in these determining factors.

Two main factors which might lead to such a development of transnational industrial relations are the growth of the multi-national corporation and of regional economic integration (the latter especially in Western Europe, but potentially in other areas of the world as well). These two factors have also to be fitted into a larger picture, to be seen as salient aspects of a gradual and far-reaching change in economic and political structures with worldwide implications. The first step in the inquiry should thus be to identify and to assess the relative strength of the basic trends which confront one another – trends in economic and political structures with worldwide implications – and to speculate concerning both their possible impact on industrial relations

[1] The IILS Symposium on International Collective Bargaining.

and, conversely, the ways in which industrial relations may influence these trends.

This is a speculative exercise, in which the subjective quality of individual judgment and individual perspectives is bound to play a big role. It is therefore important, in trying to reason about future possibilities or probabilities, to start by examining the bases upon which projections can be made about the forces conditioning the future. It is in this spirit that I put forward some initial conjectures and raise some questions.

Mention of the multi-national corporation and of regional organisation brings immediately into the picture the institution which has been the basic unit of national and international order: the State. As an institution, the State is flourishing today despite recurrent prophesies of its inadequacy to cope with the world's major issues. How will the State adjust to these two newer institutions which themselves are foci of decision-making in domains of interest to the State? Firstly, the State is a juridical form which covers, with a certain formal equality, very unequal amounts of real power, from the super-powers to the very small, from concentrations of power capable of exerting great influence over political and economic events in many parts of the world to structures which are highly dependent and highly influenced from outside.

In international terms, States now characteristically seek to influence the behaviour and goals of others rather than to achieve direct domination (they pursue milieu goals rather than possession goals in Joseph S. Nye's terms)[1] – although one can think of salient exceptions. For the more dependent and weaker powers, this objective means attempting to secure control over local events from external influences. In national terms, i.e. internally, States have tended towards more concerted intervention in their economies in more sophisticated ways. Economic growth is the link between these two aspects – external and internal – of State behaviour: economic growth is a key to external influence, and maintenance or acceleration of growth is one major reason for internal intervention in the economy. Thus the State has tended to concern itself increasingly with investment, employment, wages and prices, all of which impinge directly upon industrial relations.

Continuing economic growth has now become dependent to a large extent upon massive research and development. The future economic strength of today's super-powers may be ultimately thought of as

[1] See Chapter 3.

6

'fall out' from their current investment in essentially non-commercial lines of research like nuclear physics and space exploration. Such research and investment is in turn dependent upon public investment on a scale which is at present beyond the capability of all individual states save the United States and the Soviet Union. The large corporation has been a primary beneficiary of this investment in research and development and of the economic growth it has stimulated. Furthermore, the giant corporation has acquired the capacity itself to finance large-scale research and development so as to maintain itself in the vanguard of industrial innovation.

Access to overseas raw materials, markets and production possibilities has turned some large corporations into multi-national corporations. The large corporation has many advantages for growth in a multi-national direction:

- a flexible organisational form conciliating centralised managerial control with operations in a number of countries;
- ability to maximise profits by combining the factors of production in the most advantageous ways, taking account of geographical variations in their values;
- ability to mobilise capital for expansion derived from various sources: as a recipient of public investment, through the exploitation of new capital markets like the Eurodollar market and above all by self-financing, all attributable to the multi-national corporation's scale of operations;
- ability to use modern information science effectively as a tool of decision-making and to combine functional specialisation with central direction and control in a powerful model of national organisation.

The multi-national corporation has thus become a transnational centralised decision-making system which affects investments, employment, wages and prices in many different countries – those very things the State is trying more effectively to control. Familiar comparisons have rather loosely been made between the relative powers of some of the big corporations and the smaller States in terms of assets, production and labour force (especially skilled labour force). In such a ranking, the multi-national corporations would far outstrip in resources and growth potential the least powerful States in the present world society.[1] Thus

---

[1] Adolf A. Berle, has written: 'Many of these corporations have budgets, and some of them have payrolls, which, with their customers, affect a greater number of people

the problem of relations between the State and the multi-national corporation is posed in areas touching upon industrial relations

In this relationship, much depends upon what kind of a power the multi-national corporation is, whether it is a fully autonomous power or whether it is linked in some significant way with its country of origin. Howard Perlmutter, in Chapter 2, sees the future evolution of the corporation as being in the autonomous 'geocentric' direction. Some of the States in which corporations operate seem, however, to be suspicious. Multi-national corporations may differ in the extent to which certain aspects of their policy are decentralised (e.g., as regards staffing of local operations with nationals and local autonomy to negotiate with unions) but it seems legitimate to ask whether ultimately corporation policies are not most likely to respond to their principal market and the source of the research and development which is the motor of their continuing expansion, both of which are to be found usually in the United States.

Regionalism suggests one method whereby States in a position of relative weakness may by working together or by merging some aspects of sovereignty gain fuller control over their economic growth potential and thus create a more autonomous industrial power base. The process of economic integration has gone furthest in Western Europe, which makes it possible to test at least provisionally some claims of regionalism in this respect. But the argument is put forward elsewhere, especially for Latin America as in the paper of Marcos Kaplan.[1]

European States of approximately 50 million population do not have the capability to invest in research and development individually on a scale to compete with the two super-powers. Neither can the private industrial organisations which have grown up within them attain the scale at which they can compete in research and development with the multi-national giants home-based in large countries.[2] In a short-term period of prosperity, medium-sized national economies and medium-sized firms can share in a general advance; but in the long run many of the medium-sized may become candidates for take-over by the giants.

than most of the hundred and thirty-odd sovereign countries of the world. American Telephone and Telegraph, for example, based on combined population and wealth, would be somewhere around the thirteenth state of the union in terms of budget, and certainly larger than many of the countries of South America, and most if not all of the countries of Africa. Some of these corporations are units that can be thought of only in somewhat the way we have thought of nations.' 'Second Edition/Corporate Power', *The Centre Magazine*, (published by The Centre for the Study of Democratic Institutions, Santa Barbara, Calif.), Vol. II, Number 1, p. 82.

[1] See Chapter 9.

[2] Firms like Nestlé, I.C.I. or B.A.S.F. may be possible exceptions to this thesis.

At least some part of the motivation for European integration is the desire to create the conditions for an autonomous industrial power. Beginning with a 'sick' industry – coal – the future of economic integration is now often seen in terms of autonomous development in sectors of advanced technology.

Concentrations of European industry and the creation with State support of European scientific and industrial projects are one kind of response to *le défi americain* – the American challenge.[1] But governments in their attitudes to European mergers may be torn between the desire to preserve national control over strategic industries and the feeling that the only way to fight the overseas-based multi-national giants is to create a race of European giants – a dilemma dividing the old local nationalism from the new regional nationalism.

Only limited progress seems, however, to have been made by such regionalist industrial structures. By contrast, the European Common Market and the Eurodollar capital market have stimulated the expansion within Western Europe of North American-based multi-national corporations. Regionalism may thus in practice – and perhaps as an unintended consequence – facilitate rather than thwart the growth of worldwide industrial structures like the multi-national corporation.

We can now begin to discern the possibility of such worldwide industrial structures bridging the East-West political cleavage, although this remains a prospective question. The recent rash of enterprise-to-enterprise agreements analysed by Norman Scott[2] show that this is not a purely speculative question, however. Zdeněk Mošna's paper[3] links the possibility of further development in this direction with the structural changes taking place within the socialist systems through the reforms of economic management which tend to place effective decision-making powers in the hands of the managers of large undertakings rather than in those of the central party organs and State bureaucracy. J. K. Galbraith[4] has likened these trends in the Soviet system to the role of 'techno-structures' in U.S. corporations; and Howard V. Perlmutter heralds the multi-national corporation as a worldwide organisation transcending ideologies. It seems too early to find much evidence of transnational industrial relations crossing East-West frontiers; but it may not be too soon to begin to think about some industrial relations implications.

[1] See J.-J. Servan-Schreiber: *The American Challenge* (New York, Atheneum, 1968).
[2] See Chapter 11.
[3] See Chapter 10.
[4] J. K. Galbraith: *The New Industrial State* (London, Hamish Hamilton, 1967).

Conflict between the State and the multi-national corporation may be expected to occur especially in some less developed countries. The relations between multi-national corporations and new States are asymmetrical. The corporation is weak relative to local political pressures; it may be strong because of its control of the advanced economic organisation needed to develop local resources and because of its option to move elsewhere.

Where the multi-national corporation operates in the developing areas, it creates about itself a centre of modernisation. Those left outside – the poor – when they become articulate can seek satisfaction only through the local political authority. The local political authorities can – in the extreme case – take control of the physical resources on their soil; but they will be less able to control the human resources to develop them. The strength of the multi-national corporation, by contrast, lies in its creation of the technical organisation needed to exploit physical resources.

As in Europe, economic nationalism may be an initial reaction to the presence of multi-national corporations; and regionalism may be a second-stage effort to organise a more effective autonomous development than is possible within countries of a small population and limited resources. The explosive force of populism behind national solutions may prove to be strong in the developing areas, stronger than any comparable popular support for regionalism in a more affluent Europe, although the organisational capability for territorially-based development will be much less. Industrial relations in less developed countries may become politicised in this sense.

Industrial relations systems in the more industrialised countries will themselves affect the basic trends in world economic structures which we are examining, as well as be affected by these trends. Which are those changes in industrial relations systems most likely to be significant in this respect? Everyone will have his own preferred list of critical factors. In selecting a few, I am looking for factors which may influence the locus of decision-making about work rules and earnings.

The first is the growing differentiation in the labour force brought about by an increasing proportion of technicians and highly skilled personnel; and the accompanying differentiation of occupational interests expressed through the growth of new occupational associations side by side with the older trade unions of manual workers.

The second is the increasing importance of plant agreements in

European countries which have been used to a centralised structure of collective bargaining. There is also greater scope for personnel management and for special arrangements within the firm. J.-D. Reynaud, in a forward look at industrial relations in Western Europe, did not think the plant agreement would become the main form of collective agreement, but envisaged 'a disordered and anarchical development' in which plant-level activity would increase while the traditional industrial and national level negotiations continued.[1] This would mean more local autonomy and more flexibility in industrial relations.

The third is a seemingly contrary tendency towards enhancement of the authority of central trade union and employer association organs over their members. This is attributable mainly to the State calling in these bodies as consultants and would-be partners in shaping and (hopefully) applying certain aspects of economic policy, especially in regard to prices and incomes. How real will this 'trend' prove to be, and how will it be reconciled with that favouring greater local autonomy?

The fourth is the demand for employee participation in management. Whatever the long-range consequences, this seems initially likely to enhance the trend towards local plant autonomy.

The fifth factor concerns attitudes. Over a fairly long period, there seems to have been a lessening in the tendency to identify with class and a penetration of 'middle-class' values amongst wage-earners generally – a desire for the artifacts of the industrial society and a personal adaptation to the large organisation. By weakening a common ideological bond, this change in attitudes could favour the diversification of material interests pursued by different groups. Yet just as the end of ideology had been proclaimed and the 'organisation man' appeared secure in his quiet affluence, an anti-organisation revolt appeared spreading from the eccentric fringes of society to the streets, the campuses and even occasionally the factories. In the assertion of personal freedom against the claims of organisational conformity this revolt is akin to the contemporaneous explosions of local cultural nationalisms which aim – with perhaps equal futility – at the rejection of more powerful alien institutions and influences. However improbable is the attainment of the objectives of these movements, and it is often unclear whether they have specific objectives, they may well

---

[1] 'The Future of Industrial Relations in Western Europe: Approaches and Perspectives', *International Institute for Labour Studies Bulletin* No. 4, February 1968, p. 98.

have a cautionary and humanising effect on big organisations. The sentiments underlying them will infiltrate into the organisational world – indeed, there is every likelihood that within many a formal organisation man lurks an anti-organisation rebel.

Summarising, a number of these changes seem to be working concurrently towards a fragmentation or loosening of unified national structures of industrial relations. This may be a necessary condition for transnational industrial relations to come into being; but a further condition would be that the disintegrated elements of national structures be reintegrated into international trade union structures aligned to the multi-national corporations or perhaps into broader transnational industrial structures. Present conditions in industrial relations seem to open the possibility of this happening. Whether or not it does occur will depend in large measure upon national trade union and employer reactions to the multi-national corporation.

In purely abstract terms, three possible types of reaction by national or local trade unions and employers are conceivable:

– disappearance (leaving the field to the multi-national corporation);
– opposition; and
– symbiosis (or complementarity).

Disappearance, in the case of the trade unions, is an unlikely extreme. However, the personnel policies of some multi-national corporations which offer a high level of security and income to a predominantly highly qualified staff suggest that the trade union may not necessarily be a universal or permanent fixture of future industrial relations. As regards national employer associations, disappearance is even less likely. The recent trend has been towards the creation of such organisations in less developed countries where none existed previously.

Opposition to the multi-national corporation is a more likely possibility; and it will be important to consider the circumstances in which it may occur. Unions would tend to look for alliance with the State to bring political or legislative pressure on the multi-national corporation. They might also ally with national employer interests. As regards national employers, contrasting policies have been noted in some European countries between U.S.-based multi-national corporations and locally organised employers on such matters as wages, lay-offs and the closing of less efficient undertakings. The contrast reflects different ideologies of management, each rooted in a different pattern of economic organisation. An attitude of opposition, on the part of unions or management, would probably reflect a conflict of values or of cultures with the multi-national corporation.

Symbiosis is the reaction most likely to lead towards transnational industrial relations. For unions, it means an objective of building systems of security for employees around the corporation (rather than the State), for example through a guaranteed wage, pensions, and individual career development. For employers, it would mean that national industries would play a complementary role to the multi-national giants; and that they would accept the premises of their industrial relations philosophies. Symbiosis implies a sharing of values, a common industrial culture of universal extension.

The outcome of current mutations in world economic organisation involving the multi-national corporation thus turns upon the relative weight to be given in the future, on the one hand, to transnationally structured economic and organisational power and to nationally structured power on the other. What balance will be struck between these two structural possibilities? *Which* type of decision-making system will exert the primary influence *where* upon the location of industry, employment and earnings?

One might extrapolate from the multi-national corporation a vision of a functionally organised world based upon globe-circling economic structures, a kind of Saint-Simonian[1] dream in which control lies with technocrats in rational organisations. Towards the end of World War II, David Mitrany in his pamphlet called *A Working Peace System*[2] explained the merits of functionalism, in which men were united across national boundaries by common interests commonly perceived, over various schemes of federalism. He was thinking mainly of governmental agencies, of the kind which later grew more numerous as specialised agencies of the United Nations. However widely such organisations' activities have spread, and however useful they have become, it is hardly possible, twenty years later, to consider the specialised agencies as the foundation of world order. Now comes this new vision of a world economy twenty years from now organised by 300 giant corporations which from private origins have become of public import because of their scale and the essential character of their services.

Alternatively, one can think of a world organised in larger regional

[1] See *Doctrine de Saint-Simon – Exposition, première année* (1829), new edition, published by C. Bougie and E. Halévy (Paris, 1924).
[2] London, Royal Institute of International Affairs, 1943.

groupings, each with the capacity for further economic growth, yet retaining its own individuality. Each region would be characterised by a high intermixture of political power and industrial organisation, though different names would be given to the ideologies dominant in different regions. This vision seems to carry somewhat less conviction today than it might have perhaps in the early 1960s when regionalism had achieved its first successes in Europe and the ideological current of regionalism was running high in Latin America and Africa.

The State remains as the major territorially-based force to be reconciled with the multi-national corporation. Whether the State is accommodating or hostile will depend upon the attitudes of popular forces and local economic interests. Industrial relations seem likely to be an arena in which these attitudes are crystallised.

# THE GROWTH OF MULTI-NATIONAL CORPORATIONS AND OF ECONOMIC REGIONALISM

THE two chapters of this section are concerned with the quantitative and qualitative aspects of the growth of the two major trends which are expected to move industrial relations in a transnational direction.

Multi-national corporations, irrespective of their national origins, have grown rapidly in the last decades. Sales of overseas subsidiaries of American-based corporations are estimated at approximately $150 billion a year now; those of other origin are estimated at over $80 billion, suggesting that multi-national business is not exclusively the 'American Challenge'. Other countries, especially the United Kingdom, Germany and Japan, seem to show a 'lag' rather than a 'gap' in terms of multi-national business, as compared to the United States, which would sustain the proposition that future growth of multi-national corporations does not necessarily imply American dominance of the world economy.

There is a fair consensus of opinion among economists, sociologists, politicians, trade unionists and all types of futurologists that multi-national corporations will grow in the years ahead; opinions are mainly divided as regards the tempo of this trend. The growth of multi-national business is seen as related to the phenomenon of concentration which anti-trust legislation has not in practice effectively counteracted. Concentration is now actually promoted on a regional basis by supranational authorities and countries eager to see potential competitors to the American-based companies develop. Growth of multi-national business, combined with mergers across national frontiers, make the current assumption (by Jean-Jacques Servan-Schreiber, Howard V. Perlmutter and others) that the world markets will be dominated in the next decades by some 200–300 multi-national corporations, whatever form they may take, a likely possibility.

The basis for this evolution is the unprecedented combination of managerial and technological know-how embodied in the multi-national corporation (including aspects of finance and marketing), which is nourished by large-scale research and development. Multi-national corporations should therefore enlarge in the years to come their already substantial effect on national growth patterns, investment, employment, wages, exports and balance of payments. As a consequence, their possible impact on industrial relations, the major interest of the present book, can likewise be expected to increase.

The possible incompatibility of decisions by multi-national corporations, overflowing national boundaries, with decisions made on a national level (incorporated in development plans, national social policies and industrial relations behaviour) is a recognised source of potential conflict. Developing countries are in the centre of this preoccupation. Fascinated, on the one hand, by the growth potential and the modern technology which multi-national corporations introduce in their territory, they are fearful, on the other hand, that loss of control over resources may have negative consequences for their major concern: nation building.

The extent to which such conflicts could be resolved would determine progress towards a fair distribution of welfare in the world (a concept defined by national criteria), but also have implications for the growth prospects of multi-national business itself; it would determine whether multi-national corporations become indeed vehicles of progress which are considered both indispensable and legitimised in the eyes of those who have to deal with them: national and regional government, national and international trade unions, employers and the great public.

Resolving such conflicts would mean striking a 'balance of rights and responsibilities' for the multi-national corporation, as one speaker at the 1969 Instanbul Meeting of the International Chamber of Commerce put it. To strike such a balance, it is usually thought that all actors concerned will have to make adjustments which will require negotiations based upon the use of organised power. Unions in particular have felt the need to devise strategies to become a force capable of negotiating with the multi-national corporation about the allocation of resources.

Business circles tend to stress that commercial self-interest – rather than countervailing forces or legal sanctions – determine a behaviour of multi-national corporations compatible with the goals of the other parties involved. In the first chapter of the present section, Howard V. Perlmutter develops ideas which also explain business attitudes in relation to its own operations, but which stress functional requirements rather than interest considerations. Perlmutter's argument is that, in the process of worldwide growth, multi-national corporations will undergo

18

qualitative transformations in that their management will have to acquire worldwide outlook and attitudes, a precondition for achieving maximum efficiency of its resource allocation. Such an evolution reduces the potentiality of conflict if understood by all parties concerned. In Perlmutter's analysis, the dynamics of growth will make a company pass from an ethnocentric (home-base determined) through a polycentric (host-country determined) to a geocentric behaviour which is related to the requirements of the world as a whole. In the polycentric phase, decisions become more decentralised in that they move towards the subsidiaries of the company; they are becoming oriented towards the values and needs of the host countries. This enhances the legitimation of the corporation in the eyes of the national actors; but the competence of multi-national corporations will be fully achieved in the geocentric phase only. A geocentric corporation has a global mission. The head office management becomes really 'multi-national' in outlook, responsibility and composition, and the corporate structure of the firm tends to reflect international ownership and control. The effectiveness of geocentric corporations in creating wealth and welfare will make it an indispensable transideological institution for the nation State, labour, suppliers and consumers, the basis for a worldwide legitimacy. To fight it would be an anti-functional reflex. Processes need rather to be promoted whereby nations, unions and firms, respecting each other's roles, collaborate to reach common objectives.

Perlmutter's typology has the merit of getting away from a stereotype classification of international management according to the business culture of the headquarters country. Its predictive capacity, however, appears mainly based on untested hypotheses.

In the second chapter of this section, Joseph Nye undertakes to analyse the other major trend: the actual and potential growth of international regionalism. The impressive number of free trade areas, customs unions and common markets created over the recent decades might lead one to believe in E.E.C. president Jean Rey's assertion that the political life of the world is increasingly at the level of continents. However, Joseph Nye convincingly demonstrates that proliferation of economic regional units and increased regional co-operation are not a proof of more integration of decision-making at a regional level. One is therefore inclined to accept his conclusion that it would be mistaken to see economic regional organisation as an alternative to the functionally organised multi-national corporation, or as a force capable of controlling it.   Consequently, there remains little doubt that multi-national corporations and the nation State 'look like continuing to be the strongest structures' of world economic organisation.

It may be inferred from this that they will also be the main future potentialities for keeping industrial relations and collective bargaining within national boundaries or for allowing them to transcend these.

Chapter 2

# TOWARDS RESEARCH ON AND DEVELOPMENT OF NATIONS, UNIONS AND FIRMS AS WORLDWIDE INSTITUTIONS

*by*

*Howard V. Perlmutter*

THERE is some evidence that the leaders of three key institutions of our world society, the nation State, the trade unions and the firm, have begun to take cognisance of the world scale of events. While the earth is hardly a 'global village' as Marshall McLuhan would have it, the nature and pace of scientific and technological advance in aerospace, in communications and transportation, have revolutionised concepts of distance, and imposed a sense of political and economic interdependence the planet Earth has never known. Raymond Aron called our age 'The Dawn of Universal History', which Lord Acton explained as:

'. . . distinct from the combined history of all countries, which is not a rope of sand, but a continuous development, and is not a burden on the memory but an illumination of the soul.

'It moves in a succession to which nations are subsidiary. Their story will be told, not for their own sake, but in reference and subordination to a higher series, according to the time and the degree in which they contribute to the common fortunes of mankind . . .'

Yet this trio of institutions are not yet organised to treat the world as a total entity, with resources both material and human, to serve their clients, or constituents to contribute to 'the common fortunes of mankind'. For it is a commonplace paradox that while the Earth has shrunk along space-time dimensions, the sentiment of international solidarity between persons in different nation States does not seem to have accelerated markedly. In fact, nationalism, or its associated

21

attitudinal state, ethnocentrism (defined as a strong belief in the superiority or reliability of one's people, values, standards and ideas to foreign ways), seems to be on the rise, either as a post-colonial reflex in the developing countries or as an expression of the need for autonomy in the Eastern European countries, or as a reaction to United States power in Western Europe. For the individual, ethnocentrism may be the expression of need for a piece of territory on which one can feel roots and identity, in the complex and turbulent world society. But while this need is understandable, a worldwide orientation seems more appropriate when the fruits of science and technology of the Global Industrial System are considered.[1]

Our purpose in this paper is to raise some researchable questions on the conditions facilitating development of a worldwide (or geocentric) orientation in the leadership of society's central institutions. For despite the aforementioned ethnocentric symptoms, it seems evident that all institutions and their constituent individuals must willingly or unwillingly develop some geocentric niche in the last third of the twentieth century, either in terms of markets for the firm and State or working conditions and pay policies for unions. Just how institutions like firms, nations, and unions cope with the problems of becoming less home-country centred or ethnocentric and more geocentric in order to remain viable is both a fascinating research problem and a challenge for each kind of institution.

As a starting point in this paper, we believe a case can be made for a radical transformation over the next several decades in the world's commercial–industrial system due to the emergence of both super-giant and giant multi-national firms with extractive, processing, transportation, communication, manufacturing, marketing distribution and/or service facilities in almost every country in the world. The firms which survive will be able to reach billions rather than millions of customers with their goods and services, and could conceivably produce a significant portion of the world's gross national product.

One question for research is whether the development of a worldwide or geocentric orientation in industrial, commercial and service institutions will set in motion processes which will be seen as having, in the short and long term, constructive impacts on nation States, in the East and West, in the North and South, and on the trade unions at the

[1] See Howard V. Perlmutter 'Management Problems in Spaceship Earth', an address to the Academy of Management, 26 August 1969 (Mimeo) (Division for Research and Development of Worldwide Institutions, Wharton School, University of Pennsylvania, Philadelphia).

local, national and international levels. We can envisage a course of events where the collaborative-competitive pattern of negotiations between a multi-national firm, the State and a union will facilitate the primary objectives of each institution – higher wages, better working conditions, employment security and training for the workers, etc.; sustained economic development and a better quality of life for citizens of nation States; and higher productivity and greater wealth creation for the firm. But, since this is not the best of possible worlds, it is possible that the emergence of an essentially new, economically powerful institution like the multi-national firm can induce strong feelings of threats about the erosion of powers or the cohesion of both State and union, with consequent defensive and destructive actions.

One scenario for the future is essentially that of a pluralistic world of geocentrically oriented firms, States and unions who recognise their interdependence in a world where technological change is in itself geocentric or worldwide in character. A second scenario is that of struggle, subversion, of direct or guerrilla warfare between multi-national firms, unions and nations. And while these are extremes, I believe the seeds of both scenarios are being sown today. The central research questions are then:

1. Under what conditions will specific nations, unions and multi-national firms achieve a constructive level of collaborative interdependence?
2. Under what conditions will specific multi-national firms develop destructive, distrusting patterns of interrelating?

Our argument is divided into five parts:

1. The first in which we try to demonstrate why the multi-national firm will gain in economic strength because of its internal resources and external opportunities.
2. The second in which we try to show that in the interests of viability (profitability and growth) the multi-national firm is concerned with developing *attitudes* which lead to the optimising of its resources around the world.
3. The third, in which we indicate that the multi-national firms (unlike nations and unions) are becoming involved in transideological commercial and industrial ventures.
4. The fourth is that the leaders of multi-national firms are becoming more self-conscious about their social responsibility. As the world's

23

spotlight is placed on them, they are becoming more aware that they must deliberately engage in some kind of worldwide institution building process.

5. And in a fifth and final section we consider three propositions which relate the growth of multi-national firms to the evolution of nation States and unions:

(a) In the first proposition, we try to show that the present rate of geocentrisation of multi-national firms is greater than that of nation States and unions.

(b) In the second proposition, we try to explain that at the present time the primary responses of nation States and unions to multi-national firms are defensive, ambivalent and distrusting.

(c) In the third part, we try to envisage, with a longer time perspective, the conditions under which an atmosphere of trust and acceptance of each other's legitimacy would prevail among this trio of institutions.

1. Our first proposition is that of the three key institutions, the multi-national firm has a stronger likelihood of becoming one of the dominant worldwide economic institutions of the latter third of the twentieth century. Elsewhere I have conjectured that by 1985 we should expect to see about 300 supergiant firms of the multi-national variety, including conglomerates, in all the key sectors, from mining to manufacturing, and including commercial service sectors, such as banking.[1] I see nothing to change this view, despite increasing government concern and action. But we recognise that a very large number of efficient and innovating middle-sized and small regional or micro-global multi-national firms can find a positive niche in the world economy, as competitors to the supergiants, or as suppliers, or service industries associated with the supergiants.[2] To say that only 300 companies will remain in twenty years is absurd. But to assume that big firms will dissolve and not play a prominent role in the emerging global industrial estate appears to us unduly naive.

My reasoning for the emergence and continuous growth of the supergiants is as follows:

(1) Giant firms such as Unilever, I.B.M., Nestlé, Standard Oil of New Jersey or Philips can get capital from anywhere in the world if

---

[1] See Howard V. Perlmutter: 'Super-Giant Firms in the Future', *Wharton Quarterly*, Winter 1968 (University of Pennsylvania).

[2] Howard V. Perlmutter, *op. cit.*

they need it, although many not only generate sufficient revenue to be self-financing but on occasion lend money to banks.

(2) Supergiant firms develop worldwide production and distribution systems which make it possible to launch new products everywhere in the world. This means that potentially they can reach several billion consumers rather than those of a single nation State.

(3) Supergiant firms can diversify their risks by a global investment pattern, so that they are not vulnerable to the economic and political cycles of a given nation State. They are less vulnerable to take-overs or acquisition moves from other companies.

(4) Supergiants can afford the research and development necessary to make and exploit breakthroughs in science and technology. (Take the example of I.B.M.'s $5 billion investment in the hardware of the 360 system.)

(5) Supergiants can find highly qualified specialists and managers, afford to pay them salaries and provide a career with relatively little fear of being taken over, or financial failure. This means the corporation can attract and keep people to perpetuate the firm over many generations.

(6) The supergiant multi-national firms can project an image of confidence, of trust and reliability, by standing behind their product everywhere in the world.

(7) Finally, the giant firms generally are committed to growth and profitability commensurate with worldwide opportunities, whether by internal forces or by the acquisition route. Sustained growth will make them supergiants within a few decades.

The sheer size of giant multi-national firms can be considered an obstacle. In recent months two executives from different worldwide firms expressed doubts whether their firms could grow indefinitely. Size often means inefficiency, problems of quality control, a sense of impersonality, a greater bureaucracy, cumbersome decision-making, with lost opportunities, inflexibility to change, a less personal approach to customers and their needs, as compared with smaller firms. Is there an optimum size beyond which a firm like General Motors should not grow? G.M.'s 757,000 employees, plus their dependants, and suppliers, make it from a population view one of the world's small and very wealthy 'nations'. From an asset and annual sales view G.M. is about the tenth largest nation. My question is: How can G.M. *stop* growing?

It is more realistic to say that G.M. will continue to use a part of its resources to seek ways to make the larger systems work, to reduce unprofitable products, to introduce others which are profitable. To stop growing in sales, in production capacity, in scientific capability in a growing world market is to decline. And while organisational inefficiencies are apparent, we should not underestimate man's capacity to learn to organise, perhaps (with the help of computers) to design larger systems (including nation States, armies, churches), to find and utilise new technologies to make the large organisations work. For example, the organisational concept of a Product Division conceived as a profit centre, makes it possible for what were hitherto large businesses to be included as viable parts of a larger organisation. More recently the conglomerate has come on to the business scene. It is clear that there are both efficient and inefficient conglomerates. Thus while this way of diversifying risks (and incidentally increasing the size) is, as yet, unproved it is an organisational innovation that is not likely to disappear, because the professional managerial skills are either transferable or the process of producing relevant knowledge is too expensive for small business.

Furthermore, in Europe and the United States small and middle-sized firms are frequently one-man family businesses, which while likely to be more entrepreneurial in character during the first generation, are:

(a) not necessarily more efficient and more competitive in the second generation;
(b) not the best place to work for workers who are not members of the family but who seek some employment security; and
(c) are vulnerable, given the mortality of the *patron*, and his propensity not to train successors.

I make no plea for size but say simply that the economies of scale for giant multi-national firms are not the only criteria on which to evaluate them – the survival value and access to resources to meet global demands and opportunities are crucial. Nobody I know in a senior position in a worldwide company has specified *when* he intends to stop growing. Most business leaders, at least those in their early fifties, prefer the difficulties of growth to the insecurities of declining market shares, and a widening reputation among shareholders for being unwilling to reach for worldwide opportunities as effectively as their competitors.

The second set of reasons to support the proposition that large firms will get larger is the nature of countervailing forces in the world community. The individual sovereign States, including the United States, are not able to destroy the multi-national firm, although there are likely to be attempts to limit their powers – at least for American-based international firms and eventually in Europe through anti-trust legislation, price controls, and a host of restrictive legislative acts. But the United States Government may find that:

(1) The definition of size for American-based international firms will not be readily accepted by non-American multi-national firms and thus United States firms will be handicapped by being evaluated on ethnocentric criteria.

(2) The leadership of international firms in the United States and elsewhere will be increasingly aware that obligations to the home nation State are likely to become more and more crippling as overseas markets generate a larger proportion of the revenue. When the shareholders come from five different nation States (as in the case of Royal Dutch-Shell), or when the customers are 97 per cent outside the headquarters company as with Nestlé, or if a large proportion of the employees are outside the home country, where does the firm's loyalty lie?

There is a case for the observation that headquarters of a worldwide firm is an arbitrary location; in any event its location should not be a major obstacle to worldwide growth and profitability. And in this connection, it is interesting that in studies conducted by a number of multi-national firms, the United States is considered to be one of the least desirable places to have a home headquarters, given some United States Government attitudes towards firms based there.

Yet, in the final analysis, neither host nor home nation States are *overwhelming* countervailing forces because essentially individual States compete for the resources and capabilities of multi-national firms – a fact which leaders of multi-national firms are well aware of.

With all due respect to the international trade union movement, the union is not a countervailing force which can destroy the multi-national firm today, for reasons to be elaborated below. In fact, it is probably to the interest of the trade union movement to seek to share in the wealth produced by the multi-national firm.

These are some of the reasons to support my argument that the multi-national firms will become prominent worldwide industrial-commercial institutions. I have chosen the round and arbitrary number of 300 firms dominating the scene in 1985 (with especial focus on petroleum, data processing, food, chemical, pharmaceuticals, automobile manufacturing, transportation, steel making and banking). Mr Agnelli's (Fiat) belief that only six or seven automobile firms will be around in 1975 is obviously less conservative than my view. But I should like to repeat that small and middle-sized well-managed firms ought to thrive in the decades to come – especially if they resort to a strategy of not trying to attack the big firms in their strong areas, not trying to do what big firms can only afford to do, but capitalising on the obvious vulnerabilities that large size induces (e.g., slowness of decision-making bureaucracy, less personal attention to the customers' specific needs).

In comparison, States seem less able to function using worldwide economic systems except in worldwide empires. I am perhaps too optimistic in assuming the age of military domination of one State over many others is coming to an end!

2. My second proposition to support this view is that the leaders of this and the next generation of multi-national firms will want to become more *geocentric*, or *world centred* in ownership, in research and development, in marketing, or manufacturing, as opposed to ethnocentric (home country centred) or polycentric (host-country centred). Their management will seek every opportunity to optimise the use of men, money, markets and machines on the world scale, with the nation State as on the whole a barrier to this optimisation process. Table 1 shows in archetypal form how ethnocentric, polycentric, and geocentric attitudes are evidenced in some key decision areas. And while there are costs, risks and payoffs for each approach or mixture, and both external and internal restraining forces towards geocentrism, the net direction in most firms I have observed is towards making *more geocentric decisions* and facilitating a more geocentric approach, despite external contraints in the form of host and home governments. But there are, and will be, no purely geocentric companies for several decades (and in many instances even regressions towards ethnocentrism). More research is necessary here.

In view of our concern with relations between multi-national firm and trade unions, it may be useful to distinguish these three approaches as they might be evidenced in industrial relations policies. We should expect multi-national firms to become more aware of their options in industrial relations as well as finance, marketing and manufacturing. Headquarters and subsidiary executives can work out a worldwide industrial relations policy in a climate of mutual trust and understanding. (See Table 1.) The *ethnocentric* approach of United States firms might be described in the area of wage administration when United States headquarter executives attempt to control all policies from H.Q. in terms of United States experience, for example, a pay scheme in which the worker is paid in relation solely to his performance rather than what might be customary in some countries, where payment is made according to seniority and family size. When imposition of some of the more complex methods of time-study and job evaluation is added, the ethnocentric approach is even more pronounced in some United States firms. *Polycentrism* here would be headquarters acceptance of the status quo, a not infrequent reaction to the resistance of local workers to the inflexible application of the U.S. practices irrespective of culture or custom and economic needs. (Headquarters usually says that industrial relations programmes are solely the affair of local management, which may or may not be the case.) Central to *Geocentrism* is a collaborative approach to finding the best way, with local variations in mind. The geocentric approach is the search for the *best* industrial relations policies which promote *values* which relate to workers' pay, and organisational requirements for productivity from everywhere in the world to meet worldwide standards of price, quality and quantity. I am told Philips of Eindhoven is moving in this direction.

Research is necessary to determine under what conditions multinational firms develop geocentric industrial relations policies but we would predict that the *ethnocentric* approach (which is frequently based on the idea that foreigners are second-class citizens) and the *polycentric* approach (which limits the learning from other countries) are less likely to endure over the long term. B. C. Roberts's observations are most relevant.[1]

3. My third proposition is more controversial and only research over time will test its validity. I believe the multi-national firm is more likely to become *transideological* – it will literally rise beyond the ideologies of capitalism or communism – than unions or States. The countries of Eastern Europe must become an integral part of the world

---

[1] See Chapter 6.

TABLE 1

THREE TYPES OF HEADQUARTERS ORIENTATION TOWARD
SUBSIDIARIES IN ANY INTERNATIONAL ENTERPRISE*

| Organisation Design | Ethnocentric | Polycentric | Geocentric |
|---|---|---|---|
| Complexity of organisation | Complex in home country, simple in subsidiaries | Varied and independent | Increasingly complex and interdependent |
| Authority; decision-making | High in headquarters | Relatively low in headquarters | Aim for a collaborative approach between headquarters and subsidiaries |
| Evaluation and control | Home standards applied for persons and performance | Determined locally | Find standards which are universal and local |
| Rewards and punishments; incentives | High in headquarters, low in subsidiaries | Wide variation; can be high or low rewards for subsidiary's performance | International and local executives rewarded for reaching local and world-wide objectives |
| Communication; information flow | High volume to subsidiaries: orders, commands, advice | Little to and from headquarters. Little between subsidiaries | Both ways and between subsidiaries. Heads of subsidiaries part of management team |
| Identification | Nationality of owner | Nationality of host country | Truly international company by identifying with national interests |
| Perpetuation (recruiting, staffing, development) | Recruit and develop people of home country for key positions everywhere in the world | Develop people of local nationality for key positions in their own country | Develop best men everywhere in the world for key positions everywhere in the world |

* Howard V. Perlmutter, 'The Tortuous Evolution of the Multi-national Corporation'. Reprinted from *Columbia Journal of World Business*, Vol. IV, No. 1 (Jan–Feb 1969).

economic-industrial system and thus to become geocentric as well, for economic development within the confines of COMECON (or indeed the E.E.C.) is severely limited. The recognition of this limitation is in itself a source of anxiety and concern in many Eastern European countries. I believe that, cautiously and painfully, the forces towards a *transideological international division of labour* by country will gain momentum over the long term – not without crises, setbacks, and attempts to control the process by the political ideologists. I do not expect that the United States will lead in this direction unless a Vietnam settlement should occur soon. But Swedish, Danish, French, Italian, Federal German, Japanese and British enterprise show obvious interest in moving in this direction.[1]

During the past twenty years leaders in the East and West have been experimenting with essentially three theories, all of which are evident today in varying mixes. The first we call the *submergence theory*: belief in the West, particularly in the United States, that capitalistic systems must prevail and dominate the East, militarily, politically, industrially and commercially. Or the belief in the East, that communism will bury the Western capitalistic system from without and within, by natural evolutionary processes or by direct political-economic and military action.

There are still *submergence theorists* in key political and military positions around today – in both the East and West. But the fear of nuclear disaster hampers the acting out of these impulses.

Other options have been articulated. There are also *divergence theorists*, who see the Western market economies and the Eastern command economies as drawing away from each other under the pressure of ideological leaders of both sides, in particular the East, resulting in some kind of *competitive coexistence*.

More popular is a third theory, held by the *convergence theorists* on both sides who see the two systems borrowing more and more from each other and becoming more and more alike, in the long term (by the year 2000).

My own researches on East–West relations lead me to infer that a fourth theory of East–West relations is in its early stages: I call it *emergence theory*, a theory that acknowledges the first beginnings of a *transideological industrial zone* between East and West and viable and durable *transideological institutions* which can grow out of some of the

[1] Howard V. Perlmutter: 'Emerging East–West Ventures: The Transideological Enterprise', *Columbia Journal of World Business*, September–October 1969.

subcontracting, licensing and joint ventures between Western and Eastern industries already in existence today.

Examples are found in joint ventures of this variety:

(1) I.K.E.A., a Swedish furniture store chain supplies machinery and designs under its technical control for the semi-manufacture of furniture in Poland, which is then shipped to Sweden for finishing by I.K.E.A.

(2) Poland manufactures diesel motors under licence of one British Leyland concern. The Polish-made motors are jointly sold by Leyland and the Poles in a third country.

(3) Simmons Machine Tool Corporation of the United States has agreed with Czechoslovakia's Skoda to have the latter produce a line of specialised heavy equipment under the Simmons–Skoda trademark.

(4) Krupp of Essen and the Csepel Machine Tool of Hungary factory have jointly developed digitally controlled short lathes on German designs and drawings which are to be exported to Germany and third markets.

(5) Italy's Officine Meccaniche Gaitano Zocca has set up a 50–50 trading company in Switzerland with Bulgaria's Machine Export, the foreign trade organisation handling industrial machinery to sell grinding machines worldwide. Zocca will receive unfinished machines from Bulgaria, add parts and finish the equipment, then turn the machines over to the trading company. Zocca will service all sales outside the Eastern bloc, the Bulgarian supplier doing the same within the Eastern bloc, not only for the grinding machines but also for all of Zocca's other products that are sold to Eastern bloc countries.

And the examples are even more abundant from Yugoslavia where some joint stock companies are being planned.

Emergence theory is in its infancy and there are many political reasons to doubt its rapid rise to popularity. But in view of the inexorable logic of the world market, more managers and political leaders know they must seek to gain a worldwide niche for their goods and services and reach worldwide standards of quality and reliability. The forces in the direction of widening the *transideological industrial and commercial zone* seem irreversible.

What are the implications for a world where managers transcend ideology to do business, to build markets, and to share technology?

It is still too early to tell. But it would be paradoxical that it will be management and not labour that will become *transideological* first.

4. My fourth proposition is that some multi-national firm will deliberately seek and gain institutional status in the world economy. By this I mean that the kind of leadership that will emerge will seek primarily (a) to demonstrate the distinctive competence of a world-wide firm to utilise worldwide science and technology to create and share wealth on the global scale, to be financially *viable* in both host and home nation States, in both advanced and developing economies, in the East and West, and (b) by this route and social policies, to gain legitimacy, that is to gain the status of being perceived as an indispensable institution in view of its consumers, suppliers, nation States, and particularly labour.

Thus, it is not a surprise that some executives see themselves as engaged in worldwide institution building, with the multi-national firm potentially as a new kind of social architecture, particularly suitable for the last decades of the twentieth century.

To be *viable, legitimate and indispensable* the multi-national firm will have to be *measured* as to the degree it achieves *social architectural standards* by creating such *values* as:

(1) Goods and services around the world at a high standard and fair prices to all customers everywhere in the world.

(2) Wealth created and shared with its claimants which include managers, workers, shareholders.

(3) Enlightenment and training commensurate with the rate of technological change as it is occurring on the world scale (not just in a given country).

(4) Personnel practices and working conditions which promote the physical and psychological well-being of all employees.

(5) Justice for all employees regardless of their religion, country of origin, in (for example) grievance procedures and due processes.

(6) Respect and concern for the individual dignity of all employees as evidenced in fringe benefits, hiring and layoff policies, in comparison with State-owned or privately owned national firms.

The burden of proof will be on the multi-national firm to demonstrate that the social architectural standards of the subsidiaries of multi-national firms will not be just as good as, or poorer than, locally or nationally owned firms but significantly *better* on most of these parameters as translated into quantitative and qualitative indicators.

This means that the severest tests are likely to come in the less developed countries where providing such standards can produce a beneficial model in addition to the opportunity offered by multi-national firms to leap into the world economy.

Of course a multi-national firm which behaves like a multi-national institution in this case is very likely to have satisfied employees, and the question of what role unions and States play in regard to these same needs comes up.

5. Now we turn to the fifth area of discussion. Our first proposition reads: *The multi-national firm is geocentrising at a more rapid rate than than nation States or unions.* As a preliminary start in this problem we ask from available data these two questions:

(a) What are the perceived driving-restraining forces, external and internal, towards geocentrism in multi-national firms, unions and nations?

(b) At what rate are the obstacles being overcome, and are driving forces being increased?

Table 2 shows findings based on our research to date in a large number of multi-national companies. Among the internal obstacles to geocentrism (as defined in table 1), executives included both structural factors (a nation-centred reward system) and attitudinal factors (nationalistic tendencies in staff).

While we believe there is considerable difficulty in overcoming the obstacles to geocentrism, our over-all impression is that there are both conscious awareness of some or many of the obstacles to geocentrism and conscious efforts to reduce their strength. For example any given firm may be engaging in (a) language training courses, (b) multi-national task forces, (c) organising headquarters for a world-wide operation, (d) planning systematically for international careers, (e) widening distribution of equity to non-nationals, (f) increasing awareness and commitment of executives in subsidiaries to world-wide objectives, (g) improving the worldwide communication system and (h) building up methods for geocentrisation of policies.

By product, function and geography, there is an attempt to change the varying mixes of ethno-(E), poly-(P) and geocentrism (G), which we have termed EPG profiles, and most companies have the tools, incentives and the control to make geocentrism more characteristic of key decisions.

In many multi-national firms, for example, headquarters usually reserves the right to:

(a) establish the broad policies and objectives of the company;
(b) evaluate subsidiaries' operating plans within these policies;
(c) establish financial policies;
(d) sanction major capital investments;
(e) make senior appointments everywhere in the world;
(f) decide on the remuneration of top management.

With regard to the unions and nation States our research is in the early stages. We must rely on anecdotal evidence or specific cases. Tables 3 and 4 represent a crude and early stage of this analysis. More systematic research is needed; however, it seems clear that both the willingness, resources and structures to increase geocentrism are not available with the kind of commitment and sometimes missionary zeal one sees in multi-national firms (such as Unilever, Shell, Nestlé, I.B.M. I.T.T.) trying to build a worldwide culture. Clearly the headquarters of an international union does not have the kinds of interest described above. In comparison the international union is a very loosely organised institution more akin to a holding company where each country goes its own way.

A nation State has limited access to extra-national resources and facilities. The nation State has necessarily a narrower, often more provincial, mission than a world institution like the multi-national firm. The socio-political and military objectives of a nation make economic consideration less primary. National self-sufficiency and the need for military preparedness make ethnocentric values necessary to maintain the citizen's loyalty to the country, and maintain a level of suspicion of foreign States' motives and actions. The need and resources to define a realistic worldwide niche based on competitive advantage and distinctive competence as a country are usually rather muted. After all, only nationals can be used in key posts in comparison with the intention (if not the implementation) of multi-national firms to get the best men and ideas everywhere in the world regardless of the passport of the ideas or the men. As table 3 indicates, the nations are obliged to protect inefficient industries, to embark on import substitution programmes, to remember historical wounds from other nations. And while there is increasing awareness that a geocentric mission is

## TABLE 2
### INTERNATIONAL EXECUTIVES' VIEW OF FORCES TOWARDS AND OBSTACLES TO GEOCENTRISM IN THEIR FIRMS*

| Forces Towards Geocentrism | | Obstacles Towards Geocentrism | |
|---|---|---|---|
| Environmental | Intra-Organisational | Environmental | Intra-Organisational |
| 1. Technological and managerial know-how increasing in availability in different countries | 1. Desire to use human vs. material resources optimally | 1. Economic nationalism in host and home countries | 1. Management inexperience in overseas markets |
| 2. International customers | 2. Observed lowering of morale in affiliates of an ethnocentric company | 2. Political nationalism in host and home countries | 2. National-centred reward and punishment structure |
| 3. Local customers demand for best product at fair price | 3. Evidence of waste and duplication in polycentrism | 3. Military secrecy associated with research in home country | 3. Mutual distrust between home country people and foreign executives |
| 4. Host country's desire to increase balance of payments | 4. Increasing awareness and respect for good men of other than home nationality | 4. Distrust of big international firms by host country political leaders | 4. Resistance to letting foreigners into the power structure |
| 5. Growing world markets | 5. Risk diversification in having a worldwide production and distribution system | 5. Lack of international monetary system | 5. Anticipated costs and risks of geocentrism |

| | | | |
|---|---|---|---|
| 6. Global competition among international firms for scarce human and material resources | 6. Need for recruitment of good men on a world-wide basis | 6. Growing differences between the rich and poor countries | 6. Nationalistic tendencies in staff |
| 7. Major advances in integration of international transport and telcommunications | 7. Need for worldwide information system | 7. Host country belief that home countries get disproportionate benefits of international firm's profits | 7. Increasing immobility of staff |
| 8. Regional supranational economic and political communities | 8. Worldwide appeal of products | 8. Home country political leaders' attempts to control firm's policy | 8. Linguistic problems and different cultural backgrounds |
| | 9. Senior management's long-term commitment to geocentrism as related to survival and growth | | 9. Centralisation tendencies in headquarters |

* Howard V. Perlmutter, 'The Tortuous Evolution of the Multi-national Corporation', Reprinted from *Columbia Journal of World Business*, Vol. IV, No. 1 (Jan–Feb 1969).

## TABLE 3

### INFERRED FORCES TOWARDS AND OBSTACLES TO GEOCENTRISM IN NATIONS

| Forces Towards Geocentrism | | Obstacles To Geocentrism | |
|---|---|---|---|
| Environmental | Intra-National | Environmental | Intra-National |
| 1. Economic vulnerability of a given State | 1. Increasing know-how about overseas trade | 1. Rising economic nationalism | 1. Need to protect infant or inefficient industries |
| 2. Growing world markets; limited domestic market. (even the United States is one-third of the world) | 2. Increasing awareness of economic limitations of a State | 2. Growing differences between rich and poor countries | 2. Military needs to be self-sufficient and to guarantee physical security |
| 3. Geocentric character of world science and technology | 3. Country's desires to achieve worldwide standards | 3. Nuclear armaments race | 3. Relative inaccessibility and distrust of nationals of one country to experts in another: military secrecy |
| 4. High costs of R and D in advanced areas of science and technology | 4. Increasing awareness of interdependence of State and multi-national firm regarding managerial skills and technology | 4. Political nationalism | 4. Unclear concepts regarding national comparative advantage |
| 5. Shortage of investment capital | 5. Increasing need for foreign capital | 5. Racial turmoil | 5. Extreme of import substitution policies |

6. Global competition among nation states

7. Growth of regional supranational communities (E.E.C. and LAFTA)

8. Major advances in integration of international transport and tele-communications

9. Nuclear disaster threat

10. Internationalisation of product by multi-national firm: structural changes in the world economy

6. Increasing need to harmonise policies with other States: taxes, standards, patents, monetary policies

7. Awareness of limitations of import substitution policies

8. Increasing difficulties with balance of payments in trade

9. Need for hard currency

6. Lack of international monetary system

7. East-West Conflicts

8. War: Viet-Nam

9. Lack of worldwide information system as regards opportunities and comparative advantages

10. Poor concept of future world economy

6. Primacy of historical national sentiments plus territorial imperative

7. Historical wounds

8. Need to have one's standards, practices prevail over others in negotiations (ethnocentrism)

9. Belief each country must be econo-militarily and technologically self-sufficient (polycentrism)

10. Inferiority feelings of less developed countries leading to emulation of wrong models (xeno-philia)

TABLE 4

INFERRED FORCES TOWARDS AND OBSTACLES TO
GEOCENTRISM IN UNIONS

| Forces Towards Geocentrism | | Obstacles To Geocentrism | |
| Environmental | Intra-Union | Environmental | Intra-Union |
| --- | --- | --- | --- |
| 1. Growth of giant multi-national firm | 1. Perception that multi-national firm is exploiting national weaknesses | 1. Great differences between industries | 1. Limited identification of worker with worldwide union vs. worldwide company |
| 2. Capacity of multi-national firm to transfer production if labour climate is poor | 2. Perception that multi-national corporation is anti-union and wants to exploit worker | 2. Intergovernmental rivalry: parity of wages may lead to loss of world markets | 2. Polycentric tendencies in trade union: strong personalities at national level |
| 3. Wide differences in working conditions and industrial relations policies | 3. Belief that supergiant corporations will be free from countervailing forces of host and home States and unions | 3. Great differences in facilities and know-how between countries | 3. Fragmentation of unions at national and local level |
| 4. Structural change in world economy: inter-nationalisation of production | 4. Awareness of ineffectual character of global trade union movement up until now | 4. Wide range of pro-ductivity and managerial skills | 4. Ideological splits between unions |

5. Major advances in integration of international transport and telecommunications

6. Economic integration in Europe and Latin America

7. Emerging forms of inter-governmental co-operation

8. Some geocentrisation processes in multi-national firms

5. Fear of divide and conquer strategy of worldwide institution

6. Experiences of international union solidarity

7. Emerging leadership committed to an international approach to organisation

8. International trade union information system on worldwide firm practices

9. World Company councils

10. Technical assistance in collective bargaining

5. Variation in size of domestic markets

6. Ethnocentric and polycentric tendencies in worldwide firms, industrial relations policies

7. Progressive corporate philosophies aimed at developing the firm as a multi-national institution

8. Economic and political nationalism

9. East-West conflict

10. Growing differences between rich and poor countries

5. Distrust of international headquarters and its power objectives

6. Limited international managerial resources of worldwide unions

7. Limited understanding of how multi-national firms function and their distinctive competence

8. Unclarity of mission and distinctive competence of worldwide unions

necessary (excluding the empire concept as non-feasible in our times), there is only a limited amount of harmonisation possible with 140 or so other countries!

Table 4 further specifies some of the difficulties unions face in becoming geocentric. It is not easy to overcome such obstacles as (1) limited identification of workers with worldwide unions, (2) polycentric tendencies in the trade union movement – especially where there are strong personalities at the national level, and (3) ideological splits in the union as for example when the A.F.L.–C.I.O.[1] decides to stop co-operating with its European counterparts and leave the I.C.F.T.U.,[2] on the ground that the European members are too friendly with the communist world. Or some external obstacles, such as the great variation in practices, histories, experience of national trade unions or in the size of domestic markets.

In comparison, the multi-national firm can be either more ethnocentric or geocentric than the international trade unions because its headquarters has the power to build an organisation.

*The second proposition of Part 5* is based on the current state of distrust and threat which unions and nation States have for large geocentrising multi-national firms. There seems to be less concern about working out partnership courses with multi-national firms from each of the other institutions. This is understandable in view of the relative recency with which multi-national firms have gained prominence, and to a certain degree dominance in the world economy.

*Le défi americain* (the American challenge) is the United States-owned multi-national corporation to which the corporate response should be a European-owned multi-national corporation. But the threat stems from a growing awareness that the United States multi-national firm is often too American-oriented in its attitudes towards foreigners. In addition, United States firms are inconvenienced by actions of the headquarters country as regards anti-trust, trade with Eastern Europe, and restriction on overseas investment. The United States Government is unwittingly developing *geocentric* attitudes among chief executives of U.S. multi-national corporations.

Of course, the distrust of national political leaders is not reduced by George Ball's Cosmocorp, the United States incorporated international corporation which bypasses State influence, or by such declarations as that of Frank Tannenbaum:

---

[1] American Federation of Labour/Congress of Industrial Organisations.
[2] International Confederation of Free Trade Unions.

'If . . . a base could be found upon which to build an extra-national political institution then indeed the external role of the nation state would decline and gradually disappear. . . . This extra-national body is the corporation . . . the multi-national corporation.'[1]

The rise of the multi-national firm has been associated with the *withering away of the nation State*, an opinion that can only serve to increase the unease of political leaders for this new kind of phenomenon. Furthermore, for the leaders of multi-national firms, *economic and political nationalism* is seen as one of the principal external restraining forces in the firm as it strives for survival, growth and profitability. So the possibility that nation States will have less influence is not an unpleasant prospect.

*Ambivalence* may be a better way to describe nations' response to the emergence of multi-national firms within their boundaries since technology and managerial skill are welcome. But these gifts are usually seen as coming at a price, dependent on a distant, foreign-owned headquarters, whose values and objectives are usually different from the home country.

The reaction of *union leadership* is not very different, and in recent months even more explicit. The multi-national firm is viewed as a monolith, with its intention to destroy unions, to achieve its methods by *divide and conquer* tactics – a monolith which takes little responsibility for the unfair policies of its subsidiaries to workers, and their conditions of work. While no doubt the external threat of the multi-national firm may be best exaggerated a little in order to increase the cohesiveness of the polycentrically-oriented union, there is little doubt that the prevailing climate is one of mutual suspicion and doubt about the good intentions of the other. The union suspects the multi-national firm as seeking cheap labour, withholding the workers' share of the wealth created by the firm, and trying to alienate the worker from unions by increasing his identification with the company. The goal is to bargain at headquarters on a worldwide basis on an equal level.

The multi-national firm in turn fears that unions will price their products out of the competitive world scale by insisting on wage parity without concurrent gains in productivity.

---

[1] Frank Tannenbaum: 'The Survival of the Fittest', *Columbia Journal of World Business*, March–April 1968.

*Coalitions*

I have done little research on the possible *coalitions* and how they will contribute to this negative atmosphere. For example, the *multi-national firm could* team up with *worldwide unions* to further neutralise the *nation State*. A *State could* co-operate with the *multi-national firm* when it believes the *union*'s collective bargaining objectives will be disastrous for the national economy and its competitiveness on the world scale. Or the *union* and the *State* could team up with the intention of reducing the effectiveness of a multi-national firm by restrictive legislation of various shapes and sizes. There are instances of each kind of coalition no doubt. But I believe it is fair to say that each is inherently unstable, for no pair can destroy the other, and the consequences are further distrust and suspicion.

But an individual case analysis may be useful.

Let us examine some of the issues in the 1969 Ford strike in Britain.[1] One central issue concerned the corporation's legal right to penalise wildcat strikes. The local practice could be described by some United States or United Kingdom observers as giving in to demands to avoid labour stoppage. The difficulties stemmed in part from the multi-national character of Ford Motors. Ford had integrated its various European operations. Its purpose was to take advantage of economies and to specialise in plants that serve the whole European market. The vulnerability of Ford in the United Kingdom to work stoppage was apparent when, during the dispute, the Genk plant in Belgium had to lay off 1,500 workers because they failed to receive British components. The management of the Cologne plant made statements that in the future they did not want to be dependent on British components.

Prime Minister Wilson condemned the strike (which cost some 100 million dollars output in the United Kingdom apart from losses in continental Europe.) He warned that foreign business would start disinvesting or refusing to expand in Britain. Ford in the United Kingdom exports vehicles worth several hundred million dollars from Britain, it should be noted. Thus Britain's worldwide distinctive competence and competitive advantage in this particular area of automobile manufacture were threatened.

One central issue was whether collective bargaining agreements should be enforceable by law in the United Kingdom – a practice which

[1] See in particular *Business Europe*, 28 March 1969.

technologies, and for disseminating the best and most humane treatment of workers everywhere in the world. Both unions and firms need to understand the created wealth (e.g. profits):

(a) in terms of their multiple claimants – stockholders, consumers, managers and workers, and host and home countries;
(b) in terms of the firm's needs for tremendous investments in new technologies;
(c) in terms of the firm's desire for efficiency, productivity and competitive advantage with worldwide standards in view.

A partnership course in less developed countries for States and unions is necessary for multi-national firms and will have to be based on a more direct dialogue than has been the case up until now.

### The Need for Research on the Inter-institution Building Process

Research is needed on the process by which nations, unions, and multi-national firms collaborate to reach common objectives. Such research would necessarily be based on two assumptions:

(1) Each institution has a viable and indispensable worldwide role in the twentieth century.
(2) Each institution can help the other achieve this worldwide role in a climate of minimal mutual suspicion and distrust.

Three stages can be envisaged in such a research programme:

Stage 1:
(a) identifying the changing world environment (in its social, political, economic and technological aspects);
(b) identifying the drives towards and obstacles to geocentrisation in firms, nations, and unions as they seek to geocentrise their philosophies, policies, structures and practices;
(c) identifying the obstacles to and opportunities for reducing distrust and mutual suspicion between the two.

Stage 2:
A discussion of the findings among leaders of these institutions is held in a climate of objectivity and mutual understanding, encouraging leaders to redefine their missions and strategies with awareness of the other's missions and strategies.

Stage 3:

Research on the development of structures, policies and practices is conducted with the purpose of helping these institutions accomplish their new worldwide objectives based on reciprocative interdependence.

I recognise that some senior executives of worldwide firms are beginning to feel more discomfort as the world spotlight focuses on them more and more. Some would prefer that the publicity given them would die down, and they could assume a less prominent role in the world's economy. But time does not turn back, for with their silence and inactions, the scenario turns towards distrust and suspicion. The development of the firm as a worldwide institution requires a direct confrontation with the problems of mankind today.

### The Need for Worldwide Institutions

It is curious that man's talents in physical architecture have been improving with great steps over time – witness the skyscrapers, dams, aircraft, and aerospace feats. Building institutions that suit the worldwide scale of events is the key problem of our times.

Barbara Ward in her *Spaceship Earth* put it well. She wrote:

'The greatest institutional gap in our world is created by an inescapable planetary interdependence which builds common grievances and creates common needs and opportunities, yet is matched by virtually no instrument of worldwide order and welfare. And it is through this gap that mankind can tumble into annihilation.'[1]

Leaders of the trio of institutions could well heed the call to seek areas of interdependence, common grievances, common needs and opportunities in redefining the worldwide mission and objectives of multi-national firms, nations and unions – in a climate where mutual confidence prevails over mutual suspicion. A reflection of Amiel is relevant here:

'Each man's experience is starting afresh. Only institutions become wiser; they accumulate collective experience and, as a result of this experience and this wisdom, men who are subject to the same rules will find, not their nature changing, but their behaviour undergoing a gradual alteration.'

[1] Barbara Ward: *Spaceship Earth* (Columbia University Press), p. 17.

If the worldwide firm is helped to achieve its standards of performance, if its transideological character develops, this kind of institution could be a force for world economic integration and order. With the risks associated with its increasing economic power come the prospects of a world in which it would be absurd to bomb customers, suppliers, managers and workers and shareholders.

The seeds of the cosmic, postgeocentric era, symbolised by landing of man upon the moon must emphasise that building institutions with a worldwide orientation is a high priority task.

For the nation State, the worldwide orientation involves the primary awareness that each country is but a part of mankind, that each country cannot do everything, that it must import as well as export. A nation's resources, aspirations, and fate are interdependent with the rest of mankind. That is what we mean by the geocentrisation of the nation State.

Similar problems exist for the trade union as we have indicated – since organised labour is a direct claimant upon the worldwide firm. Its place in the era of geocentric institutions depends heavily on its resolution of the transideological mission.

There are missing worldwide institutions: for the worldwide firm is to be a central actor in the emerging global industrial estate. This will necessitate the geocentrisation of shareholders and of boards of these firms. Herein is contained the seeds of a fundamental philosophical solution: the people of the earth should own the emerging global industrial estate. Yet how should ownership be facilitated? The solution should be *transideological* in our view which means that a new vocabulary is necessary to describe those claimants on a firm who have financial interests in its efficiency and growth. Some kind of worldwide financial institutions which relate the needs of individuals, and institutions like the State to participate in the wealth creation process everywhere in the world.

The trade union's role in the global industrial estate remains to be defined.

It is obvious that the nation-oriented educational systems, which facilitate however unconsciously a nation-centred concept of truth, have been by-passed by the facts of the present geocentric science and technology, and the prospects of a cosmic science and technology. The generation gap between students and faculty can only decrease, to the degree that the faculty itself experiences emotionally and intellectually the emerging character of the planet Earth. The children born to the cosmic age could not but find great pockets of unwillingness to accept the dawn of universal history as natural evidence of crisis in the universities today. Thus, each subsystem of the world university on the earth must reach for its vision of the whole.

Research then, in my view, ought to focus on the obstacles and forces towards developing worldwide institutions – on the conditions which favour or impede the appearance of the *geocentric style of social architecture* as it can be embodied in firms, nations and unions.

No doubt other institutions need this kind of research – the university is one most certainly. We need to learn how to build and design, with wisdom, and patience the *missing institutions*. Each research should be evaluated according to its contribution to our understanding of the worldwide institution building process, and each institution should be judged according to its contribution to the 'common fortunes of mankind'.

## Chapter 3

# THE STRENGTH OF INTERNATIONAL REGIONALISM

*by*

*Joseph S. Nye*

THE rapid advance of our scientific knowledge and its technological applications have brought the role of massive research and development in economic growth into enhanced prominence. Figures, showing that the United States spends some fifteen to twenty times as much on research and development annually as a typical European State does, have been used to argue that most States in the world today are too small to be leaders in massive technology-oriented industries such as aerospace, applications of nuclear energy, and others. These technological pressures are said to be a force for the formation of regional entities larger than existing States in Europe and the Third World.

Another result of the growth of research and technology (as well as from other factors) is the growth of the large corporation, often but not always based on the United States market.

In 1965, 87 corporations (of which 60 were domiciled in the United States) had sales greater than the gross national product of 57 sovereign States.[1] Increasingly such corporations are developing global strategies and absorbing 'the business done "abroad" into the mainstream of corporate strategy'.[2] While such corporations are often popularly identified with a particular country (a fact that dramatises concerns about their possible threat to national control), the trend seems to be for them to become 'multi-national' by conforming to local conceptions of 'good citizenship' and perhaps eventually to become 'international' corporations in the full sense of the word – a form of private international organisation essentially free of any single national control.[3]

[1] George Modelski: 'The Corporation in World Society', *Yearbook of World Affairs, 1968* (London, Stevens, 1968), p. 68.

[2] Raymond Vernon: 'Economic Sovereignty at Bay', *Foreign Affairs*, XLVII (October 1968), p. 115.

[3] The three terms are developed in Charles Kindleberger. *American Business Abroad: Six Lectures on Direct Investment* (New Haven, Yale, 1969), p. 179.

These two developments (the formation of regional entities and the growth of corporations) can be portrayed as opposing trends in international organisation. The large international corporation can be seen as a transnational centralised decision system, staffed by cosmopolitan 'technocrats' responding to criteria of economic rationality in their choices as to the location of industry, employment or earnings. To some extent, they can be seen as private sector incarnations of the old functionalist dream, tying the world together along global lines of economic rationality. On the other hand, the regionalist can be seen as an updated version of the nineteenth-century nationalist, concerned about the identity and welfare of his particular part of the globe, and not willing to let decisions affecting it be made by 'cosmopolitan technocrats' even if (as may not always be the case) he could be assured that they were responding solely to criteria of economic rationality. The regionalist wants regional organisation to turn the forces of the large corporation to the benefit of his region.

The interaction between these forces is already beginning. Large international corporations (usually American, but also British and Swiss) have been the most adept in seizing the opportunities of the European Economic Community (E.E.C.) created by the Treaty of Rome. Similarly, American and other firms have been the most responsive to organising their activities in response to the regional vision as embodied in the Latin American Free Trade Association (LAFTA). One could speculate that such companies might be the means to introduce some day economic rationality into the post-colonial fragmentation of economic space into small sovereign units in West Africa.

The reaction to these experiences has often been nationalistic, and is generally ambivalent at best. Many Latin American businessmen and politicians complain that a Latin American common market must be for the benefit of Latin Americans and not of large outside corporations. In calculating benefit to Latin Americans they seem to pay more attention to the immediate benefit to Latin businessmen, and psychic benefit to the identity of the population of the region, rather than to the welfare benefits to the population as a whole. Given the concern of African elites for industry for prestige purposes and the sensitivity to anything that might suggest an increase in external control and a return to the indignities of the past, one can easily foresee charges of neocolonialism being brought against the large international corporation.

Even in Europe, allegedly in a post-nationalist phase, governments of the E.E.C. countries have frequently responded in a nationalistic fashion not only to investments by corporations from outside the region, but also to efforts by corporations from other member countries to take over national companies in the process of building larger European corporations. (Examples are the reactions of the French Government to the envisaged merger of Citroën and Fiat and of the Government of the Federal Republic of Germany to a take-over by the Companie Française des Petroles of Gelsenkirchener Bergwerke.)

In the eyes of some Europeans, these responses are curtailing the welfare of the people, and the proper response to the problems of the cost of technology and the existence of large international corporations is a 'global' one of accepting close economic linkages with the North American (and, to a lesser extent, Japanese) economy, and carving out areas of comparative advantage through specialisation. Other Europeans respond by arguing that maximising welfare is not the only goal, and that European identity and power are also important. Too close linkages to the global (or Atlantic) economy could hinder these objectives by making Europe overly dependent on imports of technological innovations. In the view of people like Servan-Schreiber, it is not enough for Europeans to live like Swiss or Swedes.[1] Rather they must build a strong European regional unity equal in size to the United States and U.S.S.R. and capable of being an independent power in world politics. Still other Europeans support such a strong European unit as source of protection against competition of outside corporations.

In Robert Cox's words, 'the politico-international aspects of structural change involving the multi-national corporation thus all turn upon the relative weight to be given in the future, on the one hand, to transnationally structured economic and organisational power and, on the other, to geographically structured political power'.[2] The task of this paper is to speculate on the strength of international regionalism as a form of geographically structured political power.

Since the Second World War, there has been a large increase in the number of intergovernmental organisations that have been called 'regional'. With a few exceptions, in particular, the Inter-American organisations, regional organisation is a post-1945 phenomenon.

[1] J.-J. Servan-Schreiber: *The American Challenge* (N.Y., Atheneum, 1968), '. . . but Sweden has no ambition to be a world power', p. 111.
[2] Unpublished memorandum, International Institute for Labour Studies, Ref. 11-2-31, p. 3.

In fact, an increasing proportion of the intergovernmental organisations founded have been regional (see table I below). Some of these organisations are very limited in scope; others are extremely broad in ambition. Of course the mere creation and functioning of an organisation does not mean that it has a significant impact on its members or on world politics. All too often international organisations seem to function in a vacuum like 'a set of wheels without power'.[1]

Yet along with the growth in the number of regional organisations there have been claims that they *do* represent an important trend in world politics. Illustrative of this sort of claim is the statement by Jean Rey, President of the Commission of the European Community, that 'the political life of the world is becoming less at the level of national states and more at the level of continents'.[2] And even Charles de Gaulle has said that 'it is in keeping with the conditions of our times to create entities more vast than each of the European States'.[3] As we shall see, however, the evidence for a clear trend towards 'regionalisation' of world politics is ambiguous at best. While further research is needed on the subject, one can at least say that it is unlikely that the creation of regional organisations is an indication of some great wave of history.

The term 'region' has become widely used in international politics, but its meaning is far from clear. There are no absolute or naturally determined regions. Relevant geographical boundaries vary with different purposes, and these purposes both differ and change.[4] Core areas can be determined and various boundaries delineated by analysis of mutual transactions or effective international organisation, but which of a large number of potential regions become relevant in world politics depends on political decisions. Physical contiguity can be misleading, not only because technology can make 'effective distance' differ from linear distance, but also because our images of what constitutes a region are affected by our different political interests. It may be true that a region 'needs essentially a strong belief . . . regionalism has some iconography as its foundation';[5] but these beliefs or icons change.

---

[1] André Beaufre: *NATO and Europe* (N.Y., Vintage, 1966), p. 33.
[2] *European Community*, No. 103 (June 1967), p. 8.
[3] Press Conference, 9 September 1965.
[4] In Bruce Russett's words, 'there is *no* region or aggregate of national units that can in the very strict sense of boundary congruence be identified as a subsystem of the international system'. *International Regions and the International System* (Chicago, Rand McNally, 1967), p. 168.
[5] Jean Gottmann: 'Geography and International Relations', in W. A. Douglas Jackson (ed.), *Politics and Geographic Relationships* (N.Y., Prentice Hall, 1964), p. 28.

For example, do 'oceans divide men' or 'oceans unite men'? For Western Europeans at the time of NATO's foundation, the Atlantic Ocean was the historic highway of Atlantic culture, though less is heard of this in recent years. For African anti-colonialists salt water made a difference, and 'France belongs to the continent of Europe; Algeria belongs to the continent of Africa'; though Algeria and France are both Mediterranean and close while, e.g., Algeria and Ghana are neither. What matters is not the geographical milieu, but how decision-makers conceive of it in making policy.

Table I gives an indication not only of the increasing proportion of regional organisations, but also a crude indication of the changing images of 'regions' as reflected in the foundation of new inter-governmental organisations.[1]

These ambiguities raise questions about descriptions of how world politics has become increasingly 'regionalised'. The evidence is varied, and different types of behaviour point in different directions. On the one hand, those who see a trend towards regionalism cite the fact that a non-regional organisation like the Commonwealth, which once represented the paragon of effective international organisation, has undergone a decline, and Britain has sought to limit its obligations 'East of Suez' and prove its Europeanness. Further evidence is that regional voting blocs have come to characterise the politics of the United Nations, and a principle of regional powers seems firmly established. The European Community has had a considerable success in expanding intra-regional trade, and its success has caused others to try to imitate it. Finally, as we saw in table I, an increasing proportion of new intergovernmental organisations founded have been regional in nature.

This evidence, however, is far from conclusive. The establishment of international organisations is not always the best indicator of effective systems or interdependences. And, in some cases, for example, the broadening of the 'Atlantic' Organisation for Economic Co-operation and Development (O.E.C.D.) to include Japan in 1964, or the establish-ment of the non-regional Group of Ten in the politically important international monetary system, the important trend does not seem to be regional. As for behaviour in the United Nations, many of the caucuses are 'regional' only in a loose sense of the word, and one can question the extent to which 'regional' caucusing behaviour in the U.N. arena

[1] This list is calculated by the author from a list kindly made available by J. David Singer and Michael Wallace.

## TABLE 1

### Regional and Quasi-Regional Intergovernmental Organisations Founded, 1815–1965

| Period | I.G.O.s Founded Total (N) | Regional (N) (%) | Quasi-Reg. (N) (%) | Inter. Am. (N) | Lat. Am. (N) | Carib. (N) | Eur. (N) | Atlant. (N) | Pacif. (N) | Medit. (N) | Arab (N) | Asia (N) | Africa (N) |
|---|---|---|---|---|---|---|---|---|---|---|---|---|---|
| 1815–1914 | 52 | 8 | 6 (27%) | 4 | 3 | | 3 | 1 | | | | | 3 |
| 1915–1944 | 74 | 22 (30%) | 6 (8%) (38%) | 14 | 3 | 1 | 5 | | 3 | 1 | | | 1 |
| 1945–1955 | 88 | 25 (28%) | 22 (25%) (53%) | 3 | 3 | 1 | 18 | 2 | 3 | 1 | 3 | 4 | 7 |
| 1956–1965 | 59 | 35 (59%) | 11 (18%) (77%) | 4 | 4 | 1 | 16 | 1 | 1 | | | 2 | 17 |

is a useful indicator of political behaviour outside the U.N. Turning to international trade, geography remains an important determinant and there have been dramatic increases in trade among members of regional organisations, especially those including a customs union or a free trade area, but there have also been dramatic increases between distant partners such as the U.S. and Japan.

The most exhaustive attempts to map inductively the extent of regional behaviour in the international system have been made by Bruce Russett. His factor analyses of socio-economic homogeneity, U.N. voting patterns, number of shared memberships in international organisations, trade, and geographical proximity between States led

TABLE 2

TRADE GROWTH

|  | 1958 $billion | 1967 | |
|---|---|---|---|
|  |  | $billion | 1958 = 100 |
| U.S./Canada | 3·3 | 13·9 | 420 |
| U.S./Japan | 1·7 | 5·7 | 340 |
| Intra E.E.C. | 7·5 | 24·5 | 326 |
| Intra EFTA | 2·8 | 7·0 | 249 |
| World Trade | 108·0 | 214·1 | 194 |

Sources: United Nations: *Yearbook of International Trade Statistics*; O.E.C.D.: *Overall Trade by Countries*.

him to observe that 'the lowest correlation for a given analysis is almost always between it and the pattern of geographic proximity'.[1] Moreover, his data provide no evidence for increasing regionalisation. The average correlation among his factor analyses for the 1960s was not higher (in fact it was slightly lower) than for the 1950s.

One of the problems of interpreting Russett's results for our purposes is that his factor analysis is designed to find the fewest (and thus often the largest) clusters of States to account for the variance in the data.[2] The resulting factors are then given 'regional' labels though in some cases the fit between the general meaning of the labels and the factors is very imperfect. However, if we take the three factors for which Russett has data over time and give regional labels

[1] Russett, *op. cit.*, p. 213.
[2] This tendency to find quasi- and macro-regional clusters also means that a number of Russett's generalisations about regions are not relevant (and sometimes misleading) when applied to micro-regions.

only to those factors of which two-thirds of the States are contiguous (i.e. fall in a recognisable region with a maximum of 6,000 miles between the most distant capitals), we find that the only important increase in regional behaviour from the 1950s to the 1960s that is apparent from Russett's data is in shared membership of international organisation and not in U.N. voting or in trade patterns.

Projections of the future on the basis of technological changes also lead to caution about concluding that there is a clear-cut trend towards regionalisation of behaviour in world politics. Indeed some observers argue that the revolution in transport, communications and defence technology is rapidly foreshortening effective distances and calling into question the basis for regionalist schemes.[1] For example, the creation of jumbo air freighters, giant supertankers, and large-scale data processing that facilitates capital movements and central control in multi-national corporations will make reduction of trade barriers and achievement of economies of scale less dependent on geographical contiguity. In the defence field, nuclear and missile technology has already reduced the role of geographical distance in military security, and further changes of a similar type can be expected from satellite technology (and possibly from development in chemical and biological warfare). In the view of Thomas Schelling, a new type of global geography may be taking over, in which earth spin and cloud cover may become as important in the world of satellites as Suez and Gibraltar were for seapower.[2] In Albert Wohlstetter's words, 'the up-shot of these considerations of technology in the 1970s is that basic interests in safety will extend further out than they ever have before'.[3]

It would be mistaken to conclude from the projection of techno-logical trends, however, that there will be no important regional systems of interaction – whether economic or military. For one thing, such a conclusion would be somewhat premature, at least for the early 1970s. Despite falling transport costs, geography will still have an impact on price. Despite missile and satellite technology, local and conventional defence techniques will remain relevant. Moreover, some technological changes may encourage regional organisation. Communications technology may make possible direct and inexpensive regional communications in areas like Latin America or Africa where

---

[1] Albert Wohlstetter: 'Illusions of Distance', *Foreign Affairs* (January 1968), p. 250. Also, Institute for Strategic Studies: *The Implications of Military Technology in 1970s* (London, Adelphi Paper 46, 1968).
[2] Speech to Foreign Policy Association, New York, May 1968.
[3] *Op. cit.*, p. 252.

TABLE 3

'REGIONAL GROUP' FACTORS COMPARED
TO TOTAL NUMBER OF FACTORS

|  | 1950s | |
|---|---|---|
|  | Number of factors | of which 'regional' |
| U.N. voting | 7 | (1957)<br>3    Latin America<br>S.E. Asia<br>East Europe |
| Group of Ten membership | 7 | (1951)<br>4    Latin America<br>East Europe<br>West Europe<br>S.E. Asia |
| Trade | 8 | (1954)<br>2    South America<br>North Atlantic |

|  | 1962 or 1963 | |
|---|---|---|
|  | Number of factors | of which 'regional' |
| U.N. voting | 7 | 4    Iberia<br>Atlantic<br>French African<br>Latin America |
| Group of Ten membership | 7 | 6    Latin America<br>East Europe<br>West Europe<br>Asia<br>French Africa<br>Arabs |
| Trade | 9 | 2    West Europe<br>Arabs |

Source: Russett: *International Regions and the International System, op. cit.*

intra-regional communications now often have to go through New York, London or Paris. In addition, the development of inexpensive breeder reactors may lead to nuclear proliferation of a type that encourages disengagement by distant powers eager to minimise their risks.

Furthermore, technology and systems of transactions are not the only determinants of the politics of international organisation. As long ago as 1943 some commentators were predicting that the development of modern transport and communications would likely 'destroy both the objective and subjective grounds for regionalism'.[1]

If the technology/transactions approach is overly mechanical, another type of projection of the future of regional organisation based on the alleged obsolescence of the nation States is overly technological. According to this view, as people become aware that the nation State is obsolete, yet world government remains unobtainable, they will turn towards regional organisation as the next logical step. As Herz describes it, the rise of the nation State followed the inventions of gunpowder and professional infantry which destroyed the impenetrability of the medieval castle. Now with air warfare, nuclear weapons, economic blockades and ideological warfare, the hard protective shell of the State has become 'permeable'.[2] Or in Boulding's terms, there are no longer any snugly protected centres of national power, and all states are only 'conditionally viable'.

But the obsolescence of the nation State is nowhere near as complete as it is sometimes claimed to be. Take, for instance, the failure to provide security. Nuclear deterrence has made viability conditional, but not as a fact of daily life in such a way as to weaken national loyalties. In terms of welfare, the argument tends to neglect the question of distribution. After all, one role of the State is to preserve inequality of welfare vis-à-vis outsiders and this it has done.

But perhaps the most important flaw in the obsolescence argument is that it ignores a third function that the nation State fulfils for many of its citizens – the provision of a sense of identity and community, or 'pooled self-esteem'. The discrediting of nationalism as an *ideology* in post-war Europe has not been true of the 'Third World', and even in Europe the argument that we live in a post-nationalist period has tended to avert attention from the persistence of nationalism in a

---

[1] Pitman B. Potter: 'Universalism Versus Regionalism in International Organisation', *American Political Science Review*, XXXVIII (1943), p. 852.

[2] John Herz: 'The Rise and Demise of the Territorial State', *World Politics*, IX (July 1957), pp. 473–93.

second sense, as a widespread consciousness of national identity. While this identity is usually not exclusively focused at the national level, nonetheless this is the level which has been most important. While there is certainly some relationship between welfare, security and national identity, the latter does not seem to be (at least in the short run of decades) merely the result of the other two. The relationship may sometimes be the other way round. De Gaulle was able to sacrifice considerable French welfare for the sake of 'pooled self-esteem' without losing at the polls.[1] Not only does this function of collective identity help to explain the persistence of the nation State, but it is also a factor independent of welfare and security in the causation of regionalism. Not only in Africa or Latin America, but in Europe as well, the desire to achieve status through large-size powers is an important (though sometimes illusory) motive for the creation of regional organisations. But the strength of the organisations that can be built on this sense of regional identity has not so far been such as to challenge the nation State, and it seems less realistic to see regional organisation as an *alternative* to the nation State than as something that will *coexist* as an auxilliary or instrument for the nation States.

If these arguments are correct, perhaps the most useful perspective on the future of regional organisations is to ask what incentives there are for the elites and statesmen to use them. And from this perspective, it would be a mistake to see the politics of regional organisations as purely the politics of co-operation. Regional organisations, like all international organisations, have latent functions as well as the manifest or declared ones of military security, political or cultural diplomacy and administration, and economic growth and aid. These latent functions[2] may include a symbolic role, for example, something comparable to statements of goodwill or non-aggression treaties; or more seriously as an indication of a weak alignment. They may also be useful as instruments of diplomacy, whether as a means of holding conferences without quibbling over schedules; gathering information; or as a means to exert diplomatic pressure on other States. Moreover, in a world in which communications make other societies 'penetrable', an aspect of power is the ability to communicate over the heads of governments (i.e., not by diplomacy alone) to create sympathy and a basis for legitimising one's policies. The conference or parliamentary

[1] At least up to the April 1969 referendum.
[2] There are also 'private-regarding' latent functions. International organisations may become cosy little clubs staffed by routineers; or be promoted by diplomats who see them as an opportunity for such personal goals as prestige, exile or corruption.

diplomacy aspects and sometimes the administrative actions of regional organisations are among the many means available for communicating to foreign populations.

These latent functions often seem more important than the manifest functions for the political regional organisations, particularly the macro-regional political ones such as the Arab League, the Organisation of African Unity (A.O.U.), the Organisation of American States (O.A.S.) and the Council of Europe. But military and economic regional organisations can be put to the same diplomatic use as well: witness De Gaulle's pressures on his partners in 1965 by threatening to break the E.E.C.;[1] or the 1969 struggle over the right of the Western European Union (W.E.U.) to discuss the Middle East (in reality a pretext for some of the E.E.C. States to associate with Britain).

These latent functions are particularly important as incentives for the formation and continuation of regional organisations, because of the nature of the current international system. As Stanley Hoffman describes it, the combination of the self-defeating costliness of nuclear weapons, the sanctification of the legitimacy of the nation State (enshrined in the United Nations), and the costliness of ruling socially mobilised (rather than colonially inert) alien populations, has reduced the role of force and enhanced the psychological components of power. Milieu goals (concern with the general environment of the international system) have become more important than possession goals (direct territorial, economic or other concrete interests). Prestige and capacity to communicate effectively have taken on special importance.[2] Regional organisations have been useful tools in terms of each of these characteristics: (1) with the diversification of power, the prestige of regional leadership becomes a useful symbol of power as the foreign policies of France, Ethiopia and Egypt in the E.E.C., O.A.U., and Arab League indicate; (2) with the increased importance of domestic populations in world politics, yet the enhanced legitimacy of national sovereignty, regional organisations provide, as we outlined above, an opportunity to appeal over the heads of governments to societal groups in other States (despite the sovereignty clauses often written in the charters), as the successful and unsuccessful efforts of the Ivory Coast and Ghana to influence their neighbours through the Conseil de l'Entente and the O.A.U., respectively, demonstrate; (3) with

[1] See Leon Lindberg: 'Integration as a Source of Stress on the European Community Systems', in J. S. Ney (ed.), *International Regionalism* (Boston, Little, Brown, 1968).
[2] Stanley Hoffman: *Gulliver's Troubles, or the Setting of American Foreign Policy* (N.Y., McGraw-Hill, 1968).

the devaluation of military force, traditional military alliances may be less attractive, but statesmen still feel the need to draw lines and introduce even a faint element of predictability into their search for security by political alliances under the guise of regional organisation – witness the Asian and South Pacific Council (ASPAC) and the Association of Southeast Asia (ASA); (4) with the predominance of milieu goals over possession goals, regional organisations may be useful tools for shaping conditions beyond one's national boundaries, whether it be creating more favourable conditions for aid for economic development (e.g., the regional development banks), creating regional balances of power (a major motive for ASPAC), or a group's assertion on the world scene of their collective identity; (5) finally, with the increased importance of communicaions and signals, regional organisations may be useful as 'no trespassing' signs, either between the super-powers (the O.A.S. or the Warsaw Pact) or from the weak to the super-powers (O.A.U.).

In short, regional organisations have increased in number, but from the mixed evidence that we have, this does not seem to be a trust-worthy indication of an automatic trend in the future, as some enthusiasts suggest. Nor does it seem likely that regional organisations will soon be relics of the past as some sceptics seem to imply.

If this is true, then it may be mistaken to see regional organisations as an alternative to the multi-national corporation or as a force capable of controlling it. Unless there is some drastic impairment of the capacity of the nation States to provide identity and security, or some other source (such as generational change) of a strong political will for the strengthening of regional organisations beyond what they now are, it seems likely that the multi-national corporation, regional organisation and the supposedly obsolete nation State will continue to coexist in the present imperfect way, with regional organisation by far the weakest of the three structures.

There is also a possibility, however, that multi-national corporations may unwittingly strengthen regional organisations. We have already noted that they are one of the important dynamic forces capable of taking advantage of new opportunities opened by regional market schemes and thus creating a pressure for further integration. The simul-taneous existence of regional market schemes, weak regional organis-ations, and alternative national jurisdictions with the market, increases the leverage of the multi-national corporations vis-à-vis the govern-ments, not only in less developed areas, but in Europe as well, as the vacillation in French policy towards foreign investment has demonstrated.[1]  Faced with such a situation, it is conceivable that governments might agree to strengthen their regional organisation.  So far, however, the multi-national corporation and the nation State look like continuing to be the strongest structures.

[1] See Raymond Vernon: 'The Role of U.S. Enterprise Abroad', *Daedalus*, XCVIIᵣ (Winter 1969), p. 123.

# TRADE UNIONS AND INTERNATIONAL MANAGEMENT FACING THE TRANSNATIONAL TRENDS

THE chapters of this section deal with the question how international management and trade unions are influenced by the transnational tendencies and the consequential change in their relationships.

Not surprisingly, unions see in the growth of multi-national corporations a phenomenon which alters the existing power balance between management and unions to the detriment of labour. One crucial problem for unions is access to the final centres of decision-making on industrial relations and related issues within the structure of the multi-national corporation. Unions suspect that in most cases the locus for such final decisions is not found at the subsidiaries of companies with which they bargain, but at their foreign-based headquarters outside the influence of local unions. At any rate, central foreign-based management will always have final decision-making power regarding economic issues of extreme interest to labour, such as location of plants, investments, pooling and location of profits.

Under the present power relationships, international management does not generally feel the need to bargain with unions on a regional or even a worldwide scale over industrial relations and related issues. Karl Casserini draws attention in the first chapter of this section to the efforts made by unions, and more particularly within his international trade secretariat (the International Metalworkers' Federation), to develop organisational forms and strategies by which unions hope to convince multi-national management of the usefulness to discuss and eventually bargain with them on a regional or, eventually, on a world-wide basis.

Economic regionalism is a much smaller challenge to unions than are multi-national corporations. There are several reasons for this. Firstly, economically co-operating regions do not offer the same economic possibilities for large-scale union action as do multi-national corporations. Secondly, in the more formally structured forms of regional economic integration, the prototype of which is the European Economic Community, trade unions have been given the right to contribute, at least in an advisory capacity, towards the development of common economic and social policies. Thirdly, unions have been, at least in Europe, much more concerned with lobbying the regional public institutions than with regional collective bargaining with their employer counterparts; harmonisation of labour conditions in the E.E.C. so far has been sought by putting pressure on the supranational authorities. Explanation for this state of affairs is attempted in section 7.

Despite the fact that unions have not yet developed worldwide organisational power or strategies, multi-national management, following the logic of 'going international' sees already the need for adjusting personnel management to its international role. Managements in the subsidiaries are confronted with the constraints of the national industrial relations system as reflected in labour legislation, employers' and trade union organisation, which largely condition personnel practices. Yet for reasons of efficiency and the image of a company, the home-based decision centre has an important role to play in establishing general principles or guidelines of personnel policy to be applied throughout the company. The main argument of Jack Lee in the second chapter of this section is that (before trade union pressure might push international management in any specific direction) there is considerable room for improving industrial relations by management initiative; already now such policies prevail to a much larger extent than is usually assumed.

Fundamental changes in attitudes can be expected in Jack Lee's opinion, e.g. by making mutual discussions between management and labour a habit, by introducing mutually accepted goals, by the acceptance of the principles for change, and by consolidating the achievements in collective bargaining. Analytical work in the multi-national corporations towards this end and more sophisticated attitudes which can be expected on the part of organised labour are viewed as allowing a new approach to collective bargaining involving negotiations for change. It is hoped that such a new approach could help to create mutually beneficial industrial relations both on the national and the international scale.

In the last chapter of this section, B. C. Roberts examines some of the internal and external factors that condition industrial relations policies of multi-national management. Multi-national corporations are not a monolithic structure type of management; the response of employers to managerial policy and the economic and social environment are determinants of the varying actual industrial relations setting.

For classifying the cultural aspects, Roberts adopts Perlmutter's attitudinal categories, but suggests that, while there seems to be a pronounced trend towards polycentric management, there is as yet no evidence of multi-national corporations undergoing a rapid process for adopting geocentric attitudes and culture; even the most advanced corporations in this respect will still seem to bear the stamp of their culture of origin, including the composition of senior management. Choosing between one or the other management approach means for a company to choose between acceptability and efficiency, the former being greatest with polycentric, the latter with geocentric management. Roberts expects multi-national corporations to obtain, in return for an adherence to local standards and a respect for national interest, the same treatment as national companies. He sees in the growth of multi-national corporations the best proof that these adjustments have been largely successful so far, but stresses likewise that this growth, especially if multi-national corporations and unions are allies, may effectively challenge the traditional structure of national sovereignty.

Chapter 4

# THE CHALLENGE OF MULTI-NATIONAL CORPORATIONS AND REGIONAL ECONOMIC INTEGRATION TO THE TRADE UNIONS, THEIR STRUCTURE AND THEIR INTERNATIONAL ACTIVITIES

*by*

*Karl Casserini*

## I. HISTORICAL FACTS AND FEATURES

*The Development of Trade Union Structure and Action*

THE historical development of trade unions has shown them to be pragmatic organisations with a definite social objective to be pursued within economic realities. They grew as a self-defence of the worker in a society in the throes of industrialisation. Workers of the same handicraft assembled to fight flagrant social injustice and to struggle for economic security.

The trade union structure which evolved from this basis followed, more or less, the pattern of industrialisation. There was a development from craft unions to general workers' unions.

Historically, there have been two levels for trade union action, one with industry and one with government. Yet the roots of free trade unionism lie in industry and in the collective bargaining process. Action with governments was a necessary complement which gained increasing importance as national economic policy evolved. In Europe, trade unions have traditionally favoured national and regional contracts. This arose, essentially, through a sense of equity and a feeling of solidarity towards all workers.

In the United States, the trade unions pursued a policy based on the greatest possible wage increases in those plants capable of meeting their claims. The United States have, therefore, a collective bargaining

70

structure based on the plant which permits them, to a large measure, to take account of the ability to pay on a micro-economic basis.

These two different attitudes, one based mainly on the principle of general equity and the other on the profitability of the plant, lead to different locations of power within the union structure and to diversity in the wage pattern; in the United States the collective bargaining rate being the real wage whilst in Europe contractual wages tend to be the minimum.

In the communist countries, trade union activity became an administrative function in the service of the economic and social aims of the communist State.

*Trade Union Diversity and International Change*

As trade unions, which were born out of the needs of the workers in a time of oppression and exploitation, developed, they were subjected to philosophical, religious and political ideas and influences. Disputes in this field were of such profundity that at times they split the union movement which suffered the harsh experience of theoretical and political divisions, weakening its unity and leaving a lasting imprint on its structure. This led to union pluralism, still existing today in some democratic countries, apart from the pluralistic structure of trade union international organisations.

Even in the early days, basically different trade union concepts had developed: the concept of close co-operation with the socialist party represented by the German, Austrian, Scandinavian, Belgian, Dutch and Swiss unions, the concept of trade unionism in Great Britain, the American idea moving towards a unionism of contest within a free enterprise system and revolutionary syndicalism in France, Italy and Spain.

Moreover, Christian trade unions were set up at the end of the nineteenth century. Their philosophy was that human beings consisted of soul and body; the trade unions, therefore, whilst aiming at procuring the material well-being of man, had to aspire to his spiritual perfection also. Without distinguishing between socialism and communism, it opposed the two ideas.

The year 1921 saw the creation of the Red Trade Union International in Moscow. This international had among other things the goal of organising the workers of the world for the revolutionary class struggle, with a view to the overthrow of capitalism, the liberation of the workers and the installation of proletarian power. It rejected the 'absurd hope for a peaceful transition from capitalism to socialism'. At the founding congress the need was underlined to create industry unions in place of craft unions, committees in every enterprise and workers' control. In the following years anarcho-syndicalists left this international and turned towards the trade union centres adhering to the International Federation of Trade Unions.

At the end of the Second World War, for a short period only, and with the exception of Christian organisations, the trade union movement united internationally. Today, there are the International Confederation of Free Trade Unions (I.C.F.T.U.), the World Federation of Trade Unions (W.F.T.U.), and the World Confederation of Labour (W.C.L.) (formerly Confederation of Christian Trade Unions).

These different trade union movements have within their structure so-called International Trade Secretariats (I.T.S.). Outgrowing their traditional denomination the I.T.S. have become real international industry organisations. Being an integral part of W.F.T.U. and W.C.L. they are, as far as I.C.F.T.U. is concerned, autonomous bodies although adhering to the same concept of free trade unionism.

A feature of increasing importance in the worldwide picture of trade unionism is the young trade unions in developing countries. Their structure is manifold, reflecting often the lack of national integration and political dissensions. In the forefront of their fight are trade union rights, independence, social justice and the economic development of their countries. They are an important element which is to play its part in the economic and social revolution of the world.

This sketch of trade union structure reveals that natural conditions, the economic physiognomy, historical developments, time and pace of industrialisation, traditions and special demographic and political circumstances have brought about special patterns of industrial relationships and of corresponding trade union structure on a national level, making international understanding and concerted action more difficult.

Yet, economic and social trends cannot be governed any more exclusively within the limits of national patterns of individual countries; the necessity for change in structure and policies thus extends beyond national frontiers.

The reason for this is the close interdependence of a world economy characterised by mass production, market expansion, widespread technological progress and industrial concentration as well as growing multi-national companies.

*The Early Desire for Practical Action in International Union Solidarity*

The early international contacts of labour unions, although different concepts of trade unionism were already evident, gave expression to the needs for international union solidarity and evinced the desire for practical action. It was advocated that the concentration of capitalism being international, trade unionism should develop action in the same field. In 1874, the International Worker's Congress in Brussels stated:

'Capital operating internationally, workers must also practice international solidarity, if they wanted to arrive at some concrete results.'

It was in the same spirit as this statement that examples of spontaneous international solidarity were shown in strike situations. There was real heroism in the fight for fundamental trade union rights and the abolition of inhuman working conditions. International trade union work, apart from solidarity actions lacked, however, co-ordination and practical application. In the field of documentation, planning of union activities and in collective bargaining policies trade union internationals served mainly as a letterbox.

The will to oppose capital and industrial power was very great throughout the whole trade union history and the individual unions struggled unceasingly with the leading companies under their own national conditions. But even after international phenomena, like the great depression in the thirties, with its worldwide political consequences, solutions were still sought nationally and the trade unions could not in a practical way come to grips with the problems and difficulties inherent in the world economy.

## II. TRADE UNIONS FACE TO FACE WITH NEW REALITIES

*The Challenge of Multi-national Corporations*

Today, trade unions are confronted with profound structural change. To a large extent the most important elements of change to the unions are constituted by multi-national corporations, their constantly increasing size, power and prevalence, their international utilisation of resources and centralisation of decisions. This is the case particularly in sectors essential to economic growth and fundamental to technical and human progress.

The production and marketing policy of management in multinational corporations is essentially to obtain, on a worldwide scale, the maximum return for their investment and production cost. The significance of these phenomena for the workers and their trade unions was expressed by Walter P. Reuther, president of the United Automobile Workers Union of America – a union among the first to face the strong impact of this trend – in the following terms:

'The corporations have internationalised and transformed the national economies where once we worked and earned our wages into an international market for our labor and our products. The companies we work for – Ford, Volkswagen, Fiat, General Motors, Chrysler, Renault, British Motors, Kaiser-Willys and International Harvester – have simultaneously automated and internationalized their production, while shaking off the restraint of national citizenship. In this situation, unions must recognize that they bargain today with corporations which are profoundly different from the companies they have dealt with historically, or we will increasingly find that our collective bargaining efforts are exercises in divisive frustration. . . . Today, we must stand together in international union solidarity or separately we will watch automation, relocation, and the erratic operation of the business cycle erode our standard of living in a process which will be exacerbated by competition between workers of different countries at the expense of their wages, working conditions and living standards.'[1]

The social and economic repercussions of the growth of multinational corporations and their policies are manifold and extensive. The concentration of power in these worldwide companies is such that their centralised investment policy and their decisions on the location of research and development constitute a source of great concern not only for workers, but also for communities as a whole and national economies. These apprehensions are all the more valid as multi-national corporations are not subject to democratic control: they may even escape national legislation and, in their endeavour to obtain maximum profit, disregard basic social considerations.

Disposing of a large capacity for self-financing as well as credit facilities all over the world, the multi-national corporations acquire or establish throughout the world new factories as soon as this promises new competitive advantages and profit. Securing strategic bases of

---

[1] Walter P. Reuther: 'Worldwide Labor Solidarity – Essential for Developing International Co-operation', *International Metalworkers' Federation Bulletin* No. 21, November 1964), p. 12.

production, they move on to the co-ordinated supply of markets with constant adaptation in their worldwide production programme. They progress towards the assembly of various components manufactured in key plants, which for cost and market considerations are widely dispersed. Thus, they institute an international division of labour between their subsidiaries.

These patterns provide management with the means to threaten trade unions in local or national collective bargaining with the transfer of production elsewhere if it is confronted with labour demands.

Furthermore, by a continuous process of integration, a number of important competing firms is absorbed by multi-national corporations and fitted into a worldwide production programme. Even agreements between large companies on technical co-operation and marketing have the effect of modifying, increasing or reducing production lines and employment patterns as well as changing vocational qualification requirements. The internationalisation of production by allotting specific activities to the different plants is not leading, however, to a fixed and final over-all programme. On the contrary, it is a process of constant evolution accompanied by frequent and often abrupt adjustments, which might result in the sudden closure of firms, the curtailment of production or rapid expansion.

*The Challenge of Economic Integration*

Mass production and mass consumption are corollaries and the stimulus for the growth of multi-national companies. The volume of goods produced by modern manufacturing methods cannot any longer be absorbed within the limits of national boundries. The creation of large free markets through free trade areas and customs unions has become essential both for industrial and developing countries. These trade areas necessitate, however, the elaboration of common economic policies, the creation of a real economic community with common institutions (including investment banks, social funds, etc.), the drawing up of international legislation and the harmonisation of social conditions in constant progress.

In the last two decades, centres of economic integration have taken shape in many parts of the world, such as the European Economic Community (E.E.C.) and the European Free Trade Association (EFTA), the United States – Canada common market for automobiles, the Latin American Free Trade Association, the Central American

Common Market, and economic unions in various parts of the African continent.

These integration processes will expand and intensify with the concentration and rationalisation of production on an international scale which itself is spurred on by the advancement and prospects of economic integration. The setting up of the E.E.C. and the EFTA has in the last ten years stimulated companies to plan in global terms and to establish a foothold in all important market areas of the world.

## A World in the Process of Change

On a worldwide scale, the rapid conquest of all boundaries and distance by modern technology, the incredible rise in the productivity of human labour through automation and advanced mechanisation, the application of atomic energy, advances in medicine, chemistry and other sciences, set in motion dynamic changes which have continuing repercussions on all sectors of society. Yet, expansion of the world economy and of trade does not by itself bring the solution to basic problems.

The great disparities between industrialised nations and those still in the process of development continue to increase, and economic growth still suffers recessions.

To cope with the increasing problems of an interdependent world important inter-governmental organisations were set up and expanded their activities, like the United Nations, the General Agreement on Tariffs and Trade, the Organisation for Economic Co-operation and Development, etc. New agencies were founded, among them UNCTAD (the United Nations Conference on Trades and Development) and the United Nations Industrial Development Organisation. Others, like the International Labour Organisation, have assumed increasing importance.

The basic aims of economic and social progress pursued by these organisations correspond widely with the aspirations of the trade union movement.

A new inter-governmental structure has emerged which offers large opportunities for practical worldwide co-operation that needs encouragement, support and stimulation not the least by such an important organised social force as the trade unions.

## III. TRADE UNION RECOGNITION OF THE
## NECESSITY OF COMMON ECONOMIC POLICIES

After the Second World War, the trade unions, having suffered from world depressions in the past, were more than ever aware of the direction which economic policy should take on an international scale to secure full employment within the new industrial potential of a world restored to peace. It is worth remembering that the breakaway of the democratic unions from the World Federation of Trade Unions in the early post-war years was to a great extent over the argument of the co-operation of the trade unions in the economic reconstruction of Europe through the Marshall Plan. The free and democratic trade unions were resolved to contribute actively to the shaping and pursuance of policies designed to achieve maximum worldwide economic growth, to help developing countries and to bring about regional economic integration.

In the latter field democratic national trade union centres of Western Europe which had constituted a Trade Union Advisory Committee to the Organisation for European Economic Co-operation (O.E.E.C)[1] held a conference in 1950 to draft a trade union programme for European revival. This programme launched the idea, even before it was mooted by governments, of creating economic communities for key industries such as coal, iron and steel and transport.

Specific trade union bodies were created as economic integration in Europe proceeded. They were set up to ensure the participation of the workers within the European Coal and Steel Community and later also within the European Economic Community. A new office has been created in Brussels by the EFTA trade unions.

On the other hand, the European regional organisation of the I.C.F.T.U. lost in significance, as governments have not been able so far to overcome the splitting of Europe into two economic areas.

Today, when unions are meeting the challenge of multi-national corporations in the industrial field, it is as well to recall that trade unions have always been protagonists of a united Europe, actively supporting the creation of the European Economic Community and desiring, indeed, the creation of an integrated market for the whole of Western Europe.

---

[1] This Advisory Committee still exists with the succession organisation, the Organisation for Economic Co-operation and Development (O.E.C.D.).

With the establishment of the necessary trade union structures an unrelenting pressure was brought to bear on governmental institutions to take account of well-defined trade union policies. They demand that European economic integration, commencing with internal trade liberalisation, should aim at a common economic policy, harmonisation of social conditions within constant progress and maximum economic growth, in order to ensure a steady increase of the standard of living based on full employment. Other specific concerns, which are in the forefront of trade union action for economic integration, are measures for dealing with the economic and social implications of the growth and policies of multi-national corporations. These measures include control of cartels and monopolies, economic programming, regional development and industry-sector policies as well as an active labour market policy, creating the necessary facilities for adequate training, re-training and manpower mobility in an economy undergoing more and more fundamental structural changes.

## IV. THE QUESTION OF EFFICIENT TRADE UNION ACTION

Government efforts at worldwide co-operation and regional economic integration projects constitute one area of action to provide the framework for industrial development and to meet human and social needs within economies. Yet, decisions about production activities and their development are taken to a wide extent in the private sector of manufacturing and more specifically in the individual companies.

This poses to the trade union movement decisive questions as to the kind of action to be taken and the new structures to be developed for its effective implementation. Apart from participation in the shaping and application of economic policies at all levels, trade unions must equip themselves to be able to respond to the powerful international concentration of companies through international trade union solidarity. But this solidarity must be translated into practical action. It needs to force upon international management an industrial relationship that will take account of world-wide problems of employment and social policy within multi-national companies, allowing their solution in constant negotiations and co-ordinated collective bargaining between these companies and the unions.

To forge in solidarity the tools required to meet the human needs of the time, the trade unions have to bear in mind the following questions:

- How can an efficient exchange of information be organised?
- How can the maximum possible impact on negotiations and the upward harmonisation of legislation in constant progress be achieved?
- What is to be done to improve company practices in the individual plants?
- What measures must be taken to reinforce trade union organisations, which in different countries group the workers of the same company, in order to give them the benefit of the full force of a united trade union movement?
- What priority should be given to the separate projects undertaken to realise ultimate goals?
- What measures can be taken now to prevent the workers and communities in the new worldwide economic environment from being victimised, rather than liberated, by the advance of automation?
- How can the political authority which trade unions have achieved in their respective countries to be brought to bear upon the world economy for the achievement of international full employment?
- Last but not least, can the trade unions, as they strive to build a sense of world labour solidarity, resist more effectively the efforts of some employers and governments to divide the workers and their organisations and drag them back to negative and self-defeating protectionism and nationalism?

All this constitutes part of one principal question: How do the trade unions build the machinery they require to serve the needs, not simply of their members, but of the people of the world in the new environment of internationalised production?

All these questions have been of considerable concern particularly to the metalworkers' organisations which constitute the International Metalworkers' Federation (I.M.F.).


## V. NEW STRUCTURE TO OPEN NEW AVENUES OF ACTION

*New Initiatives: The Creation of Automotive World Company Councils*

In the metalworking industry where in certain branches (auto, electrical engineering, agricultural machinery, aluminium) multinational corporations dominate, the principle of worldwide automotive councils was launched after lengthy discussion and a good deal of preparatory groundwork at the I.M.F. Automotive Conference in Frankfurt, in November 1964. For the chemical sector, the International Federation of Chemical and General Workers' Unions is drafting an international collective agreement as a basis for negotiations to be conducted in different countries with the individual plants belonging to the same company. On a regional scale, the Metal Committee of the I.M.F. unions in the European Economic Community has set up an international committee which acts as a forum for the discussion of all the problems of the employees working for the giant Philips concern. A delegation of this metal committee has met with top management of the Dutch mother company at Eindhoven, at a time when activities in several Philips plants in E.E.C. countries were cut back, to seek assurance that the company would take the necessary action everywhere to prevent avoidable social hardship and to extend to all plants the best social measures which had been implemented in some of its subsidiaries.

It is quite logical that the world trade union councils at company level first saw the light of day in the automotive industry; their creation was felt necessary because of the high degree of concentration in this sector, its pioneering management in internationalisation of production and a substantial proportion of manufacture for export. In the course of the meetings which took place from 31 May to 3 June 1966 in Detroit, the metropolis of the automobile industry, the first three councils – Ford, General Motors and the group Chrysler–Fiat–Simca–Rootes were constituted and immediately began work. The trade union leaders representing the workers in the plants of these corporations throughout the world first studied and compared the problems, achievements and objectives of the workers as well as the possibilities for common action existing in each undertaking. Moreover, they met international management of General Motors and Ford, led by the vice-presidents of these corporations, to direct their attention to basic questions shared by all unions representing workers in their employ.

The new instrument of world company councils having rapidly proved its validity, the I.M.F. established a fourth one in the automotive industry at a meeting in Wolfsburg in November 1966 for some 230,000 production and white-collar workers employed throughout the world in the plants of Volkswagen and Daimler-Benz. This council, like its predecessors, set out a programme of work and had an exchange of views with the central management of Volkswagen.

*Other I.M.F. Activities concerning Multi-national Companies
in the Metal Industry*

To answer the challenge of multi-national companies in other important metal industry sectors, the I.M.F. decided to create a commission for multi-national corporations. This new body is the outcome of deliberations at the last I.M.F. world conference on the machine and electrical engineering industries in September 1967. For this conference a list of the principal multi-national companies in these two sectors was drawn up containing basic indications on manpower, profits and wages.

Previously, in May 1966, the I.M.F. called the first international meeting of unions in General Electric undertakings. Delegates examined and compared wages and working conditions in various plants of the different countries. This meeting concerned itself particularly with the tactics applied by General Electric in the United States where this company sought to impose a policy of 'Boulwarism', called thus after one of its top managers. This policy consists of applying unilateral management decisions based on the old principle of 'take it or leave it'. This management attitude tries to reduce collective bargaining to a mere formality. Reports from other parts of the world revealed that General Electric was pursuing the same tactic in several other countries.

In March 1967, trade union representatives of 300,000 agricultural implement workers from eight countries met to share mutual experiences. Previously, delegations of the United Automobile Workers' Union of America (U.A.W.) had visited the plants of subsidiaries in Europe of the mother company with which they are the leading negotiators. A comparative document had been established on such items as average wages and wage costs, premium payments, payments for incentives, profit-sharing systems, wage groups and job evaluation, working hours and payments for overtime, break periods, vacations and vacation bonuses, guaranteed earnings and severance pay, pensions for workers, and union representations in each plant. Some interesting conclusions could be drawn on the differences which manifested themselves between different plants of the same company in the various fields of employment, wages and social policy. It was revealed that there was considerable scope for upward harmonisation internationally and even between different plants in one country belonging to the same company.

Through these new structures within the I.M.F., the metalworkers' unions have now at their disposal a modern means of action permitting practical work at the level of multi-national corporations. They are thus in a position to develop more intensely and co-ordinate effectively union activities in the field of organisation, collective bargaining, union training and documentation.

*Action Programmes of World Company Councils*

The meetings of world company councils showed the strong will of the trade unions to reply to the challenge of multi-national companies by a carefully thought out and co-ordinated programme of action.

These programmes conform to the concepts of the free trade union movement which conducts its struggle through the medium of collective bargaining. They insist on the need, without neglecting especially urgent problems that exist in specific countries and companies, for co-ordinated worldwide concentration by the I.M.F.–affiliated organisations upon issues that are of high priority. Such issues are defined as follows in the Declaration at Detroit of 3 June 1966:

- Full recognition of the right to organise, bargain collectively on wages, working conditions and social benefits and negotiate grievances.
- Upward harmonisation of wages and social benefits to the maximum extent permitted by the technological development of the industry in each country.
- Humanise the industrial process by the immediate establishment of adequate premium pay for such overtime as can be justified.
- Adequate implementation throughout the world of the vacation bonus principle already conceded by the Big Three in certain countries.
- Pensions sufficient to assure the security and dignity of workers who are too old to work and too young to die.
- Guaranteed income for workers affected by production fluctuations or technological change.
- Reduction of working time through a compensated shorter work week, more paid holidays, longer vacations, and early retirement, in the light of technological progress and the increased dehumanisation of industrial employment.

*The Problems of Anti-labour Policy to be Taken up with Management of Multi-national Companies*

It is the experience of I.M.F. that multi-national companies have permanent recourse to threats and reprisals against organised workers in plants located in developing countries with the aim of paralysing and destroying the trade union movement there. In the automotive industry, for instance, there have been concrete examples of anti-democratic practices and violence against trade unionists as well as – even in industrialised countries – of pressure used on immigrants to force them to join pseudo-unions if they wanted to obtain or keep a job.

Another practice to be vigorously opposed through top trade union intervention is the inhuman speed-up of the production pace – best revealed by a comparison of working conditions – notably evident in the breaks allowed for the workers on assembly lines. Cases have come to light where the elementary physiological necessities and the right to relief are absolutely ignored.

In taking up these grievances it is the trade union experience that local management in subsidiary plants of multi-national companies hide themselves behind central decisions. A main object of I.M.F. interventions with top management is therefore to clarify the real importance of centralised decisions and to locate the centre of policy bearing the responsibility for anti-labour practices and personnel policy in general.

In this regard, in answer to questions put by trade union representatives during the I.M.F. Company Council's meetings with General Motors and Ford, management alleged that responsibility was placed on local management, for instance in the case of decisions regarding the cut-back of personnel or the reduction of working hours without compensation of wages. On the subject of the threat of a transfer of production from a plant in a developing country to one of another country, top management denied any knowledge of such incidents.

Trade union experience, notably in the case of English and Australian plants, confirms that decisions on working conditions are often referred to Detroit and that the same tendency, to concentrate the power of decision in the hands of central management in matters of investment, production, exports and employment, is being reinforced.

*Trade Union Training and Creation of New Unions*

In the framework of its world company council activities the I.M.F. undertook special courses for the training of trade unionists in subsidiary plants of multi-national companies, particularly in the automotive industry of Latin America. These courses related essentially to questions of collective bargaining and trade union organising. They were carried out with the participation of trade union experts knowing thoroughly the problems arising in plants of industrialised countries belonging to the multi-national company concerned. Such courses are preferably organised in connection with a collective bargaining round in order to be connected with practical experience. The union experts from industrialised countries give their advice also to local unions in the course of negotiations.

Steps have also been taken to strengthen the trade unions in subsidiary plants and to create new unions wherever new establishments are opened in developing countries. For instance, workers engaged for the new plant of Ford in Peru founded their union with the help of the I.M.F. while the new installations were still in construction.

*Assistance in Collective Bargaining*

One of the most effective forms of co-operation that can be put into practice is in the context of collective bargaining. In this field plant-level documentation is essential. It is obtained with the help of questionnaires sent to competent local and plant-level union officials. These questionnaires embrace all main subjects covered by union contracts.

Such surveys encountered, of course, many problems: language, the comprehension of questions applying to different situations and the comparability of data. In this regard the Councils and the permanent contact with the people on the shop floor are of great importance.

A special endeavour to facilitate the collection of specific comparable data was undertaken by the I.M.F. automotive department which set up an expert group to define a given number of typical automotive manual and non-manual jobs. Definitions for each job, and aspects for comparison of wages and certain working conditions including requirements (such as speed, rest, training, safety measures) in different factories in Europe, were agreed upon. This is an example of the difficult groundwork to be undertaken.

Apart from the continuous systematic collection of data, an information service on specific issues is provided by means of correspondence.

Furthermore, an instructive role is fulfilled by analytical reports on important bargaining in sectors of multi-national corporations. These reports describe the economic background at the time of bargaining, the principal issues involved, the arguments invoked, the strategy of negotiation and the results obtained as well as their significance within the trade union action programmes.

Essential background material for collective bargaining comprises international profitability studies on a continuing long-term basis in highly concentrated sectors and with special regard to multi-national corporations. For a long time, this kind of work has been characteristic of the assistance provided by the Economic Department of the I.M.F. It also includes exhaustive studies on economic, technical and structural developments.

Mutual assistance in collective bargaining can be decisive particularly with regard to multi-national corporations. For instance, an American trade unionist, sent through the I.M.F. to Australia, was able to draw the attention of an arbitration tribunal to the fact that methods of production and work-pace at General Motors Holden were not only comparable but often absolutely identical with those applied in the American plants of the mother company; whilst the profitability of the Australian works was largely above that of the whole combined corporation, yet wages had improved over the last ten years far less in Australia than in the United States.

It is evident that such interventions confer a new force to trade union arguments in negotiation. Through co-operation of this kind the central management can be confronted with clear and irrefutable facts which can play a considerable role in efforts aimed at improving collective agreements and bringing about upward harmonisation in constant progress.

Collective bargaining is also greatly helped by the establishment of contacts between trade unionists of different countries. This allows them to understand better the practical implications of the growing tendency towards the internationalisation of production. Such contacts and visits to foreign plants have confirmed that the grip of modern companies on their subsidiaries is much greater than generally admitted or known. In fact, plant management is in constant contact with central management and constantly called to headquarters to participate in conferences on general planning and to discuss specific problems arising in individual plants. In trade union circles the need is all the more felt to obtain some of the same facilities which constitute a counterpart to the international conference on management problems.

*The New Structure as an Instrument to Bring about Equality of Forces*

It is no exaggeration to say from practical experience that concerted international action in the framework of world company councils opens avenues for improving the balance of forces between multi-national companies and the trade unions in their individual plants.

The best proof of this is that this organic set-up of international trade union solidarity acts as a deterrent to the threat of transfer of production from one country to another. This is borne out in practice. A striking example is the unsuccessful threat of General Electric at their Rome plant in Georgia, United States.

There is no doubt that the world company councils constitute a new instrument of modern trade unionism which will adapt itself at the industrial level to the demands of the inter-penetration of economies and the rapid changes arising therefrom. The creation of these councils is, therefore, of historical importance. They are the tangible expression of an active international trade union movement supplying the proof that it goes far beyond the simple denunciation of monopoly by worldwide capitalism.


## VI. THE NEW TRADE UNION STRUCTURE IN ITS WIDER IMPLICATION

### *The Discrepancies in Wage Costs and the World Company Councils*

The significance of multi-national companies must be viewed from still another angle. Obviously, the internationalisation of production leads these corporations to produce in ultra-modern factories throughout the world, thus constantly promoting rationalisation to the utmost. Central management sees to it that this high level of productivity is attained in all plants. Provided that the necessary investments are made everywhere, the gap in plant efficiency is not a determining factor for higher competitiveness of one plant against the other. However, the gap between wages and social conditions remains considerable. This is enhanced by the fact that the settlements made by unions in highly profitable plants in developing countries – the general level of wages being still extremely low in these countries – do not correspond by far to the financial possibilities of such modern plants.

This situation, in a world economy tending towards trade expansion, places the trade unions before difficult and delicate problems. It is absolutely necessary that they have their means to act wherever there is a flagrant disparity between the level of productivity and wage costs in order to prevent sweated labour and to safeguard working conditions in advanced countries without being forced to support moves towards protectionism.

In applying such a policy the metalworkers' trade unions have drawn up, through their International, a whole procedure for the safeguard of fair labour standards at international level which provides notably for intervention through the offices of the General Agreement on Tariffs and Trade (GATT). Governments would thus be exposed to international moral pressure obliging them to ensure that the exporting industries of their country do not benefit from an unfair advantage obtained by an inadmissibly low wage level. This calls, however, for government interference in low-wage countries. Although such intervention might be unavoidable in a country with a weak or developing trade union movement, it is doubtful whether government interference strengthens the trade unions, since it is precisely outside State intervention that unions must avoid if they are to fulfill their role in free negotiations which remain the best guarantee for a social evolution towards fair wages. In fact, trade union action for an improvement in living conditions in those countries where the living standard remains backward, is only possible by a continuing effort to bring about a better balance of forces. In this regard world company councils offer the possibility of direct practical assistance from unions in industrialised countries to unions in developing countries.

This does not mean any reduction in the importance of other trade union measures such as practical, material expressions of solidarity; the intervention at all levels in support of a policy of full employment and social progress; the demand for the retraining of workers affected by unemployment due to technical progress and foreign competition without loss of income; and trade union insistence on the right to negotiate before transfers of production to plants in other countries are envisaged. On the contrary, all these means for the defence of the workers in every country are reinforced by the setting up of world company councils.

*Basic Conditions to be Included in Supra-national Treaties*

Trade unions are already facing attempts towards a new development on the multi-national company scene. These companies are pressing for the adoption of international corporate law or the issuance of international charters providing exemptions from certain clauses of national laws, including those relating to labour and social legislation. This policy was probably best expressed in the following statement by

George W. Ball, former United States Under-Secretary of State, while chairman of Lehman Brothers International Ltd: 'There is an inherent conflict of interests between corporate managements that operate in the world economy and governments whose points of view are confined to the narrow national scene.' This illustrates the feeling of international corporations that being chartered by a national government limits their freedom of action. As examples of obstacles which limit the freedom of action of such companies are taxes, impediments to mergers, employment regulations and the manner in which capital is employed.

The same problem has also arisen as an aspect of regional economic integration. In response, the European Economic Community has already embarked upon studies for the drafting of a European corporation law.

In the eventuality of the adoption of such treaties, particularly on a world level, provisions to be included for the safeguard of the workers were worked out by the 21st I.M.F. Congress of May 1968 in Zürich. These provisions would oblige companies:

– to honour the rights of employees, in whatever the national political entity, to organise, to bargain collectively over all matter affecting wages, hours, working conditions and employment and income security, and to strike;
– to abide by all provisions of all I.L.O. Conventions, whether or not ratified by the country in which the multi-national corporation may be operating;
– to harmonise wages and social benefits to the highest level allowed by the technical development of the industry in each country;
– to honour all protective labour and social legislation in each country where multi-national corporations may be operating;
– and to refrain from racial discrimination even if (as in the case of South Africa) national law may require it.[1]

*Contract Termination Dates to Coincide*

The fight for the recognition of such conditions by the multi-national corporations is another specific task of the trade unionism of today. Such obligations to be observed by multi-national corporations constitute only a basis for further action. Supra-national legislation

---

[1] The full text is reproduced at the end of this chapter.

created through treaties will have to be supplemented by collective bargaining activities – as is so widely the case today nationally. A first step towards this end, greatly emphasised at the I.M.F. World Automotive Conference of May 1968 in Turin, constitutes the coincidence of the termination dates of collective agreements. By this means pressure could be brought to bear on major companies to help solve the problems of weaker unions in industrially developing countries where those same companies have plants. This would lead to worldwide settlements of wages and working conditions within big corporations. International strike action could become a new feature.

*The Trend towards International Collective Contracts*

A further objective, which was again mentioned at the I.M.F. Automotive Conference in Turin, is the negotiation of international collective bargaining contracts within economic regions. For this, some arduous groundwork is still to be done and the trade unions must succeed in persuading the employers to play their part. Activities such as those carried out by the Metal Committee of the unions from the European Economic Community representing the workers of Philips might lead to such an international contract with this company. Obviously such contracts which are to be an instrument for harmonisation would include minimum conditions only. For instance, the number of working hours would be one of the first subjects for regulation, but clauses for employment guarantees and safeguards in case of rationalisation could also be well suited for inclusion in a first contract.

*Necessity of Greater Bargaining Flexibility*

The changes with which the trade unions have to cope, affecting in each country their traditional structure and established policy, are numerous and profound. Above all there is the necessity for greater flexibility in collective bargaining. In Europe in particular the systems of collective bargaining have become too rigid to contend with the social problems arising from economic and technical dynamism. It is absolutely essential that the actual structure of the contract system be modified. National contracts, extremely valuable in themselves, have to be complemented by local and plant-level agreements to give workers the fullest possible contractual guarantee. General agreements, too, should be reinforced and form the backbone of the whole contractual structure. Furthermore, the content of these various contracts must be extended to new fields and specially adapted to the problems which are facing the contracting parties at the different levels. Only in this way can collective bargaining adapt itself to the challenge of our time and overcome an anachronism which could dangerously handicap the agreement of the two parties on rapid social progress compatible with economic development.

*Equity among Workers and the Ability to Pay*

The principle of equity among workers and the union objective to exhaust fully the firm's 'ability to pay', will provide a constant see-saw in negotiations. Upward social harmonisation through negotiations must do away with wide social discrepancies to provide for an over-all level of progress to be constantly stimulated through new social advances obtained by exhausting the 'ability to pay' inherent in high profits. For both levels trade unions must mobilise the greatest possible solidarity and militancy.

In this regard, a remarkable success has been achieved by United States and Canadian auto workers in their negotiated elimination of the last vestiges of wage differentials in the auto industry between these two countries, where a common market for automobile producers has been established and where technological variations affecting costs have virtually disappeared. Comparable productivity in the auto industry made it possible to achieve wage parity for the workers of this industry in the two countries despite considerable differences in over-all national productivity. This achievement in international harmonisation will no doubt spur on attempts to narrow differences in wages in other Canadian industries.

*Need to Make Workers in Multi-national Companies Conscious of the General Role of Unions*

Multi-national companies are often in the forefront of attempts to weaken the trade union movement by building company unions and taking unilateral decisions on such matters as the promotion of hourly paid workers to staff status as part of a policy of paternalism. The answer to such practices lies not only in the contest of the union with these companies over the greatest possible social progress, but also in making workers understand the full significance of trade unionism and its role as a force acting on industry and the economy for employment security and the betterment of society.

*Industry Unions, Coalition Bargaining and Group Conferences*

To give the trade unions the necessary strength to face large corporations a streamlining of trade union structure is indispensable. The move to industrial unions including both production and white-collar workers imposes itself more than ever in view of the growth of big corporations and the drift towards an increasing white-collar workface, particularly evident in these corporations. The handicaps found in the fragmentation of the workers' representation through different unions with the same company are to be overcome by union amalgamations and by coalition bargaining, which results in a united front.

As this leads to greater organisational units, trade unions have to devote more attention to the particular problems of branches of industry and to the concern of large groups of workers employed by a same group of employers. Industrial branch conferences and meetings of large bargaining units have, therefore, become a common feature in many large, industry-wide federations. In such meetings the effects of large corporations on the general economy are also examined and guidelines elaborated for trade union intervention.

*Solution of Shop-floor Problems and Involvement of the Workers*

The larger the trade union, the greater the need for effective and widespread communication with the membership. As multi-national companies create their own powerful image and promote workers' identification with the company, the unions in their organisational work and education endeavours must make new efforts to build up the personality of the union and make the worker feel an organic part of the movement which defends his rights and embodies his aspirations.

It is also a feature in big companies or in plants belonging to subsidiaries of international corporations that the workers feel isolated and subject to the dictates of autocratic power. Here again, big unions have to meet a need felt by workers individually. Consequently, at the very base of an expanding trade union structure some reforms have to be undertaken to strengthen union relationships, to increase the efficiency of union representation on the shop floor and to ensure greater participation of the members.

Whilst new forms are added to the trade union industrial structure at the international level, there is a necessity, particularly in respect of multi-national corporations, to relate realities on the shop-floor to the social industrial and economic issues to be examined and acted upon with top central management.

## Democratisation of the Multi-national Companies and Economic Life

One big problem which unions and society have to tackle in the future is economic democracy and in particular the democratisation to be imposed on large units of industrial and economic power. Moves in this direction have already been undertaken, but the whole democratisation process is still largely in a stage of discussion and requires more rapid practical application at all levels from plants to economic communities.

In this regard, while unions must endeavour to adapt themselves to cope with new problems, democratisation demands important changes in companies and in society.

## Unions, Ideologies and Multi-national Corporations

The trade union movement in facing its new tasks is still hampered by pluralism. Ideologies which split the movement find themselves confronted with a changing society and with highly concentrated powerful forces in an economy based on mass consumption. For the labour movement of today bargaining power in industry and a determining influence on economic policy are the decisive factors. Recognition of this will be more essential than ever for the effectiveness of trade union action in the realisation of union ideals. In this context unions, in adapting their structure and policies to the requirements of the present-day world, seek to make a constructive imprint on society.

This growing attitude strengthens the will towards practical union action. This is evident in the evolution of the Christian trade unions. The decision of the metalworkers from the French Democratic Confederation of Labour to affiliate with the I.M.F. is indicative of this trend. One of their motives in joining the I.M.F. was the knowledge that the I.M.F. had engaged in constructing a countervailing force to meet the challenge of multi-national corporations and disposed of the ways and means to translate international trade union solidarity into concrete results.

Increased bargaining power and a forceful role in economic policy can only be achieved by an independent, free and democratic trade union movement as a contesting and responsible force in society. The gap between conflicting ideologies over this basic issue cannot be bridged.

*New Structures in a Democratic Movement*

In conclusion, it is to be emphasised that the different forms of workers' organisations and their internal democratic structure were shaped in the course of a long struggle. They are an empirical response to the problems which trade unions meet in their countries

Today, faced with the impact of a rapid economic evolution exceeding the former national framework they must forge new structures which complement their national effort. These structures establish new bases of action to draw the maximum effect from international trade union solidarity. This is a necessity which in confrontation with the internationalisation of production has become inescapable.

Given the profound democratic character of the trade union movement, these new structures will rest in the will of its members. It is the responsibility of the leadership and a task to be fulfilled through organised workers' participation to see that the new structures serve to their utmost the achievement of the objectives of full employment and social progress for the workers of all countries.

# APPENDIX

## Resolution on Multi-national Corporations

The International Metalworkers' Federation holding its 21st Congress in Zürich from 27 to 31 May 1968 and celebrating its 75th Anniversary,

– points out that the growing concentration of capital and production is causing far-reaching structural change in the world economy;
– draws attention to the fact that in the metal sector, especially in the automobile and electrical industries, gigantic power groups are growing up;
– is aware that these large corporations in their effort to make profits by ruthlessly exploiting every political, economic and social weakness of a country, seek to play the workers of different countries one against the other;
– notes that these corporations, wherever they settle, strive to avoid the trade unions, exclude them, or strangle them at birth;
– knows from experience that the arbitrary decisions of these corporations to transfer production facilities and research centres from one country to another, can have serious consequences for workers and the economic, social and scientific position of a country;
– draws attention to efforts presently being made by major corporations to provide by treaty or international charters for multi-national corporations under which such corporations would be exempted from certain provisions of national laws, including those relating to labour and social legislation;
– is determined to oppose the united front of capital with the united strength of the trade unions and will continue to resist everywhere the efforts of multi-national corporations to exploit their workers;
– is resolved to strengthen the co-ordination of its activities and to further intensify the work of the various I.M.F. world company councils and committees covering various multi-national companies.

In the light of the dangers for democracy and social progress arising from the abuse of private economic power, the International Metalworkers' Federation demands:

– effective action in the collective bargaining and legislative fields, including international action, through which the multi-national corporations can be compelled to assume their social responsibilities;

– recognition of the trade unions, their right to bargain collectively and to strike, by the corporations at all levels – parent company, subsidiaries and branches;

– progressive working and social conditions, corresponding to the above-average returns on capital characteristic of the international corporations;

– conformity by the national subsidiaries of these corporations to the economic policies of the countries within which they operate, and tax measures which will require these corporations to bear their fair share of the costs of promoting social progress;

– renunciation by the world corporations of any kind of racial discrimination, even in countries where this is prescribed by law;

– democratisation of the plant, industry and economy and the planning of economic life to serve human ends;

– promotion and maintenance of healthy competition wherever possible, effective control of trends to monopolies and concentration, and measures to ensure socially responsible behaviour by the managers of large aggregations of capital;

– effective participation by the trade unions in all national and international economic bodies;

– enlargement of the power of supra-national economic communities for the control of the business policies of multi-national corporations;

– in the event that treaties are negotiated providing for international corporate law or the issuance of international charters, such treaties should require as a minimum that the companies subject to them comply with the following conditions:

(a) to honour the rights of employees, in whatever the national political entity, to organise, to bargain collectively over all matters affecting wages, hours, working conditions and employment and income security, and to strike;

(b) to abide by all provisions of all I.L.O. Conventions, whether or not ratified by the country in which the multi-national corporation may be operating;

(c) harmonisation of wages and social benefits to the highest level allowed by the technical development of the industry in each country;

(d) to honour all protective labour and social legislation in each country where multi-national corporations may be operating;

(e) and to refrain from racial discrimination even if (as in the case of South Africa) national law may require it.

## Chapter 5

# INTERNATIONAL LABOUR RELATIONS
# AND
# COLLECTIVE BARGAINING

*by*
*Jack Lee*

THE marked increase in co-operation and cross-fertilisation among unions through the effective media of the international labour federations, implies that at the bargaining table and elsewhere in their relations with the unions, employers can expect to find more knowledgeable negotiators and more sophisticated attitudes and demands on the part of organised labour.

Companies with far-flung international operations are carrying out their own training, surveys and research in the field of the behavioural sciences with a view to improving their efficiency through better personnel management.

The rapid spread of knowledge through better communications and information systems makes it possible for the developing countries to draw increasingly upon the wealth of experience gained in highly industrialised societies.

Inevitably, however, each country evolves its own labour relations pattern to suit its own economic, social and political environment.

In the developed countries of Northern and Western Europe, and in Australia and New Zealand, collective bargaining is to a large extent conducted between industry-based employers' associations and industry-wide or country-wide unions. The individual employer participates very little in the bargaining and is required to adapt the settlements made on his behalf by his association. Traditionally, unions in these countries have sought gains through legislation and they have achieved for their members a high level and variety of benefits coupled with relatively low wages. In the United States the trend is towards high wages coupled with relatively fewer benefits.

Traditionally the unions in Europe have put the emphasis on political and legislative action and have not concerned themselves to any great extent with activity at local plant level. However, as unions have become increasingly independent of political parties and substantial legislation has been obtained, they have increased and developed their interest at the local level. Union interest in such things as grievance procedures, industrial safety, and in aspects of the economic viability of enterprises has increased substantially during the last few years. In part the trend towards local action is due to present union disenchantment with the approach to incomes (and prices) taken by governments with inflation, e.g. the United Kingdom – and productivity bargaining.

Practically everywhere in Europe wages have been rising much faster than provided for in government guidelines, which themselves frequently exceed the current growth in productivity. Increasingly governments are turning to wage and price controls but they are having limited success in making them hold. With the supply of available labour practically exhausted, and labour costs rapidly rising, further growth will depend almost exclusively upon advances in achieving greater productivity. A growing number of companies and unions, particularly in the United Kingdom, are implementing mutually agreed productivity deals to break down inflexible working habits in exchange for higher earnings, greater stability, etc. Such an approach represents a significant breakthrough towards increased efficiency.

Over-generalising somewhat, the rest of the world is characterised by these two major labour relations problems: political unionism and under-employment.

In most of Latin America and part of the Arab world, unions are relatively well established, politically orientated and are subject to considerable ideological influences. By law, custom and other local circumstances, employers in these countries are frequently obliged to provide benefits for the employee and his family which exceed those found in Europe and the U.S.A. They frequently include free medical and dental care, free education, free transportation and free or highly subsidised housing and pension benefits.

In some parts of Africa and much of Asia, unions are numerous but small and there is little or no labour legislation, and practically no collective bargaining to speak of.

Politics is amongst the strongest factors affecting labour relations in many of these nations; and some governments have sought to reduce the threat from unions by suppressing them severely, by circumscribing their activities or by developing conciliation and arbitration procedures dominated by the government.

Perhaps the major factor affecting labour relations in the developing countries is under-employment; and this is frequently accentuated by high rates of population growth and by migration from rural areas to urban centres. In this context governments have tended to resist all attempts by industry to reduce the labour force in order to meet competitive demands or benefit from technological progress. In parellel the unions are equally resistant to reductions in surplus personnel and have frequently pressed for restrictive lay-off and dismissal contract provisions and laws, e.g. Middle East, Africa, Latin America.

As is to be expected, the union situation varies considerably from country to country, but in general it can be said that the level of union development inevitably reflects the level of economic development and the growth of employment.

The content of collective agreements in developing nations inevitably varies considerably. At one end of the scale are agreements limited only to a few items and at the other are agreements which cover as wide a range of subjects as the most advanced agreements to be found in the United Kingdom or the United States. In fact, in a number of respects, collective agreements are more comprehensive than is usually found in either of these two countries. It will also be found that a great many matters normally open to collective bargaining in one country are part and parcel of the labour legislation in another and therefore of compulsory application to both labour and management.

The principal subject of negotiations in the developing countries as in industrialised nations is remuneration and it is in this respect that collective bargaining poses considerable problems. There is a danger that under the pressure of the unions, wages will rise more quickly than is desirable for economic stability and rapid growth, and some politicians in these areas fear that inflation will be generated and that rising labour costs and strikes will deter overseas investors. However, there is no real evidence that the free trade union movement has had an adverse effect on economic growth and indeed the very opposite may be the case. A strong and healthy labour movement may well bring a much more rapid adjustment of the social organisation of developing countries to the exigencies of a modern industrial society than is likely to be achieved if such pressures are non-existent. In any event, the fear that foreign investment will be discouraged by healthy union activity is also almost certainly misplaced. Most international companies are well used to dealing with trade unions and to settling issues through an orderly industrial relations procedure.

At this juncture, I should like to sound the warning that what *will* deter private investment and the progress that goes with it, are the extremist political aims that some radical unions seek to achieve through this movement. And let us be brutally frank, there are unions that, rather than seek the improvement of the working conditions of their members through good union-management relations and competent bargaining, prefer to foster discontent and create conflict, in order to exploit the pent-up frustrations of the workers by directing them towards propagandistic campaigns for the nationalisation of private industry. Where such unions exist, private investment will cease. Paradoxically, this situation is more frequently observed in the very areas where massive private capital investment is called for to bring about economic and social progress.

Country-to-country variations in the union situation are paralleled by wide variations in company policy concerning their international personnel and industrial relations. It is suggested, however, that if the various operating companies of a worldwide commercial organisation are to function efficiently, a decentralised system of management is the more appropriate because a considerable degree of local freedom and operational flexibility is essential to operate competitively, since conditions of investment, products, supply and demand, import and export restrictions, local taxation, transport facilities, climatic conditions, nationalistic feelings and other local environmental factors, besides the local labour legislation and labour relations to which we have already referred, are different in each country, and therefore for every operating company within the international complex.

Under these circumstances, the function of the home office of an international corporation is to act as a catalyst for the co-ordination of supply and planning, the provision of specialist services and functional and economic advice, the pooling of the knowledge and experience of each of the operating companies for the common benefit of all, the unification of basic policy and the assessment of worldwide trends in demand and of the best investment opportunities.

In essence then, the home office is the common denominator whereby the individual companies of a worldwide industrial set-up are provided with the means to integrate and thereby maximise the use of their resources.

What, specifically then, is the role of the home office of an international corporation in the field of personnel?

As suggested, the co-ordination concept of the home office provides, among other things, a means of utilising expert talent – specialised human resources – most economically (in the measure in which they are required by one operating unit or another). A major factor concerned with the function of the home office or a supplier of talent is to provide the quantity and quality of management to meet the present and future requirements of the business.

Where one enterprise succeeds and others fail, the significant – the ultimate – difference is in the quality of management. Therefore the personnel management of managers, i.e. the need for deliberate and systematic attention by management to the problem of replacing itself, is one of the tasks deserving of top priority in the home office. Following up on this concept, a significantly challenging role of management itself is the development of programmes and practices which will provide the most effective utilisation of manpower.

If there are any useful lessons that we have learnt in this respect, they may be summarised in the following basic precepts:

For personnel and industrial relations to have effective direction and consistency, to be a fully integrated part of general management, they must work to a clear common policy which should be:

(1) applicable throughout the enterprise in all countries;
(2) in writing;
(3) couched in sufficiently broad terms, thus permitting application to meet varying local conditions;
(4) justifiable on an assessment of its longer-term impact on profit:
(5) approved and authorised by the highest authority within the organisation;
(6) regarded as inviolate as to its underlying principles, in so far as this is within the power of management.

Properly formulated personnel and industrial relations policy orients all operating management to defined goals, giving practical effect to the philosophy of management by objectives. Viable personnel and industrial relations policy provides operating management with a basis for consistency and integrity in its relations with employees, employees' representatives and government labour authorities, while at the same time it allows flexibility to operating managements by providing a framework within which to act promptly, decisively and confidently on problems as they arise. It helps to build a concerted management group of executives at all locations and finally, it provides a medium for consistent control at the corporate or operating level.

Successful industrial relations require the acceptance by management that it is just as accountable for the quality of labour relations in the plant as it is for the other major responsibilities of management. This implies management planning, initiative and decision-making in labour relations, rather than merely expedient response to the demands or claims initiated by unions.

The greatest opportunity for contribution by the personnel function lies in its service to the process of manpower planning.

Personnel and industrial relations administration, to make its greatest contribution, must be an integral part of management and directed by executives who first and foremost are members of senior management and only secondly specialists in their field.

Up to this point this chapter has been principally based on and related to the traditional patterns of labour relations that have evolved in advanced industrial societies and have subsequently formed the basis for such relationships in the developing countries.

However, the changes that are taking place in Europe, America, Australasia and other similar industrial environments make it necessary for us to think in terms of challenging the traditional patterns of collective bargaining; of searching for a means to break out of it and away from its accompanying rigid patterns and attitudes; and of developing new practices aimed at replacing the traditional approach with something more dynamic and flexible.

The traditional manner in which collective bargaining has been conducted usually results in a settlement under which employees are granted increased pay and benefits in exchange for a guarantee that industrial peace will be maintained for the duration of the agreement. This type of bargaining has usually been conducted in an atmosphere of conflict and the succession of agreements arising from it has led to the acceptance of the inevitability of regular increase in wages and fringe benefits. This has become almost a 'natural law' largely unchallenged and rarely involving a greater degree of commitment or activity from employer or employee. This kind of bargaining has tended to breed mutual distrust and to create a 'them and us' attitude, thereby fostering resistance to any changes in the manning of plants and offices on the part of labour, while posing restrictions on the nationalisation of skills, the use of new tools, new materials and new methods of work. But although it may be delayed, the progress of time cannot be stopped. The traditional approach has therefore been increasingly challenged in recent years by management. Government and public opinion have also criticised the present system of bargaining on the grounds that by means of it some sections of the community can acquire undue benefits regardless and often at the cost of the over-all interest of the community, and furthermore because it is often a major contributory factor to inflation. A point to be borne in mind is that in a number of countries a continuation of the traditional approach to bargaining is apt to invite greater government intervention in the bargaining process.

In many cases in recent years, management have tried to break out of the traditional pattern by taking the initiative in negotiations. This has generally taken the form of management making demands on unions for the removal of some restrictive practice known to be inhibiting productivity and therefore tending to make the company uncompetitive. In return, financial inducements or other improvements in conditions of employment have been offered. In some countries, especially in the United Kingdom, this has come to be known as 'productivity bargaining' (a better term would be 'efficiency bargaining') and it has required management and union representatives at the bargaining table to obtain an intimate knowledge of the details of the working arrangements being negotiated. They must be familiar with what is involved in technological change, new equipment, new techniques and work methods; they must understand what this means in terms of redundancy, re-training and new wage structures.

While some solid achievements have been made, it is becoming increasingly evident that there are limits to the amount of progress that can be obtained solely by this type of bargaining. Evidence is beginning to accumulate which indicates that the productivity bargaining approach can be considerably enriched if the involvement and participation of all employees are secured.

Studies and experiments carried out in various parts of the world, together with the research work of behavioural scientists indicate that an approach along the following lines can produce encouraging results:

(1) The bringing about of a fundamental change of attitude on the part of management, unions and employees, through the encouragement of a habit of discussion.
(2) Establishment of parallel objectives.

(3) Encouraging a joint solution of problems.
(4) Identification of barriers of resistance to change and of motivational factors.
(5) Acceptance of change in principle and identification of specific changes.
(6) Consolidation of the foregoing in collective bargaining.
(7) A continuous implementation during the life of the collective agreement of the principles agreed to and preparation for further change by a continuous non-crisis joint approach to problems of the more effective use of manpower.

It is evident that an approach along these lines is an uninterrupted process. A great amount of preparatory work is needed before management meets the union at the bargaining table. In fact, negotiations with the union under such circumstances would become merely the formal process whereby agreed principles and changes emerging from a continuous 'dialogue' are from time to time consolidated and recorded.

Indications are that it is fundamental to encourage dialogue and a habit of discussion. This can be a long, complex and often frustrating process which can be embarked upon only when top management is fully committed and when line management and supervisors on the one hand and union officials and individual employees on the other are fully and personally involved.

There can obviously be little detailed guidance on how to establish the habit of discussion but it could well be directed towards such things as:

(1) Encouraging thought about the common interest of employees, management and the community in the economic health of the company.
(2) Improving understanding of competitive and other difficulties of the company.
(3) Introducing the notion of mutually accepted goals (parallel objectives) as between employer and employees.
(4) Avoiding telling employees how the objectives, once identified, can be reached, but rather ensuring that they accept them for themselves and inviting them to work equally and freely with the company in finding ways in which the objectives can be achieved.
(5) Drawing out underlying principles for change, rather than getting too involved in details of specific short-term changes.

(6) Avoiding heated argument or confrontation on controversial subjects which will serve only to harden attitudes.

All of this sounds simple on paper but there are many dangers and risks and in practice the process calls for unfailing constant effort and a personal conviction of all concerned (and, needless to say, a union that is not involved in a political campaign for the take-over of the company). It must be recognised that there will be setbacks and misunderstandings as well as progress. Nevertheless, several companies have either embarked on this route or in retrospect have wished they had.

There are indications that a re-orientation of objectives of management, employees and unions can be conducive to building a climate of understanding and trust and any dialogue must be directed towards the identification and establishment of mutually acceptable goals. Top management must carefully consider its fundamental objectives and philosophy and attempt to define them in a form which can be communicated to and understood by managers, supervisors, employees and union representatives. Attempts to establish parallel objectives must stress the mutual interest of management and unions on the grounds that improved productivity, for instance, can mean 'more for both'. Any restatement of objectives is likely to be achieved only through management initiative and unions will tend to need the help of management to clarify their own objectives. Resultant collective bargaining must be a success in the eyes of management on the one hand, and unions and employees on the other, in the form of benefits for both sides as opposed to one side gaining at the expense of the other.

Experience of a number of companies together with studies of social scientists indicates that there is a tremendous latent interest in a knowledge of work practices throughout an organisation. A re-orientation of objectives and habit of discussion should provide an opportunity of releasing and using this, and gradually there should emerge a clearer concept of mutually beneficial goals and targets. A degree of initiative from unions and employees directed towards the solution of operational problems is likely to appear at this stage from which there should emerge a joint solution of problems.

It must be faced that this means that there should be genuine joint examination of job content, work methods, pay systems, working hours and so forth, rather than management telling employees what it has already decided. At each level positive efforts need to be made to involve each subordinate fully in his work, among other things, by giving more scope to his initiative and a greater variety of tasks. This process should not be equated with 'soft' management – management still takes the decision but there is true participation by subordinates and consequently a greater use made of their potential. Neither should it be confused with the concept of 'co-management' or 'co-determination'. What is involved in the first instance is a change in every-day informal relationships.

Management must be prepared throughout this and subsequent stages to show a thorough and sympathetic understanding of the human problems and attitudes to change, it must encourage thought about how such problems can be tackled and how there can be benefits in terms of the job satisfaction of the individual. To do this, management must identify the obstacles preventing the full and effective use of manpower in both the present and the planned operational situation. In the light of this, plans can be made for overcoming these barriers and for motivating employees to accept the resultant changes.

Management must therefore try to determine what the employees' own perceptions are of the problems being dealt with and what their attitudes to work and the company are. Besides having an understanding of the perceptions and attitudes of employees in order to identify barriers to change, management must also understand those factors which motivate employees. A good deal of research has been and is being done in this field, but more study and experimentation are needed before anything more than tentative conclusions can be reached. Already, however, it would appear that behavioural scientists are agreed that there are limitations to what can be achieved by financial inducements alone.

From the lengthy preparatory period of creating a climate conducive to change by encouraging the habit of discussion and the joint solution of problems and establishing parallel objectives should emerge specific ideas for change. It is only at this stage that there is much likelihood of achieving genuine fundamental change in the collective bargaining process.

In some circumstances, of course, it may be possible to implement some changes before going to the bargaining table. Many other changes are too detailed to be spelled out in a collective agreement and often are of such a nature that they can only be gradually developed and implemented.

The new approach to collective bargaining tends to be one of getting agreement with union officials on identifying the general subjects to be discussed – for example, those about which there will be normal bargaining, those which will confirm specific changes already implemented or clearly understood, and those which will concern matters of general principle which will serve as a guide to the implementation of changes on a broad front during the life of the collective agreement.

While at this stage there will probably be negotiations over general adjustments to wage levels, etc., in the light of such factors as increased cost-of-living, the important point is that rather than disputing at great length over every minor change proposed, the parties at the bargaining table would be likely to draw up a joint statement of agreed principles and the provision of a procedure for their gradual implementation. Hence the layout and format of such agreements are likely to be different from the traditional ones and the agreement, rather than 'freezing' pay, conditions and jobs at a new level, should pave the way for constant development which can be beneficial both to management and employees.

It is not envisaged, however, that all of this should lead to 'open-ended' agreements. Agreements should invariably be of fixed duration to ensure a period of industrial peace and stability and should, on re-negotiation, incorporate and consolidate changes already put into effect. Neither, of course, should negotiations be re-opened before expiry date merely to incorporate innovations put into effect during the agreement.

The experience of various firms is that negotiations of this kind seem to be more easily carried out at the plant or local level. The reason is that the types of change needed, firstly, to elimate practices inhibiting the most effective use of manpower and, secondly, to meet technological innovation, differ from plant to plant. Hence the greatest possible flexibility on a local basis is needed in negotiating for change. A further element is that it is likely that it is at plant or local level that a climate conducive to change can best be created.

However, while this has been found by a number of companies to facilitate the reaching of agreement on change, they have generally maintained 'bargaining relationships' with unions at the national level. In a number of cases it has been possible to reach agreement with a union on fundamental principles at national level which have provided an acceptable framework within which local, more detailed agreements can be reached.

Written agreement with a union, or acceptance by union and employees of new principles and goals, is unlikely to result in immediate implementation of all the detailed changes flowing therefrom, even when the appropriate climate has been created and new employer/ employee relationships forged. In fact, once agreement on principles is reached, putting these into effect is probably the most difficult task of all. All manner of issues and conflicts can arise:

(1) The rate at which it may be possible to train or retrain employees to undertake jobs of wider scope, especially 'multiskill jobs'.
(2) The time it may take employees to accept or become accustomed to change, to work out for themselves how it will affect them and to adapt themselves to it.

A sustained, co-ordinated and enthusiastic 'follow-up' by management and supervisory staff is essential. The original principles agreed to must not be lost sight of in detailed problems of implementation, or the impetus will be lost and effective change will only be partial.

It must be evident from the foregoing that special training programmes will be required to implement changes agreed in collective bargaining, especially in relation to supervisory and 'multiskill' training and it is worth noting that governments in a number of countries are increasingly taking a hand in this by such means as setting up special training programmes for specific industries in order to keep pace with technological change.

Management's task to foresee and understand changes in environmental factors and to meet them by planning and implementing corresponding changes in organisation and operations is a formidable one.

It must be tackled in social as well as technical terms. A new approach to collective bargaining – involving negotiation for change – can play a major role in achieving progress in this field. Those in the personnel function must therefore be of sufficient experience, training and calibre to play an effective role in both planning for and implementing change in relation to its human aspects. The full commitment and involvement of management at all levels is also vital if the human problems of change are to be overcome on both a national and international scale.

Chapter 6

# FACTORS INFLUENCING THE ORGANISATION AND STYLE OF MANAGEMENT AND THEIR EFFECT ON THE PATTERN OF INDUSTRIAL RELATIONS IN MULTI-NATIONAL CORPORATIONS

*by*

*B. C. Roberts*

THIS paper will seek to explore some of the factors that shape the industrial relations policies of management within the central and peripheral undertakings that together comprise a multi-national corporation. The factors involved can be classified into two groups: (1) those that are internal and are generated within the corporation; (2) those that are external and influence the corporation's industrial relations from outside. There will be, of course, an interaction between the internal and external factors which will determine the dynamics of the corporation's industrial relations at each location of its activities and through time.

The internal and external factors that will be examined will be grouped as follows:

(1) the influence on the corporate structure of different types of economic activity carried out;
(2) the culture and style of management;
(3) the response of employees to managerial policy;
(4) some economic, social and political problems.

## TYPES OF ECONOMIC ACTIVITY

The economic activities of multi-national corporations may be classified into extractive; plantation cultivation; processing; manufacturing; transporting and communicating; trading and marketing and the provision of financial and other types of services. Some multinational corporations may be engaged in only one of these activities: others may be engaged in a number or possibly even all of them.

Whichever kind of economic activity is being carried on by a multinational corporation it will necessarily involve an investment in fixed assets such as offices, plant and equipment, and in an organisation that will involve the employment of personnel. The scale of the capital investment, its location and its mobility, will vary with the nature of the activity and its technological features. An oil, mining or manufacturing company will have to make fixed investments on a considerable scale in order to conduct its activities, whereas a corporation supplying expertise may require to invest in no more than organisation. The type of economic activity carried on by the corporation will, therefore, have an important influence on its organisational structure, its pattern of management and the character of its industrial relations.

## Oil Companies

An oil company must by the nature of its purpose, which is to find, process and market oil and its derivative products profitably, make investments in geological surveys, drilling equipment, transportation, refineries and chemical plants and marketing services. Since oil is located only in certain specific areas, but consumption is worldwide, companies engaged in the production and sales of oil products must, therefore, become multi-national corporations if they are to extend their control over supplies and extend their markets.

The activities of an oil company which is operating on a multinational scale must be carefully co-ordinated if optimum economic results are to be achieved. It follows that the timing and scale of investment decisions, the inter-relationships of exploration, extraction, processing and marketing must be effectively controlled. This requires a pattern of organisation that will allow for a high degree of centralised decision-making on major investment and operational decisions, and at the same time permit a substantial degree of local flexibility to meet the different circumstances that exist for a corporation operating in a great many different countries under very different political and economic conditions. The vertically integrated technology of oil production, processing and marketing will make any stoppage of work extremely costly. It is, therefore, essential for an oil company to establish a pattern of industrial relations, so far as this is possible, that will safeguard it from industrial unrest. The empirical evidence indicates that oil companies tend to be wage leaders and to provide above-average conditions of employment. Since labour costs as a proportion of total costs are relatively low oil companies are in a favourable situation to give their employees high wages and good employment standards. They have also been helped in this respect by the rising world demand for oil, petroleum and chemicals. The increase in the output of the industry has been accompanied by considerable improvements in the labour efficiency which have been brought about by advancing technology and economies of scale made by the multi-national corporations.

*Mining Companies*

Mining companies are in important respects in a similar situation to oil companies. They have to locate their extractive activities at those places where the ores they wish to mine are to be found. As in the case of an oil company they will have to make large-scale fixed investments, but their activities are generally more labour-intensive than in the case of oil companies. Organisationally, mining companies, with the exception of aluminium companies, are not dominated by the same degree of vertical integration from prospecting to the marketing of the final consumer product. Mining and smelting often go together, but it is also quite common for the ores to be bought by a completely different company. This means that there is not the need for multi-national mining companies to develop the same degree of centralised decision-making and organisational co-ordination as oil companies. It is not uncommon in the mining field for companies to be relatively small. Even where companies are large, such as Rio Tinto-Zinc, Alcan or Anaconda Copper, local subsidiaries have a high degree of local independence in labour matters.

Mining companies frequently have the reputation of being hard employers. As a type mine managers tend to be rugged, authoritarian and little concerned with applying modern personnel management techniques. The stereotype they have, of the miners they boss, is of men who will only respond to harsh directives and unrelenting pressure. This is in part due to the fact that mining is generally a tough, dirty, dangerous occupation. Labour costs are a substantially higher proportion of total costs than in the case of oil. Since individual companies have relatively little control over the general supply and demand situation for their products, price and profits tend to fluctuate much more than is the case with oil. These factors have tended to make mining companies harder bargainers; they are also less vulnerable to the pressure of their employees than oil companies, since ores and metals can be stockpiled much more easily than oil. Whereas oil companies rarely have strikes, industrial conflicts in mining tend to be bitter and sometimes result in violence as both sides refuse to compromise.

There are, of course, different types of mining and it is worthy of note that bauxite mining tends to produce a pattern of industrial relations that is closer to that of the oil companies than to the shaft and tunnel types of mining. This is due to the fact that bauxite is generally produced by open cast methods, where the numbers employed are relatively small and are engaged driving mechanical diggers and other types of machinery. Thus the bauxite miner is in fact a skilled operator of large-scale mechanical equipment working under totally different conditions from a man underground.

A second factor is that the mining of bauxite tends to be like the extraction of oil; it is the first stage of a vertically integrated process that is carried on through the reduction of the bauxite to alumina, which is then smelted into aluminium, which is in turn finally manufactured into finished products by a single company. The multinational corporations which produce aluminium tend to follow positive industrial relations policies which they endeavour to pursue consistently at all stages of their activities.

*Agricultural Products*

A large proportion of the products of tropical countries is produced by multi-national corporations that are engaged in growing coffee, tea, sugar cane, bananas, sisal and rubber. These activities have some similarities with the production of oil and mining of metallic ores, in that they have to be carried on in specific areas with the appropriate climatic conditions, and these are usually under a different national sovereignty from the country in which the corporations involved have their headquarters.

The products of tropical agriculture are even more vulnerable to vagaries of supply and demand in world markets than mining products. Moreover, labour costs account for a very high proportion of total costs, in this type of enterprise, thus making the problems of wages and conditions of employment factors of crucial importance.

In the past most of the countries in which plantation production is carried on were colonies and this has inevitably had an important influence on the relations of workers and their employers. Management was, and to some extent still is, drawn from the country in which the company owning the estates and plantations had its headquarters. With changing political circumstances and rising educational levels there is a rapidly growing tendency to recruit and train locally born staff for managerial posts. Capital control continues to be determined at the corporate headquarters of the companies concerned, but political as well as operational factors compel a high degree of local autonomy.

The multi-national corporations engaged in plantation agriculture tend to set higher standards of wages and provide superior conditions of employment by comparison with locally-owned estates and plantations. The reason for this is in part a need to avoid political criticism, but more importantly the foreign-owned companies tend to manage their estates and plantations more efficiently. However, in this respect they face an extremely difficult problem, since if they use the most modern methods of cultivation and harvesting, substituting capital for labour, they put out of work great numbers of their employees. The technology used by multi-national corporations has to take into account therefore the social situation in the country in which it is being applied, and some or all of the economic gains to be made by the corporation in introducing advanced technology may have to be devoted to ameliorating the immediate impact on the level of employment.

*Manufacturing Industries*

Multi-national corporations engaged in manufacturing cover a very wide variety of products. They differ greatly in the scope and scale of their activities. Some are amongst the largest employers in the host countries in which they have located plants. Others may have only small operations which have little local significance.

In general manufacturing companies will find themselves much less locked in than oil, mining or tropical product companies. They will have a greater freedom of choice in whether and where they manufacture overseas. This element of flexibility will be an important factor in their relations with the host countries and it will have an important bearing on the structure of organisation and pattern of industrial relations.

The technological situations to be found in manufacturing vary so widely that it is impossible to generalise about their effects on the structure of management and the inter-relations between the head-quarters and the peripheral companies. Every kind of corporate structure can be found, ranging from a very high degree of centralised control over every type of operating decision to the allowing of almost complete autonomy to the subsidiary companies.

The way in which a decision to invest in a manufacturing activity overseas is carried out will have an important influence on the degree of local control granted to the subsidiary. If the activity involves the manufacture of a particular product which is highly developed and requires the use of advanced technology of which the parent has unique experience, and the establishment of a new factory in a foreign country, the corporation making this investment is likely to use as managers men already trained and familiar with the parent organisation. If it is simply taking over an existing establishment it may continue to use the local management and make other arrangements to ensure co-ordination. In both cases the balance between central and local control will depend upon a variety of factors.

Differences in technology arising from type of activity in which the multi-national corporation is engaged will influence its organisational structure and its pattern of industrial relations.[1] The effects of the technology will, however, be independent of the fact that a plant is part of a multi-national corporation. The same effects would be observable if the particular plant were differently owned; they may, however, have a different significance if the management is drawn from a cultural environment different from the work force and is subject to remote and alien control.

*Transport and Communication*

The multi-national corporations that fall into this group include shipping companies, airlines, telecommunications, press, radio and television and films. Shipping companies and airlines have certain features in common. Though operating internationally they both tend to represent their country of origin. They are financially controlled from one point, and their operating decisions are taken at the head-quarters. Nevertheless, the pattern of operation may be determined by the national likes and dislikes of the countries they serve rather than the country whose flag they show. For example, the passenger liners, the *Queen Elizabeth* and the *Queen Mary*, were both managed

---

[1] See J. Woodward: *Industrial Organisation: Theory and Practice* (Oxford University Press, 1965).

from the point of view of providing their mainly American clientele with the kind of service these passengers desired.

Shipping and airlines are both subject to a high degree of international control, through well developed and accepted maritime and air laws and conventions. In this respect this kind of multi-national corporation is quite different from any other type. The principal reason for the development of the international regulations of shipping and air traffic stemmed from the factors of safety, national security, and the need to come and go across the oceans and skies of the world with the maximum of freedom. Nevertheless, in economic matters, as distinct from factors affecting safety, the national States attempt to regulate in their own concept and image. This is particularly true of the United States, which has sought to impose its own rules relating to competition and fixing of rates on non-American vessels carrying goods and passengers to and from the United States. In spite of the international character of shipping and airlines, levels of wages and conditions of employment have been primarily determined by reference to national rather than international standards. The fact that most of the shipping companies and airlines represent national economic interests and are generally strongly supported by national governments, on whom they rely to obtain rights of passage, deters their managements from looking at their own jobs in international terms. However, there is some sign that airmen are beginning to see themselves as belonging to an international fraternity employed in an international labour market. This idealist conception has, however, a materialist basis: it is the foundation of a claim to secure higher pay and better conditions of employment because most pilots earn substantially less than Canadian and United States pilots. There has also been some tendency for ships' crews, particularly on oil tankers, to compare their rates of pay and to seek to move towards a common standard, though relatively little success has been achieved.

Telecommunications firms are generally firmly controlled from their national headquarters. In this respect there can be no doubt but that they are primarily influenced by the national standards of the country to which the company concerned belongs. Television and film companies have become increasingly international. Television is primarily directed at a national market, but there is a growing international element in the production of television material. The film industry, though nationally based and showing strong national cultural characteristics, has become increasingly international as a commercial activity and in its financial and managerial control. The entertainment world in general has moved in this direction. Salaries and conditions of employment are greatly influenced by international factors. As a consequence of the increase in the mobility of entertainers, managerial and technical staff, the national interests of employees affected have been protected by the use of work permits. This device to regulate the labour market by denying entry, except on very narrowly-defined terms, has become an important factor influencing the pattern of industrial relations in this field.

*Trading and Services*

Trading companies were perhaps the first multi-national corporations. The great chartered trading companies of the seventeenth and eighteenth centuries played a vital part in opening up the world and were largely responsible for the early settlement and government of North America, India and South East Asia under British sovereignty. They were also important in the nineteenth century in Africa.

The problems of trading companies are clearly different from oil, mining or manufacturing companies. They are not called upon to make massive investment in plant, but they have to acquire warehouses, shops and offices. Trading is an activity in which local initiative and managerial flexibility are essential. It is difficult to exercise a high degree of central control, but this has been achieved by some companies such as Campbell or Booker, who have been concerned to ensure that their image as fair traders in the West Indies, Africa and elsewhere was not tarnished by local deviations. Foreign trading companies in relatively poor countries are in a particularly vulnerable situation, since they are an easy target for popular hostility and are generally held responsible for the price of the goods in which they trade.

Banks, insurance and finance companies have become increasingly multi-national in their service activities. The management of the overseas branches of a bank or other type of financial institution is generally given a good deal of local autonomy in the type of business they might accept. However, in the field of employment policy much more central control has been exercised. In the past in the less-developed countries, this has sometimes meant a decision not to employ members of certain races or colours. This type of policy was ostensibly framed on the operational need to present a certain image, in particular of reliability and security. These are no longer policies that can be justified and multi-national corporations have had to change their policies in these respects.

From this brief examination of the different types of economic activity carried on by multi-national corporations it is possible to say that the structure of management is greatly influenced by the technical requirements of the activity. This factor will interact with broader cultural influences on the style of management. It is, therefore, possible to find multi-national corporations in the same field of economic activity behaving in the area of industrial relations in ways that differ significantly.

## CULTURAL INFLUENCES ON
## THE STYLE OF MANAGEMENT

The culture and style of management are factors of critical importance in the determination of the policies of multi-national corporations. In examining the nature of this problem it is of advantage to use the classification of multi-national corporations devised by Howard V. Perlmutter and published in a celebrated article in 1965.[1]

Perlmutter grouped multi-national corporations into three types: ethnocentric, polycentric and geocentric.

*Ethnocentric* multi-national corporations generally wholly own their overseas subsidiaries which are managed by nationals of the country in which the parent corporation is based. They are in effect a cultural, as well as an economic, extension of the parent corporation.

*Polycentric* multi-national corporations often have local participation in the capital ownership of their subsidiaries, which are managed by citizens of the countries in which they are located. The culture pattern of management is predominantly that of the country in which they are situated.

*Geocentric* multi-national corporations are international in their management structure. Staff are appointed purely on the basis of the best man for the post irrespective of nationality. The cultural climate of the corporation is like an international agency of the United Nations, divorced entirely from the pursuit of the national interests of any ethnic group or nation State.

There are in fact no truly geocentric corporations in being at the

[1] Howard V. Perlmutter: 'L'Entreprise internationale – Trois conceptions', *Revue Economique et Sociale* (Lausanne), May 1965.

present time, but Perlmutter believes that by the end of this century the world's trade will be dominated by three hundred corporations of this type. Such corporations as I.B.M., Nestlé, Unilever and Shell have come close to being *geocentric*, but all of these corporations at the present time are in the last resort dominated by the interests of their primary shareholders, who are highly concentrated, and not spread evenly over the areas of the world in which these corporations engage in their activities. They are also at the top managed, in terms of cultural style, and to a large extent in ethnic composition, by persons drawn from the countries in which the parent organisations had their origin and are located.

Perlmutter is convinced that technological, economic, political and social factors will bring a progressive transition from *ethnocentric* and *polycentric* corporations to *geocentric* corporations. In the long run Perlmutter may be correct, but in the immediate future there are substantial obstacles to the development of truly *geocentric* corporations.

At the present time the countries in which multi-national corporations have their legal headquarters and majority shareholders would be extremely reluctant to agree to a transfer of the ultimate control of these corporations' activities elsewhere. For example, under existing law, no British company can sell its assets to an overseas buyer without the approval of the government.

Moreover, there are technical reasons why multi-national corporations are becoming in certain respects more, not less, centralised in their decision-taking. The development of modern communications (the aeroplane, telex and telephone has made it possible for the head office of a multi-national corporation to exercise a more immediate and direct control over subsidiaries and the men on the spot. The computer has, at the same time, provided the rationale for centralised decisions, since it increasingly enables a central board to manage its total resources in the most efficient way. These developments suggest that whilst the corporation of the future may be *geocentric*, in the sense that its trading and its staff may be increasingly international, its capital and its critical decisions are likely to remain under highly centralised control, and thus highly influenced by the culture and the economic, social and political pressures bearing on to the parent corporation.

Using Perlmutter's classification we now turn to examining some of the influences of cultural factors on managerial behaviour.

The essential characteristic of the ethnocentric corporation's managerial philosophy is that it prefers to employ as managers of its subsidiary companies nationals of the country in which the corporation has its headquarters. The reasoning behind this preference is (1) that the managers of the subsidiary companies should possess a certain knowledge and experience which can only be acquired by first working in the headquarters organisation; (2) a belief that home-recruited staff are more to be trusted and will be more efficient than staff recruited from other countries; (3) the highly-skilled staff required are most easily found in the country in which the corporate head-quarters is situated.

The extent to which United States companies operating overseas hold these views has been revealed in a survey of 646 such companies, which together employed 24,659 United States citizens overseas, virtually all of them in key management posts.[1] Since the cost of sending an American manager overseas has been estimated to be substantially greater than the cost of employing a locally-recruited manager – in the case of Latin American countries up to four times as great – it is clear that United States-based multi-national companies regard United States managers as considerably superior.[2]

The use of staff from head office as managers of overseas subsidiaries is particularly marked (1) where the investment is large and the product produced is one involving the use of secret technological know-how; (2) where the overseas activity is an entirely new venture in the country concerned.

The multi-national corporation with a *polycentric* type of organisation is willing to employ managers recruited locally. It accepts this situation in the belief that local managers will be more capable of understanding the local situation; they will not be an alien element and come into conflict with other staff or the environment in which they work. These factors, it is assumed, will make them more efficient than outsiders. Behind these assumptions, however, may well lie the fact that the multi-national corporation has bought a going concern, rather than created a new enterprise. Where a multi-national corporation buys in, either to extend the market for its own product, to obtain control of a rival, to secure technical knowledge, or simply to participate in a successful business that is vulnerable to a take-over, and it leaves a substantial element of local capital holding, it is also likely to leave a considerable degree of local management.

[1] Syracuse University, Maxwell Graduate School of Citizenship and Public Affairs: *American Business and Overseas Employment* (Syracuse, N.Y., 1957).

[2] John C. Shearer: *High Level-Manpower in Overseas Subsidiaries* (Princeton University, 1960).

It sometimes happens, however, that multi-national corporations become dissatisfied with the performance and profitability of their subsidiary under local management. They then may seek to improve the performance of the subsidiary by shifting from a *polycentric* situation to an *ethnocentric* situation or something close to it. Good examples of developments of this kind are to be found in the United Kingdom in the history of the General Motors Corporation and the Ford Motor Company.

The history of the Vauxhall Motor Company, which was bought out completely by General Motors Corporation in 1925, is of a shift from a rather paternalistic British-style management which prided itself on its harmonious industrial relations based upon an elaborate machinery of joint consultation, to a more aggressive dynamic policy concerned with the raising of efficiency and payment of high wages. This change was associated with the replacing of senior British managers with Americans who spoke a different language and adopted a different style. Since this also meant uncertainty about jobs, changes in established practices and conventions, the advent of an American managing director was greeted with an outburst of anti-American feeling and an aggressive, militant opposition to some of the changes introduced.

The Ford Motor Company had until 1961 British shareholders, when the United States company decided it should obtain the total ownership of the capital. This step aroused considerable fears as to Ford's future policy. A refusal by the government to allow the company to expand on its existing site at Dagenham gave rise to rumours that the company was considering transferring much of its British activity to Germany.

In its manufacturing and labour policies the company had been much influenced by Detroit, but having a British manager it had created the image that it was essentially a British company. Following the lead of its United States parent the company did not recognise or bargain with trade unions until compelled to do so by official pressure during the Second World War.[1] When the company agreed to bargain with unions it refused to accept the national agreement for the engineering industry and, following the United States pattern, insisted on the establishment of a separate negotiating procedure for the Ford Company. With the help of the Trades Union Congress (T.U.C.), which assisted the unions involved, an agreement with the company was eventually signed.

---

[1] In fact the British company did not commence negotiations with unions until 1944 – some three years after Ford in the United States made its first agreements.

The insistence of the Ford Motor Company on a separate company agreement with the unions followed from the reluctance of the company to join the Engineering Employers' Federation. Many United States-based corporations operating in Great Britain and other countries, such as Kodak, Thomas Hedley, Esso Petroleum, have followed the same course, which has been based upon their experience and philosophy developed in the United States.

In addition to the influence of anti-trust legislation, the refusal of many American firms to join employers' associations has been determined by the great emphasis they have placed on the virtues of company independence, competitiveness and freedom to be a jump ahead of the market. This attitude has put the subsidiaries of United States-based companies in Britain into the position of wage leaders. They have traditionally sought to stay ahead of British firms and to anticipate national negotiations in their settlements with trade unions.[1]

The attitude of multi-national corporations with parent organisations in countries other than the United States to joining employers' associations and in recognising and negotiating with trade unions has been somewhat different. In the case of British-based corporations they have, with the exception of oil companies, generally favoured joining employers' associations. In former colonial territories British-based companies have in fact played a major role in the development of employers' organisations. They adopted this policy as a measure of self-protection against governments which have regarded them as a legitimate source to be exploited in the interests of economic development. These developments culminated in the establishment of the worldwide Organisation of Employers' Federations and Employers in Developing Countries. The attitude of non-American-based multi-national corporations to union recognition in so far as it is culturally influenced will be, as it is in Britain, empirical. Companies recognising unions in their home countries are likely to do so overseas. This is almost certainly a general rule that can be applied in most cases, irrespective of the country in which the corporation is based.

The history of the Organisation of Employers' Federations and Employers in Developing Countries is in itself an interesting aspect of a shift from a predominantly *ethnocentric* style of management in British-based companies operating in Africa, Asia, Middle East, Pacific and West Indies, to a *polycentric* pattern, a change that was

[1] See J. H. Dunning: *American Investment in British Manufacturing Industry* (G. Allen & Unwin, 1958).

clearly signified in the change of name from the Overseas Employers' Federation to the Organisation of Employers' Federations and Employers in Developing Countries. French policy has been conspicuously different.[1] The Centre National du Patronat Français and its overseas offshoots have always been, and remain, the undiluted expression of an *ethnocentric* policy.[2]

## Developing a Geocentric Culture

As multi-national corporations reach a certain size and scale of operations and they begin to take on the characteristics of the *geocentric* organisation they are faced with problems of creating a corporate culture which is appropriate to their role as geocentric corporations. This means that they have to weld together teams of managers who have been educated in different national environments and who will have absorbed the basic cultural values of these environments. Mr. Vansina, at the University of Louvain, has recently demonstrated that managers from different cultural backgrounds have different perceptions of the attributes that effective managers should possess.[3] He has also pointed out that these differences are likely to have some influence on the pattern of promotion within multi-national corporations, though he is not yet in a position to demonstrate the significance, in this respect, of the stereotypes held by the technic groups who are in a position to determine career developments in multi-national corporations.

In each of the four multi-national corporations that have already significantly developed some of the characteristics of the *geocentric* organisation, namely I.B.M., Shell, Nestlé, and Unilever, the major cultural influence is still that of the parent organisation and senior management is predominantly drawn from the countries in which the parent organisation is based. This situation is gradually likely to change as multi-national corporations become more geocentric. However, there is little concrete evidence available which would confirm that this process will be as rapid as Howard V. Perlmutter seems to think likely. The dominant national groups have a natural reluctance to

[1] See B. C. Roberts and L. Greyfié de Bellecombe: *Collective Bargaining in African Countries* (London, Macmillan, 1967; publication of the International Institute for Labour Studies, Geneva).

[2] The cultural chauvinism of the French may be a major reason why they have not developed any multi-national corporations on a similar scale to those founded in Britain, Germany, Holland, Switzerland, Sweden and the United States.

[3] *Cultural Issues within Multi-National Organisations*, paper presented at XVIth International Congress of Applied Psychology, Amsterdam, August 1968.

appoint from outside for the reasons that emerge from Vansina's work, and also for the simple technical reason that recruitment at the bottom is mainly in the headquarters countries. Since promotion from within is regarded as an essential feature of large-scale corporations this tends to maintain the strength of the dominant national groups.

In a recent paper given to a conference organised by the British Institute of Management, Max Gloor, Director, Nestlé Alimentana, S.A., discussed this aspect of his company. He agreed that there was 'a certain predominance of Swiss nationals in executive positions without monopolising these anywhere to any extent'. Nevertheless, he added, 'we have in each case, and at all times, done what we thought is in the best interests of the company. Adapting itself to the local scene has generally been facilitated by the type of man appointed and it is this factor more than any other which has determined the recruitment of overseas managers.'

A powerful instrument which the multi-national corporation can use both to provide an opportunity for many of its employees to develop their latent talents and have the opportunity of achieving the corporation's most senior posts is management education and training. In this respect most of the large multi-national corporations make a considerable provision. The Nestlé Company in particular has made a major contribution to management education in the establishment in 1957 of the now famous I.M.E.D.E. Although courses at business schools cannot entirely eliminate national differences, they can and do correct the cruder stereotypes and demonstrate that the techniques of modern management science are applicable in all circumstances and can be used without cultural bias. Indeed, one of the most necessary requirements for successful management in a multi-national corporation is the inculcation of what has been called Factor X.[1] This is the creation of managers who possess all the personal qualities and attributes needed for success in a different cultural environment. 'These include friendliness, lack of racial or religious prejudice, adaptability, cultural empathy, and the over-all ability to achieve the firm's goals through gaining acceptance and co-operation from nationals who might be suspicious and atangonistic.'[2] *Ethnocentric* corporations have often signally failed to develop in managers sent overseas Factor X. This is not surprising since one of the main reasons why companies

---

[1] Harlan Cleveland and Gerard J. Mangone (eds.): *The Art of Overseasmanship* (Syracuse, N.Y., Syracuse University Press, 1957).

[2] John C. Shearer: *High Level Manpower in Overseas Subsidiaries* (Princeton University, 1960).

send their own management personnel overseas is because they believe they are superior to the locals of the host country in those virtues which the company rates highest, namely, knowledge, efficiency, hard work and effective performance. The multi-national corporation which has adopted as its goal a *geocentric* orientation is in a better position to develop in all of its employees the qualities of Factor X and the abilities to achieve an effective performance; indeed, the integration of these two elements is an essential feature in the manager of a geocentric corporation.

An appropriate corporate philosophy is one of the most important factors in the creation of the cultural conditions that are necessary to make true *geocentricity* possible. I.B.M. has for some long time sought to create and to realise an ideal concept of the corporation and relationship of its employees to it. This concept has been based upon the notion that I.B.M. is a kind of community to which a person is admitted if he satisfies the tests of ability and personal qualities which I.B.M. consider essential in its employees. I.B.M. is almost a way of life, and loyalty to the corporation is a first requirement. Once a member of the corporation it offers an opportunity for self-fulfilment in terms of a worthwhile career, opportunities for personal development, a good income and a high degree of economic security. A distinctive feature of membership of I.B.M. is that an employee should not engage in trade union or political activities that might be in conflict with the aims and objects of the corporation. Although its application is intended to be worldwide, there is much about the philosophy of I.B.M. which is similar to that of other major American corporations that sought in the 1920s and 1930s to offer an alternative to the trade union and socialist ideologies that were blossoming under the stress of capitalist economic collapse and large-scale unemployment.

It is a significant question whether conducting the business of a multi-national corporation in the future will require it to recognise and bargain with trade unions. The philosophy of I.B.M. and other companies which do not recognise and negotiate with trade unions is in fact an alternative concept to the dominant notion that has pervaded the industrial relations systems of most advanced industrial countries for the past century, namely that there are two sides to industry, employers and unions, management and workers. It remains an open question whether this traditional pattern will survive in the light of changes in the structure of industry and society that are taking place. The growth of the multi-national corporation raises the question whether national-based trade unionism and its tactics and strategies designed to cope with a very different kind of industrial structure, within the confines of a nation State, can make the adjustments that will be required to maintain the classic role of the unions in the future.

The Shell Company, which has operations in 110 countries, has also developed during the past few years a distinctive corporate philosophy which it is seeking to inculcate throughout its organisation. The essence of this philosophy, which is different in one important respect from that of I.B.M., is the view that while the company is primarily concerned with maximising the profitability of the company the resources to which it has legal rights of privileged access are nonetheless part of the total resources of society as a whole and are, in this sense, social resources; the company believes that they must be protected, developed and managed as such. It furthermore believes that its use of these resources must be such as to contribute to meeting society's requirements for products and services.[1]

If the company is to be managed efficiently its employees must be committed to this objective. It will only be possible to achieve this commitment through individuals developing within themselves a willingness to accept responsibility and to take the initiative required. This means that every Shell employee, irrespective of his national origin and country in which he works, should have the opportunity to achieve self-fulfilment through involvement in the company's activities.

The implications of this philosophy in terms of personnel policy include the placing of responsibility on senior management to see that the personnel function is effectively carried out. The company accepts that it is its duty to ensure, so far as this is possible, that every employee should be able to earn a good income by the standard of the country in which he is employed and that, if he is transferred to another country, he shall not suffer in terms of the standards that he would be entitled to enjoy in his home country. The company recognises that its employees have a right to join trade unions and, unlike I.B.M., the right to have their interests protected by collective agreements. However, since the shutting down of operations in a capital-intensive, continuous-throughput industry, such as oil, is extremely costly to employees, company and the community, the company seeks to promote as an alternative to periodic demands, dramatic confrontations and bouts of bitter conflict, a continuous dialogue between manage-

[1] C. P. Hill, Shell Refining Company, London School of Economics Conference, July, 1968.

ment, workers and unions. In short, it is the objective of the company at all times 'to conduct its affairs in a socially responsible way'.

## THE RESPONSE OF EMPLOYEES TO MANAGERIAL POLICY

The *ethnocentric* multi-national corporation is likely to have a greater problem in maintaining good relations between its management and its employees than either *polycentric* or *geocentric* organisations. In the *ethnocentric* firm any conflict over conditions of employment is always in danger of being exacerbated by the cultural gap that is certain to separate management from workers. This problem is particularly acute when companies are operating in the less-developed countries, especially if they are former colonial territories.

The type of situation that can arise is well illustrated by one of the most bitter disputes to occur in Britain for many years, that was settled only a few months ago. The dispute arose when the American chairman of an American-owned textile plant in Britain insisted on making certain changes to bring about an improvement in productivity, including, among others, the replacement of male workers by women in a small number of jobs that had hitherto always been done by men. The men's union refused to agree to the changes proposed and insisted that they should not be put into effect until an agreement had been reached. Following American practice, the management of the company refused to heed the voice of the unions and it went ahead with the changes, stating that these would benefit the company, which would expand its production, and benefit the workers who would receive higher pay, and ultimately more jobs would be created. A substantial number of workers were ready to continue working at the factory, where they had been employed for many years, under the new arrangements, but those who were hostile to the changes were able to rouse opposition to them outside of the mill. As a result, the district committee of the union decided to call a strike and to picket the factory. The strike was only partially successful, but a series of violent incidents occurred and the management of the firm was fiercely attacked in the press and in Parliament for behaving in an un-British way. In fact many British firms have forced changes through in exactly the same way as the management of Roberts–Arundel, but they have not had to face the extreme hostility that was generated by the latent xenophobic nationalism, based on a stereotype of America and American management. This strike-cum-lockout lasted twelve months in which the company suffered serious damage before an agreement was eventually reached after intervention at the level of government, the United States Embassy and the T.U.C. It is quite clear that the basic problem arose out of an acute difference of culture patterns manifested in the clash between an alien managerial style and an entrenched trade union that feared it would lose influence and its control of the jobs that had been the prerogative of its members.

There have been a number of incidents of a similar if not so violent kind in Germany which have involved the United States. At the John Deere-Lanz plant the workers went on strike when the American management reduced the breakfast break which was regarded by them – since they were not used to such a meal-break – as unnecessary. Procter and Gamble were also the subject of strong criticism by the Chemical Workers Union when they introduced a system of tight factory discipline. 'We don't live in Vietnam', wrote the paper of the union.

John H. Shearer, after examining the policy of a good many United States companies operating overseas, has concluded that 'American firms which operate in foreign countries usually premise their industrial relations policies on the basis of values, assumptions and habits they have developed in the United States. They may or may not modify them in response to different circumstances.'[1] The same point might well be made about British and European firms when operating in under-developed countries, but not when operating in advanced industrial countries such as Australia, the United States or European countries.

Considering that there are some two thousand foreign-owned firms in the United Kingdom, of which 80 per cent are American-owned, the degree of conflict arising out of national antagonism has been extremely small. It would have been much larger had the management of these companies insisted on foreign standards and practices. Even though not compelled to follow British patterns by law, most foreign companies have accepted them. However, the management of United States companies have complained bitterly of the attitudes of British trade unions, restrictive practices, long meal-breaks and a relatively low total performance.

[1] John C. Shearer: 'Industrial Relations of American Corporations Abroad', *International Labour*, I.R.R.A. Series (New York, 1967).

Some United States firms, however, have had notable success in making major changes and considerably increasing output without running into the unfortunate consequences of the Roberts–Arundel affair. The negotiation of the Fawley productivity agreements, which was initiated by Esso Petroleum, involved massive changes in established practices. These were carried through by an organisation that would be classified as *polycentric*, but this particular exercise was to an important extent a reversion to *ethnocentrism*. The concept of buying out the restrictive practices, that had produced a situation in which it took twice as many men in Britain as in America to produce the same volume of output, was developed in the United States. The measurement of the saving possible, and the tactics pursued by the company to persuade the workers to accept the changes proposed for their own benefit and that of the company, were worked out by an American. Their acceptance, however, was due to the confidence that had been created by a group of British managers who fully backed the American initiative and played a major part in translating it into British cultural terms.

There has been little or no attempt by European-based unions to seek to level-up to wage standards and other conditions of employment in the most advanced firms. Certain initiatives have been taken by trade unions, but these have mainly come from American unions. The steel workers' union in the United States have done a good deal to help the unions organising bauxite workers in the West Indies. There can be no doubt that the prime motive of the union has been to raise the standards of bauxite workers so as to raise the cost of aluminium, which is a substitute for steel and therefore a threat to the jobs of American steel workers. The union has felt morally justified in supporting the bauxite workers, not only because they were lowly paid by American standards, but also because the companies concerned were American-based multi-national corporations.

Another instance of the same type of response is to be found in the efforts being made by the United Automobile Workers' Union (U.A.W.) to persuade the unions organising workers employed by the overseas companies of Ford, General Motors and Chrysler to co-ordinate their bargaining strategies to secure higher levels of pay and improved conditions of employment. In the opinion of the U.A.W. the overseas plants of the American car companies are similar to the so-called runaway companies that have established plants in the deep south to take advantage of lower labour costs.

128

## INFLUENCE OF ECONOMIC, SOCIAL
## AND POLITICAL FACTORS

Labour costs will be a factor of critical importance in the decision of a multi-national corporation to locate a new plant, or extend an existing activity. These will be affected by a variety of factors, including the level of development of the labour force and its cultural characteristics, type and degree of trade unionism, legal regulations and political environment in the country concerned.

In deciding whether to put down a new plant the corporation will have to take into account the advantage of this step against that of supplying the market of the country concerned from elsewhere. Even if labour costs are comparatively high it may still be of net advantage to establish a new plant, since transport and other costs may offset the adverse level of labour costs.

Comparative labour costs will be of particular importance in the choice of a manufacturing centre from which a large number of important markets are to be supplied. In theory research studies should establish the optimum location, but in practice the less-tangible factors of union hostility, labour indiscipline, legal constraints and political instability, will be of prime importance. In these matters the stereotype of the behaviour patterns of the labour situation in each country held by the management of the multi-national corporation will be a major factor in the making of its decisions.

Whatever the stereotypes, and how far they truthfully reflect the actual realities of particular countries, there can be no denying that the industrial relations systems vary greatly from one country to another. A multi-national corporation will have to face this fact and come to terms with its implications. It will be more difficult for an *ethnocentric* organisation to make the adjustments necessary, especially if the management it sends overseas have not had an appropriate experience or training, than for *polycentric* or *geocentric* corporations.

The decision where to site a plant is a matter that often gives rise to conflict between national interests and multi-national corporations which are seeking to achieve the maximum economic advantage. The site chosen by a multi-national corporation to commence new operations may not be regarded by those who wield political power in the host country as the most suitable. Objections may be raised on the score of the effect which the satisfying of the corporation's interests will have on the employment situation, or on amenity in the district concerned. If the situation is one in which the host country is seeking to persuade a multi-national corporation to locate a projected major investment in its territory, it may have to accept, as the price that it has to pay, the site chosen by the multi-national corporation, even though it is less than ideal. When, however, a multi-national corporation has already made a large investment it may be in a weaker bargaining position and, therefore, more willing to establish the location of further plant in places that would meet the social case advanced by the government of the country concerned.

The laying-off of workers, and the closing down of plants are also decisions that will touch upon sensitive issues and give rise to acute conflicts of interest. These will arise in particular if the subsidiary of the multi-national corporation is entirely owned by the parent corporation and its senior management is from overseas. *Polycentric*, but to a lesser extent *geocentric*, organisations will not have to meet the same degree of national concern. If the lay-off is brought about by a general deterioration in the economic climate and the multi-national corporation is clearly reacting to circumstances which are affecting indigenous firms in the same way it may avoid some of, but it is unlikely to avoid altogether, the hostility which its foreign ownership is likely to arouse.

The greatest difficulty will arise when a multi-national corporation seeks to improve its efficiency by reducing its labour force to the most efficient scale. The problem will be most serious if this involves the complete shut-down of a plant which is the sole or main source of employment in a district. In under-developed countries it is not uncommon for a multi-national corporation engaged in mining, agricultural or manufacturing activities, and having a substantial investment at stake, to be carrying on its payroll a much larger labour force than it requires. If, however, it seeks to make the maximum economic gain by reducing its labour force to the most efficient level it will encounter strong opposition and even social and political action to prevent its carrying out its decision.

It may well be that a multi-national corporation is more favourably placed to weather locally-adverse economic circumstances and its ability to do so will create a public opinion sympathetic to its activities. So, too, will the payment of wages and the granting of conditions of work above the standard normally applied in the countries in which it is operating. If, however, the country concerned is seeking to prevent wage and salary increases from rising faster than the average rate of economic growth it will be looked upon by the government as an unfriendly act if the company attempts to purchase the goodwill of its employees by raising pay levels above the norms the government is wishing to impose. By the same token foreign-owned corporations will be expected to observe other rules or limitations that a government may be seeking to impose in order to prevent inflation, or to achieve a particular social policy.

Particular difficulties for a foreign-owned firm may arise, especially if the firm is *ethnocentric*, when a government decides to embark under local political pressure on a policy of staff localisation. This has happened in most former British colonial territories. Governments have often laid down strict rules limiting the immigration of the parent company's nationals to those in a category regarded as absolutely essential if the particular enterprise is to remain in business. This policy is not, of course, confined to under-developed countries; protection of jobs and wages is carried on in the advanced countries by restrictions on immigrants. In these industrially advanced countries the problem is often no less acute for the foreign-owned company, although senior management personnel are usually free from restrictions on entry. This may not be true, however, in the entertainment field where even quite high-level technical and artistic staff may be refused entry on the grounds that a local person is available to do the work involved.

There are certain developments in the legal regulation of company management that multi-national corporations may be reluctant to accept. If the appointment of worker directors were to be made mandatory this might well give rise to a serious conflict of interest and could be an important factor in a multi-national corporation's decision to begin or continue activities in a particular country. Legal compulsion to recognise and negotiate with unions organising management grades would also pose difficult questions for corporations that do not normally enter into negotiations on matters concerning these grades.

In all of these conflicts of economic and social interests the multi-national corporation should in principle be placed in the same position as a national corporation. In practice, however, if the multi-national corporation is engaged in an activity which is of vital concern to the host country and the corporation can choose between different countries in which to locate its activities, it will have an advantage over the locally domiciled company and be in a strong position to resist policies to which it is opposed. On the other hand, if it must locate its operations in one particular place in order to gain access to particular raw materials its bargaining position may be quite weak. So far as it is possible to judge on limited information available, it would seem that in most cases the conflicts of interest that arise are resolved without a serious rupture of relations between the multi-national corporation and the trade union and other interests in the host country. The best evidence for this lies in the growth of multi-national corporate activity. However, the situation may be different in the future, if the activity scale of the multi-national corporation continues to rise, and, as envisaged by Perlmutter, *geocentric* multi-national corporations come to dominate world economic activity as a new kind of supranational entity. In these circumstances the nation State and such interested groups as the trade unions may fear that their social concerns will be over ridden by the power of the multi-national corporations to decide on the terms on which they will operate within a particular territory. Faced by a threat of this kind it is certain that the nation State will seek to preserve its sovereignty. How far it is able to do so may well depend on the degree to which the development of the *geocentric* multi-national corporation has been accompanied by a similar pattern of development on the part of the trade unions. Acting together multi-national corporations and trade unions might successfully challenge and change the established structure of national sovereignty. Much, then, might depend on the future development of the unions as well as the multi-national corporations.

# CANADA AND JAMAICA: TWO CASE STUDIES OF TRANSNATIONAL INDUSTRIAL RELATIONS

BOTH countries, so different in size, geographical location, culture and level of economic, social and political development, have one major aspect in common: they are both exposed to the pronounced influence of American-based multi-national management and international trade union federations. The two chapters presented in this section are attempts to analyse for each of the two countries the effects of this exposure of industrial relations, as well as to shed light on the wider societal repercussions.

For the first time in history, fully fledged international collective bargaining has occurred between a multi-national firm (Chrysler) and the Canadian and U.S. Chrysler workers organised in the U.A.W.[1] This collective agreement has been facilitated by a particular set of circumstances, including a high degree of economic integration with the U.S., whose investors control a large part of the Canadian industry, similar levels of productivity in the Chrysler plants on both sides of the border and the special trade union structure grouping workers of both countries in the same organisation. For the Canadian and U.S. Chrysler workers, the political border separating both countries will become meaningless to a large extent; they will be treated as an entity in respect of wages and other work rules, as well as union strategy.

David H. Blake, who undertakes in Chapter 7 to study the political, social and economic implications of the Chrysler/U.A.W. agreement, underlines that henceforward three peaks of authority will exist for the Canadian U.A.W. workers; the Canadian Government, the multi-national corporation and the bi-national union. Perhaps somewhat surprisingly, David H. Blake found Canadian Government officials fully aware, but on the whole not overly concerned, about the potential for collision between the policies of U.S.-controlled corporations and national policy goals. However, this may reflect the assumption that the similarities in economic conditions, social and economic organisation and culture of the two countries would mitigate possible disruptions.

[1] United Automobile, Aerospace and Agricultural Implement Workers of America.

135

Jamaica offers in this respect an obvious antithesis. Jeffrey Harrod's essential concern in Chapter 8 is the implications of the presence of powerful forces from a very different culture manifested in the operation in a key industry (bauxite) of an American-based multi-national corporation and the influence of a likewise American-based union. In Harrod's judgment, these forces alter not merely industrial relations, but affect dramatically the total political situation through a modification of nature, structure and leadership role of the local unions. In his analysis, the interference of the foreign-based multi-national corporation and unions has split and depolitised the local trade union movement, curtailing its importance as a group pressing for meaningful social and political change. The latter judgment naturally contains elements of speculation, as it is impossible to predict what would have actually happened in the absence of transnational influences; but the Jamaican case study appears to carry the general lesson that, particularly in developing countries, the presence of a foreign-based multi-national corporation, as well as the influence of international unions, cannot be seen in economic isolation. Therefore, while in similar environments transnationalisation of industrial relations might occur nearly unnoticed, whatever the total repercussions might be (as the Canadian case until recently suggested), their possible distorting effects in dissimilar environments need to be closely watched.

Chapter 7

# MULTI-NATIONAL CORPORATION, INTERNATIONAL UNION AND INTERNATIONAL COLLECTIVE BARGAINING: A CASE STUDY OF THE POLITICAL, SOCIAL, AND ECONOMIC IMPLICATIONS OF THE 1967 U.A.W.–CHRYSLER AGREEMENT

*by*

*David H. Blake*

## INTRODUCTION[1]

IN 1970 representatives of the United Automobile, Aerospace and Agricultural Implement Workers of America (U.A.W.) will sit down with Chrysler Corporation personnel to hammer out a master agreement which will cover workers in Canada and the United States. Should a strike be called by the union, Chrysler workers in Canada and the United States will walk off the job, effectively closing down the corporation's productive facilities. Furthermore, upon reaching an agreement, the proposed contract will be voted upon by all the Chrysler–U.A.W. members in the United States and Canada. If a majority of the workers, regardless of nationality, accept the agreement, then a new master contract, governing corporate and employee relations, will have been reached, and the many U.A.W. locals can proceed to bargain with plant representatives about various local

[1] The research for this paper was supported by a grant from the Wayne State University–University of Michigan Institute of Labour and Industrial Relations and by a National Science Foundation Institutional Grant from Wayne State University.

I want to thank Mr Charles Tripp for his aid with the U.A.W. survey which is only partially reported here. Appreciation is also expressed to the many union, government and business officials who talked freely with me about the issues at hand. A final word of thanks must go to the men of U.A.W. Local 444 in Windsor, Ontario, who completed the questionnaire.

issues. The important point is that for the first time in the crucial automobile industry true international collective bargaining will have occurred. The Canadian and United States Chrysler workers will have been treated as one group with no distinctions corresponding to political boundaries.

The provisions of the new contract will also emphasise the trans-national nature of the union-corporation relationship. Wage parity between United States and Canadian workers performing the same tasks will be achieved. Other provisions of the master agreement will apply equally to all the workers, no matter which country they are located in. The locals in Canada will basically have the same status as locals in the United States in their confrontations with the corporation, and they will have the full weight of Chrysler-U.A.W. members behind them in their disputes. Thus, as from 1970, to a very significant extent, the political boundary between the United States and Canada will be non-existent for Chrysler-U.A.W. relations.

It is this relationship, the development of international collective bargaining, as well as the larger and more general problem of the influence of international non-governmental economic organisations on host States that fascinate me as a political scientist. We in political science and other social sciences have too long ignored, in terms of empirical research, the actual and potential impact of these trans-national groups on international and domestic political systems.[1] If the relationship is explored, it is usually done in a polemical or intuitive manner. Some have looked upon the activity of these transnational groups as an extension of imperialism. Others, happily or hopefully, foresee the growth of transnational interest groups leading to the development of international loyalties, values, and interests which by commanding more loyalty than the nation State may culminate in a greater possibility for peace in the world. However, I am interested in observing the structure, behaviour, impact and consequences of these non-governmental international economic organisations on the economic, social and political systems of States. It is this interest that leads me to explore international collective bargaining and wage parity as it occurs in the Chrysler Corporation-U.A.W. relationship. In this case, in 1970, a multi-national corporation and an international union, both of which are headquartered in the United States, will engage in

---

[1] See *Plenary Sessions of the Conference on the Politics of International Business*, sponsored and published by *Daedalus* in 1969, for an interesting discussion of some of the questions which need to be researched.

activity that will have significant effects upon the economy and politics of Canada.

The first part of this paper will consider the nature of Canada's union and industrial structure as well as the characteristics of the Canadian automobile industry. With the economic and industrial environment explained, it will be possible then to turn to a discussion of the wage parity provisions of the contract and the international collective bargaining arrangement. This will be followed by an analysis of interview and survey data on the reactions of officials of the Canadian Government, the corporation, the union, and of the rank and file Canadian–Chrysler union members, to wage parity and international collective bargaining. The concluding section of the paper will be a speculative look into the future based on the implications of the research reported herein.


## ECONOMIC AND INDUSTRIAL ENVIRONMENT

Although the differences between Canada and the United States are often overlooked or underestimated by Americans, it certainly is true that there are a great many similarities that have been produced by similar colonial and cultural backgrounds. In addition to this, though, there has been the constant influence of United States institutions and processes on the development of Canada. Probably in few areas has the influence of the United States been greater than in the development and organisation of the Canadian economy. For instance, United States residents own 44 per cent of the manufacturing industry, 54 per cent of the petroleum and natural gas industry, and 54 per cent of the mining and smelting industry.[1] To be even more specific, in 1963 United States residents controlled 97 per cent of the Canadian automobile industry, 90 per cent of the Canadian rubber industry, 54 per cent of the chemical industry, and 66 per cent of the electrical apparatus industry.[2] Obviously, American economic penetration is of major proportions, and this has been a source of concern to many Canadians, as evidenced by the recent Task Force on the Structure of Canadian Industry.

[1] Report of the Task Force on the Structure of Canadian Industry, *Foreign Ownership and the Structure of Canadian Industry*; Melville H. Watkins (Ottawa, Queen's Printer, 1968), p. 422.
[2] *Ibid.*, p. 11.

The major problem, as Neil Chamberlain has put it, is that the United States subsidiary in Canada is faced with two peaks of authority – the Canadian Government on one hand and the parent company in the United States on the other. Problems arise for both the corporation and the sovereignty of Canada when the interests of the two peaks of authority conflict.[1] The question becomes then: 'What is the nationality of the United States subsidiary in Canada?'[2] The seriousness of the conflict is increased if the parent company requires the subsidiary to carry out policies favourable to the United States Government but inimical to the interests of Canada.[3] As the Watkins report states, 'Insofar as subsidiaries become instruments of policy of the home country rather than the host country, the capacity of the latter to affect decisions, i.e. its political independence, is directly reduced.'[4]

Thus, the very large amount of United States activity in the Canadian economy suggests the possibility of direct or indirect infringements upon the ability of Canadians to control aspects of their own economy, politics and foreign relations. But Canada is also faced by another force, another peak of authority, which has the potential to encroach upon Canadian sovereignty in these areas. This force is the international union, with the great proportion of its membership and officialdom as well as its headquarters in the United States. Based on 1965 figures, the 110 international unions operating in Canada had a Canadian membership which was 70·8 per cent of the total numbers of Canadian trade union members.[5] Furthermore, eight of the ten largest unions in Canada are international unions.[6] While these figures do not testify to the degree of influence the international unions have over Canadian politics or economics, they do emphasise the potential which lies therein. Indeed, a number of Canadian scholars, government officials, some union officials, and journalists, have expressed

---

[1] Neil Chamberlain: 'The Concept of Economic Sovereignty in Relation to Business', in *Domination or Independence? – The Problem of Canadian Autonomy in Labour–Management Relations*, ed. by Shirley B. Goldenberg and Francis B. Bairstow (Montreal, McGill University Industrial Relations Centre, 1965), pp. 3–4.

[2] Watkins, *op. cit.*, p. 311.

[3] For instance, the United States forbids its corporations to engage in trade with Red China or Cuba and this prohibition applies to subsidiaries in Canada. Similarly, there are domestic measures which infringe on the economic sovereignty of Canada, as evidenced by the fact that American anti-trust legislation applies to the activity of subsidiaries in Canada too. See Chamberlain, *op. cit.*, pp. 5–6, and Watkins, pp. 312–13.

[4] Watkins, *op. cit.*, p. 311.

[5] John Crispo: *International Unionism: A Study in Canadian–American Relations* (Toronto, McGraw-Hill Company of Canada Limited, 1967), p. 4. There are 1,124,241 Canadians who are members of international unions.

[6] *Ibid.*, p. 5.

concern over the central position in the economy which the international unions have.[1]

John Crispo, Director of the Centre for Industrial Relations, at the University of Toronto, has explored in *International Unionism: A Study in Canadian–American Relations* the influence of the international union, mainly on the basis of interviews with international union officials. He found that generally the Canadian branches of international unions have a significant degree of autonomy from the union headquarters, and even where the international must approve a decision to strike, the amount of international deference in this area is great. Crispo also suggests that the international unions generally view their membership and activity as a whole and that they pay little attention to the fact that Canadian members belong to a separate political entity.[2] This does not seem to concern the Canadian membership, for the controversy over international unionism exists largely because of the desires of some groups to profit by the conflict.[3] Crispo found that, 'By and large, the Canadian members of international unions do not think twice about the fact that they belong to an international union.'[4] A mixture of loyalty, contentment and apathy brings about the disinterest in the development of national unions to rival the internationals.[5] Crispo goes on to say that large employers generally look kindly upon international unions although they are very much concerned about the issue of wage parity, but the smaller employer is more hostile to the internationals, probably because of a feeling of being overwhelmed by a much larger union.[6] As regards

---

[1] It is interesting to note that most Europeans and Americans who are concerned about protecting a State's sovereignty from the influence of 'foreign' or multi-national organisations do not recognise the potential threat from the truly international union. While attending the Symposium on International Collective Bargaining held at the International Institute for Labour Studies in Geneva from 29 April to 2 May 1969. I observed that many participants were deeply disturbed by the pervasiveness of international, particularly American-owned, private enterprise. However, the idea that an international union engaging in international collective bargaining and other such activities might also compromise a State's sovereignty was not perceived by them, and attempts to seek consideration of this possibility were largely ignored.

[2] *Ibid.*, p. 31. Some international unions, by not being sensitive to the political divisions, have given very poor service to their Canadian members. One such union serviced its Quebec members from a regional office located in Philadelphia by representatives who neither spoke nor understood French. Another major international union, which should have known better, found that the international president before the union's convention for the Canadian membership spoke on the necessity of electing Hubert Humphrey to the presidency of the United States.

[3] *Ibid.*, p. 165.
[4] *Ibid.*, p. 23.
[5] *Ibid.*, p. 29.
[6] *Ibid.*, pp. 279–280.

141

the attitudes of the Canadian Government, Crispo feels that there is a willingness to live with international unions even though they are not particularly welcomed.[1] In general though, this scholar of the Canadian labour movement gives the impression that international unions do more good than harm and that the degree of American control is overshadowed by the amount of Canadian local autonomy.

However, Crispo essentially agrees with the hypothesis of Bryan Downie[2] that the influence of United States union officials on collective bargaining will be the greatest when exports from Canada threaten American wage standards, when there is at least one competing union in the industry, when the industry is 100 per cent controlled by American residents, and when the Canadian and United States industries are located in the same area. Under the extreme conditions represented here, it is felt that international union influence on the nature of Canadian demands and on the process of negotiating would be quite large.[3] But, Crispo has found that American union officials usually do not enter Canadian collective bargaining unless it is by invitation of the union local, the government, or the employer.[4] Even though United States Union participation is frequently by invitation only, the Canadian locals usually use the United States settlements as guidelines or goals. Eugene Forsey expressed it this way:

'Canadian employers sometimes assert that Canadian workers adopt wage and other policies which are not suited to Canadian conditions. They sometimes go on to assert that this is because most Canadian workers belong to international unions. The first assertion, true or false, does not concern us here. The second does. The theory seems to be that if the Ford workers in Windsor, Ontario, for example had not belonged to an international union, the U.A.W., it would never have occurred to them to ask for the guaranteed annual wage. If they had looked across the river and seen what the American employees of the American Ford Company were asking for, and in part getting, they would just have said, "Well, well! Most interesting!" The idea that Canadian workers have to eat, and pay rent, and clothe themselves all the year round, just as much as American workers, would never have crossed their

[1] *Ibid.*, p. 294.
[2] See Bryan Downie: 'International Union Influence on Collective Bargaining in Canada', in *Domination or Independence? – The Problem of Canadian Autonomy in Labour – Management Relations*, ed. by Shirley B. Goldenberg and Frances B. Bairstow (Montreal, McGill University Industrial Relations Centre, 1965).
[3] *Ibid.*, p. 192.
[4] *Ibid.*, pp. 221-2.

minds. Nobody would have thought of asking: "If it's good for the man on the Ford assembly line in Detroit, why not for the man on the Ford assembly line in Windsor?"

'Of course, the international union's policy for its American members influenced its Canadian members. But, short of erecting a Chinese Wall, or an Iron Curtain between Canada and the United States, there is just no way of preventing Canadian workers from finding out what American workers are doing; and when they find out, they are very likely to think that what is good for American workers is good for Canadian also, and ask for it. If every single union in Canada were Simon Pure Canadian, if not a single unionist in Canada had ever so much as laid eyes on an American union member, the result would be precisely what it is now, or so nearly the same that it would need an electron microscope to see the difference.'[1]

Even the Canadian national unions usually follow the patterns established in the United States.[2]

Thus, we can summarise our discussion of Canadian industry, Canadian trade unions and Canadian collective bargaining by recognising the very great influence of the American institutions. Some of the influence is calculated and directed by the United States organisation involved but, just as often if not more often, the influence seems to occur merely because of the existence of these institutions in a State which has friendly, frequent and open interactions with Canada.

The problems faced by the Canadian Government and people revolve around the question of maintaining economic and political independence in the face of the combined, though not necessarily colluding or similar, union and corporate pressures. As the Watkins report[3] attests, this is a difficult task under the most favourable conditions. This paper describes a case where a United States headquartered corporation employing about 12,000 people in Canada will bargain internationally, not locally or regionally, with a United States headquartered union about matters that may directly affect the political, economic, and social patterns of Canadians. The following statement from a *New York Times* editorial[4] about the achievement of wage parity for Canadian automobile workers is an appropriate commentary about the possible implications of this particular relationship for Canadians and the Canadian Government:

[1] As quoted in Crispo, *op. cit.*, p. 185.
[2] *Ibid.*, p. 193.
[3] *op. cit.*
[4] 'Exporting Wage Rates', *New York Times*, 11 November 1967, p. 32.

'The bad part of it is that the decision was made, under coercion of a strike deadline, by American corporate and union leaders much more concerned with their own interests than the immediate consequences for Canada. This is a type of economic imperialism no country can welcome.'

## THE CANADIAN AUTOMOBILE INDUSTRY

Having considered in a general way the economic and industrial environment, the specific case of the automobile industry must be discussed.[1] Basically, the tendencies noted above about the general structure and patterns of Canadian industry are represented in the extreme in the Canadian automobile industry. The United States parent companies of General Motors, Ford, Chrysler and American Motors control their Canadian subsidiaries, even though there is some Canadian ownership of Ford. Thus in essence, the big four in the United States own the big four in Canada, and these four companies dominate the Canadian automobile industry just as they do in the United States.

The employees of the Canadian subsidiaries are organised in the U.A.W. just as their American brothers are, and in the past the Canadian locals have had the same rights and as much or more autonomy as United States locals. The Canadian union officials were kept closely informed of the bargaining sessions for American workers in Detroit, but the Canadians themselves bargained at a later date with corporate representatives for their own contracts. Thus, while there was much pattern setting in the industry, formally the collective bargaining was strictly on a national and not on an international basis.[2] Chrysler Local 444 in Windsor, Ontario, for instance, was perfectly free to formulate their own demands and strategy without checking with the international; and they did. It must be admitted, though, that the international U.A.W. headquarters has the ultimate authority to approve a strike but, according to Downie, this 'has

[1] In the ensuing discussion, note how closely the nature of the Canadian automobile industry meets the conditions which Downie suggests will lead to a significant degree of influence by the international union officials.

[2] The international U.A.W. often provided technical staff men to aid the local bargaining committee during the negotiations, and the corporations frequently did the same. However, sometimes United States corporate personnel would actually perform the bargaining for the Canadian subsidiaries.

never been used as an instrument of control' with respect to the Canadian locals.[1]

Thus, prior to the events of 1967, the Canadian automobile industry was characterised by complete United States control of the Canadian subsidiaries; by a large degree of local and regional union autonomy, although there was much co-operation and help available from the international union headquarters; by differing wage scales, fringe benefits, and car prices, even though the directions in which each of these moved were similar in both countries; by geographical proximity; and by a high degree of product substitutability.

One other very important aspect of the industry has significant bearing on the problem at hand. In January 1965 President Lyndon B. Johnson and Prime Minister Lester Pearson signed an Automotive Products Agreement which, after action by the Congress of the United States and the Canadian Parliament, entered into force on 16 September 1966. In essence, this agreement completely eliminated the tariff on automobiles and automotive parts used in the manufacture of new cars between the United States and Canada. Canadian citizens could not purchase cars in the United States and bring them back into Canada without paying a duty, but the automobile manufacturers could ship new cars and parts for new cars between the two countries without payment of a tariff. In addition, in letters of agreement with the corporations, Canada established certain stipulations that ensured the maintenance of the Canadian share of the market.

This agreement enabled the corporations to rationalise their production facilities. Costly duplication of processes and short 'runs' required for the production of many models were no longer necessary. As a result the Canadian and American facilities became integrated, with production specialisation occurring between the two countries. Thus, cars assembled in the Chrysler plant in Windsor, Ontario, were shipped to both Canadian and American destinations without payment of duty. This was also the case with the products of the Chrysler assembly lines in Detroit. In terms of the production and sale of new cars and new car parts, the Automotive Products Agreement eliminated the Canadian-American boundary. For the industry, the two countries became but one.

---

[1] Bryan Downie, *op. cit.*, p. 118.

## WAGE PARITY AND INTERNATIONAL BARGAINING

Given the nature of the Canadian automobile industry and the Automotive Products Agreement, the achievement of wage parity lay but a
short time ahead. George Burt, the recently retired U.A.W. Canadian
Director, said:

> 'We have in our hands for the first time in our history, and with
> the courtesy of the governments of the United States and Canada,
> if you please, the key to perhaps the oldest and greatest collective
> bargaining objective of our union: the right to equal pay for equal
> work with our American brothers.'[1]

Mr. Burt made this statement in October 1965 and, in the next round of
negotiations in November 1967, wage parity was achieved.

On 8 November, 1967, after much hard bargaining and under the
threat of a strike, a 'Wage and Production Parity Agreement' was
reached by the union and Chrysler representatives in Detroit. This was
an agreement which signified the company's willingness to grant
parity in their forthcoming negotiations with the Canadian region in
January next. This agreement was not part of the contract achieved for
United States employees, even though it was likely that the United
States U.A.W. members would have been called out on strike if
the agreement on parity had not been reached. Rather it signified that
the corporation had conceded the parity question. The agreement
also suggested that in their Canadian negotiations Chrysler could
'press vigorously for parity between said plants [United States and
Canadian plants] with respect to working conditions, plant practices'.[2]
This was pursued by Chrysler and a few revisions were achieved but,
after a short strike of Canadians in January 1968, the company had to
give up their major objective of instituting relay relief-time practices,
as in United States, instead of the Canadian practice of closing the
plant down for relief-time.

Wage parity, as it was agreed upon, is to take place gradually over a
period of two and a half years. By June 1970, in similar jobs Canadian
workers will make the same hourly rate in Canadian dollars as Americans make in United States dollars and thus the forty cents average
hourly rate difference between Canada and the United States will be

[1] As quoted in Crispo, *op. cit.*, p. 200.
[2] Mimeographed copy of 'United States and Canada Wage and Production Party
Agreement', p. 2.

erased. The parity achieved, though, is based on the respective currencies of the two countries.

Chrysler was the first to agree to wage parity, but in short order Ford and General Motors also agreed to the establishment of parity. Thus, in one of the major industrial sectors of the Canadian economy, the wage rates of Canadian employers were tied directly to the rates achieved by United States employees. Parity already existed to an extent in the pulp, and paper and paper-products industry, in the West Coast longshoremen's union, and in a few scattered steel and car plants.[1] But, the achievement of parity in the automobile industry was certainly a major breakthrough – particularly when one considers that the Canadian automobile industry employs about 62,800.[2]

The second major development agreed to (but not on a contractual basis) was the decision to initiate international collective bargaining between Chrysler and the U.A.W. in 1970. At that time, the union will have a single International Negotiating Committee which will meet with the corporation representatives to negotiate an international agreement. Although the union has not decided exactly how to establish this international committee, it is likely that the current nine-man negotiating committee based on representation of various functions performed by U.A.W. members will be expanded to include one or two Canadians, who will represent in the first case an all-inclusive Canadian sub-council or in the second case a skilled and a non-skilled Canadian sub-council. Thus, Canadian representation will be assured on the International Negotiating Committee. However, the American and Canadian workers will be acting as a single unit with no differentiation.[3] If a strike should be called, all the union members working at Chrysler, whether in Canada or the United States, would go on strike. In addition, approval of a contract would require a majority vote by all the Chrysler-U.A.W. members, with no veto for either the Canadians or the Americans. True international collective bargaining will therefore occur.

While the concept of an international collective agreement being negotiated internationally is not completely unique in Canadian and United States labour history, it is certainly the first time that it has

[1] Crispo, *op. cit.*, 198–9.

[2] The significance is even greater when one realises that there are 44,200 more U.A.W. members in Canada who do not work in the auto industry. Some of their workers are employed in both office and production jobs by such firms as Massey-Ferguson, General Springs Limited, and the Northern Electric Company.

[3] Walter P. Reuther, *Report of President Walter P. Reuther to the 21st U.A.W. Constitutional Convention*, Part I, p. 77.

occurred with a major corporation and union in a crucial industry. Previous international bargaining arrangements have been entered into by a small operation of the Continental Can Company and by the Bethlehem Steel Company iron-ore mine in Mormora, Ontario.[1] A discussion as to whether the Chrysler breakthrough will lead to similar developments will be taken up later in this paper, but suffice it to say at this point that neither Ford nor General Motors nor the respective union locals in Canada wish to initiate international collective bargaining.

## ATTITUDES OF CANADIAN GOVERNMENT OFFICIALS

The establishment of wage parity and the achievement of international collective bargaining were considered by many to be quite momentous developments. Therefore, in order to pursue my concern with the implications of these events, I have attempted to explore the actions and reactions, the hopes and fears of Canadian Government officials, corporation executives, union officials, and rank-and-file union members. Obviously, the attitudes of the Canadian public also would have been of interest, but scarce research resources prevented such an attempt.

The issue of wage parity is one that the Canadian Government had quite carefully studied and considered even before the agreement of November 1967. In addition, the prestigious but non-governmental Economic Council of Canada explored thoroughly the topic of wage parity in its third annual report. In this, the Council said:

'If one could imagine parity of money income for every Canadian citizen being decreed by Order in Council at ten o'clock in the morning, one could equally well imagine parity of real incomes being effectively repealed in the foreign exchange market before three o'clock the same afternoon.'[2]

The Economic Council of Canada went on to suggest that wage parity was not desirable in those industries where there was no parity in

---

[1] Crispo, *op. cit.*, p. 183.

[2] Economic Council of Canada, Third Annual Review: *Prices, Productivity and Employment* (Ottawa, Queen's Printer, 1966), p. 70.

levels of productivity. However, 'if the gap [of productivity] can gradually be narrowed, the number of situations in which parity could become a reality will increase'.[1] Thus, the Economic Council seems to have based its resistance to wage parity on the fact that disparities in levels of productivity would continue to exist. This situation would result in inflationary tendencies within the economy and in Canadian dollar instability in the international money market.[2]

The Economic Council's evaluation of the cause of the productivity differentials is based upon factors which are not easily or rapidly corrected. The poorer quality of Canada's productive resources and the less efficient methods by which these resources are used are thought to be the major causes of the lower level of productivity.[3] More specifically, the smaller and therefore less efficient production runs, the inability to specialise in production activities, and the lower level of managerial and labour skills all contribute to a less efficient production process.[4]

By and large, the officials in the Ministries of Industry and of Finance, as well as a number of economists and newspapers, were most concerned about the demonstration effects of wage parity in the automobile industry. They feared that other workers in sectors of the economy related and unrelated to the automobile industry would also seek parity, and the overall consequence would be an acceleration of the already severe inflationary movements in the Canadian economy. These officials thought that unless the inflationary trend was halted the result would be a devaluation of the Canadian currency. Thus, they foresaw a wage-price spiral leading to very undesirable actions and consequences.

Another argument used by government officials and some news-papers was aimed more directly at convincing the rank-and-file Chrysler employee that wage parity was not a reasonable goal at this time. This point, based on the Economic Council's analysis, suggested that equal wages coupled with a lower level of productivity would cause the corporations to expand their operations in the United States, at the expense of Canadian production. 'After all,' the argument went, 'if we equalise wages when we have a lower level of productivity, then the unit cost of production relative to that in the United States will be greater. Given this, what is the advantage for the corporations to expand production in Canada when it is actually cheaper to manu-

---

[1] *Ibid.*, p. 72.  [2] *Ibid.*, p. 71.
[3] *Ibid.*, p. 70.  [4] *Ibid.*

facture in the United States?' Following this line of reasoning, it was pointed out to the workers that the result would be at least a freeze in jobs, if not an actual decrease in employment in the Canadian automobile industry.[1]

C. M. Drury, the Minister of Industry during the bargaining, made several speeches pointing out that the Canadian automobile industry's level of productivity was approximately 20 per cent lower than that in the United States. For this reason and the attendant consequences of less employment in the industry and the push on inflation, Mr. Drury was quite critical of the wage parity demand. His opposition to parity was mentioned with a degree of bitterness by some union officials, for they saw his actions as a potential threat to union solidarity on this issue. Therefore, the union officials expended some effort to counteract any influence that his arguments had over the workers. Speeches by local and international officials, pamphlets handed out in the plants, and stories in Local 444's newspaper, were some of the actions taken by union officials to convince the membership of the beneficial nature of wage parity.[2]

Officials in the Department of Labour also were aware of possible negative effects of widespread parity of wages, but they were not at all convinced that parity in the automobile industry alone would lead to increased inflation, decreased exports and instability of the Canadian dollar. While it was felt that widespread parity of wages would be harmful to the Canadian economy, the demand for or achievement of parity was unlikely in most industries, particularly those where the productivity differences were great.

Each official interviewed in the Ministry of Finance stressed the statement on the repercussion of wage parity on the foreign exchange market quoted above from the Economic Council's *Third Annual Review*. However, in contrast, the personnel in the Department of Labour drew attention to the succeeding two paragraphs of the Economic Council's review which stated that wage parity did exist in certain industries, that the Canadian economy could support a limited number of parity situations, and that wherever the productivity

---

[1] Of course, the Chrysler Corporation could have financed wage parity from the revenue of its combined Canadian and United States operations, but if the productivity levels were as unequal as was claimed, Chrysler might have little incentive to expand production in Canada.

[2] Local 444 is the main Chrysler—U.A.W. local in Canada. This local in Windsor, Ontario, has nearly 10,000 members. Since the two other Chrysler locals are comparatively quite small (about 1,500), my research has focused on Local 444 only. A fourth Chrysler local for salaried personnel has not been studied either.

gap could be narrowed or eliminated parity could occur.[1] Interestingly enough, these points, were *never* mentioned by persons in the Ministry of Finance.

During discussions with persons from the Department of Labour and related agencies, it became clear that they discounted the dangers resulting from parity in the automobile industry. It was felt that, in most other bargaining situations, the demand for wage parity would be used merely as a bargaining weapon – something to be given up in return for the achievement of a more important demand. In addition, great faith was expressed in the good judgment of union leaders not to make a core issue out of wage parity when indeed the company or industry could not afford it.

Thus, as far as personnel interviewed in the Department of Labour and other labour-oriented agencies were concerned, the Chrysler-U.A.W. wage parity agreement was not by any means a threat or even a worrisome trend. Indeed, they felt that the difference in levels of productivity in the automobile industry was not great and definitely was declining; therefore wage parity might well have been justified.[2]

Although it may be somewhat surprising that such disagreement on the wage parity issue exists in different areas of the same government, (particularly when the official government position is that wage parity is acceptable if productivity is equal), the differences of opinion can be explained by the differing clientele and areas of concern of the particular departments involved. Thus, it is likely that officials of the Department of Labour identify to a significant extent with the interests of the workers and the unions, persons in the Ministry of Finance relate to the opinions and needs of those in financial circles, and personnel of the Ministry of Industry respond somewhat to the views of industrialists and manufacturers. At least, officials in the respective departments have far more in common with their own clientele than they do with the clientele of other departments.

The interviewed government officials, in the different ministries, were either unaware of the international collective bargaining agreement or unconcerned about it. They did not seem to be concerned by the fact that henceforth many decisions affecting the 12,000 Canadian Chrysler employees – including wage rates – would occur during bargaining sessions located in Detroit between officers of the

[1] *Ibid.*, pp. 70–1.
[2] Department of Labour personnel, as well as union officials, were quite critical of the corporations for not making public the productivity figures.

United States Chrysler Corporation and a predominantly American U.A.W. International Negotiating Committee. Whereas most of the governmental officials were alarmed by the possibility of wage parity occurring in other industries, none feared the consequences of increased international collective bargaining. This was quite surprising, particularly since more than half of the people interviewed were concerned by the great potential for control over the Canadian economy which belonged to the United States-owned and controlled corporations.

Another question put to the government officials was what the Canadian Government could do to maintain a greater degree of control over international union-multi-national business contract negotiations which threatened to harm the economy of Canada. The answer from all parties interviewed was a resounding 'Nothing'! The Canadian Government is in a particularly difficult position to manage the economy because union-management collective bargaining and wage rates are by law the concern of the provincial governments – except in those areas where the Federal Government has jurisdiction over labour relations, e.g. Crown corporations, banking, finance, railways, lake shipping, radio, television, other communications and a few other industries. Only by engaging in drastic indirect manipulations such as tariffs and taxes might the adverse effects of an inflationary settlement be prevented. The picture, therefore, is of the Canadian Government standing aside, unable to enter into the international (primarily United States) collective bargaining process for the sake of the national economy. Here then are all the ingredients for a case in which a sovereign State is caught between the interests of a multi-national corporation and an international union, without the ability to do much about it except by initiating drastic measures. However, the government does not seem overly concerned, for as one very high official put it:

'Even without the international bargaining agreement, we have little enough influence over the negotiations anyway. We have had no direct influence over the unions, for they look upon the Government as an enemy. Thus, we are unable to work together as partners in any way.'[1]

[1] It is worth mentioning, though, that a Task Force on Labour Relations has been established to examine industrial relations in Canada; presumably some of the questions raised in this study will be considered by the task force.

## ATTITUDES OF BUSINESS

Unfortunately, the reaction of Chrysler Corporation officials to the wage parity and international collective bargaining agreements could not be probed because of their unwillingness to co-operate in this research effort. However, secondary accounts and interviews with executives of other large corporations have been used to attempt to gauge the reaction of the business world to these developments.

A high official of a Canadian subsidiary of a United States automobile company suggested that the achievement of wage parity, although inevitable, had been premature because of the differing levels of productivity. However, he did feel that the companies could make the necessary adjustments so that productivity equality could be obtained several years after wage parity went into effect in 1970. He thought, though, that the companies would have a difficult time for the next five or six years because of the higher labour costs.

This executive was quite concerned about the demonstration effect of wage parity and the consequent increase in inflation. This fear was supported by an official of a strike-bound Canadian tyre and rubber company, also a subsidiary of a United States corporation. He described how contracts between the U.A.W. and the automobile manufacturers had a great influence on the negotiations between the United Rubber Workers (U.R.W.) and the tyre and rubber manufacturers. Indeed, initially, one of the main issues of the strike between his corporation and the U.R.W. was over the question of wage parity. Although this issue had declined in importance as the strike became lengthier, he did feel that it would continue to be a union demand and would be achieved within the next four or five years.

Wage parity was the crucial issue during the 1968 negotiations and ensuing strike between the United Automobile Workers and Massey-Ferguson Industries, manufacturers of agricultural machinery. The corporation, a Canadian one with plants in both Canada and the United States, suggested that in order to keep its Canadian plants in operation and still sell to the main market in the American Mid West it could not afford to pay Canadians the same rate as United States employees were earning. The corporation claimed that the transportation costs associated with shipping farm implements from Ontario plants to the Plains states of the United States prohibited the payment of equal wages if the company was to remain competitive.[1] Therefore, as was frequently emphasised during the negotiations and the strike, if wage parity were achieved, the company would be forced to close down its Canadian plants and relocate closer to the market in the American Mid West. Even though the long strike was eventually settled without the achievement of parity, some executives of the corporation did not feel that they had heard the last of the wage parity demand, and they were rather uncertain about the chances of remaining in Canada.

In summary, wage parity in the automobile industry and the example it set were feared by many Canadian businessmen. They were concerned about the likelihood that wage parity would become a demand in many union-management negotiations throughout the country. If wage parity was granted in a significant number of cases, they shared the concern of governmental officials over the Canadian economy and the Canadian dollar. Indeed, wage parity has been a real demand in a number of situations since Chrysler succumbed to the U.A.W. in November 1967. As has already been mentioned, wage parity was demanded of Massey-Ferguson and a major tyre and rubber manufacturer. In addition, the Canadian Saint Lawrence Seaway workers sought and achieved wage equality with their American brothers on the opposite side of the Seaway.

The international collective bargaining agreement was not greeted with as much concern as was exhibited over wage parity. The executive in the tyre and rubber corporation did not feel that the U.R.W. would seek such an agreement because of the fundamental differences between the two industries. In the first place, while a continent-wide strike could close down the automobile manufacturers, the tyre and rubber manufacturers could import tyres made for them in other parts of the world and sell them for nearly the same price. Secondly, there is not a Canadian-United States free trade area with respect to tyres, as there is for the automobile manufacturing industry. Thus, the possible achievements of Canadian-United States rubber worker solidarity would be quite unimportant compared to the benefits which could be gained by the unity of Canadian and American auto workers.

The official of the automobile manufacturer, where international

---

[1] Massey-Ferguson commissioned a study on the problem of wage parity, which presents the company's economic position. See *Wage Parity and Massey-Ferguson in Canada*, prepared by Hedlin, Menzia & Associates Ltd. at the request of Massey-Ferguson Industries Limited, Toronto, Ontario, 20 July 1967.

collective bargaining was desired neither by the corporation nor the Canadian local unions, considered the Chrysler-U.A.W. agreement to be an infringement on the ability of Canadians to make decisions which have potentially great consequences for Canada.[1] It seemed to him that with the advent of international collective bargaining the most crucial industrial relations decisions faced by Chrysler-Canada would be made by executives of the parent company in the United States. Decision-making on these matters would be removed from the Canadian subsidiary.

Interviews with international U.A.W. officials suggested that Chrysler personnel were pleased to conclude an international collective bargaining agreement, for they felt that to do otherwise would merely be a duplication in effort with little likelihood of differences in outcome. On the other hand, the U.A.W. men said that General Motors and Ford were not in favour of bargaining internationally because of their concern about the reaction of vehement nationalistic elements among their Canadian employees. Thus, while the attitudes of Chrysler about wage parity and the international bargaining arrangement are not certain, it does seem clear that generally business interests in Canada were unhappy with both developments. The best expression of this response was given by an important member of the Canadian business community who suggested that he was not surprised to hear that Chrysler did not wish to co-operate in this research project 'because they know that the other companies feel that they sold out to the union' and that, therefore, the less said about the matter the better it would be

## THE REACTION OF UNION OFFICIALS

The generally negative reactions of businessmen and government officials to the wage parity and international bargaining agreement will serve as a contrast to the attitudes of many union officials. An important staff member of the Canadian Labour Congress suggested that the widespread achievement of wage parity was not the overall goal of his organisation but that the automobile industry was a rather special case because of the industrial structure and the Automotive Products Agreement. He felt that wage parity was certainly justified in the

[1] Surprisingly, he also was quite disturbed, possibly even bitter, about the high degree of control wielded by United States corporations over their Canadian subsidiaries.

155

automobile industry but would not be possible in most other sectors of Canadian industry, even though wage parity might be increasingly used as a slogan for the rank-and-file worker. In addition, regardless of whether wage parity became widely accepted as a goal for many unions, he did feel that the gap between United States and Canadian wages would be decreasing. Thus, there might be movement towards wage parity in fact, if not in terminology.

This official of the Canadian Labour Congress was also questioned about his attitudes towards the international collective bargaining agreement. In the first place, he thought that it would strengthen the bargaining power of the Canadian members in their dealings with the international corporations. No longer could Chrysler, or any other company where such an agreement exists, use a strategy of divide and conquer in the collective bargaining process. Henceforth, the ability to rely upon production in the United States to lessen the economic disruption while Canadian workers were on strike would be denied to the corporation.

However, on the other hand, this official was rather concerned lest the Canadian members become overwhelmed by the great dominance of the American sector in internal union politics and decision-making. While he did not mean to imply that the international union would discriminate against Canadians, he was aware of the possibility that it might lose contact with the problems of the rank-and-file Canadian member. Prior to the international bargaining agreement, the local and regional union leadership bargained directly with the corporation. However, under the agreement, the Canadian representative is merely a small part of a larger international bargaining committee. Thus, the demands and needs of Canadian members may be ignored or perhaps even voted down by the full international committee.

In general, although excluding the U.A.W., the official of the Canadian Labour Congress was somewhat sceptical about the faithfulness of most Canadian unions to the concept of internationalism and international union solidarity. Thus, he felt that Canadian members in most international unions would not do much to support a strike by their United States brothers. As an example, he cited the case of the United Packinghouse Workers of America (U.P.W.A.), an international union. In 1966, the international executive board assessed the United States locals in order to help support a strike against one of the largest Canadian meat-packing companies. Apparently, with some reluctance, the United States locals finally raised the extra money and turned it over to their Canadian brothers. However, subsequently, the executive board attempted to assess both Canadian and United States locals in order to support a strike by some United States farm workers who were trying to organise migrant workers. This time, contrary to the spirit of international unionism and brotherhood, just two Canadian locals supported the Americans on strike by raising the money after a donation had been pledged by the district director for Canada.

In summary, this staff member of the Canadian Labour Congress applauded both the wage parity and international collective bargaining agreements as they applied to the automobile industry. However, he perceived this industry and the U.A.W. to be a rather unique case in which these agreements were quite beneficial. In other industries and with other unions, he doubted whether these agreements were either feasible or advantageous. Because of this doubt, he did not think that the U.A.W. agreements with Chrysler would establish a trend which would be followed by other unions in the near future.

The Canadian Labour Congress executive found himself in agreement with fellow Canadians who were either officers of Local 444 or officials of the U.A.W. Canadian region, with respect to the reasons why the international union advocated and fought for wage parity. They felt quite strongly that Walter P. Reuther, President of the U.A.W., and the international had sought wage parity as a means of protecting the jobs of American workers. Indeed, Reuther quite often expounded this theme in speeches, reports, and the like. United States union members were frequently told that it was necessary to gain wage parity in order to ensure that lower Canadian wages did not take jobs away from them.

In contrast, all the United States officials of the international union who were interviewed stressed that this was merely a legal and a political ploy and was not the prime motivation for parity. Emphasising the necessity of protecting United States jobs served as the necessary legal fiction by which the U.A.W. could bargain with Chrysler in Detroit over an essentially Canadian matter. Without relating the issue of parity to United States interests, the U.A.W. could not legally discuss the question with Chrysler during a United States bargaining session. Secondly, this argument was used to gain the support of the United States membership for an issue that would mainly benefit Canadians. By showing how wage parity could help United States job security, the rank-and-file United States member was made more willing to go out on strike, if need be, to obtain this demand. If the connection was not made clear to the United States members, the sought-after solidarity in the face of corporate intransigence might not be achieved.

It is difficult to explain why the Canadians and the Americans disagreed over the reasons why the international fought for wage parity. However, a tentative suggestion can be offered. It may be that both the United States and the Canadian officials were attempting to picture their group as being as altruistic and responsive to the Canadian membership as the other group. Thus, the United States international officials desired to give the impression of advocating wage parity on the basis of equity and justice, as opposed to United States self-interest and job security. As far as the Canadian officials are concerned, they may have been attempting to play down the altruistic and concerned image of the international so that their members would realise that it is their local president and their Canadian director who are most concerned about them, whereas the international headquarters will only help when it is in their own interest to do so. These are tenuous propositions, though, for there is no evidence to support such an explanation.

As would be expected, Charles Brooks, President of Local 444 in Windsor, Ontario, and George Burt, director of the Canadian Region until May 1968, were delighted with the achievement of wage parity and the international bargaining agreement, for both men had been seeking wage parity for Canadian workers since 1940. Neither man saw any evidence of direct Canadian Government pressure on the bargaining sessions, but they were very much aware of the possible impact on the workers of the arguments against wage parity as expressed by some government officials and the local newspaper. Thus, Charles Brooks called several mass meetings in order to counteract these viewpoints, some of which seemed to be based upon exploitation of nationalist sentiments among the workers. Both George Burt and Charles Brooks observed that the younger Chrysler employees were more susceptible to the arguments of the government than the workers with more service in the company. The reason for this, Charles Brooks asserted, could be explained by the content of the statements of some government officials which threatened a job freeze and possible job reductions if parity went into effect. Naturally, these predicted consequences would affect the young short-term employee without much seniority, as opposed to the more senior men who were well-protected in their jobs. However, in spite of the arguments of the government against wage parity, 88 per cent of the Local 444 membership heartily approved of the provision in a vote on the issue.

Charles Brooks and George Burt were also strong supporters of the international collective bargaining agreement. With this agreement, the company could no longer rely on United States production in order to break a Canadian strike. International union solidarity would be able to match the strength of the multi-national corporation. Charles Brooks pointed to recent United Rubber Worker strikes against several tyre corporations as an example of the need to develop union action and co-operation on an international basis. When the United States workers were on strike, in 1967, the corporations' subsidiaries in Canada were making tyres at an increased pace, thereby reducing the economic impact of the strike on the corporations. Similarly, in 1968 the Canadian subsidiaries were closed down by a strike, and the United States plants expanded production to take up the slack that occurred. This, Charles Brooks suggested, is a case in which members of the same union working for the same corporation but on different sides of the border were in effect acting as strike-breakers. As Charles Brooks views it, the international collective bargaining agreement will end this kind of situation. Furthermore, he feels that eventually the General Motors and Ford workers as well as other unions will also seek such an agreement.

Actually, the possibility of an international bargaining agreement had been discussed independently by both the local leadership and the international headquarters in the year or two preceding the 1967 negotiations. In late 1967, the international officials asked Charles Brooks and the leadership of Local 444 whether they desired to have such an agreement. The international union was mildly in favour of this bargaining arrangement but was not going to exert any pressure on the local to adopt it. However, the leadership of Local 444 felt that it would be a beneficial move, and at a vote taken on the question in a union meeting on 21 January 1968, the membership overwhelmingly supported the proposal with only a very few dissenting votes. With Chrysler in favour of such a proposal at this point, the international bargaining arrangement was concluded.

As has been mentioned earlier, for all but local issues the Canadian and United States members of the U.A.W. who work for Chrysler have become essentially a single bargaining unit. The political boundaries are virtually non-existent as far as the union and its actions are concerned. However, the Canadian and American sections are subject to different governmental regulations and controls. From the standpoint of the union, the most unacceptable constraint is an Ontario law that prohibits unions from striking during the life of a contract. Thus, it is illegal for the Canadian U.A.W. members to go on strike during the contract period to protest against an unfair action by the corporation, such as an abuse of the grievance procedure. This, the union feels, is a great disadvantage. To remedy this situation, Douglas Fraser, Director of the U.A.W.-Chrysler Department, sent a letter to the corporation which made the following points:

> 'The International Union takes this means of notifying the Chrysler Corporation that it cannot tolerate a situation in which the Chrysler management takes advantage of the Canadian workers because they do not have the right to strike.
> 'The International Union will take all necessary steps and commit the full resources of the International Union to assist the Canadian workers with regard to issues that might arise during the life of this agreement in which they are being disadvantaged because they do not have the same right to strike as do their fellow employees in the United States.
> 'In addition, we will call upon all the Chrysler Local Unions in the United States to lend every assistance to the Canadian workers should they be confronted with any situation described above.'[1]

This letter was supported by a statement of Dennis McDermott, the Canadian U.A.W. international representative, who said that the union would strike against the parent company if the Canadian subsidiary would not resolve local problems during the life of the contract.[2] Thus, the international nature of the Chrysler-U.A.W. membership is enhanced by Fraser's letter and McDermott's statement. Henceforth, the Chrysler workers will be bound together as a single force ready to use their combined strength to correct abuses and support contract demands whenever they occur.

None of the interviewed local, regional and international officials saw much difficulty in obtaining co-ordinated and co-operative action by the Canadian and United States members. They felt quite certain that the workers would be able to rise above national or parochial

---

[1] Quoted in *Local 444 News*, 22 February 1968, p. 3.
[2] *Ibid.* Upon the retirement of George Burt as Director of the Canadian Region of the U.A.W., Dennis McDermott became the Canadian Region director.

feelings, and understand that the existence of common interests which transcend political boundaries requires international solidarity. One official of the international union, though, did express the view that extreme feelings of Canadian nationalism might cause a Canadian withdrawal from the international collective bargaining arrangement. However, this would only occur if relations between the two countries became so severely strained that it became quite unpopular to have any dealings with Americans.

Before leaving the topic of the reactions of union officials, it is worth mentioning that, in June 1968, Local 444 had an election for the leadership of the union. The election campaign was a rather spirited one with the main opposition to the Brooks administration, the Blue and White ticket, attempting to make a major issue out of the close ties to the international U.A.W. The Blue and White wished only to reduce the amount of co-operation between Local 444 and the international but had no intention of severing ties. Apparently, they hoped that the anti-international stance would be a critical issue to the membership, for, just several years before, this group had been even more supportive of the international union than Charles Brooks was. Indeed, the real difference of opinion between the incumbent administration and the Blue and White slate seemed to be a strictly political one – who should lead the union. A second opposition group, the Independent Progressive slate, was exceedingly anti-international. Indeed they supported the idea of a Canadian autoworkers union, for they viewed the international union as an agent of a foreign power.

The approximate results of the union election gave Charles Brooks and his slate 4,500 votes, the Blue and White ticket 2,500 votes, and the Independent Progressive group 150 votes. Even assuming that voting took place only on the issue of the degree of closeness with the international U.A.W. (a false assumption to be sure), those in favour of maintaining the current close co-operation with the international union outnumbered all the others by 9 to 5. The number of workers favouring something approaching outright withdrawal was a minute figure. Thus, on the basis of the above-mentioned election, the membership strongly supported the policies of Charles Brooks, which included the achievement of wage parity and an international collective bargaining agreement.

161

## OPINIONS OF THE LOCAL 444 MEMBERSHIP

Rank-and-file voting in the union election is not a good measure of the degree of support for either wage parity or the international bargaining agreement because of the numerous other factors involved. Therefore, a rather extensive questionnaire was sent to five hundred randomly selected Local 444 members in order to obtain their views on a number of issues, including wage parity and international collective bargaining.[1] To date, 94 members (or 18 per cent) had responded to the questionnaire.

Of the respondents, 57 per cent favoured wage parity for the Chrysler employees, 29 per cent were against parity, and 14 per cent were undecided where they stood on the issue. Note that this is significantly less than the 88 per cent of the members who voted in favour of parity. When asked to explain why they favoured wage parity, the predominant answer involved some variation on the 'equal pay for the same job' theme. Indeed, 55 per cent of the 54 who favoured parity responded to the question in this way. Of the 26 against parity, 12 men felt that jobs would be eliminated or the company would squeeze more work out of them. There were nine workers who were against parity because of the likelihood of inflationary pressure and damage to the economy.[2]

From this very brief descriptive analysis, it seems that most members in favour of wage parity adopted the rationale of local and international union officials. Similarly, most of those objecting to parity seemed to accept the arguments of government officials although only 42 per cent of the 92 persons answering this question knew that the government actually opposed wage parity. Given the fact that one of the major arguments of the government officials against wage parity involved the pressures it would cause on inflation, it is interesting to note that 62 per cent of the respondents said that inflation was one of the most urgent social economic, or political problems facing people in the Windsor, Ontario, area. Yet 57 per cent favoured wage parity. It seems as though the attempts of the government to link parity with the threat of inflation were not very successful for most of the union membership.

[1] At the time of writing, the analysis of the data is in a preliminary stage; therefore only tentative and descriptive findings can be reported in this chapter.

[2] There is some overlap here because a few of the respondents gave more than one reason for their objection to wage parity.

It was more difficult to explore the workers' attitudes on the international collective bargaining agreement because of the complicated nature of the concept. Therefore, questions were asked which attempted to probe the feelings about international unionism. Of the 90 respondents, 55 per cent felt that an international union probably or definitely would be more effective in representing their interests in collective bargaining than an independent national union. There were 32 per cent who thought that an independent national union would probably or definitely be more effective than an international union. There were 12 per cent who were either undecided or felt that it made no difference. I think that the local and international officials would be quite surprised at the relatively strong support shown by this sample for the concept of an independent national union.[1] At the same time, it appears that there is a pretty solid base of support for the international union and a small but still significant degree of apathy and indecision, which of course aids the status quo.

Another question asked the respondent to estimate what he would do if the international U.A.W. headquarters urged him to support striking Chrysler employees in the United States, the United Kingdom and in Mexico. The alternatives specified in the questionnaire were: (1) go on strike yourself (assuming such action was not illegal); (2) engage in a work slowdown; (3) pay increased dues for financial support; (4) give moral support; and (5) not do anything for 'that is their problem'. The results are reproduced in Table 1 below. First the idea of 'doing something' to help fellow Chrysler employees who are on strike in other countries is quite abhorrent. There seems to be an awareness of the existence of some kind of responsibility for their brothers in other countries. However, doing something about this responsibility depends upon the cost to the Canadian worker for, as the action taken increases in cost to the worker, the number of men willing to take such a step decreases. Giving moral support is not too costly but going on strike is.

The willingness to 'do something' varies quite noticeably with what appears to be the degree of similarity, identification and interaction with other countries. More than half of the respondents would be willing to go on strike in support of their United States brothers; very few would for Chrysler workers in the United Kingdom

---

[1] With this question, as with the others, it should be noted that only those rank-and-file members motivated to complete the questionnaire did so. Therefore, there is the possibility that co-operating with the survey was a means of registering protest for some of the men.

or Mexico. This greater willingness to support Americans may be caused by the closeness and similarities of the countries; or perhaps the common tie through the international U.A.W. is the explanation. In either case, I find this degree of internationalism to be quite surprising.

It is difficult to explain why more Canadian workers would not engage in a work slowdown to support their United States brothers, but a possible explanation might lie in the acceptance by so many of the concept of the single international bargaining unit. It may appear

TABLE I

How Canadian U.A.W. Members Are Willing to Support Fellow Chrysler Employees in the United States, United Kingdom, and Mexico
N = 94

|  | United States | United Kingdom | Mexico |
|---|---|---|---|
| Percentage of respondents who would: |  |  |  |
| (a) go on strike | 52 | 13 | 12 |
| (b) slowdown | 35 | 15 | 14 |
| (c) pay increased dues | 69 | 44 | 40 |
| (d) give moral support | 69 | 70 | 62 |
| (e) do something | 94 | 81 | 72 |
| Percentage of respondents who would *not*: |  |  |  |
| (a) go on strike | 48 | 87 | 88 |
| (b) slowdown | 65 | 85 | 86 |
| (c) pay increased dues | 31 | 56 | 60 |
| (d) give moral support | 31 | 30 | 38 |
| (c) do something | 6 | 19 | 28 |

to the workers that they now have the strength to close down Chrysler; therefore, why take a serious yet only a half-way measure? Be that as it may, a major implication of the findings reported in Table I is that Walter Reuther and the international U.A.W. have a great deal of support for their attempts to increase international autoworker co-operation. Large numbers of the Canadian U.A.W. members are willing to 'do something' to help their fellow workers in other countries. In the case of the United States workers, they are willing to do quite a lot.

The results of the survey of Canadian members of Local 444 suggest that there is a good deal of support for wage parity – much of the support based upon the fairness of 'equal pay for equal work'. However, the questionnaire also uncovered a rather large amount of resistance to parity, especially by those who felt that it would add to the inflationary problem in the economy. Other tentative findings point to a high degree of willingness to co-operate with fellow Chrysler workers in the United States in case of a strike. The potential, then, for concerted action by the international U.A.W. seems to be great. Similarly, while the workers were less enthusiastic about helping fellow Chrysler employees in the United Kingdom and Mexico, they were in favour of at least some expressions of support. Thus, it seems that the workers sampled are quite 'internationally minded', for they are aware of the need for at least some degree of co-operation among automobile workers of the world.

## CONCLUSIONS

International collective bargaining has been achieved by about 12,000 Chrysler workers in Canada and 107,000 Chrysler employees in the United States. Beginning in 1970, with respect to contract negotiations they will act as a single bargaining unit; already they are working essentially under a single contract with slight variations for local practices. In 1970, the Canadian workers will achieve wage parity with the Americans, thus eliminating one more distinction between the Canadian and American employees. Basically, the political boundary between the United States and Canada will find no counterpart in the relations between the multi-national corporation, Chrysler, and the 119,000 Canadian and American Chrysler employees who are members of the U.A.W.

The study uncovered great concern in business and government circles about the achievement of wage parity, where it was felt that the economic problems of Canada would become more severe by having Canadian wages tied to a United States standard. Basically, they thought that the countries were dissimilar enough to require different treatment with respect to wage rates. Thus, the resistance of business and government officials seems to rest on the uniqueness of the Canadian economic and industrial sectors.

Given this attitude about wage parity, it is surprising that there was little knowledge about and fear of international collective bargaining.[1] Certainly, if the achievement of wage parity reduces Canadian uniqueness, international collective bargaining is even more likely to ignore the difference between Canada and the United States. For the most part, the uniqueness of Canada and the Canadian situation would become lost in the international collective bargaining arrangement and the need for international union solidarity. This is not to say that there would be a totally American settlement, for the special problems of both countries might take second place to the problems of the common industrial and labour sector which is transnational in scope. However, it may well be that when the implications of international collective bargaining in a transnational industrial and labour sector become understood, the degree of resistance fostered by a spirit of nationalism may be increased, and political obstacles may be erected to inhibit the growth of such economic internationalism.

In contrast to businessman and government officials, the local, regional and international U.A.W. officials were quite aware of the political, social and economic implications of international collective bargaining. Indeed, they seemed to be quite idealistic about the development of common interests by auto workers of the world, and some explicitly stated that they hoped that the development of international interests would undercut the divisive forces of national loyalty.

The President of the U.A.W., Walter Reuther, is very much aware of the international character of the corporation and the need for international co-operation among trade unionists. In his report to the 21st Constitutional Convention[2] he cited the fact that in 1962 Chrysler produced only 18,811 units in countries other than Canada and the United States while 528,692 units were produced abroad in 1967. Therefore, given the growth of the multi-national corporation and expansion of automobile production around the world:

'The U.A.W., as a matter of trade union solidarity in its own immediate self-interest, is obligated to co-operate with the metal-working and auto workers' unions in the rest of the world in establishing systems of wage harmony within regional marketing

---

[1] John Crispo predicted in his book that continent-wide bargaining would follow shortly after the achievement of wage parity or parity would follow international bargaining. While making the connection between the two phenomena, he does not discuss in much depth the implications of such a bargaining arrangement (Crispo, *op. cit.*, p. 201).

[2] Reuther, *op. cit.*, p. 136.

areas which substantially eliminate wages as a factor in world market competition.'[1]

To help implement this co-operation, the U.A.W. has become a strong supporter of the International Metalworkers Federation (I.M.F.) and of the World Automotive Council, a part of the I.M.F. In addition, the U.A.W. has offered to help automobile unionists in other countries with respect to training, strike assistance, and whatever else may be helpful. In his recent report[2] Walter Reuther relates how the U.A.W. helped bring together three competitive auto unions in Mexico into a single National Autoworkers Council. He mentions the strike assistance given to Mexican Ford workers and the training and technical assistance given to automotive unionists in Mexico and Venezuela. U.A.W. action in Japan helped to consolidate competing automobile unions there too. An example of more direct intervention by the U.A.W. occurred when a Ford subsidiary in Venezuela fired certain employees for attempting to organise the plant. The U.A.W. applied pressure on the parent company in Detroit, and the men were shortly reinstated. The possibilities of this kind of international help are, of course, quite interesting, and the step from Douglas Fraser's letter to Chrysler promising U.A.W. action if Canadians should be disadvantaged to pressure on the behalf of workers in more remote countries does not seem to be too great. In addition, the survey suggested that at least Canadian U.A.W. members are willing to support to some degree their fellow workers in other lands.

One of the implications of this case study suggests that the Canadian Government will have no opportunity of controlling or influencing the collective bargaining between Chrysler and the U.A.W. As has been discussed, there will no longer be any 'Canadian' bargaining, for it now becomes a transnational matter beyond the realm of Canadian influence. The Government of the United States will undoubtedly have a greater opportunity to influence the negotiations and contracts because both the union and the corporation are located in the United States and the majority of employees and officials are Americans. Thus, a possible Canadian strategy might involve asking the Government of the United States to intercede on its behalf if a particular contract appears capable of causing severe damage to the Canadian economy. However, it must be said that the United States Government itself has frequently been unable to influence contract

---

[1] *Ibid.*, p. 137.  [2] *Ibid.*, pp. 137–8.

negotiations in domestic bargaining situations. Of course, if the Canadian Government becomes desperate about its lack of influence, there is always the possibility of restrictive legislation which would prohibit international collective bargaining. Although such action is not at all likely, it should be repeated that the extent to which the Canadian economy is influenced by patterns set in the automobile industry is also the extent by which Canadian control over the economy is reduced. This relationship, then, is a source of potential concern and action by the Canadian Government.

Before attempting to generalise from the particular case of the Chrysler-U.A.W. agreement to the likelihood of international collective bargaining occurring in other situations, an assessment of the factors which contributed to this achievement in this case seem in order. One of the underlying factors is that there already was a high degree of United States participation in the Canadian corporate and union structures. In addition, the great cultural, social, ethnic and economic similarities, and the long tradition of frequent, friendly and open contacts between the two States and their citizens, provided fertile ground for further economic integration in the form of international collective bargaining. The historically based 'we–they' attitudes which characterise the relations among many countries are largely absent,[1] and their absence removes the very real psychological barriers which so often inhibit greater integration between countries. Thus, in such a favourable atmosphere international collective bargaining could be achieved far more easily than if the attempt were made in a more hostile environment.

Another factor contributing to the achievement of international collective bargaining involves the long-standing United States participation in the Canadian automobile industry and automobile worker unions. Both the U.A.W. and the manufacturers have underplayed the differences caused by the Canadian–American boundary. The manufacturers, for instance, built the same cars for Canadians as they did for their United States customers; they standardised parts and production practices; the dealer organisations were similar; and the publics of both countries were subject to the same mass advertising campaigns. The manufacturers, therefore, were willing to exist in the two-nation environment, but they were not going to

---

[1] It may well be that Canadians are more conscious of differences than Americans, but in this type of relationship where the much larger partner is unaware of or ignores national distinctions, the smaller country has to make a continuing and concerted effort to worsen relations. Obviously, Canada and Canadians have not behaved in this manner.

allow different customs and different governmental practices to hinder the expansion of their operations in both countries. Thus, the multi-national corporations successfully adapted to the bi-national character of the market.

In a similar way, the U.A.W. has historically refused to allow the boundary to interfere with its activities. The union has been committed for some time to existing in an international or at least a bi-national environment. Not only has the U.A.W. rejected being a parochial, solely United States, union, but it has also actively sought to extend its membership and influence across the border into Canada. It, too, has successfully adapted to the two-nation market, and thus it has been able to meet the challenges offered by a multi-national corporation. The major point is that in the limited case of Canada and the United States the U.A.W. has organised itself to be a bi-national union with the ability to meet the bi-national strength of the corporations.[1] In addition, as was mentioned above, the U.A.W. does not seem to be content to stop here, for it is supporting efforts to increase international co-operation and solidarity among the automobile workers of the world. But it is flexible in its approach to this increasing internationalism and is not merely trying to export United States practices and unionism. Rather, it is attempting to advance worldwide worker co-operation within the constraints of the existing political and social environments.

The previously discussed Automotive Products Agreement also facilitated the achievement of international collective bargaining. The Agreement allowed the free flow of new automobiles and new automobile parts between the two countries, thereby promoting the integration and rationalisation of the industry. Specialisation of production processes was instituted on both sides of the border, with the consequence that a car purchased in Pittsburgh might be composed of parts manufactured in both Canada and the United States but assembled in Ontario, Canada. With the rationalisation of production, the labour force in essence became integrated. This quickly led to the achievement of wage parity, but it also contributed to the development of international collective bargaining. Except for the symbolic but nonetheless very important arguments essentially caused by Canadian nationalism and a desire to control one's own affairs, the

---

[1] Even where international collective bargaining agreements have not been instituted, the U.A.W. has devised ways to practise successfully bi-national unionism. It should be noted that there are many historical reasons for the development of bi-national unionism by the U.A.W. and other unions in North America.

integration of the autoworker labour force and the achievement of wage parity leave little justification on the part of the workers or the other automobile manufacturers for refusing to accept an international collective bargaining arrangement.

All of the these factors contributed to the achievement of international collective bargaining between Chrysler and the U.A.W.; yet it is difficult to identify one as being the major cause of this development. Certainly, the high degree of integration in the automobile industry and the friendly environment in terms of the general social, cultural, economic, historical and political interactions between the two countries provide a favourable atmosphere for international collective bargaining. Undoubtedly, situations where a strained or hostile atmosphere existed would not be as conducive to cross-national negotiations.

However, accepting the importance of a favourable milieu, the ability of the U.A.W. to match the international expansion of the corporation by adapting itself to bi-national unionism was a major reason for the achievement of international collective bargaining. More specifically, an international collective agreement might well be concluded in a less favourable environment (though not in a hostile environment) by an equally adaptable and internationally committed union, but it is doubtful that international bargaining could be instituted in the most favourable of environments when the union remains parochial, single-nation oriented, and inflexible. Thus, the flexible, bi-national character of the U.A.W. was a necessary although not a sufficient cause for the achievement of international collective bargaining.

Given this assessment of the situation, it seems likely that Ford and General Motors shortly will be negotiating international contracts. Furthermore, if the Chrysler-U.A.W. agreement proves to be a useful or successful tool for both the United States and Canadian workers and barring, of course, any significant growth of Canadian nationalism, international agreements will probably be concluded in other industries which have structures somewhat similar to that of the automotive industry. The achievement of wage parity will facilitate this process, as will the establishment between the two countries of other free trade arrangements similar to the Automotive Products Agreement. However, regardless of the existence of wage parity and free trade sectors, it is thought that intelligent, flexible and internationally committed union leadership will be able to institute bi-national collective bargaining or a much higher degree of bi-national co-operation during contract negotiations. Thus, it is concluded in the case of the United States and Canada that international collective bargaining will increase where industrial ownership and structure is quite concentrated, where production processes and problems are similar in both countries, and where the union leadership proves to be adaptable and committed to intra-union co-operation and solidarity across the boundary. (This, of course, assumes the continuation of a propitious social and political environment.) In addition, it is expected that the expansion of international collective bargaining and of wage parity will serve to integrate further the economies and industrial decision-making structures of Canada and the United States, with greater economic integration both causing and being stimulated by the establishment of free trade sectors between the two countries.[1]

While an increase in international collective bargaining is expected in the United States–Canada situation, there seem to be several obstacles to such a trend in most parts of the world. In the first place, the favourable environment that exists between Canada and the United States seems to be largely missing in the relations of other States. Instead of a tradition of frequent, friendly and open relations, there usually exists a long history of national distrust and animosity. In addition, in the countries of the European Economic Community, for example, private enterprise was for a long time only national in scope. As a result, and quite importantly, the unions of these countries historically have limited their activities to only one country; meaningful internationalism or even a commitment to international union co-operation is largely missing. Thus, the unions in these States have failed to meet the challenge of an industrial structure which increasingly encompasses multi-national corporations operating in many States. The continuing single-nation orientation of most unions prevents them from adapting to the changing economic environment.

The normal internal political processes which national unions can use to represent their interest to the domestic corporation and central government are not very successful when dealing with an apolitical or transpolitical multi-national corporation. As a result, it is likely that there will develop patterns and procedures for international co-opera-

---

[1] Most of the Canadians interviewed in this study felt that a fairly high degree of economic integration between the two countries was both likely and desirable. However, they thought that efforts should be made now to explore the means by which Canadian independence and individuality could be maintained and fostered within an integrated economic structure.

tion among unions. These informal and formal means of aiding each other will present the multi-national corporation with at least some degree of international union pressure. Although such co-operation will expand, it is not likely that it will evolve into international bargaining except between countries where there are many political, social and economic similarities. However, it must be stressed that since the rise of the multi-national corporation has largely defined the economic system within which unions must operate, it is incumbent upon the unions themselves to change their structure, orientation and modes of operation in order to adapt to the new system. This will be a difficult and slow process, and while international collective bargaining may not be achieved for a variety of reasons, certainly an increase in the co-operation of unions and workers of many States is a realistic method of confronting the strength of the multi-national firms.

If indeed the prediction that there will be a large increase in international co-operation among unions is correct, there are a number of possible implications for international and domestic politics. For instance, if unions are successful in their attempts to form a counter-vailing power, which is international or regional in scope, to the multi-national corporation, where does that leave the nation State? How can the nation State continue to be responsible for the welfare of its citizens when the major economic decisions are being arrived at in some form of international collective bargaining to which no government is a party? Will major domestic and international decisions involving economics and politics be removed from the influence of the nation State and reside instead in these international but non-governmental economic organisations? What will be the consequences for political organisation, domestic politics, and international affairs? Indeed, will the nation State wither away and become obsolete, or will it adapt to the new system? Will new and larger political organisations, regional or even international in scope, develop to counteract the decision-making power of the multi-national corporations and international unions? These questions and many others like them suggest the wide scope of problems that may eventually arise from an internationalisation of production, distribution, ownership, management, and worker representation. As such, they represent challenges to the research skills of political scientists, economists, and social scientists in general.

Chapter 8

# MULTI-NATIONAL CORPORATIONS, TRADE UNIONS AND INDUSTRIAL RELATIONS: A CASE STUDY OF JAMAICA

*by*

*Jeffrey Harrod*

THE impact of foreign corporations on less-developed countries has usually been considered in relation to national income, capital accumulation, balance of payments and technological transfer while the more general aspects have received less attention. The purpose of this chapter is to examine some of the broader social and political effects of the foreign corporation with special reference to trade unions and industrial relations.

From this standpoint the corporation cannot be considered in isolation. Its presence brings the involvement of national and international trade union organisations, governments and international organisations. The objectives, methods and policies of these additional organisations substantially affect the nature and extent of the total impact of the corporation.

For this reason a large part of this chapter is historical, dealing with the record of the involvement of foreign corporations, trade union organisations and international organisations in Jamaica. Although the essential interest here is the effects of foreign corporations on industrial relations and trade unionism, the findings are also important to the theories of organisational transfer and functional international integration.[1]

## THE JAMAICAN BACKGROUND

Jamaica is a tropical island in the Caribbean of approximately 4,500 square miles and a population in 1968 approaching two million.

---

[1] These subjects and other aspects of the Jamaican experience with foreign organisations are dealt with extensively in J. Harrod: *Trade Union Foreign Policy* (Macmillan, 1972).

173

For nearly 300 years a colony of the United Kingdom, it became a nation State with full powers in 1962.

There are five identifiable divisions in the Jamaican economy: tropical produce for export; smallholdings and farms for domestic agriculture; manufacturing; extraction and processing of bauxite; and the tourist industry. The first two divisions may be termed the traditional sector and the latter three the modern sector.

The traditional sector has been dominated, since the seventeenth century, by sugar cane growing and milling. The modern sector is of recent origin, dating from approximately 1950, and has shown spectacular growth. From 1950 to 1960, mainly as a result of growth in this sector, per capita income doubled to approximately US$400. The percentage increase in gross national product between 1950 and 1965 has been 7·2 per annum and therefore one of the highest in the world.

This growth, however, has hardly affected the traditional sector in which the bulk of the population is engaged and it has not reduced the levels of unemployment, estimates of which range from between 13 and 25 per cent of the labour force. The growth in the modern sector has accentuated a pattern of income distribution which was described in 1958 as placing Jamaica 'among the countries with the highest recorded rate of inequality of incomes'.[1] The study showed that the upper 10 per cent of households accounted for 43 per cent of income while the lower 60 per cent of households shared only 19 per cent of income.

Jamaica's main trading partners are the United States, United Kingdom and Canada which together supplied 66 per cent of imports and received 81 per cent of exports in 1965. The United States is the chief purchaser and supplier for Jamaica.

*Jamaican Society and Culture*

Jamaica is described as a multi-racial society although over 75 per cent of the population is designated 'African', while 'coloured' accounts for approximately 17 per cent. Other minorities, including Europeans, all have less than 1 per cent each of the total population.

The labour force in 1960 (classified as persons over 14, employed or

[1] A. Ahiram: 'Income Distribution in Jamaica 1958', *Social and Economic Studies*, Vol. 13, No. 3, September 1964, p. 335.

unemployed) was 500,000, and in 1968 estimated at 700,000. In 1967, 40 per cent of the population was under 15.

The majority of the labour force is in the traditional sector with at least 50,000 in the sugar industry. Less than 20 per cent of the labour force is in industry.

Although there is some academic dispute over the issue, Jamaica can be described as having two cultures.[1] The class description, often loosely used, is inadequate as an explanation of the divisions within Jamaican society, although occupational and income differences closely follow cultural differences.

The two cultures have been described as 'European and African' or 'cultured and primitive', but a more accurate description would be 'imitative' and 'evolved'. The imitative culture finds its highest achievement in the imitation of the life style of the industrial societies of the United Kingdom and North America; the evolved culture resulted from the necessity of African slaves to reconcile African cultures with the new environment of slavery and Jamaica, while being denied the possibility of moving into the imitative culture. The two cultures are separated by language, family structure, religion, custom, colour, and also usually by income and occupation. The evolved culture embraces the majority of black Jamaicans, about 70 per cent of the population, while the imitative culture has within it the smaller percentage of those whose background (including colour) has permitted a successful emulation of the British/American culture. It is impossible in a paper of this nature to deal extensively with these cultures but an awareness of them is important for an understanding of the evolution of trade unions in Jamaica.

*The Trade Union and Industrial Relations Situation prior to 1950*

The Jamaican colonial government passed a basic Trade Union Law in 1919 which provided for the registration of trade unions but did not make provision for peaceful picketing and protection from liability in tort arising from a trade dispute. These omissions were rectified by a spate of legislation in 1938 when Acts were passed which provided for

[1] See H. I. McKenzie: 'The Plural Society Debate, Some Comments on a Recent Contribution', *Social and Economic Studies*, Vol. 15, No. 1, March 1966, pp. 53–60.

government participation in conciliation, non-compulsory arbitration, appointment of boards of inquiry, workmen's compensation and minimum wages. Collective bargaining was practised early in the history of Jamaican unions, but its greatest impetus came with the formation of the powerful Bustamante Industrial Trade Union (BITU) in the early forties. One of the earliest collective agreements was signed between the BITU and the Sugar Manufacturers' Association in 1942. The Jamaican laws, however, were based on those of the United Kingdom and so a collective agreement has remained unenforceable at law.

Trade unionism in Jamaica, up to 1939, had been confined to dock workers, printers and other small crafts. When riots occurred on a sugar estate in 1938, Alexander Bustamante, at the age of 54 and described then as a 'volunteer political agitator', assumed a leadership position and eventually created the BITU. Bustamante, who had spent much of his life outside the British Empire, talked the language linguistically and emotionally of the evolved culture and brought the mass of rural workers within the framework of a political organisation. Bustamante's union, despite its leader's imprisonment by the British authorities for seventeen months, became the most powerful in Jamaica. Bustamante listened to no arguments concerning the 'proper' model of trade unionism and refused to co-operate with those who argued that unions should adopt the British model. He stated he had no conception of trade unionism when he founded his union and that he called it 'industrial' merely to distinguish it from other unions at that time. The BITU was in fact a blanket union and for many years operated without a known hierarchy, structure or policy.[1] Bustamante made himself life president and when executive committees and branch structures were created they were constitutionally staffed by the President's nominees, or at least subject to his veto. The union had no outside affiliations and refused to participate in the early trade union educational projects sponsored by the British Government. On the union base, Bustamante founded the Jamaica Labour Party (J.L.P.) and won the first popular election contest in 1945. His Party has formed the Government of Jamaica for seventeen out the of twenty-four years of self-government.

In contrast, the rival union which emerged in the early forties, was

[1] An *industrial union*, in pure form, is one which embraces workers in a particular industry. A *general union* has members from many industries but makes internal divisions on industrial lines. A *blanket union* is a general union which, deliberately or by force of circumstance, does not give substantial internal recognition to industrial divisions.

led by persons whose milieu was the imitative culture. The Trades Union Congress of Jamaica (T.U.C.J.) (originally the Trades Union Council) was led by professional people such as accountants and lawyers, and clerical workers. Their union membership was basically from the administrative and clerical occupations and they modelled their organisation on the British Trade Union Congress, rejected the already established blanket structure of the BITU, and kept contact with and received aid from British unions. The union was associated with the People's National Party (P.N.P.) which had been founded in 1939 but which lost the first election in 1945. This failure caused the leaders of party and union to rethink the applicability of the federation of craft and industrial unions model to the political reality of Jamaica. For the next election, in 1949, the T.U.C.J. changed its form from a federation of unions to a blanket union but was still not successful in winning for the P.N.P. Thus by 1949, the union structure in Jamaica was that of two blanket unions, one virtually merged with a political party and the other closely associated with and a basic supporter of a political party. It is clear that it would be impossible to alter the structure, leadership or nature of the unions and leave the political situation unaffected.


## THE FOREIGN CORPORATIONS

Although Jamaican sugar estates and manufacturing concerns have always been foreign-owned to a large extent, the most important of the modern corporations are the North American-based aluminium companies mining bauxite in Jamaica. Bauxite is the basic ore from which aluminium is produced and has approximately a 4 to 1 reduction ratio. The production of aluminium occurs in three stages: first, the open-cast ore mining; second, a partial reduction into alumina; and third, a final smelting into the metal. The alumina stage is a chemical process and can be located almost anywhere, while the smelting has so far required large amounts of electricity and is therefore located near to hydro-electric plants.

Bauxite was discovered in Jamaica in 1942 and the first shipment despatched in 1952. The first company in Jamaica for bauxite extraction was a wholly-owned subsidiary of the Aluminium Company of Canada (ALCAN). It was followed at a later date by Reynolds Aluminium

Company, Kaiser Bauxite and Chemical Company, and finally the Aluminium Company of America (A.L.C.O.A.). Bauxite in North America is of much poorer quality than that of Jamaica and the reserves are not substantial; thus the convenience of Jamaica to shipping lanes made it a desirable ore supplier to North American plants. In 1965, for example, only 13 per cent of ore needs in the United States came from domestic production, while 57 per cent came from Jamaica. To cut transport costs to its smelting plant on the Canadian west coast, ALCAN reduces bauxite into alumina in Jamaica, having two plants which started production in 1952 and 1959. According to ALCAN data its total investment in Jamaica was £65 million in 1968.

For mining operations, the basic investment is in heavy open-cast mining machinery, construction of railways, roads, port facilities, drying kilns and storage sheds. Bauxite mining and alumina reduction are capital intensive and the corporations, once past the initial construction stage, have never employed more than 5,000 Jamaicans, representing less than 1 per cent of the labour force.

*Foreign Corporations and National Trade Unions*

At the construction stage the bauxite companies were prepared to accept the trade union structure and industrial relations systems in Jamaica as they found them. The corporations dealt with the unions through the local construction companies and wages were paid at roughly the same level as that of other construction workers on the island. One important factor was clear from the beginning – the corporations were reluctant to deal with the BITU. As we have seen the T.U.C.J., by virtue of its leadership, was technically more competent and was well-versed in the industrial relations system and legal niceties of the metropolitan centres. The BITU had none of these advantages, its style of operation would be unfamiliar and its leader, despite his political power, could not have the same rapport with an American corporate official as could a T.U.C.J. leader or, for example, Oxford-educated lawyer, N. W. Manley, leader of the P.N.P. and T.U.C.J. legal adviser. The refusal to recognise the BITU as a serious union and bargaining agent in the bauxite industry has persisted, with minor exceptions, throughout the history of the corporations on the island. In 1967, the BITU did not represent one bauxite worker, either in mining or plant construction.

Thus, the first corporate contact with a Jamaican union was with the T.U.C.J. and this union was successful in concluding a contract with Reynolds in 1950 which included a provision not to use strike breakers and a dues check-off arrangement. The possibility of continuing and undisturbed negotiating between the corporations and the T.U.C.J. was ended by events following the general elections of 1949. It was obvious to all political actors after the election that the party which had the strongest union base would continue to win the political elections. Thus, both the T.U.C.J. and the BITU began to seek more union members, and in the course of this process representational disputes and strikes occurred. These events brought to the fore two issues, a specific one concerning the machinery for union recognition, and a general one concerning the political nature of unionism in Jamaica. The first corporate voice heard publicly on these issues was an attorney for Reynolds, who gave evidence to the government-organised Board of Inquiry into Labour Disputes Between Unions. The attorney presented almos thalf of the recorded evidence at the Board, which amounted to a long account of labour practices in the United States with special reference to procedures relating to poll-taking and union recognition as a bargaining agent although Reynolds at that time had not had any representational disputes in Jamaica. The corporation spokesman also pointed out that an unstable wage rate and union situation would discourage private capital from coming to Jamaica. Two years later, a mission sponsored by the International Bank for Reconstruction and Development (I.B.R.D.), in a report on the Jamaican economy, used almost the identical words to warn Jamaica that private foreign capital would be deterred by an unstable labour situation.[1] The evidence at the Board and the I.B.R.D. report are two of the first instances where United States labour practices and procedures were advocated by foreign sources.

As a result of the Board, a non-compulsory poll procedure was established for settling representational issues and the T.U.C.J.–acquired bargaining rights with ALCAN and started negotiations with Kaiser, together with the BITU. But once again the T.U.C.J. corporate relations were disturbed by political events.

---

[1] I.B.R.D.: *The Economic Development of Jamaica* (Baltimore, Johns Hopkins Press, 1952), p. 82.

The T.U.C.J. and the P.N.P. both claimed to be socialist organisations, but the leaders began to have political differences and the two organisations began to split. While such a breakup can be explained in terms of power or ideological disputes within the T.U.C.J-P.N.P. complex, it was inextricably involved with. the representation of the bauxite workers. A leader of the T.U.C.J. formed a breakaway union, which he announced at a meeting of bauxite workers was to be a separate bauxite union, although it was in fact a rival blanket union.

A party purge eventually took place in which four major leaders of the T.U.C.J. were charged with anti-party activity by propagating Marxist doctrines and forming a Marxist cell in the party.[1] At that time in Jamaica there was no accusation that the people involved had foreign communist bloc connections, especially after the T.U.C.J.'s withdrawal from the World Federation of Trade Unions (W.F.T.U.). For at least two of the expellees there is doubt that they were ever communists or Marxists, although most subsequent histories of the Jamaican labour movement refer to both the T.U.C.J. and the expellees as communist.

The expulsion of the T.U.C.J. leaders from the P.N.P. still left the T.U.C.J. with a large number of workers as members and still holding the bulk of bauxite workers. The P.N.P. then created a new union, the National Workers Union (N.W.U.). Once again, although the N.W.U. was created as a blanket union, it is obvious from its early history that its immediate and prime objective was to wrest representation of the bauxite workers from the T.U.C.J. The latter union had been involved in an arbitration with Reynolds, claiming a cost-of-living wage increase and negotiations with Kaiser for representation had collapsed. The N.W.U. soon obtained representation of the workers in construction and mining at ALCAN and Kaiser, but a N.W.U.-promoted representational strike at Reynolds resulted in the BITU gaining the poll. It should be remembered, to put the activities of both the breakaway union and the new N.W.U. into context, that the bauxite workers were still few in number and were not paid wages much higher than the island level. Thus representation would not have brought significant financial benefits to the representing union.

---

[1] Newspaper reports of the purge refer always to 'Marxist' doctrines and 'Marxist' cells. Party reports of a later date, however, refer to 'Communist' doctrines and cells. See: People's National Party, *Man of Destiny*, Kingston, 1954.

The creation of the N.W.U. was a multi-nation and international operation. Before the N.W.U. was legally registered as a union under Jamaican law, and despite previous aid given to the T.U.C.J., the British T.U.C. made a £500 organising grant which was further supplemented by another grant of £1,500. The Cuban Confederation of Labour gave an undisclosed amount of financial aid to assist in the organising of sugar workers and the I.C.F.T.U. gave £250 for general purposes. When a Caribbean Area Division of the Inter-American Regional Organisation of Workers (ORIT) was created a few months before the N.W.U. was registered, the Assistant Secretary of ORIT for International Relations and Education, Serafino Romualdi, records that 'One of the CADORIT's first organizational tasks was to assist in the development of the Jamaican N.W.U.'[1] Although ORIT and its division CADORIT were officially regional organisations of the International Confederation of Free Trade Unions (I.C.F.T.U.) they retained their autonomy and were largely financed by United States national trade union centres.[2] But the most involved organisation in Jamaica was a United States industrial union, the United Steelworkers of America (U.S.W.A.).

The first appearance of the U.S.W.A. was soon after the N.W.U. was registered in October 1952, when the international representative, the ex-president of the Aluminium Workers of America which merged with the U.S.W.A. in 1945, visited the island. It was clear from a speech he made to striking workers on a bauxite construction site that he was in Jamaica to assist the N.W.U.–P.N.P. As a result, his actions were the subject of a complaint to the U.S.A. State Department by the BITU–J.L.P. government at that time and he was also denied entry to the island for the purpose of labour activities in March 1953. The U.S.W.A. then sent a Canadian from its Canadian division who was permitted entry because, according to the U.S.W.A. newspaper, he held 'Commonwealth status'.[3] Another U.S.W.A. executive later told a conference, however, that the order against the first representative was revoked with the aid of the British Labour Party.[4]

[1] S. Romualdi: *Presidents and Peons* (New York, Funk and Wagnalls, 1968,) p. 354.
[2] See P. Reiser: *L'Organisation Regionale Interamericaine des Travailleurs (ORIT) de la Confederation Internationale des Syndicats Libres (C.I.S.L.) 1951–1961*, Geneva, Droz, 1962.
[3] 'It's Not All Calypso!', *Steel Labour*, April 1957, p. 7.
[4] R. Aronson and J. Windmuller (eds.): *Labor Management and Economic Growth* (Institute of International Industrial and Labor Relations, Cornell University, 1954), p. 216.

What initial and specific action caused the entry of the U.S.W.A. into Jamaica is in doubt as accounts differ. Officially, the 'workers' of Jamaica requested aid from the I.C.F.T.U., and as the Canadian director of the U.S.W.A. was on the executive the matter was referred to him. An ex-U.S.W.A. executive interviewed, however, stated that a participant on a United Nations technical assistance mission suggested that the U.S.W.A. assist the N.W.U. Another ex-U.S.W.A. official said that one of the bauxite companies called the U.S.W.A. headquarters and said that the union should send someone down with whom they were used to negotiating. The individual was named and in fact sent.

Regardless of the immediate reasons why the U.S.W.A. became involved, the level and means of involvement is a matter of record. An immediate cash grant of $3,000 was made in 1953.[1] At the same time a Jamaican N.W.U. official was put on the U.S.W.A. payroll to organise the bauxite workers on the N.W.U.'s behalf. He remained on the payroll for over four years, serving during that time in both national and international capacities.[2]

U.S.W.A. negotiators were present at most N.W.U.–bauxite corporation negotiations. An important arbitration occurred in 1953 between the N.W.U. and Reynolds concerning wage rates. The U.S.W.A. Canadian research director presented the N.W.U.'s case and argued that the bauxite industry was a special case and that the companies should conform to an 'ability-to-pay' doctrine rather than have the wages pegged at the all-island level. The United Kingdom arbitrator rejected this argument although he awarded pay increases higher than those offered by the corporation. In another arbitration in 1955 the ability-to-pay doctrine was accepted and the bauxite workers' wage rates freed from the all-island level. This met opposition from local Jamaican employers but the immediate beneficiaries were the bauxite workers and the N.W.U.; the latter, owing to the establishment of dues check-off in the industry at an early date, now had a source of income which was disproportionate to the number of workers it represented.

The N.W.U. by this time had gained representational rights for all bauxite workers in mining and construction but had very few paying members in other industries.

In 1955, the U.S.W.A. suggested that the bauxite workers should

---

[1] *Daily Gleaner*, 22 April 1953, p. 2.
[2] From *National Workers Union Annual Reports* (Kingston, Jamaica), 1955 and 1956.

become a direct affiliate of the U.S.W.A. and for two years the N.W.U. leadership considered the proposal positively.[1] However, the Minister of Labour in the P.N.P. government, an ex-executive member of the N.W.U., opposed it on the grounds that with the coming independence of Jamaica its unions should all be independent. The internal politics of the U.S.W.A. also affected this situation, as one Canadian executive interviewed said that he opposed the idea as it would mean that the Jamaican workers would come under the control of the U.S.W.A. headquarters in Pittsburgh.

The failure of this proposition resulted in a change in the constitution of the N.W.U. The original 1953 constitution was based on a branch structure with a high degree of central authority at union headquarters and was similar to a British general union. In 1959 this was changed to a 'local' structure in which certain locals under certain conditions could become 'chartered locals' and have greater autonomy. The draft of the later constitution has inserted in the basic 1953 document a 'chartered local' section, which uses American terminology and language, in contrast to the British usage throughout the rest of the document. The main provisions of the chartered local section is that such a local can have its own bank account and have fees returned from the central office to the local. The bauxite workers of Jamaica are the only chartered local in the N.W.U.

Thus, by the late fifties the corporations were dealing with a section of a blanket union which had a high degree of autonomy and with a union which was, in general, prepared to co-operate in collective bargaining with the unions of the national corporate base.

*Foreign Union and Corporate Objectives*

While the natural resources of Jamaica clearly supply the incentive for the presence of the aluminium corporations in Jamaica, the objectives of the unions are not so clear.

The stated purpose of the U.S.W.A. in Jamaica, as expressed by speeches of its executives, was to protect the labour standards of workers in the United States by raising wages in the industry in Jamaica. Referring to iron ore in Guatemala and Venezuela, and bauxite in Jamaica David J. McDonald, U.S.W.A. President, noted in

[1] *N.W.U. Annual Reports* (Kingston), 1955 and 1956.

his inaugural address in 1953 'great rich fields of ore owned by American corporations are being developed by American corporations to be worked by the natives of those countries at miserable wages . . . I am going to have a study made of these situations because we must protect the standards of our people here at home'.[1] Another U.S.W.A. executive told a conference in 1954 that the activities in Jamaica were 'placing the members of the United Steelworkers under a competitive handicap'.[2] This explanation has been accepted by several academic commentators on the situation.[3]

These explanations, however, are not consistent with either the economics of the aluminium industry or the actions and statements of union executives in Jamaica. First, the domestic production of bauxite in the United States has since 1950 only supplied a small proportion of total consumption, ranging from 30 per cent in 1950 to 13 per cent in 1965 and throughout the period employment in bauxite mining has been less than 1,000. (The U.S.W.A. has over a million members.) Secondly, the labour cost of bauxite mining is not a significant part of the total production costs of aluminium. In 1962 bauxite mining labour costs in Jamaica represented less than 1 per cent of the market price of unwrought aluminium.[4] Thus a naturally superior ore produced with low labour cost in Jamaica could not really be considered labour-cost competitive with an inferior ore produced with high labour cost in the United States.

Furthermore, in a 1955 arbitration the Canadian research director of the U.S.W.A. claimed – on behalf of the N.W.U. – that the corporations were *not* in Jamaica to take advantage of low wage rates and could not use the low-wage argument to resist the claim for a much higher wage rate in the industry.

In conclusion, the actions of the U.S.W.A. in Jamaica can thus be seen as one of ensuring the supply of bauxite, rather than increasing labour costs to protect workers in the United States. The Union represents many thousands of workers in primary aluminium production and fabrication, most of whom are dependent on Jamaican

---

[1] *Steel Labour*, April 1953, p. 4.
[2] Aronson and Windmuller, *op. cit.*
[3] See G. Eaton: *Trade Union Development in Jamaica, W.I.*, unpublished dissertation (McGill University, 1961); and W. Knowles: *Trade Union Development and Industrial Relations in the British West Indies* (University of California Press, 1959), p. 136.
[4] Calculated from figures in H. D. Huggins: *Aluminium in Changing Communities* (London, Andre Deutsch, 1968). p. 124 and N. Girvan: *The Caribbean Bauxite Industries*, Studies in Regional Economic Integration, Vol. 2. No. 4, Institute of Social and Economic Research University of the West Indies, Kingston, 1967, Table A, p. 3.

bauxite.[1] The obvious requirement then is a continuous and un-interrupted supply of bauxite and alumina to the alumina and smelting plants in North America.

The corporations clearly have the same interest. After less than three years of full-scale production the corporations were prepared to pay the Jamaican workers salaries and wages twice or three times the island average for unskilled workers, and even more for skilled workers, which often placed them in the top 1 per cent income bracket in Jamaica.

The strategic nature of aluminium meant that the United States Government likewise had an interest in the continuous supply of bauxite. This was a subject of much concern in Washington between 1949 and 1951; a typical lobbyist pointed out that 'action must be taken now to provide reliable and expanding sources of aluminium supply to defend ourselves and our allies to carry any war that may be thrust upon us to a successful conclusion'.[2] A Presidential Materials Policy Commission was established and its report 'Resources for Freedom' was published in 1952 and advocated a stockpile programme and examined in detail the bauxite position in the world.[3] In Jamaica, the United States Government had already financed a loan of £2,500,000 to ALCAN for its Jamaica operations in the early forties to be repaid by shipments of alumina.

The corporate response to the strategic value of the material in the framework of the cold war is permanently inscribed on an aluminium plaque unveiled by Walter L. Rice, President, Jamaica Mines Ltd., in 1952: 'On this property in 1942 the Hon. Sir Alfred D'Costa in the hope of improving the agricultural productivity of the sterile soil took the sample which on analysis proved to be aluminium ore, thus bringing to the people of Jamaica a new industry and to the peoples of the free world a new resource against aggression.'[4]

The U.S.W.A. also accepted the national effort in the cold war: President McDonald claimed that U.S.W.A. executives would 'talk to anyone from the national administration if we can be of assistance not only to the United Steelworkers of America but to our world economy', and that the union's representatives 'travel to the four

---

[1] When the aluminium union merged with U.S.W.A. in 1945 it had 30,000 members.

[2] H. D. Anderson: *Aluminium for Defense and Prosperity* (Washington Public Affairs Institute, 1951), p. 9.

[3] *Resources for Freedom* (Washington, D.C., 1952), Vol. II, 'Outlook for Key Commodities – Aluminium', pp. 65–73.

[4] Reynolds Jamaica Mines Ltd: pamphlet commemorating the event.

corners of the world . . . to combat Communists in their lair for what they are, men without truth in their being'.[1] An article by an international trade unionist stated that the Caribbean 'has lately become an important source of minerals, mainly bauxite. These are essential for the rearmament efforts of the western world. Undoubtedly this explains the Communists' efforts to gain a foothold in these industries.'[2] J. K. Galbraith has specifically mentioned bauxite as a resource which a modern corporation attempts to free from all market uncertainty, either of price or supply.[3] Another writer, referring to the needs of the State, records that although bauxite reserves are '. . . found largely outside the industrial centers, they are in areas to which non-Communist industrial countries should continue to have access. . . .'[4] It should not, therefore, be surprising that, given the international political climate of the time, a multi-national corporation should call on the relevant union of its national base to assist in effecting such operations.

The ultimate objective of all parties involved in the Jamaican bauxite industry must therefore be seen as the most efficient control of a resource essential to the industry in North America. The immediate objectives were to secure local organisations, industrial relations and economic practices which would facilitate such control. It is in this process that the presence of foreign corporations made a wide impact on Jamaican society.


## INDUSTRIAL RELATIONS AND LABOUR EFFECTS

It is clear that corporate management was anxious to see American industrial relations practices established in Jamaica, at least in their specific industry, and that they were assisted in this policy by foreign and international unions and international governmental agencies. Particular aspects advocated were representational polls, autonomous local or branch structures, dues check-off, collective bargaining, and a shop-steward-based grievance procedure.[5]

[1] *Proceedings of the 7th Constitutional Convention of the United Steelworkers of America*, 1954, pp. 11 and 12.

[2] S. Romualdi: 'Labour in the Caribbean', *The American Federationist*, Vol. 60, No. 4, April 1963, p. 14.

[3] J. K. Galbraith: *The New Industrial State* (Hamish Hamilton, London, 1967), p. 39.

[4] S. Brubaker: *Trends in the World Aluminium Industry, Resources for the Future* (Baltimore, Johns Hopkins Press, 1967), p. 149.

[5] See W. Knowles: *Trade Union Development and Industrial Relations in the British West Indies, op. cit.*, pp. 73–5.

Up to 1950, the industrial relations legislation and practices were basically British, thus the American elements had to be grafted on to this structure and the basic resistance to this alteration of the industrial relations system came from the local Jamaican employers.[1] While they were prepared to agree with foreigners' opposition to political unionism, they were opposed to compulsory polls, recognition of trade unions and union shop. The enthusiasm of outsiders for American practices sometimes also met opposition from the union as the proposals ran counter to union politics in Jamaica. Thus the I.B.R.D. recommendation for dues check-off in 1952, had it been implemented, would have been disastrous for the newly-formed N.W.U. which had few paying members. The U.S.W.A. Jamaican organiser for the N.W.U. had to explain that while he was for dues check-off in principle, it would always have to be postponed until the union was strong enough. The result of such resistance was that some American practices, which have the force of law in the United States, became voluntary in the Jamaican system. Thus there is provision for representational polls but on an unenforceable and non-compulsory basis, collective bargaining is not enforceable, there is no widely accepted union shop principle, minority union rights may be recognised, and the unions have remained blanket rather than becoming industrial.

Conditions in the bauxite/alumina industry, however, have given rise to a *de facto* United States system. Representational polls have not arisen since the early fifties as all the workers are represented by the N.W.U. which extends great efforts to ensure that the BITU does not represent any workers in the industry, not even those only tangentially associated with bauxite/alumina. Union shop is accepted and minority union bargaining rights, a possibility in the rest of the economy, does not occur. The same may be said of plant-by-plant versus industry-wide negotiating. Plant-by-plant negotiating is the basic practice in Jamaica but in the bauxite/alumina industry the same negotiators are involved with all corporations and a body or arbitration precedent treats the industry as a whole, which means there is *de facto* industry-wide negotiating. Collective bargaining in the industry is detailed in comparison with that prevalent in the rest of the economy, as the agreements contain arbitration provisions and extensive clauses on fringe benefits.

[1] See 'Joint Statement for Public Information by Jamaican Employers Federation and the Jamaican Chamber of Commerce', *Daily Gleaner*, 18 January 1961.

Since the early fifties, the corporations have had virtually no strikes and the largest bauxite mining installation none at all. The reason for this is found in the extremely high wages the bauxite workers receive and in the good relations which exist between the corporations and the N.W.U. The wage level, so far above the average, diminishes the likelihood of workers changing unions or striking in breach of contract. Reporting that the N.W.U. enjoyed 'amicable relations' with the companies, a researcher who interviewed corporate management reports that 'the trade union is accepted as a useful social institution serving a police function which is valued by the company'.[1] The workers, however, show a lack of positive attitudes towards the corporation; a survey of attitudes conducted in 1960 showed that 60 per cent were indifferent to the corporation, 20 per cent loyal and 20 per cent hostile.[2]

The existence of a very small and highly paid group of workers does not seem to have affected the labour situation in general. Entry to the industry is on political lines, BITU members or J.L.P. members being effectively banned, a situation which has led to violence at bauxite construction sites.[3] The possibility of working in bauxite is sufficiently rare to prevent any skilled workers from waiting for such opportunities rather than taking lower paid jobs elsewhere. At least one corporation has a school for training skilled workers and, unlike the rest of the economy, the wage rates have been high enough to prevent a large loss of trained men through emigration. All companies and the N.W.U. co-operate in training union delegates for the industry.

From both the labour and industrial relations standpoints then the bauxite/alumina industry is an enclave, although there have been some spill-over effects in these areas. Despite the industrial peace established on a *de facto* basis in the industry, there are still attempts to extend the system by legislation to the rest of the economy. In 1967 the N.W.U. requested the legal department of the U.S.W.A. in Pittsburgh to prepare a model industrial relations act which was to be presented to the government for consideration.[4]

---

[1] G. Eaton: *Trade Union Development in Jamaica, W.I.*, *op. cit.*, p. 624.

[2] *Ibid.* p. 715, and see R. Aronson: 'Labour Commitment among Jamaican Bauxite Workers: A Case Study', *Social and Economic Studies*, Vol. 10, No. 2, June 1961, pp. 156–72.

[3] See 'Strong-Arm Men at Bauxite Project', *Public Opinion*, 7 July 1967, p. 1.

[4] *N.W.U. Annual Report*, Kingston, 1967.

*Organisational Effects*

The operational problems of effective control of the bauxite/alumina workers in Jamaica in 1950 were found in the unfamiliar and difficult nature of the BITU and its leader, the socialism and nationalism of the leaders of the T.U.C.J., and the blanket structures of both unions.

The BITU members were predominantly the rural people of the evolved culture and the organisation reflected this culture. The verbal and cultural impossibility of communication with the BITU experienced by a succession of British colonial labour advisers was duplicated in the succeeding North American corporate manager and trade unionists. Thus, even though the BITU was the most powerful union at the time, the corporations opted to deal with the more familiar structure of the T.U.C.J. and communicative members of the imitative culture. In the first instance the BITU was ignored and subsequently its nature attacked.

But the leaders of the T.U.C.J. were both socialist and nationalist and made no secret of their opposition to the development of the Jamaican economy by direct rather than indirect foreign investment. Eventually a coalition of domestic and international actors destroyed the T.U.C.J. by designating its leaders as communists and creating a rival union which would be a more amenable organisation for the new bauxite/alumina industry. The accepted interpretation of these events, as well as an indication of the policy pursued, is given by an international trade union official describing the situation in Jamaica in 1953: 'The BITU is a personal instrument of Mr. William Alexander Bustamante himself . . . his popularity is fast decreasing [the BITU that year represented 70 per cent of the unionised labour force and Bustamante was the island's chief minister] . . . the Jamaica T.U.C. is following the Communist-ruled W.F.T.U. [the T.U.C.J. applied for membership of I.C.F.T.U. in 1952 and its leaders were active in Moral Rearmament] . . . the N.W.U. . . . has made very strong progress in a very short time [N.W.U. paying membership was 1,842 compared with 46,260 for BITU and 7,140 for T.U.C.J.]. It now has the workers of two bauxite companies which are operating in the island.'[1]

The blanket nature of the unions, both the new N.W.U. and the BITU, could however be said to have brought unwanted involve-

[1] S. Romualdi: 'Labor in the Caribbean', *op. cit.*, p. 14 (this author's brackets).

189

ment in the larger aspects of unionism in Jamaica. The U.S.W.A.
attempt to associate formally the bauxite workers with the United
States union can be seen in this light.

Although from the standpoint of the corporations the creation of
the N.W.U. solved the immediate problems, foreign unions and sometimes foreign employers in Jamaica continued to mount attacks against
the political nature of Jamaican unions. From 1955 almost all the
trade union educational activities, whether by the P.N.P. government,
the British Government, the University College of the West Indies,
or the American Institute for Free Labour Development, emphasised
the problems of political unionism and placed emphasis on the
technical aspects of unions. Bustamante consequently saw all education
attempts as a frontal attack on his union and refused to participate.
With his retirement and with the influence of industrial-country labour
relations practices in the N.W.U., both unions have lately become more
technically oriented. The N.W.U. still opposes the BITU on the
grounds that the N.W.U. is less close to the P.N.P. than the BITU is
to the J.L.P.

The result of these activities was the destruction of a union with
radical and nationalist leadership; the creation of a union leadership
intent on imitating stuctures and functions derived exclusively from
an industrial country's trade union experience; and the depoliticisation
of the trade union movement (in the sense that unions became less
important as groups pressing for meaningful social and political
change).

The broader impact of these developments cannot be precisely
determined and in any case could only be derived by the dangerous
device of comparing an historical 'might-have-been' with a current 'is'.
Within a more theoretical framework, however, some organisational
effects can be suggested. The Jamaican unions in their early stages were
the results of, and were responsive to, the social and economic conditions
in Jamaica. They consequently served emotional and welfare functions
and articulated grievances arising from conditions not usually the
concern of an industrial-country union.[1] They often agitated on
behalf of the unemployed, the unpaid rural worker and the seasonally
employed, many of whom were associated in some form of 'member-

---

[1] A description of these functions found in another union in the Caribbean is in S.
Rottenberg: 'Labour Relations in an Underdeveloped Economy', *Economic Development
and Cultural Change*, December 1962, pp. 25–260. Rottenberg's description is applied to
Jamaica in G. E. Cumper: 'Labour and Development in the West Indies', *Social and
Economic Studies*, Vol. 10, No. 3, p. 298.

ship'. The unions fitted a particular social type in the Caribbean which one scholar has called 'neither peasant nor proletarian'.[1] Charisma in leadership, obvious in the case of the BITU although less so in the T.U.C.J., is considered by Max Weber and some of his contemporary admirers as the necessary creative element in organisation building.[2] The history of the BITU would be an example of the process by which an organisation is created which reflects in its structures and functions the cultural and social demands which are at the base of the leader's charism.[3] The T.U.C.J., in a not totally disimilar process, accepted the BITU-developed structure as suitable to local conditions and in the early 1950s moved towards absorbing the technical competence necessary for dealing with the foreign corporations.

In the early period then, between 1938 and 1952, the union leaders, despite the imitative culture origins of the T.U.C.J., were schooled in the necessities of responding to mass demands and the problems of organisation building in accordance with local conditions. By compaiison the political parties were artificial creations, the bulk of the leadership intent on conforming to the available external industrial-country two-party model and operating mainly within the framework of the imitative culture. The insistence that 'political' functions should be transferred from unions to parties, which came from both internal and external sources, eventually brought organisational development to a halt and left some of the original functions of the unions unfulfilled, the unemployed unrepresented and the rural workers, demands less vigorously presented. The result is that to some extent the unions have become dysfunctional in relation to their environment.

It should be made clear at this point that it is not argued that this process was solely the result of the arrival of foreign corporations. There were obviously other social, psychological and economic factors involved, but it is suggested that the role of the foreign corporations and unions in this process must be considered as important.

[1] R. Frucht: 'A Caribbean Social Type – Neither "Peasant" nor "Proletarian"', *Social and Economic Studies*, Vol. 16, No. 3, September 1967, pp. 295–300.

[2] See S. N. Eisenstadt: *Max Weber on Charisma and Institution Building, Selected Papers* (Chicago, University of Chicago Press, 1968). For a writer who does not altogether agree with the Weber formulation when applied to the Caribbean see A. Singham: *Hero and the Crowd in a Colonial Polity* (Yale University Press, 1969).

[3] On the relation between the basic cultural order and charisma, see S. N. Eisenstadt: 'Introduction', in *Max Weber on Charisma and Institution Building, op. cit.*, p. xix.

*Political and Economic Effects*

Between 1960 and 1965 the bauxite/alumina industry contributed an average of nearly 10 per cent of Jamaica's gross national product and in 1965 represented over 45 per cent of export earnings. The taxes and royalties provide a large amount of revenue which the government could use for development purposes.

The other economic impacts are less obvious, and sometimes speculative, as they relate to political and social phenomena. Economists have argued that an impediment to continued growth in Jamaica is the lack of growth in the agricultural sector and the poor distribution of income. Thomas Balogh has noted that in Jamaica the 'discrepancy between rural farmers and urban industrial incomes, shocking as it is already, is growing' and that 83 per cent of farmers account for less than a quarter of the total income.[1] Correction of these imbalances requires political organisations attuned to the needs of those on the bottom of the scale. The removal of the more radical elements from the Jamaican political scene in the early 1950s, plus the depoliticisation of the unions, may be seen as two reasons why Jamaican society has not moved to create a more economically healthy distribution of income and land.

The demonstration effect of a small group of extremely highly paid industrial workers is also difficult to assess. It can be said with certainty, however, that it has added to the traditional distaste for, and low status of, rural life and occupations. At the same time, the government has launched expensive programmes to discourage the move to the urban centres in the mostly hopeless search for industrial work. [2] Politically, the representation of bauxite workers or the achievement of bauxite rates for other workers has become a triumph important in party politics. In a recent arbitration concerning the payment of bauxite rates to BITU workers on a bauxite construction site, court proceedings were started because the arbitrator told one of the parties he must decide in favour of granting the rates partly because 'it is well known that he was a Labour Party man and that the award of bauxite rates would be of tremendous help to his Party'.[3] Shortly afterwards a J.L.P. minister complained in a letter to the opposition

[1] T. Balogh: *The Economics of Poverty* (London, Weidenfeld and Nicolson, 1966), p. 293.
[2] See M. G. Smith: 'Education and Occupational Choice in Rural Jamaica', *Social and Economic Studies*, Vol. 9, No. 3, September 1960, pp. 332–54.
[3] From an affidavit published in the *Daily Gleaner*, 20 April 1967, p. 3.

leader that, as a result of the P.N.P.-N.W.U. activities, he had not been able to get employment in the bauxite/alumina industry for 'a single worker from his constituency'.[1]

Economic integration within the Caribbean has been advocated by economists as beneficial for the area and governmental attempts have been made towards that end, as they have in Central and Latin America.[2] From the standpoint of the bauxite/alumina industry Caribbean economic integration would most likely mean the more extensive use of various Caribbean productive resources, an increase in the number of alumina plants, location of smelting plants in the area and creation of fabricating facilities.[3] Such a programme would be complicated by the vertical and individual integration of the competing corporations in the area and by their international trading patterns.[4] More relevant to the material presented in this case study is that it would also appear that any political programme for such integration would have to take cognisance that policies in the various country units may be substantially influenced by foreign-based trade unions and corporations which may have both deep involvement in the domestic political system and direct interests in the outcome of the integration policies.

*Conclusions*

This paper has shown in a specific case that the impact of the multi-national corporation on a society in a less-developed country is far wider than is readily apparent; that although the immediate effects of the corporation may be in segments of the economy, industrial relations and trade unionism, there are important long-term political, economic and societal effects; that there can be an identity of interest between multi-national corporations and national and international trade union organisations and that the *total* impact of the corporation must be considered as an important factor in any policies dealing with economic development or regional integration.

---

[1] *Daily Gleaner*, 7 August, 1967, p. 1.
[2] See H. Brewster and C. Thomas: *The Dynamics of West Indian Economic Integration* (Institute of Social and Economic Studies: Kingston, 1968).
[3] See the arrangement proposed by A. McIntyre: 'De-Colonisation and Trade Policy in the West Indies' in F. Andic and T. Mathews (eds): *The Caribbean in Transition* (Institute of Caribbean Studies, 1965), p. 212.
[4] See M. Girvan and O. Jefferson: 'Corporate versus Caribbean Integration', paper at 'Conference on Latin American and Caribbean Integration', University of West Indies, 1967 and reprinted in *New World Quarterly*, Vol. IV, No. 2, 1968, p. 53; see also H. D. Huggins: *Aluminium in Changing Communities* (London, Deutsch, 1965).

A case study such as this cannot claim universal validity but it can stand as a criticism of prevailing theories and patterns of academic and administrative thought. The findings in this case are directly critical of the practice by which international capital transfer by direct investment has been considered in economic isolation and divorced from its broad cultural, societal and political aspects.

# A POSSIBLE REGIONAL SOLUTION FOR LATIN AMERICA TO THE 'AMERICAN CHALLENGE'.

INTENSIFIED regional economic co-operation, mergers of firms with home bases in the region, and regional pooling of governmental resources to enable large-scale research and development are some of the recipes promoted particularly in Europe for meeting the challenge of American-based multi-national corporations. The envisaged creation of a legal statute for private multi-national corporations of European nationality is another potential device for strengthening the power of regional firms, so as to enable them to compete with the foreign supergiants.

Obviously, any realistic attempt to create countervailing forces will have to take into account the particular conditions in the region and especially the availability of private and public resources, the prevailing political and cultural preferences.

In the following chapter, Marcos Kaplan suggests (in line with the experience in the European Common Market) that the process of Latin American economic integration, in particular through LAFTA, far from being a countervailing force, has actually contributed to the growth of foreign-based (American) international corporations. To put it sharply, economic integration has entailed a strengthening and proliferation of outside international decision–centres with prime importance for the economic and social development of the region; it has therefore, in a sense, been self-defeating.

The relative economic and political weakness of the Latin American countries, in Marcos Kaplan's opinion, exacerbated by excessive economic liberalism, puts Latin America, nevertheless, in a very different position from the European Common Market. Reliance on national private firms is unlikely to generate sufficient economic development, viewed as a prerequisite of economic and political independence, an area sensitised by the economic predominance of the United States. Marcos Kaplan sees in the conscious enlargement of the public sector the potential driving force for regional development. The creation of multi-national public corporations, operating in a variety of fields, is the proposed agent for such an evolution and is viewed as a locally relevant alternative model of integration 'from within and below' to the present model of integration 'from without and above'.

The success of these proposals appears to depend both on the political will to put them into practice as well as on the solution of the inherent problem of comparative efficiency of multi-national public ventures in fields so far clearly dominated by private multi-national corporations. This problem is a particularly formidable one in a developing region, where not only shortage of capital but even greater shortages of entrepreneurial skills are major limiting factors for development.

Potentially, inter-state co-operation in the regional setting, especially in fields involving advanced technology, whether in the form of a multi-national public corporation or in any other form, seems to be a natural counterpart of the deep involvement of the U.S. Government with the private sector as regards research and development (highlighted in J. K. Galbraith: *The New Industrial State*). Such co-operation, involving changes in the locus of decision-making on industrial relations issues and on allocations of resources, should open similar avenues for transnationalisation of industrial relations as the operations of private multi-national corporations.

Chapter 9

# MULTI-NATIONAL PUBLIC CORPORATIONS FOR DEVELOPMENT AND INTEGRATION IN LATIN AMERICA

*by*

*Marcos Kaplan*

THIS chapter sums up the progress made towards integration through the Latin American Free Trade Association (LAFTA)[1] and proposes multi-national public corporations as one of the means by which that integration may be further promoted.

## I. A PATTERN OF INTEGRATION IN DEPRESSION

Like any similar experiment, Latin American integration has to be effected not only between areas with huge total surface, but also between a diversity of nations, each having its own social, economic, institutional, political and cultural systems. Such integration efforts must also take place within the texture of a general process of events in which there is constant interaction and interpenetration between the various aspects and levels of public affairs.

A review of achievement to date justifies the statement that neither of the two experiments in the region – the Latin American Free Trade Association and the Central American Common Market[2]—has an inherent dynamic which could fully guarantee its continuous advance.

The origin, progress and pattern of LAFTA (to which, as the bigger and more important of the two, reference in this paper is restricted) are not the result of deliberate, consequential action; they are the incidental by-product of pragmatic reaction (direct or indirect) to the

---

[1] LAFTA has the following membership: Argentina, Brazil, Chile, Colombia, Ecuador, Mexico, Paraguay, Peru, Uruguay and Venezuela.
[2] Membership: Costa Rica, El Salvador, Guatemala, Honduras and Nicaragua.

structural and conjunctural depressions which have plagued Latin America in recent years. It seems fair to describe LAFTA as having been, from the outset, a precarious combination of abstract theory and narrow short-term empiricism. This conclusion is justified by the following brief enumeration of the real motives for the experiment and the doctrinal arguments which seek to justify and explain it.

*Real Motives and the Theoretical Background*

Regional economic integration is usually presented as a device for the promotion of economic growth and efficiency through economies of large scale and intensified competition. It is not thought of, however, as an option which excludes either national development or greater integration into the world market. Some of its claimed results are more rapid and diversified internal growth, modernisation and mobilisation of dynamic social groups.

In the Latin American context, in particular, it is held that integration permits simultaneous enjoyment of the advantages of the national and of the regional market, and also assists in creating conditions for better access to the markets of the advanced countries; at the same time it is suggested that there is a strengthening of the international position and the real independence of the countries in the region.

There were many reasons for attempting this economic integration, especially the demographic perspectives and, on another level, the revolutionary challenge (particularly that of Cuba) inherent in the prospect of economic stagnation. LAFTA, officially created in 1960, was inspired by progressive conservatism. For its advocates, it seemed above all to be a prerequisite for acquiring a new potential or of creating a new economic entity with worldwide implications. Seen in this perspective, the large North American companies have a direct interest in Latin American integration because the experiment could considerably expand their outlets.

The process of integration therefore tends to stimulate, as a side effect, establishment and growth of national and international undertakings; it will also contribute, in this way, to the creation, proliferation and strengthening of international power centres situated outside the region, these latter taking more and more decisions of prime importance for the structure and development of each Latin American country and the region as a whole as regards investments, location and variations of production, applied technology, employment, foreign trade, internal integration of national economies, equilibrium between countries, areas and social groups.

*Achievements and Gaps*

The positive aspects of LAFTA are obvious. It provides a framework for the needed integration of economic structures, increased trade and interchange on the human level, and, also, the setting up of an indispensable common basis for comparable statistics.

LAFTA has served as a place of negotiation for freer trade, and has instituted machinery by which problems can be solved and obstacles overcome. Seven particular agreements for complementary industrial development have been signed and have come into force. Many sectoral meetings have been held and special committees and working parties established to deal with various aspects of integration. LAFTA is also concerned with the problems of infra-structure in the region. Furthermore, within its set-up, it promotes contacts and mutual acquaintance between entrepreneurs of the region and ensures greater participation on their part.

There are, however, many gaps. Latin America is not the European Common Market and it is not just a question of harmonising economic policies – as is the case in Europe – but also, and especially, of making up for a significant lag in the development of the region. In addition, the economic, social and political heterogeneity of the Latin American countries is very pronounced (without mentioning geographic obstacles) and the feeling of continental solidarity is weak. Moreover, no single country, even among the three largest (Brazil, Argentina, Mexico) is in a position to take the lead in promoting a common policy. It is also necessary to stress internal resistance (pressures of social groups) and external resistance (foreign powers and interest groups) to more organic integration. These forces cannot be overcome by the political (State) powers in a Latin America which is at present dominated by an economic liberalism that is ineffective except in creating obstacles to planning.

Looking at the LAFTA experience of integration as a whole, one has to contend that a single pattern has been selected which excludes *a priori* a series of alternatives. In the LAFTA concept, economic integration is conceived as a necessary *and* sufficient requisite for development. It assumes the possibility of imitating, stage by stage, the classic pattern of Western capitalist development, neglecting certain regional characteristics of economic (e.g. centrifugal orientation towards Europe and the United States) as well as of social and cultural nature.

The State in Latin America uses inefficiently the public sector which can be such a powerful agent for development and also an instrument for countervailing certain possible disruptive effects stemming from the growth of multi-national firms. What the State actually does is not aimed at enlarging the public sector, nor at stimulating it in order to make it a driving force for development. On the contrary, despite the absence of clear options, the State favours, on the whole, large private enterprises.

Lastly, no political strategy for an over-all development and integration has been drawn up, specifying possibilities, forms and successive stages of growth, and ideologies capable of attracting wide support. The implications and consequences of a constant process of development and integration or a common and dynamic goal for society are rarely considered.

## II. AN AGENT FOR A NEW STRATEGY:
## THE MULTI-NATIONAL PUBLIC CORPORATION

The Treaty of Montevideo[1] was a useful minimum point from which to start the first attempt at Latin American integration including the principal countries of the region. Because it has enabled LAFTA to perform an experimental catalytic function and because of all that has been achieved, and even because of the obstacles and shortcomings which it has revealed, the advantages of the treaty cannot be denied.

However, as a result of the above-mentioned defects and limitations the LAFTA system has fallen into a state of crisis and exhaustion from which no escape seems likely for the moment. So it is indispensable to move beyond the form chosen and the stage reached so far, and proceed to formulate the rules and lay the foundations of a customs union, a common market and an economic integration or community in the true sense. If this is to be done, those features of the system which correspond to the initial period of development must evidently not be discarded *en bloc*, but rendered more flexible and complete – starting with transitional measures for the short and middle term; above all, it is necessary to inject a whole new strategy of development

[1] Setting up the Latin American Free Trade Association (signed in February 1960).

and integration, to which more explicit reference will be made hereafter.

It may be said at once that in addition to preparing the total integration of Latin America and creating the appropriate machinery it is possible and necessary also to prepare and to create machinery for partial strategies and tactics which will not counteract the general strategy but on the contrary will enrich and strengthen it.[1] Such partial measures should take the form, chiefly, of multi-national projects for the establishment and operation of poles or centres of integration which would stimulate, diffuse and multiply appropriate action at all possible points and levels in the areas, organisations and groups surrounding them, dependent on them, or influenced by them. More specifically, the principal concrete function of such centres would be to produce movements of real solidarity with a strong multiplier effect and the greatest possible degree of participation in different areas and by various organisations, groups and individuals – movements which would induce and stimulate new attempts at integration, merge with the general dynamic of integration, prepare, strengthen and extend it. That kind of integrating action could at the same time provide an instrument for intellectual planning, analysis and operation, produce a more real and specific understanding of the need, advisability and viability of integration for the countries, regions and groups involved; it would strengthen sectoral integration, reduce overhead costs, permit material, financial and human resources to be better used; and it might help towards reducing the differences in levels of development among the LAFTA countries and so lead towards a better equilibrium between them.

It will be necessary to start the process by ascertaining what kinds or classes of relations have – effectively or potentially – the capacity for spreading integration. Further questions are: how to build these relations up into general systems and specific projects with a high multiplier effect; what are the conditions – economic, social, institutional, political, cultural – on which the feasibility of such an undertaking depends. Among the many possibilities in this connection, and as examples of what might be bases for extending integration, one may mention: sub-regional groups of countries (Greater Colombia, the Southern Cone, the Plata Basin, the Andean group); development sectors (basic or dynamic industries, infra-structure); frontier associ-

[1] See: 'Hacia una Estrategia de los Polos de Integración', *INTAL*, Boletín de la Integración, Buenos Aires, March 1966.

ation; specific multi-national programmes and projects. The following pages discuss one possible multi-national project, i.e. the feasibility, structure and problems of the multi-national public corporation as an agent or pole of integration and development.

*Integration of the Public Sectors*

The State, the public sector of the economy and the enterprises belonging to it, can and must play a decisive role in the process of Latin American development and integration.

This problem is real and important, primarily because of the sustained tendency towards an increase in State intervention, the public sector and government undertakings which has occurred in Latin America in the last few decades. Since the early years of the twentieth century and above all since the 1930s, this process has become evident and been accelerated due to a great number of factors which include the following: the decline of the traditional methods of geographical expansion – stimulus from abroad and purely private action; the new phase of more rapid urbanisation and industrialisation; the emergence of new social groups with a strong drive upwards (middle classes, industrial proletariat); substantial changes in the power relationships prevailing in the world economy and politics, with direct internal implications for Latin America; changes in methods of obtaining and exercising political power; growth of a nationalistic climate of ideas, stressing the importance of internal factors and the need for instruments and machinery calculated to promote the rational organisation and expansion of an independent economy; resistance to change on the part of traditional structures and groups; disorganisation, weakness and lack of leadership in the sectors theoretically interested in structural change and modernisation (industrial employers, labour movement). All this helped to motivate an increase in State intervention and public enterprise as a means of compensating or replacing – in whole or in part – the weakened traditional sources of growth, and of promoting some degree of development with the urgency required by the exhausted and critical state of the traditional structure.

So, in the principal countries of Latin America, there has been a steady increase in the number and scale of governmental action and agencies of all kinds, aimed not only at the direction, regulation and deliberate promotion of economic and social activities which are considered as of public interest, but also at direct engagement therein. The State has thus greatly contributed to the emergence of a kind of mixed economy in which the growing extent of public control and the decentralisation of decision-making are major characteristics. The most striking feature of the process is the great increase in the number and scope of public development and finance corporations, central administrative departments, State commercial companies, public undertakings in the proper sense of the term, and mixed organisations. There is abundant statistical evidence – not reproduced here for lack of space – on the high degree of participation by the public sector in the formation and distribution of the gross domestic product and income, in capital formation and investment, the development of the infra-structure and basic industries, transactions regarding goods and services, the creation of additional employment, subsidies to consumers and producers by means of reduced prices and charges, support for the purchasing power of the market and the regulation of its structure and operation – more briefly, in the development of the national economies by way of internal stimulus and machinery.

The above will suffice to show how important the public economic sectors and State enterprise can become in the integration process; but it does not exhaust the argument, which may be strengthened by the following considerations. The role played by government initiative in the birth and growth of the European Economic Community (E.E.C.) should not be forgotten. Experience within the E.E.C. shows that the State has a natural aptitude to impose its policy despite narrow regional or sectoral viewpoints. Every supranational power must start from and work through the existing nation States.

Furthermore, the public sector in the Latin American countries can and must contribute decisively to unifying economic policies – an essential element in the progress of regional integration. It can contribute of itself, because of its share (and often exclusive engagement) in important sectors and branches of the economy (transport, communications, electricity, oil, basic industries); indeed, some of the principal forms of international co-operation have been emanations of the public sector. The State should also countervail or replace the private agreements which tend to seek and obtain monopolies; it should compete against private undertakings, with which it will have strong and irreversible social-economic relations. Co-operation between public sectors is the proper method by which to undertake such essential tasks as the integration of infra-structures, the establishment or strengthening of key industries, progress in theoretical and applied technology, sub-regional planning (border areas, international river basins). Lastly, the public sectors can help to harmonise currency, credit and banking policies, to equalise social standards (employment and conditions of work; a common code for State employees which might be used as a model for the private sector), and in general to bring national legislations into closer concordance.[1]

Joint action by the public sectors should be undertaken as part of regional investment plans for the chief branches of the economy in which, in Latin America, the public sectors operate – regional plans that would extend and harmonise the various national plans and by bringing the parties tangible profit would help to generate a community of intention and a lasting solidarity of interest among the participating countries severally and in the region as a whole.

It may be assumed that, as a result, joint economic activities will be undertaken and persistent exchanges develop, which should, in their turn, have a favourable effect on the balanced growth of the countries to be integrated. Such co-operation will also contribute towards the emergence of a new social, economic and political geography, to be deliberately and consciously promoted by the following means: pooling and diffusion of scientific and technological advances; stimulating specialisation and augmenting multi-lateral exchanges within the region; eliminating imbalances and distortions; encouraging inter-dependence between the countries; inducing habits of co-operation; making international borders less rigid and adjusting them to social-economic realities.

This kind of collaboration through the public sectors may develop on lines similar to those which the experiments in co-production have begun to take in recent years, and of which the following characteristics are relevant to our present subjects:[2]

(1) contractual association between public authorities or enterprises belonging to different nations or systems, each of which under-takes to make its specific contribution with a view to reaching certain objectives by concerted and mutually adjusted action;

(2) permanent institutional linking of interests and productive and

---

[1] See André Marchal: *L'Europe Solidaire* (Editions Cujas, Paris, 1964); and *L'Intégration Territoriale* (Presses Universitaires de France, Paris 1965).

[2] Maurice Byé: 'Co-operación en la Producción y Convergencia de los Sistemas Económicos', and R. Demonts: 'La Co-producción', *INTAL*, Boletín de la Integración, Buenos Aires, July 1966 and March 1967 respectively.

commercial processes through governing bodies made up of representatives of the public (the State, decentralised public corporations);

(3) establishment of the co-production unit in virtue of an international agreement which either merely envisages the possibility of starting such a scheme and sketches the general conditions, or embodies a specific commitment;

(4) indication of certain conditions in the instrument which sets up the scheme and forms the association (how the plans, programmes and projects will be determined; financing; contributions; position regarding markets; distribution of financial yield; arrangements for reinvestment).

Without prejudice to the common objective of the two or more bodies taking part, each of these retains its own purposes and logic. For a period of unforeseeable duration, co-production by public sectors will inevitably be the scene of competition and dispute. It may give rise to the pooling and mutual reinforcement of convergent powers, or to confrontation and tension between powers in opposition. On the other hand, accommodation between the various levels and classes of interests of the States, national economies and nations is emerging and gaining strength. Such an experiment should therefore have regard to the associates' own objectives and never contradict them. The structure and operation of the scheme, and the other similar movements which it causes or promotes, must be compatible with general development conditions in the participating countries.

One important problem immediately arises, namely the composition of units fit to undertake regional integration and development schemes, having the form of joint or multi-national enterprises, and enjoying – within limits specified in advance – some degree of organic and functional independence. Such units may be based on purely private or purely public participation and contribution, or on a combination of the two. Accordingly, various solutions are possible: private enterprises, bound by contract to public authorities; mixed enterprises, partly public and partly private, whether bound by contract to public authorities or not; intergovernmental enterprises, set up either by Latin American governments only or with the participation of some from outside the region. In the present paper the method of *multi-national corporations set up by Latin American countries* is proposed because it is regarded as the most appropriate and viable approach to co-operation for integration.[1]

## A Range of Possibilities

It should be pointed out first of all that a wide range of possibilities lies open in this respect. The governments participating in such an experiment of co-operation may wish to avoid financial, legal and administrative burdens and complications, and may therefore refrain from setting up a new and independent body. In that case, a previously existing international organisation could take on the new job, provide the requisite material facilities and administer the scheme or enterprise as a 'special programme' or under a 'special agreement'. It may also happen that the governments, without creating a new corporation, will appoint a national service to execute the project, acting as their agent and on account of them all ('agency agreement').

On the other hand, the governments may prefer to create a new organisation which will give their co-operation a permanent, independent frame. In that case the type and structure of the organisation will depend largely on the task or project to be undertaken. If the work is to consist solely in the elaboration of documents (surveys, reports, resolutions, proposals), the machinery required will be similar to that of an ordinary government department – a permanent secretariat and a council of representatives of the participating States. But a more complex and extensive operational organisation will be needed if the intention is to administer a big establishment or installations, requiring a wide range of activities (such as also arise in some countries in connection with the application of national law); that would involve a large budget, and multifarious relations with individuals, private undertakings and public bodies.

Organisations of this last kind have been increasing in number and size in recent years. They carry various titles – multi-national public corporation, international public establishment. Most are economic rather than political in scope, and may operate in such diverse fields as the creation, construction and/or administration and operation of infra-structures, production plant and the provision of public services –

---

[1] See Paul Reuter: *Organisations Européennes* (Presses Universitaires de France, Paris, 1965); Louis Cartou: *Organisations Européennes* (Dalloz, Paris, 1965); Claude-Albert Colliard: *Institutions Internationales* (Dalloz, Paris, 1966); Carlos Fliger: *Multinational Public Enterprises* (International Bank for Reconstruction and Development, June 1967 (multigraphed edition)); and 'Creación de Empresas Multinacionales', *INTAL*, Boletin de la Integración, August 1966.

transport by land, air, sea or river, roads, communications, other public services, industry (steel, petro-chemical, heavy machinery), fuel and energy, hydraulic works, education, scientific and technological research, health, increase and diversification of agricultural and mining production for the regional market, agrarian reform and land settlement. Those are examples only. As will have been seen, such work usually requires big human, material and financial resources, drawn from several nations, and extensive markets. It involves long-term plans, programmes and projects of a public character which need to be undertaken by a permanent multi-governmental organisation able to carry out substantive operations and having powers and means of direct action.[1]

Such agencies must have a territorial competence corresponding to the areas or activities covered and to the multi-national programmes and projects concerned. They must have organic and functional independence and combine possession of governmental powers with enjoyment of a high degree of freedom, flexibility, initiative, ability to take risks and to innovate; accordingly, anything that implies the rigidity, caution and routine characteristic of traditional public authorities will be unsuitable. Multi-national public enterprises must be secure from the influence of purely national political or private considerations and pressures. They must be enabled, further, to attract an elite for the senior posts and in general a capable, enterprising personnel, dedicated to the objectives and requirements of regional development and integration. Independence is also required so that a balance may be struck between the interests or objectives of the particular countries, and each is prevented from obtaining privileges at the expense of others.

Corporations of such a kind would find it easier to secure financial assistance from international organisations and agencies because they would combine the advantage of a guarantee by the participating States with those of coherent control by a single management and

[1] See Konstantin Katzarov: *Teoría de la Nacionalización (El Estado y la Propiedad)* (Institute of Comparative Law, Mexico City, 1963); William A. Robson: *L'Industria Nazionalizzata e la Proprietà Pubblica* (Edizioni di Comunità, Milán 1962); *Nationalization – A Book of Reading*, edited by A. H. Hanson, George Allen and Unwin Ltd., London, 1963; *Le Fonctionnement des Entreprises Nationaliséese n France – Travauxdu 3e Colloque des Facultés de Droit* (Dalloz, Paris, 1956); Pierre Bauchet: *Proprieté Publique et Planification (Entreprises Publiques Non-Financières)* (Editions Cujas, Paris, 1962); A. H. Hanson: *Public Enterprises and Economic Development* (Routledge and Kegan Paul Ltd., London, 1959); Ignacy Sachs: *Patterns of Public Sector in Underdeveloped Economies* (Asia Publishing House, New York, 1964); Marcos Kaplan: *Países en Desarrollo y Empresas Públicas* (Editorial Macchi, Buenos Aires, 1965).

simple procedures for administering the project or supervising the use of the loan.

*Structure Relevant to Origin and Purpose*

Multi-national public corporations are set up by treaty between two or more States – the partners in the joint undertaking (participation by independent public bodies in the respective countries may also be acceptable). Such a treaty requires a special international system to be established; this may reflect various situations and take various institutional and juridical forms. The treaty – or agreement or convention – is subscribed in accordance with the established procedures of the particular States – i.e. with or without authorisation by the legislature – and so becomes the 'constitution' of the multi-national public corporation. The form chosen will have regard to a number of material circumstances: whether the bulk of the work done by the corporation will be in a single country or in several; whether the danger that one country will control or excessively influence the corporation and its activities is great or small; etc. In general terms, it may be stated that the form chosen begins to take shape in the light of the 'constitution', the law which is to apply, the legal status and capacity of the corporation, and its nationality. Several variants, pure or mixed, are possible.

(1) The treaty may bind the signatory States only as regards the principle of engaging in the joint enterprise, which it will define by stating the objective, the area of operation and the participants' rights and obligations. Particulars regarding the establishment of the corporation, its structure and operation, the law which will apply to it, grant of legal personality and capacity, and nationality, may be set out in a protocol to the treaty itself or in subsequent conventions.

(2) Alternatively, the treaty may relate directly to the establishment of the corporation, specify what law is to apply to it, determine its legal personality and capacity, its nationality, structure and mode of operation. This variant divides, as regards the subjects mentioned, into several possibilities, which include the following:

(i) The type or class of corporation chosen may belong to the legal system of one of the participating States. The enterprise will then become a national corporation of that country, which provides it with a headquarters, gives it legal personality (fully recognised by the other associated States), applies to it the national laws covering other public corporations as regards its status and internal affairs.

(ii) The treaty itself may establish the corporation, provide that an international regime shall apply to it, and determine the type or class of regime. The 'constitution' itself, and not any national provisions, is then the applicable law. The treaty also gives the corporation international legal personality and capacity within the territory of the signatory States, and it has the nationality of all of them.

(iii) On each and every one of the above-mentioned points there may be various solutions and combinations. Some of the points may be settled in a separate instrument, a protocol or annex to the treaty. The 'constitution', whatever form it takes, may provide that modifications on certain matters can be introduced in the future without the need for ratification by the national parliaments. The legal personality and capacity of the corporation may become international, not by virtue of its constitution, but objectively (either for functional reasons, so that it may do its work, or because of the large number of member countries). Legal personality may be granted, not by the treaty or by only one of the participating States, but by each or several of them. The corporation may be governed by one national legal system with restrictions or modifications deriving from the treaty, or inversely the treaty or protocol may lay down special legal rules with subsidiary application of one national system.

Multi-national public corporations usually share many features with national public and private organisations. However, the fact of having been established by or in virtue of a treaty, with a consequent combination of national and international elements, modifies – in some cases and in some respects – the results which such features would have against a purely national background. In particular, the function assigned to the corporation determines the scope of its jurisdiction and the extent of the powers required to put this into effect.

I consider it advisable to adopt, with the necessary modifications, the prototype of public corporation which William A. Robson describes as 'the most important invention of this century in the field of public institutions[and] likely to play, in the nationalised industry of the twentieth century, a role as important as that of private enterprise in the capitalist organisation of the nineteenth'[1] The main characteristics of that prototype, adjusted to the particular regional conditions in which the corporations will have to operate, are as follows.

### Characteristics and Problems

1. The constituent treaty should provide for the establishment of the multi-national public corporation, determine its general character and objective, specify the law under which it is to act, and define its legal personality and capacity, and state its nationality. The treaty should also indicate, at least in general terms, the corporation's structure, functions and mode of operation, its rights and obligations (and those of the participating States), its property and privileges, its relations with the governments and with other public and private undertakings. Detailed regulation of matters directly linked with structure and operation may be handled in protocols and annexes to the original treaty, or in subsequent conventions or statutes. The treaty should specify who is to issue administrative and complementary rules and how this shall be done, making it clear that further diplomatic agreements at the same level are not required. It should also indicate the method by which any conflict between the 'constitution' and the national laws having subsidiary application is to be settled.

The provisions on the points mentioned above will relate mainly to the legal personality and capacity of the multi-national public corporation in the territory of the signatory States. Outside their territory, legal personality and capacity will be determined by the extent to which its character as an international corporate person is accepted elsewhere, and by the powers stemming from its original status. The corporation's international personality may not be recognised by countries outside the region, but in such countries the State, public enterprises and private undertakings may consent to the establishment of certain kinds of relations with it (purchase and sale, hire of services, hire of plant, loans). To the above must be added problems respecting the liability of the participating States for the acts by the multi-national corporation outside their territories and the corporation's right to diplomatic protection if required.

The position is complicated by the fact that neither the constituent instruments nor international public law at its present stage of develop-

[1] William Robson: *Nationalised Industry and Public Ownership* (London, Allen and Unwin, 1961).

ment can foresee all the contingencies, all the situations which may emerge from the activity of a multi-national corporation, nor are there any international courts having compulsory jurisdiction in such matters. The relations between multi-national corporations and countries not participating in them – as well as individual nationals of such countries – can only be governed by the principles and rules of international private law regarding conflicts between national provisions.

2. A multi-national public corporation has a public purpose. It is the common instrument of the participating national States and it is imported into the public sector of their economies. Consequently the corporation brings together and combines functions, activities and institutions which either already belonged to the public sector of the participating countries or are included in it for the particular experiment in integration. Such inclusion may be effected in various ways – expropriation, nationalisation with or without conversion into state property, confiscation (under the penal laws or by revolutionary act), or socialisation. Decisions regarding such inclusion and regarding assistance in setting up the corporation will be taken in accordance with the laws and procedures applying in each participating country.

3. The creation of a multi-national public corporation need not involve any big transfer of sovereignty; it will merely require the constitution of a joint authority and the adoption of a common policy for a given sector, programme or project. It is true that the multi-lateral corporation must be an independent unit, with legal personality and capacity, administrative autonomy, its own liability, the right to figure in lawsuits, and broad powers of decision regarding economic and financial management, accounts, property, acquisition and disposal of goods and services, personnel management and contracts in general. The objectives sought and the functions to be performed will help to determine what powers are needed and the scope with which they should be exercised. The corporation's powers and their scope may be stated in the provisions of the treaty, its annexes, etc., or regulations issued thereunder, or they may arise by inference from the said provisions or from the objectives and functions of the corporation. Furthermore, the signatory States may promise to take such action, regarding law, property, finance, fiscal and customs matters as will facilitate normal operation.

4. On the one hand, a multi-national public corporation is outwardly distinct from the States which set it up, having its own person-

ality and relative independence. On the other hand, it remains linked to the States which jointly own and use it, is subject to control by them and responsible to them. The link originates from the very fact that the participants created the corporation, adopted its constitution, formed its share capital; the control is exercised, accordingly, by amendment of the constitution and rules, vote in the general meeting of partners, appointment and removal of directors.

If there are several corporations with the same membership, control should be centralised in some kind of supra-national organ comprising representatives of the associated States.

Such supervision by the executive branch of government should relate to the most important matters of general policy or special significance, as precisely defined – over-all or in detail – by the treaty or applicable law. On the other hand, there should be no supervision or *a priori* restriction as regards the normal activities or current administration of the enterprise.

Apart from the supervision by the national executives, there may be others – parliamentary, judicial or financial, efficiency investigations, surveys by planning organs, etc. Some of the operational activities may also be subject to supervision by an external body, either already existing or established for the purpose, and comprising representatives of the associated States.

Of course, the supervisory organs and procedures must be precisely and efficiently regulated.

5. A multi-national public corporation should naturally have its own governing bodies and management. These may include: a general meeting of the partners (States or independent public bodies) or their equivalents; a supervisory board, as mentioned above; a president; a board of directors; and a general manager or executive director. The president and members of the board of directors should be appointed by the governments for a certain number of years. The general manager or executive director may be appointed in the same way, or by the general meeting or board of directors.

The powers and functions of the various organs, the relations between them and the participating States, and their mutual relations must be defined in the constitutional instruments, its annexes or regulations issued thereunder. The question is particularly important, as will be evident if one remembers that multinational corporations are on the one hand relatively independent of the national States, their provinces and local authorities, and on the other hand are imported into the public sectors of the countries where they operate: so they must keep up a close network of relations of various kinds, both with national public establishments and with political and administrative authorities in the associated countries.

In any case, it is indispensable for the governing bodies and general management to enjoy independence and be protected against political vicissitudes and private pressure groups; they must not be removable save in certain specified cases, and must have the right to defend themselves.

A multi-national public corporation should have considerable freedom to determine its own staff regulations, which will be different from those applying to national officials and employees. Members of its personnel are indeed not civil servants in the strict and traditional sense – neither the president, board of directors and principal officers, nor the junior supervisors and ordinary wage or salary earners. As a rule there should be no general code or prior decision by the governments, fixing conditions of recruitment, dismissal, pay, work and discipline. The corporation should have entire freedom in those matters.

Selection of the managerial and intermediate staff and of the rank-and-file should be directed towards securing skilled personnel, as dedicated as possible to the corporation's purposes of development, integration and public advantage. They should be recruited as a rule from among citizens of the participating countries, with some regard for distribution by nationality but not making this an absolute or exclusive criterion. The quality of personnel and the style of management may contribute as much as anything to the emergence and success of integrated development in Latin America.

6. The 'constitution' must specify the general lines along which the corporation is to operate. The corporation must be completely independent as regards the administration of its economic activities, finances and property. This raises a number of complex problems, not at all easy to solve.

First of all, it is indispensable for the original instruments to settle, at least in their essential terms, a number of important points: how plans, programmes and projects will be established; how the corporation is to be financed; how contributions, markets and profits will be distributed; and how investments will be made. A major inevitable difficulty arises out of the fact that a multi-national public corporation is usually set up by countries of unequal development and economic potential. The common enterprise will absorb resources provided by all the participating countries, but its operations may tend to favour one nation, region or branch more than others. The object must be to find methods of operation which will produce something like an equilibrium between sacrifice and benefit for each of the countries taking part.

The contributions of the participants may consist of the following: natural and material resources; land and buildings; infra-structure; labour; finance; science and technology; information; markets. As regards finance in particular, funds may come from sources within the multi-national corporation itself (through prices and charges for the goods produced or services provided) or from outside it (government contributions or loans; yield of taxes earmarked for the joint enterprise; loans and credits from other public corporations; issue of stocks to the public; recourse to the money market, bank credits; authority to contract debts by overdraft or in other ways; international institutions or foreign governments).

Distribution of the fruits of the joint enterprise is a problem which may arise at two stages. First, the corporation can be obliged to hand over all its profits to the participating States; or – once it has met its liabilities, including advances from the governments and other bodies, taxes, etc. – it may freely dispose of the profits under its own powers: by reinvestment, increases in remuneration or bonuses for the personnel. Second, the governments may decide on various methods of distributing the fruits; they may share out the profits, the markets, the goods produced and services rendered, or combine all three.

A multi-national public corporation must have its own property, but the extent and character of this may vary. According to a restrictive view, which I consider erroneous, any property in the possession of the corporation belongs, not to it as a separate legal person, but to the participating States in proportion to their respective contributions; they are the real owners; the corporation merely has the usufruct of the property in its possession, including the right to use this, for purposes of business; it possesses working funds with which to carry out certain tasks and discharge certain obligations; the States authorise disposal of the property, determine the conditions for its employment and set limits thereto; they may even deprive the corporation of all or part of the property at any time, or increase it without any real influence over these matters on the corporation's part. I consider, on the contrary, having regard to the objects of a multi-national public corporation and the way in which it acts, that such a corporation should own property and have the fullest right to dispose freely of it within the general limits defined by its rules.

The corporation's finances should be independent, its income being separate from the ordinary budgets and its profits not as a rule going to the national treasuries. Because of its public purpose, although such a corporation is set up to engage in industry or commerce or provide a service and to be financially self-sufficient, it should not operate merely with a view to obtaining profits like any private undertaking, but should act as the custodian of the general interests of the participating countries and the region. However, it should seek to produce an income equal or superior to its expenditure; if a surplus arises, this should be reinvested, paid into reserve, or used to reduce prices, increase efficiency or improve remuneration and conditions of work. The corporation should administer its own reserve fund, with due regard for any general instructions which the governments or the joint supervisory organ may issue to that effect. In any case, self-financing should be the rule – i.e. the corporation should handle its current expenses and investments from its own income. As already stated, it may have recourse to credits or subsidies from governments or international bodies, and to public loans. If it issues stocks on the ordinary capital market, the holders will have no vote or say in its affairs. In general, the search for a balance between the social, economic and political objects of a multi-national public corporation on the one hand and considerations of profit and financial self-sufficiency on the other, as well as the choice between aiming at a profit, a loss or a balanced budget, are among the main questions regarding the structure and operation of undertakings of this kind.

7. Lastly, various special problems arise which deserve mention, although strictly speaking they lie somewhat outside the limits of the present paper.

(i) A multi-national public corporation can and should have privileges and immunities commensurate with its objectives, operational requirements and the degree of independence given to it, and intended also to secure an equilibrium between the various participating countries and national interests involved. The privileges and immunities may relate to the following: fiscal status (partial or total exemption from taxes); exemption from customs duty or other restrictions on traffic between participating countries in raw materials, capital goods and equipment for the corporation's establishments and activities, on goods produced or handled and the services provided by it; removal of restrictions on purchase, possession and use of foreign exchange and the transfer of funds; protection of the corporation's property (particularly safeguards against requisition, expropriation and confiscation); liability towards the States, other public bodies and individuals within and without its own territorial limits.

(ii) Subjection to or exemption from provisions regulating free competition or preventing or checking monopolies.

(iii) Jurisdiction and procedures for interpretation of agreements and settlement of disputes between the participating States, between the States and the corporation, between it and public and private undertakings, or involving governments and nationals of States not taking part in it. The organs in question may be: a board of conciliation; an independent standing court of arbitration, either previously existing or established for the purpose; an ad hoc arbitration procedure; an emergency umpire with powers of decision.

(iv) Entry into force of the constitution; termination of the scheme and winding up the corporation.

(v) Multi-national public corporations may have various purposes and operate at various levels. One may be conceived and set in motion as a *general development corporation*, in which case its most important functions will be: to study the national economies of the participating countries or of the particular region in which it is to work; co-ordinate development efforts and give them a coherent pattern; raise and mobilise capital to finance plans, programmes and projects, and carry them out directly or by establishing secondary public undertakings; participate in mixed companies; promote private undertakings, making contributions of various kinds (capital, credit, technical and administrative assistance); buy and sell materials and equipment for production or services. Another may be a *promotion and finance corporation* for a particular branch of industry or agriculture or a particular service. Others may organise and implement programmes for the *integral development of river basins*. Classified from a different standpoint, multi-national public corporations may operate throughout the territory of the countries participating

218

in a particular experiment at integration (as for instance the Andean Corporation set up by the Bogota Agreement) or only in respect of certain branches or regions.

Last of all, it should be pointed out that pure theory and formal legislation regarding this type of organisation may be misapplied in practice, in either of two opposite directions: on the one hand, bureaucratic over-centralisation, due to excessive interference by the participating governments or to conflict between them and rivalry for the control of the corporation; on the other hand, excessive independence, causing dispersal of effort, irresponsibility and disorder. Experience in many countries has shown that it is difficult to put the letter and spirit of the law into real effect, and also to follow a satis-factory middle course between autonomy and control, initiative and uniformity. However, difficult does not mean impossible.

## III. SUMMARY, CONCLUSIONS, PROSPECTS

The multi-national public corporation is proposed as an agent or instrument for the combined process of integration and development – as an instrument by which that process can be promoted and strengthened. Whether such a corporation will be really able to perform its function, and how efficiently it can do so, depend in turn on what is happening to integration and development themselves. The interaction is easy to understand. Although the corporations can help towards integration and development, it is also true that the Latin American countries and their public sectors suffer from a series of defects and limitations. This fact, together with the resistance put up by traditional forces and structures, may hamper the emergence or the effective action of multi-lateral public corporations, or convert them into mere fashionable gadgets surrounded by a reality which they cannot change and which neutralises or defeats them. The present and immediate future will have been a time of alternatives and options of choice between possible models and patterns. At the risk of over-simplification, and in order not to exceed the limits of the present discussion, suffice it to say that two basic possibilities are open.[1]

---

[1] Within the abundant literature on patterns of development and integration, reference may be made to *Obstacles to Change in Latin America*, edited by Claudio Véliz (London–New York–Toronto, Oxford University Press, 1965); *The Politics of Conformity in Latin America*, edited by Claudio Véliz (Oxford University Press, 1967); *Latin America, Reform*

*Existing Model*

On the one hand, the Latin American process may continue for a period of unforseeable duration, along the lines followed in recent decades. In other words, let us assume the continuance and the unrestricted operation of private property, enterprise and profit, the free play of market forces and an unchanged external situation. In that case, a particular kind of development and integration, having some very special features, may continue and have some effect. It will occur in the interest, on the initiative and under the control of the great international corporations with North American capital and of the Government of the United States. It will be carried out according to a new pattern of international division of labour, now being elaborated in and for the metropolis, which will confer privileges on some social classes, industries and regions of the Latin American countries to the detriment of the rest. The dominance of the United States concerns and government will be intensified, and extended over the key sectors and main sources of economic strength, over the most important machinery for production, sales and finance, over peoples and markets, over the selection, development and use of scientific and technical advance. Since a process of that kind and its direct or indirect consequences involve rejecting or suspending any profound social change, it will generate a wide range of tension and conflict. Consequently, United States dominance will have to be exercised through absolute control of the political and military apparatus; totalitarian repression will become the almost exclusive pattern of social organisation and equilibrium. Centres of decision will be increasingly transferred to the metropolis. Latin America will be obliged to form part – much more so than hitherto – of an inter-American satellite system. What are now the states of the region will lose not only the remainders of real autonomy which they enjoy at present, but also

*or Revolution – A Reader*, edited by James Petras and Maurice Zeitlin (Fawcett Publications Inc., Greenwich, 1968).

See also the vast bibliography on Latin American integration, e.g., *Integración de América Latina – Experiencias y perspectivas*, edited by Miguel S. Wionczek (Fondo de Cultura Económica (F.C.E.), Buenos Aires – Mexico City, 1964); *Hacia la Integración Acelerada de América Latina* (F.C.E., 1965); *Factores para la Integración Latino-americana*, edited by the Inter-American Development Bank (F.C.E., 1966); Institute for Latin American Integration; *La Integración Latino-americana – Situación y Perspectivas* (Buenos Aires, 1965); Sidney Dell: *Experiencias de la Integración Económica en América Latina* (C.E.M.L.A., Mexico City, 1966); Inter-American Planning Association: *Hacia una Política de Integración para el Desarrollo de la América Latina* (San Juan, Puerto Rico, 1967).

the minimum prerequisites for national viability – even if they retain some external vestiges of purely formal independence. The result – as Antonia García has said – will be integration from without and from above, development in dependence and distortion, the source of manifold stresses and inbalance between countries, regions, industries and classes.

*An Alternative Model*

The other, the opposite alternative, stems from the premise that integration is inevitable and irreversible anyway, and must not be shaped and dominated from outside the region. Acceptance of that premise requires the elaboration of a strategy, the imposition of a pattern, which reflect the view that development and integration have to be general, unified and indigenous. In other words, they must be applied at all levels (economic, social, political, cultural, ideological); they must interact as the linked halves of a single process; they must be operated from within and from below. Profound internal structural change and regional integration must be mutually assumed at the outset and combined in practice so that each may reinforce the other. More specifically, the following tasks must be undertaken in a realistic spirit and carried out with precision:

1. to adopt a set of values which may serve as basis and criterion for choice between the various alternatives, for selection of targets and priorities, for rejection of the model followed hitherto, for creation and adoption of the new pattern;
2. to elaborate and disseminate an ideology capable of providing the intellectual frame, the guidelines, the stimulus which may mobilise dynamic and progressive groups and the mass of the people, shake up political parties and transform institutions;
3. to decide what are (actually and potentially) the interests and forces behind the desired integration and development, who are its advocates and agents, what are their relative strengths, their possible articulations and alliances, and which of them will take the lead; to decide also which are the enemies, and how they can be neutralised or defeated;
4. to determine the objectives, conditions, methods and instruments of development and integration; the successive stages, the requirements and results, the concomitant and consequential social changes; the types of economy, of society, of political regime, of institutions

and of culture, the place in the international system, that are sought or expected as part of the double process.

The development and integration of Latin America *from within* and *from below* must start with analysis and diagnosis, made in a critical and inventive spirit, of the problems ahead. Solutions fitting the particular background and real conditions of the countries of the region must then be worked out and put into effect – on original lines, without imitating foreign patterns. All this implies a plan, and therefore a strategy embodying a reasonably coherent set of decisions an certain related economic social, political, ideological and cultural questions.

Latin America needs a united policy which will ensure the following: a big step forward in development, taken soon; structural changes and greater productivity in agriculture and mining and at the same time an industrialisation going beyond the mere replacement of imports; progressive redistribution of income; national economic independence, not precluding regional integration but making it possible; priority for national finance, a subsidiary and strictly controlled function being performed by foreign capital and assistance; better balance between the various parts of the region. Economic development must be accompanied by substantial changes in the social structure, more equality and justice in social and economic matters, an equitable sharing of effort, sacrifice and profit; changes in the present status and power relationships between classes and groups; shaking up the apathy and indifference of the masses, gaining support and direct and active participation on their part; establishment of full democracy in economic affairs, society, the State and education. The prevailing uncertain and erratic economic growth under more or less liberal regimes must be replaced by total development at all levels, induced by the State and other organisations, acting as authentic representatives of the majority of the people, by means of an increasingly imperative plan: for the Latin American States may be powerful agents of development and integration if their social and political make-up and their administrative structure are profoundly modified. The object and justification of the above strategy amount, in effect, to the creation of economic, social, political and cultural structures which can meet as fully as possible the mounting needs of the people and enable individuals to develop their technical skills and personalities.

Success in reaching the above objectives will help to provide the conditions and meet the requirements for integration itself. The requirements include:

1. increasing control of the machinery of power and decision by dynamic reforming groups which do not fear or resist integration but need it and promote it;
2. a steadily increasing degree of internal organisation and more or less general agreement in favour of development and integration, so as to provide a basis for action to that effect by representative, solid, efficient States;
3. mutual adjustment of internal and regional structures and machinery; viable, effective national policies and planning; greater co-ordination with regional plans and policies provided the latter are compatible with the former;
4. more or less gradual creation of supra-national or common authorities with power to make political decisions, to plan and to take diplomatic action;
5. severance of the present dependent relationship between the United States and the Latin American bloc which it dominates; recovery of political and diplomatic freedom; elaboration and effectuation of a Latin American foreign policy which will permit joint negotiation with the great powers and other international blocs.

In still more general terms, the pattern sketched above requires conditions of three kinds to be fulfilled:

(a) an active alliance between the more or less dynamic and progressive classes and groups – the industrial proletariat, the working masses of the towns and countryside, intellectuals, professional men and women, technicians, small and medium domestic entrepreneurs; and the gradual assumption of leadership over that alliance by the sectors most thoroughly predisposed in favour of continuous and profound reform;
(b) the emergence and self-assertion of a vanguard of political and administrative elite with ideological and political lucidity and a clear view of objectives, priorities and means dedicated to the interests of society, the nations and the region, unshakably determined to carry out the above task; and at the same time conscious of the danger of themselves becoming a privileged class, losing touch with the people and promoting a bureaucratic state capitalism which would falsify their objectives and prevent success;

(c) a high degree of awareness, interest and direct active participation by a great body of the population in the search for change, in its achievement and in the reorganisation and conduct of the State.

The alternative pattern which is no more than roughly sketched in the preceding pages can be tried and may be translated into reality if the men and women who promote and direct it understand that development and integration mean rapid, profound, disruptive change in all fields and at all the levels of national society and of the region as a whole – change which must be a continuous process for a period of unforeseeable duration and can hardly fail to involve conflicts between powers and forces both inside and outside Latin America, unrest, social and political convulsion and violence. Moreover, in theory and logic, the pattern seems likely to clash for a time with the framework of a mixed economy. Its own character and inherent dynamic, in the conditions and perspectives I have mentioned, tend to bring it into contradiction with the system of private property, enterprise and profit, and to place society before the fundamental double dilemma of capitalism or socialism, reform or revolution.

Neither of the two models or patterns outlined here is assured of success or permanence. In the Latin America of today, as at all times and places, history has no predetermined or inevitable outcome. The course it follows and the choices it appears to make are results of the actions of living individuals and groups, the relations between them, the interaction of conditioned forces, conscious volition and chance. Confrontation of the two patterns and a decisive choice between them are a basic element in the profound crisis which Latin America is experiencing and a necessary subject for the collective examination and action which will be increasingly expected of its men and women in the present and immediate future.

# EAST-WEST ECONOMIC CO-OPERATION
# AND INDUSTRIAL RELATIONS

ALREADY facilitated by the political détente, the possibilities of economic co-operation between East and West have been tremendously enhanced and fundamentally modified by the results of economic reforms, which have given the management of individual enterprises in Eastern European countries the possibility of direct contact with Western enterprises. In this way, the stage has been set for future increased utilisation of the potentialities of East-West trade and several types of economic co-operation at the enterprise level involving Western multi-national corporations.

Eastern European countries' main motivation for exploring these possibilities is firstly the recognition that maintaining the high rates of economic growth obtained in earlier years with a system of central administration and directives is at the present stage of sophistication of the economy feasible only with enhanced decision-making power at the enterprise level. Secondly, it is recognised that growth can be facilitated by the productivity effect resulting from co-operation with multi-national corporations which have modern technological, managerial and marketing know-how. Western multi-national corporations on the other hand, are primarily interested in the exploration of the fast-growing Eastern European markets, the main basis of which is consumer demand. However, other driving forces, such as prestige, the challenge of production and marketing organised on a global scale, might also play a role. But there are indications that increasingly the productivity effects may go in both directions and also that interest in foreign markets is felt by both sides.

As Norman Scott puts it in the second of the two chapters of this section, the new type of East-West co-operation at the enterprise level appears to be 'an ingenious means of imparting to East-West economic relations sone of the elements of contemporary industrial progress without infringing the ground-rules of economic management proper to each system'.

What are the prospects of industrial relations becoming modified in the process of growing East-West enterprise relations? Zdeněk

Mošna, who relates in Chapter 10 the nature of economic reforms and corollary internal transformations of labour relations in socialist countries, does not believe in any such changes in national patterns of industrial relations at present; but he does not exclude that with an increasing free movement of labour and capital, both inside COMECON countries and on an East-West scale, transnational features of industrial relations might emerge. Scrutinising somewhat more closely such possibilities, Norman Scott perceives of wage movement in enterprises co-operating with Western multi-national corporations as possible levers by which transnational influences on industrial relations might come to bear. Relative income and productivity advances in such enterprises over others not participating in East-West co-operation could permit wage rate adjustments with implications for the national systems of wage structures and industrial relations.

Admittedly, available evidence does not allow us at the moment to predict with certainty any specific change of industrial relations in a transnational direction. However, its potentialities being recognised, the field is worth further observation and study.

Chapter 10

# ECONOMIC REFORMS AND LABOUR RELATIONS IN THE SOCIALIST COUNTRIES OF EASTERN EUROPE

*by*

*Zdeněk Mošna*

## I. NATURE AND CHARACTERISTICS OF THE ECONOMIC REFORMS

THE socialist countries of Eastern Europe are making substantial changes in the management of their national economies. These changes are usually called 'economic reforms' or 'new economic systems'.[1] They are also accompanied by changes aiming at a better functioning of the socialist society as a whole, thus contributing to further promotion of democracy in all areas of social life.

What is the basic content of the economic reforms which are being carried out in the socialist countries of Eastern Europe? It is a gradual transition from a directive model of management, based on the use of administrative managerial methods, to an economic model of management, which is based on the use of economic managerial instruments.

For many years the application of the directive system of management (under which all fundamental economic activities are predetermined by central bodies and imposed on individual enterprises in the form of a detailed planned targets) was associated with successful economic development.[2]

[1] The principles of the new economic system in the German Democratic Republic were adopted in 1963. Those of the Czechoslovak new system of planned management were adopted at the beginning of 1965, and, in the same year, basic ideas concerning changes in the existing models of management were introduced in Poland, the U.S.S.R., Bulgaria and Hungary. At the beginning of 1967 Rumania also declared its intention of introducing a new economic model.

[2] Let me give only some examples to illustrate the fast industrial development of the socialist countries of Eastern Europe after the Second World War.

From 1958 to 1965 the industrial production of the U.S.S.R. increased by 84 per cent. Also, during 1965 the Soviet industry was producing 5 times more steel, 5·5 times more

However, the rapid progress in bringing about complicated transformations of the productive and social structures in the socialist countries of Eastern Europe was not achieved without overcoming difficulties and obstacles.

Serious economic difficulties began to emerge at a certain stage of economic development in almost all the socialist countries of Eastern Europe. The rate of growth of national income slowed down. And in Czechoslovakia stagnation actually set in and something happened which had never before occurred in any socialist country: in 1963 the absolute volume of national income dropped below that of the previous year.

The negative trend which emerged after so many years of successful economic development began to be analysed critically and this gave a strong impetus to thorough and open discussions on the operation of the existing model of management. These discussions, encouraged by the highest organs of the respective Communist Parties, led to the conclusion that the directive model of managing the socialist economy ceased to be effective once there was a change in the conditions which had brought it about. With the growth of the economic potential of the socialist countries of Eastern Europe and the increasing satisfaction of demand, some of the negative features of the directive model started to come more and more to the fore. Production processes proved to be insufficiently elastic to satisfy growing social and individual needs, because production reacted only with difficulty and often very late to changes in the pattern of demand. It was proved that the directive system of management did not provide sufficient scope for raising

rolling stock, almost 8 times more oil, practically 13 times more cement, 4·2 times more motor vehicles, over 11 times more tractors and 10·5 times more electric power than in 1940.

The post-war industrial output of Poland increased twice as fast as that of England and France; and in 1965 it showed a 50 per cent increase over 1960. In 1963 the industrial output of the German Democratic Republic amounted to almost 90 per cent of the pre-war industrial output of Germany as a whole. Bulgaria, a backward agricultural country twenty years ago, has been converted into a country where now 51 per cent of the national income is created by industrial production. This transformation is also true of Hungary, where now 62 per cent of the national income is contributed by industry. The process of industrialisation in Rumania can be expressed by figures showing a continuous flow of the agricultural population to industry: in 1945 almost 80 per cent of the total active population was employed in agricultural production, whereas in 1964 this proportion had fallen to only 52 per cent.

Czechoslovakia was before the Second World War one of the most industrially developed countries in the world. Since 1948 its national income has increased by 265 per cent and its industrial output has risen by more than four times. In 1968 the share in national income of industrial output (including the building industry) accounted for 78 per cent; and Czechoslovak industrial output represented 2 per cent of world industrial output.

the efficiency of production and that it obstructed a consistent application of the principle of economic rationality.

By limiting to a substantial extent the economic functions of markets, the directive model of management deprived itself of important criteria for measuring the economic results of individual enterprises; and it did not provide strong material incentives for continuous technological and organisational innovations in the production processes because enterprises were not financially encouraged to introduce such innovations.

The most important features of the economic reforms which are being put into effect in the socialist countries of Eastern Europe are:

- to stress the significance of central long-term economic plans and to make their preparation more scientific;
- to gear the function of central planning to market relations and categories;
- to increase the autonomy of enterprises or groups of enterprises by enabling them to create and accumulate their own financial resources and funds;
- to strengthen the material incentives of both enterprises and individual workers;
- to introduce a more flexible system of prices capable of reacting to changes in the supply-demand relationship;
- to reduce to a substantial degree the number of centrally fixed directives and to replace them by indirect tools of economic management; and
- to increase the significance both of professional and participative management.

In this connection two principal elements are involved: first, the new role of central management and of the national economic plan; and, secondly, the use of economic instruments of management resulting from the growing role in economic life of the socialist market.

The key functions of central management in the economic management system of a socialist economy can be summed up as follows:

1. to elaborate long-term (prospective) concepts of economic development based strictly on a scientific assessment of future development trends in both internal and world markets;
2. to furnish to lower management levels, and in the first place,

to individual enterprises, a comprehensive range of information on development trends in national and international markets as well as all those relevant data which otherwise lower management levels find it difficult to obtain;

3. to provide a comprehensive set of economic tools and rules promoting the long-term interest of enterprises in their optimum development and exerting effective economic pressure for rational decision-making at the enterprise level;

4. to regulate directly through mandatory assignments some long-term and socially significant economic processes – by using, for example, the most important capital investments with a view to bringing about structural changes in the national economy.

The basic instrument of central management is the long-term national economic plan, which outlines fundamental objectives of the whole national economy as well as the principal guidelines for achieving them.

A growing use of economic instruments is becoming characteristic of socialist management of the economy. By using economic instruments central management authorities influence the decision-making process of enterprises in a way that is advantageous for both the enterprise and the national economy as a whole. At the same time economic instruments of management exercise sound economic pressure on enterprises and encourage them to use productive factors more rationally.

Economic instruments of management, i.e. prices, taxes, wages, credits, interest rates, etc., will go on gaining in importance and gradually replace centrally fixed directives.

All the economic reforms which are being carried out in the socialist countries of Eastern Europe attach great significance to the long-term national economic plan. This is why all of them place emphasis on drawing up prospective plans (for 15–20 years) based on a full understanding of future economic and technological world trends. These long-term forecasts are then detailed in five-year and annual plans.

With the help of economic instruments central management authorities guide individual enterprises or groups of enterprises towards the achievement of these objectives outlined in the long-term economic plan. However, where necessary they do so through directly fixed (mandatory) targets as well.

One of the characteristic features of all the economic reforms is a substantial reduction in the number of centrally fixed targets. This may be illustrated by the following examples.

The new system of economic planning in the Soviet Union decreased the number of centrally fixed indicators from some 20 to 30 to only eight.

In Poland, the mandatory character of central planning is now expressed in the form of limits which relate to three main areas:

(a) the number of employees and the wage fund;
(b) investments; and
(c) foreign trade relations.

In the German Democratic Republic the centrally fixed targets cover:

(a) production assignments for the most important items;
(b) the wage fund, the number of employees and the increase in the productivity of labour;
(c) limits for materials and technical supplies;
(d) profits and the decrease in production costs; and
(e) the volume of investments.

In Czechoslovakia, centrally fixed targets now relate only to the following areas:

(a) production assignments for the most important commodities (52 items in 1965 against 1,300 in 1964) which safeguard the satisfaction of basic social needs;
(b) decisive capital formation; and
(c) the total volume of exports and the volume of individual export deliveries resulting from inter-state contracts.

Under their new system of management, Bulgaria and Hungary have also reduced sharply the number of centrally fixed targets.

In the countries where the economic model of management is applied in a more advanced way, so-called transfers from the financial incomes of enterprises to the state budget are effected. This is the case, for example, with the Czechoslovak model of management, which imposes on enterprises the duty to transfer to the State a share of their gross income or profits.

The enterprise is considered to be a relatively independent economic unit which derives all its revenue from sales and places a certain share at the disposal of the State. The latter uses the financial resources thus obtained for financing the basic needs of society as a whole.

In those countries where the State still retains its function of financing basic needs of the enterprise (e.g. capital investment, wages, etc.) there are no taxes on the financial income of the enterprise, which transfers to the State all its revenues. Under the changes introduced by the economic reforms in such countries, the State does not withdraw all the financial income of an enterprise but places part of it at the disposal of the enterprise.

Charges on productive fixed assets (capital charges) have also been introduced in all the socialist countries of Eastern Europe. The basic objective of these capital charges is to encourage a more economical utilisation of fixed assets such as machinery, equipment, buildings, vehicles, etc.

There have been substantial changes in the price system of the socialist countries of Eastern Europe. In some countries, various categories of prices are being used. In Bulgaria and Hungary there are fixed, limited and free prices; and in Czechoslovakia there are mandatory (fixed), regulated and free prices.

The economic role of credits and of interest rates is growing with the introduction of new management conditions. Outright investment grants from the State budget are being gradually abandoned in all the countries. Every enterprise can now finance its investment needs either from its own financial resources or with credits from the banking system. The purpose of this measure is to raise the effectiveness of capital investment.

Substantial changes are being introduced in the principles underlying remuneration policy. All the socialist countries of Eastern Europe have now adopted the principle that the level of wages and salaries of individual employees has to depend partially on the economic results of their respective enterprise.

## II. ECONOMIC REFORMS, PARTICIPATIVE MANAGEMENT AND TRADE UNIONS

The first socialist country to introduce quite a new pattern of participative management was Yugoslavia, which developed a system of self-administration in order to eliminate bureaucratic tendencies in the State apparatus. The system of self-administration serves as the basis for Yugoslav management both in the economic sphere (in the form of workers' councils) and in the over-all social sphere.

The managing director of an enterprise is responsible for all fundamental management questions to the workers' council which is elected by all the employees of the enterprise. A managing director has, of course, full authority as regards all the technological aspects of production.

In Yugoslavia the one-man executive pattern has thus been replaced completely by a collective pattern of management.

Similar forms of management are partially applied in Hungary and in Poland. In Hungary works councils were established in 1957. They were given the right to take decisions binding upon the director of enterprises in relation to certain questions. The works councils have been operating under the leadership of the trade union organisations, which are now expected to replace them.

Polish workers' councils, which were introduced in 1956 with extensive rights, have gradually been transformed into entities which no longer manage the enterprise but which now represent the interests of trade union bodies.

In Rumania and Bulgaria, there is a strong tendency to set up in individual enterprises collective organs of administration which, for instance, would have an influence on the appointment of top managers selected on the basis of competition.

In Rumania managing committees have been established in all State enterprises. The managing committee is headed by a managing director; 70 per cent of its members are managers and 30 per cent are representatives of trade unions and employees. The managing committees decide all fundamental questions concerning the development of enterprises.

Trade union organisations act only as advisory bodies to management as regards most managerial questions. There are, however, some areas of enterprise activities, mainly social questions, where they often have powers of decision.

With the introduction in Czechoslovakia of economic reform and under the impact of changes in the social system as a whole, a new role began to emerge for the trade unions.

The Czechoslovak trade union movement, which is a unified voluntary and independent organisation of both manual and professional workers, has the responsibility for defending and advancing the social and human rights of its members.

The new role of the Czechoslovak trade unions is reflected mainly in the independent policy position which they take up in relation to the State and to all the social organisations.

Trade unions implement their active and independent policy within the framework of the National Front, where they strive to subject to sound criticism all the proposals presented by the State or social organisations concerning social and human rights of workers. Having their own programme, the trade unions act as a partner of the State and of the economic organs; and they put forward their own proposals for achieving a higher standard of living for the population.

Trade unions play an active part mainly in relation to the following economic and social matters:

- development of wages and salaries;
- protection of consumers in the context of the State's prices policy;
- cultural and vocational progress of employed persons;
- occupational safety and health;
- social insurance, including maternity leave, health and old age insurance, etc.

At the enterprise level, trade union organisations act as representatives of groups of employees in relation to the management of the enterprise.

There are some questions which the trade union organisation has the right by law to co-decide with management; and in this context the trade union organisation has the right to suspend the implementation of decisions made by the management.

Under the new system of management the application of this principle is clearly apparent as regards the creation of resources for running the undertaking and the manner of using them (after the mandatory transfer to the state budget). The trade union body co-decides, for instance, what kind of material incentive is to be introduced in order to increase the material interests of workers in production; it also co-decides all measures relating to remuneration, including the amounts to be paid into the fund for cultural and social needs and into the wage fund. The trade unions, moreover, have the power of co-decision regarding the use of these funds. In addition, economic management bodies cannot take a decision as regards questions of labour legislation (working hours, number of employees, their composition, etc.) unless and until they have obtained the agreement of the trade unions.

Trade union bodies and management conclude collective agreements in order to safeguard the development of the economic organisation; improve the working, health, cultural and social conditions of the workers; and ensure co-operation at the shop, department, plant and undertaking levels. Collective agreements can also be concluded between higher-level trade union bodies and higher-level bodies of the economic administration; and this means that the influence of the trade union organisations is safeguarded at all levels of management. Failure by management to meet its obligations under a collective agreement is considered a breach of the labour contract and may result in disciplinary action against the offender. On the other hand non-fulfilment of obligations by a trade union organisation always implies a moral-political responsibility.

## III. INTERNATIONAL ECONOMIC OPERATIONS AND COLLECTIVE BARGAINING

One of the main objectives of the economic reforms is to establish closer links between producers and both the domestic and foreign markets.

Under the directive system of management, producers were kept completely apart from foreign markets. Trade and all foreign contacts were the exclusive competence of foreign trade corporations. These monopoly corporations purchased goods from home producers at fixed prices (domestic wholesale prices) which had no relationship to the prices they would obtain abroad. The difference between wholesale prices and actual prices on foreign markets were compensated by the trade organisation and, in the final analysis, by the state budget.

This practice led to big differentials between domestic and foreign prices and created a permanent danger that the structure of production (the range of goods, quality and technical level) would diverge from market requirements.

Home producers, who were economically insulated from foreign markets, were not interested in winning contracts on them through high quality and low production costs. At the same time, the monopoly trade corporations had to face alone competition on world markets; consequently they ran into many difficulties.

The new system of management does not imply the elimination of the foreign-trade state monopoly, which plays a useful part as a 'shock-absorber' and which protects the domestic economy against price flunctuations on world markets; but it provides scope for linking economic production interests with foreign trade. Foreign trade has to be organised so as to expose the economy to the impact of trends on world markets resulting from technological advances and rising productivity. The foreign trade corporations will make progressive adjustments in the purchasing prices of home products after assessing prices fetched abroad; and the same principle will apply for imports. Ultimately, the home producers will be able to sell their export goods at price levels more or less matching foreign prices.

With the introduction of economic changes far-reaching organisational measures were also taken. These include the representation of industrial plants in the directorates of foreign trade corporations; the grouping of foreign trade corporations and industrial enterprises; and direct contacts between domestic producers and foreign clients.

The economic reforms, in helping to develop market relationships in the national economies of individual socialist countries of Eastern Europe, are at the same time creating favourable conditions for promoting real and economically motivated processes of integration within the framework of the Council for Mutual Economic Assistance (COMECON). However, these processes have not yet reached a stage of development which would lead to the creation of multinational economic units; and problems of international collective bargaining have not yet come to the fore in the field of economic co-operation among Eastern European countries. This is mainly a result of the fact that in these countries an international labour and capital market has not yet emerged.

There can be no doubt that the economic reforms analysed above will promote East-West trade. They have introduced a system of management which should be able to satisfy in a more flexible way the growing and changing social and individual needs; and this calls for a systematic development of East-West trade.

The necessary structural changes in the national economies of the Eastern European countries and the desire of these countries to satisfy some of the so far deferred needs of the population create a basis for growing East-West trade. In some socialist countries, like Hungary or Czechoslovakia, the promotion of East-West trade is also regarded as a factor helping to create more competitive conditions for domestic producers.

On the other hand, highly competitive conditions in world markets tend to induce Western companies to switch their goods and capital to Eastern European markets.

The mutual interest in expanding trade relations can be met in different ways. There is emerging scope not only for a simple exchange of goods but also for some more complex types of economic co-operation, such as joint ventures in which Eastern and Western enterprises combine their respective skills and resources to serve both Eastern and Western markets. Such joint ventures usually combine supply and licensing with co-production and sales agency arrangements.

There are already some examples of this kind of venture:

- Poland manufactures diesel motors under a licence from the British Leyland Motor Company. These motors are jointly sold in third countries.
- A Swedish furniture chain supplies machinery and designs to Poland for the manufacture of unfinished furniture which is shipped to Sweden for finishing and resale.
- Bulgarian grinding equipment is shipped to Italy for finishing and assembly; and then sold through a Swiss-registered trading company owned jointly by the co-operating entities.
- A Hungarian and a Federal German firm combine their respective generators and steam engines to make steam generators for their own markets.

These ventures are only initial examples of the possibilities of co-operation. In the future, even more extensive co-operative arrangements can be expected; but there are as yet no indications that growing East-West trade and co-operation – whatever form they take – bring about any change in national patterns of collective bargaining. However, the growing international division of labour, based on a rapid introduction of scientific and technological innovations into the production process, coupled with the free movement of labour and capital, tend to link all countries more closely together, and an emergence of international bargaining can thus not be excluded.

Chapter 11

# SOME POSSIBLE IMPLICATIONS OF EAST-WEST ENTERPRISE-TO-ENTERPRISE AGREEMENTS

*by*
*Norman Scott*

## I. INTRODUCTION

THE Pythagorean cosmos was threefold, as is, from a speculative point of view, the contemporary world economy – East, West and South pursuing sometimes parallel, frequently divergent, paths of development. The most powerful integrative force, whether of systems of ideas or of institutions, tends to be the advance of compatible knowledge. In contemporary international economic relations the compatibility of scientific and technical progress in the Eastern and Western systems is leading to the multiplication of new forms of productive and trading links. These new forms – which go under the name of 'scientific, technological and industrial co-operation' – owe their origin to the fact that modern techniques of industrial production have tended to impose similar patterns of industrial organisation on enterprises *within* each set of countries. In the Western developed economies, the tendency has been for big enterprises to grow still bigger by means of mergers, fusions, etc., so that the *share* of total manufacturing output provided by, say, the hundred largest enterprises has roughly doubled in recent years. The striking growth of the multinational companies has been due to the internationalisation of this process, as enterprises have sought to protect themselves from the competitive pressures, and to seize the competitive opportunities, generated by the creation of larger, sometimes regionally integrated, markets. Similar forces have been at work in the socialist countries. There, industrial concentration and intra-COMECON industrial co-operation have taken place by administrative decree, not by market mechanisms,[1] but the end result is very similar. To echo Voltaire,

[1] The creation of government-sponsored bodies to promote industrial reorganisation and rationalisation in Britain, Italy and France serves as a reminder that the process is not entirely spontaneous in the 'market' economies.

if channels of communication and interlinkage between similar technical and industrial trends in the two areas did not exist, it would be necessary to invent them. East-West industrial co-operation does seem to have been invented as a means of modernising economic relations between the two groups. Some of the possible implications for industrial relations of the further development of such industrial co-operation are examined in this paper.[1]

At the outset, it should be emphasised that the central issue is not directly related to the celebrated, and unproven, theory of 'convergence' of the Eastern and Western systems. Trading ties between the two were maintained for over a decade at artificially low levels by the strategic embargo, by the recourse of the Eastern European countries to a quasi-autarchic regional trading network, and by reciprocal political distrust which prevented any very serious or sustained attempt by either side to overcome the obstacles to trade created by incompatibilities of the distinct commercial and payments arrangements practised by each group. Subsequently, over the past ten years, East-West trade has been one of the most dynamic sectors of international trade, yet it is still far from attaining its potential share of world trade, or even from reattaining the share it held before the political map of the world was redrawn at the end of the Second World War. Before proceeding, therefore, to a brief review of the possible role of multi-national corporations in the ' Western' side of East-West exchanges, it is worth while trying to identify the economic forces which have nourished the growth in the volume of trade and shaped the channels through which it develops.[2]

---

[1] The corollary of the strengthening of economically integrative forces, via intensified East-West industrial co-operation, is the risk of a widening North–South technological gap. Hence the decisive importance for the future of better mechanisms for the transfer of technology in the targets and strategy of the Second Development Decade, 1970–80. Multi-national corporations could in theory make a major contribution to an accelerated transfer of technology, provided certain revisions were made both of their tendency to centralise research and marketing decisions and of most developing countries' reluctance to welcome private capital inflows in sectors where control over sensitive plan sectors of investment and employment would be located outside their frontiers: the danger, as the latter see it, of resurgent 'economic colonisation'.

[2] The process of political *détente* in East-West relations has been, of course, a necessary, but not a sufficient, condition of closer economic ties. Consequently, any reversal of this process would almost certainly react unfavourably on the steady expansion of East-West trade. Although the political dimension is not considered here, it is necessary to observe that trade between the Soviet Union and the United States is exceptionally small in volume and slow to grow. To the extent that political factors are decisive in this context, and given the fact that the major multi-national firms have their headquarters in the United States, an improvement in political relations between the two great powers would seem to be a *sine qua non* for a 'breakthrough' in the scale of sales of multi-national firms in the Soviet market.

Foremost among these economic forces explaining the dynamism of East-West exchanges has been the search among the Eastern European countries[1] for forms of economic planning and management permitting the maintenance of high rates of economic growth through the speedy diffusion of technological innovation – either in the producers' goods sector or in that of final consumers' goods. An outstanding early example was the decision of the Soviet Government in 1957 (followed by several smaller Eastern European countries) to proceed to the 'chemicalisation' of the economy; output of basic chemicals was to be given priority in investment planning and foreign-exchange allocations in order greatly to increase output of, *inter alia*, artificial fertilisers (thus boosting production of foodstuffs) and plastics – for both intermediate uses (replacing non-ferrous metals in some branches of engineering) and consumers' goods. In that case, as in the more recent decision to commission large automobile plants, on the basis of Western know-how, contracts were signed with very large Western companies (I.C.I., Courtaulds, Fiat, etc), whose scale of operations and self-financing was compatible with the large-scale requirements of the Eastern European state trading monopolies.[2]

This is one of the points of contact with the second contemporary tendency making for the dynamism and diversification of East-West economic relations – namely, the growing strength of multi-national corporations in science-based branches of industry or in the manufacture of research-intensive products of more traditional industries. The principal characteristics of these firms in respect of research, financing, manufacturing and marketing operations, are the subject of other chapters in this volume. Their features most relevant to the development of East-West relations, and which call for mention here, are threefold: first, their *scale* of operations, which provides access to finance and technological expertise commensurate with the requirements of Eastern European purchasers; second, their *technological leadership*, which often gives them what has been called a 'monopoloid' position as suppliers of new products or processes, as well as providing Eastern European customers with access to the best available contemporary technology; third, their *managerial* and *marketing*

---

[1] Unless otherwise specified, this term is used to denote the Soviet Union too.

[2] It has been reported that the Swedish Volvo enterprise was a strong candidate on *technical* grounds for the contract subsequently signed with Fiat, the smaller financial capacity of the former having been a decisive disadvantage. If true, this report lends support to the argument that it is the *combination* of scale of production, technological leadership and financial, managerial and marketing strength which confers unique trading advantages on the multi-national corporations.

*expertise* – skills which the Eastern European economies now know they need if the secular aim of 'catching up and surpassing the most advanced capitalist countries' is to be realised.[1] Consequently – and taking refuge behind the economist's customary defensive formula of 'other things being equal' – a continuation of the tendency towards industrial concentration within the market economies, as well as among them (regional integration as in the E.E.C., and essentially trans-Atlantic multi-national enterprises), might be expected, *a priori*, to promote more numerous East-West trade and production ties.

Here, however, two questions must be allowed to disturb the 'other things being equal' assumption. Are decentralising tendencies in the planning and management systems of the East European economies liable to diminish the attractiveness of multi-national firms and other large industrial concentrations (such as Krupp) as trading partners? In other words, if enterprises in Eastern Europe (such as the Czech Skoda automobile enterprise) are authorised to enter directly into foreign contracts, without the intermediary of foreign trade corporations (as is already the case in Yugoslavia), will they not prefer to deal with Western enterprises of compatible scale?[2] Preference for equality of bargaining power, and avoidance of the risk of being too closely tied to capitalist oligopolies (painful memories of pre-war experience being relevant here) might incline them to such a policy. Second, and perhaps more important, what are the inducements to multi-national corporations to extend their activities to Eastern Europe: are such inducements – prospective economies of scale, expanding markets and lower-cost sources of supply – likely to gain or lose in strength? Plainly, the answers to such questions depend on many complex and interesting factors, the future evolution of which does not lend itself to confident prediction. It follows that the issues taken up in this chapter belong to an unknown future, and therefore to the realm of

[1] One addition too, and subtraction from, this general description make it more accurate. First, Eastern European countries tend to find it more administratively convenient to deal with a large-scale firm which is big enough to manage efficiently its own subcontracting, etc., and thus enter into a 'package' contract, thereby reducing the number of parties to negotiation; second, political limitations are still imposed on the transfer to Eastern countries of advanced technology in militarily sensitive spheres such as aerospace and electronics.

[2] In fact, the Skoda plant is one of the first, and best known, Eastern European enterprises to have been authorised to conclude contracts with foreign customers without the direct intervention of the Czechoslovak Ministry of Foreign Trade. It used this freedom in July 1968 to reach an agreement with the main comparable Yugoslav engineering combine for exchange of technology and specialisation of production. Joint marketing and the merger of some productive operations were envisaged at later stages of co-operation.

speculation. Nevertheless, the assessment of probabilities must rest on the correct identification of the relative strength of already discernible market and organisational tendencies. An attempt to identify them is made in the following pages, although the difficulties of the undertaking have to be admitted at once, inasmuch as the information publicly available on the terms of many of the contracts entered into by multi-national corporations with Eastern European enterprises is quite inadequate for the purpose.


## II. SOME SALIENT FEATURES OF
## EAST-WEST TRADE

East-West European trade turnover amounted to just under $9 billion in 1968 – almost twice as much as in 1960 (though still only 5 per cent of total world trade) – and thus was one of the most dynamic flows in world trade. The annual rate of growth in the 1960s has been 11·3 per cent on average and in 1966 was as much as 16 per cent, compared with a rise in total world trade of 9 per cent. This rapid expansion in East-West exchanges obviously could not have occurred – particularly in view of the many institutional impediments thrown up by the differences of economic system – unless considerable unexploited trading potential existed. That this was so, and an idea of how much still remains, emerges from the statistics showing the importance of each market in the total trade of the two groups: in 1968 the Eastern market accounted for only 4½ per cent of the total trade of the Western European economies, while the share of the latter in the total trade of the socialist countries amounted to some 20 per cent. When it is recalled that the socialist countries now produce about one-third of world industrial output, it becomes evident that trade between the two groups is still at a much lower level than would be dictated by economic forces alone. In a sense, however, this is a false criterion, since the *raison d'être* of the economic planning practised in Eastern Europe is to steer economic forces in the direction sought by the political authorities over the medium term – Stalin's advocacy of 'two separate world markets' being a particularly relevant example in the present context. Consequently, the imperatives of central planning, besides giving rise to such institutional factors as the traditional preference for bilateral trade agreements, the foreign trade monopolies and the inconvertibility of the Eastern European currencies, all point to a level of trade between the two groups below what would be considered optimal, or even natural, in a broadly homogeneous market system such as obtains in Western Europe.[1]

Examination of the changing commodity composition of East-West trade confirms the impression left by the above figures for total trade – some features of dynamic change, remaining unexploited potential and a certain structural skewness; it also introduces some new factors relevant to the scale, marketing and research-intensive characteristics of multi-national corporations. In the first place, East-West trade consists preponderantly of the exchange of manufactures and semi-manufactures from the market economies (64 per cent of their total exports in 1965) against food, raw materials and fuel from the socialist countries (63 per cent of the latter's exports) – a structure of trade which contrasts sharply with the degree of industrialisation of the two areas, the large share of manufactures (over 70 per cent) in each group's intra-trade, as well as with the composition of the exports of socialist countries to all destinations. In 1965, for example, machinery and transport equipment made up 28 per cent of the socialist countries' exports to all destinations, but only 6 per cent of their exports to the West. This means that only 4 per cent of Eastern European exports in this category went to the world's largest market for machinery (the O.E.C.D. region) and accounted there for less than 1 per cent of total machinery imports.

It is by inspecting the finer detail of East-West trade in manufactures that the more significant changes, relevant to the general theme of this chapter, can be singled out. Breaking down all manufactures into three groups – semi-finished goods, investment goods and consumers' goods – the following longer-term rates of change are found:

| | Western imports from East (c.i.f.) | | Eastern imports from West (f.o.b.) | |
|---|---|---|---|---|
| | Average value 1966–8 (million $U.S.) | Change 1966–8 1957–9 (percentage) | Average value 1966–8 (million $U.S.) | Change 1966–8 1957–9 (percentage) |
| Semi-finished goods | 1,092 | *159* | 1,644 | *140* |
| Investment goods | 324 | *165* | 1,567 | *284* |
| Consumers' goods | 258 | *147* | 328 | *525* |
| All manufactures | 1,674 | *158* | 3,539 | *209* |
| All commodities | 4,508 | *139* | 4,246 | *171* |

Source: E.C.E., *Economic Bulletin for Europe*, Vol. 21, No. 1, Appendix Tables B and C.

[1] The reform of planning priorities and methods in Eastern European countries has been, as will be seen, a potent factor favouring trade expansion.

245

By far the most dynamic expansion is seen to have occurred in Western exports of consumers' manufactures (textiles, footwear, motor-cars, etc.), followed by investment goods (mainly transport equipment other than ships, and metal-working machinery). A shift also appears to be taking place in the established structure of trade towards a larger share for manufactures in the socialist countries' exports to the West, and from basic industrial equipment in the reverse flow towards chemicals, plastics, complex plant and consumers' manufactures. The explanation for this must be sought in changes in plan priorities and management methods in the socialist countries, as well as in the greater awareness in both groups of the new trading frontiers opened up by the onrush of contemporary technical progress.[1]

## III. REFORMS OF PLANNING PRIORITIES AND METHODS

The phrases in most common currency concerning economic development in eastern Europe in recent years have been 'reform', 'profits', 'increased incentives' and, ubiquitously in the West at least – 'Libermanism', 'decentralisation of decision-making', and 'market forces'. Loosely strung together they convey a roughly accurate impression of the direction taken by the changes introduced or contemplated in Eastern Europe but fail to bring out the great differences in the degree of experimentation resorted to by each country, or the very real constraints, under present price systems, on the scope for giving freer play to market forces.

At the risk of formulating too loose generalisations which fit no single country of the region exactly, it may be appropriate for present purposes to lay stress on the search throughout the area for increased factor productivity, as claims on resources (the pressure of rising consumers' expectations, the housing backlog, the need for modernisation of obsolescent productive capacities, etc.) grow faster than

---

[1] The figures shown in the text table also reflect the West's considerable export surplus in manufactured goods with the East, which is balanced by an import surplus in other commodities. Consequently, a condition of the transformation of the slightly archaic structure of East–West trade must be an increase in Western imports of manufactures from the East. Multilateralism and convertibility might make this condition less essential if a more triangular pattern of East–West–South trade were achieved – but progress in that direction is not likely to be quick. It may be added that lack of convertibility sets limits on the attractiveness of Eastern European markets for multi-national corporations.

investible funds, while the reservoir of transferable agricultural manpower diminishes. The quest for higher productivity has been pursued in a number of directions, notably by changing investment priorities, by according increased autonomy to enterprise management, by relaxing the binding force and reducing the number of central plan indicators, by accelerating the rate of innovation and by revising foreign trade objectives and procedures. Obviously this list (which is not, of course, exhaustive) comprises measures which are highly interdependent; for example, greater freedom for the enterprise manager to adjust his investment programme with a view to profit maximisation can result in increased pressure to import capital equipment embodying advanced technology. Here, the important point is that the pursuit of higher productivity via enhanced decision-making powers at the enterprise level must mean close surveillance of the external balance. This is especially true of those Eastern European countries such as Czechoslovakia or Hungary whose economies are most heavily dependent on foreign trade.[1]

The prominent architect of economic reform in Czechoslovakia, Professor Ota Sik, has stated that an essential goal of the reform is 'correlation between international trade and the national economy', while the role of foreign trade in the Hungarian reform is defined as follows in the official announcement:

'The faster development of the Hungarian economy presupposes more active participation in the international division of labour and the more efficient exploitation of the resultant economic benefits. Economic co-operation with other socialist countries . . . will continue to be a factor of first importance. But economic ties with non-socialist countries must also be extended. The necessary measures must be taken to permit foreign markets to exert an efficient stimulative effect on the production, trade and development of Hungary.'

The 'necessary measures' referred to in the above quotation are still the subject of experimentation, the scale of which varies from country to country. In Hungary the reforms so far introduced in this sphere are intermediate in innovating 'boldness' between what was envisaged in Czechoslovakia in 1968 and what has been implemented in eastern Germany, and may therefore be taken as broadly representa-

---

[1] As much as 40 per cent of Hungary's national income is generated by exports, and each increment of 1 per cent in national income necessitates a 2 per cent increase in imports and exports.

tive of the present reforming tendency in the region. They have been designed to satisfy three requirements:

(a) the creation of organic links between the domestic and foreign markets;
(b) the enlargement of enterprise autonomy; and
(c) the provision of incentives such that enterprises will mobilise to the maximum their 'internal reserves' (i.e. output per unit of existing inputs measured in terms of productivity growth and profitability).

To that end, the foreign trade targets of the enterprise plan are now specified in a more flexible manner, with less detail and for attainment over a longer period (five years); above all, prices and exchange rates have been so modified (by the use, in respect of the latter, of varying co-efficients equivalent in effect to multiple exchange rates) as to make it easier to assess by means of the volume and rate of profits, the worthwhileness of exporting or importing activities. This is a most important departure from earlier practice of maximising foreign exchange earnings (or minimising foreign-exchange expenditures) regardless of domestic costs. It is safe to conclude that the resultant generalisation of cost-consciousness (including opportunity costs) in enterprise manufacturing and trading, coupled with the stronger links that have been established between enterprise profitability and incremental personal earnings, could lead to a faster expansion of East-West trade,[1] with stronger emphasis on the transfer of technology (including managerial and marketing know-how) and on relatively new forms of enterprise-to-enterprise agreements.

To sum up, the long-range objectives of higher productivity and increased efficiency sought by the current reforms of Eastern European planning and management, together with the greater importance attached to satisfying consumers' demand for more sophisticated commodities, may be expected to result in a lengthy process of enlarging both the role played by foreign trade in national economic development and the technological and managerial component of East-West exchanges. Some of the reasons for believing that multi-national

---

[1] The closer alignment of domestic and international prices can only proceed by gradual stages (cf. Yugoslav experience), is difficult to reconcile with traditional Eastern European methods of planning (price flexibility increases uncertainty in plan formulation) and may be accompanied by wider short-term fluctuations in the rate of growth of East-West exchanges. Moreover, a steady growth in Eastern imports from the West can be sustained in the long run only by a commensurate increase in the Eastern countries' capacity to pay – which means, in practice, greater success in selling their manufactures to the West.

companies may participate actively in this development, as well as some of the limitations on the prospects for extending their activities, are discussed in the remainder of this note.

## IV. THE DEVELOPMENT OF EAST-WEST ENTERPRISE-TO-ENTERPRISE AGREEMENTS

It is difficult to ascribe a precise date to the emergence of industrial co-operation as a new form of East-West economic relations, but already in 1963 an increasing number of enterprise-to-enterprise agreements was being reported and the rising trend has continued since then.[1] As a rough estimate, the number of East-West European enterprise-to-enterprise agreements on industrial co-operation can be put at 350–400 in early 1969. The chemicals and pharmaceutical industries, electronics and engineering seem to be the branches of production most actively involved. Five broad types of arrangement may be distinguished:

(1) The first consists of sub-contracting agreements providing for the continuing delivery by the Eastern European partner to the Western company. Poland, for example, delivers refrigerator parts to Western Germany and tractors to Italy, according to the Western partners' specifications and technical documentation, the final products being assembled and marketed by the latter.

(2) A second type of co-operation makes provision for product specialisation and exchanges meeting reciprocal requirements. An example is provided by the agreements reached between Austrian and Hungarian producers of chemicals and pharmaceuticals, the latter supplying basic chemicals for drug-making, technical know-how and certain finished products in exchange for a number of specialised commodities produced only by the former.

(3) A third type provides for agreed specialisation by each partner in the manufacture of units or components which are then exchanged, each party assembling the final product.

(4) Fourthly, a number of East-West enterprise-to-enterprise agreements provide for co-operation in selling in third markets. Polish organisations have, for example, a contract with a British-based

---

[1] Agreements of this type were already a feature of Yugoslavia's trade with the West towards the end of the 1950s.

company for installing diesel engines in the export models of Polish-made cars and commercial vehicles, the Western partner providing also spare parts and technical servicing facilities in all of Poland's export markets.

(5) Finally a numerically important category of enterprise-to-enterprise agreements consists of technological arrangements ranging from an exchange of know-how (including the exchange of personnel) to joint research and development projects in specific fields. Such agreements tend to be concluded with large-scale Western enterprises on account of their ability to concentrate and self-finance big research and development resources, thus enabling them to bear the high 'threshold' or 'entry-price' costs imposed by many branches of advanced technology. Taking Soviet agreements with Italy as an example, by the end of 1965 thirteen agreements of this type had been concluded by some of the largest Italian companies, providing for joint research in specific commodities, exchange of production experience and exchange of specialists. The co-operation agreements with Montecatini and Fiat, for instance, envisage, respectively, joint research in polypropylene synthetic fibres, and scientific and technical co-operation in the construction of large-scale automobile plants capable of producing at least 400,000 cars a year.[1]

The interests of the types of arrangements distinguished above consists less in their originality – after all, analogous co-operation has existed *within* each sub-region of Europe for many years – than in their novelty in the context of economic relations *between* the two groups, East and West. Plainly, the forms of industrial concentration and specialisation practised within each group are unsuitable, without adaptation, for arrangements between enterprises belonging to different systems. The mergers, fusions, 'take-over mechanisms', etc. so characteristic of industrial organisation in the market economies in the 1960s cannot be extended over the East-West economic frontier for the simple reason that private ownership of productive assets (outside the artisanal and peasant farming sectors) is prohibited by law. Similarly, the co-ordinative mechanisms employed by the Eastern European countries under the auspices of COMECON rest on the principle of state ownership and planning and do not lend themselves

---

[1] See United Nations Economic Commission for Europe, *Economic Survey of Europe in 1967*, Chapter II, and *Economic Bulletin for Europe*, Vol. 21, No. 1.

to transplantation to the Western industrial market-place. East-West enterprise-to-enterprise agreements on industrial co-operation thus represent, when viewed in this light, an ingenious means of imparting to East-West economic relations some of the elements of contemporary industrial progress without infringing the ground-rules of economic management proper to each system.

Generalising the characteristics of industrial co-operation present in the majority of reported agreements,[1] the following can be singled out as being specially important: first, the long-term (five–eight years, on average) nature of the contracts, and their provision for a 'complex barter' system of settlements, whereby a flow of goods and services in one direction (often component parts and related know-how) is compensated by a reverse flow of complementary goods and services;[2] second, the provision made for the transfer of technology, often unilateral to begin with but potentially reciprocal; third, the built-in possibility for each side to market its products throughout its partner's trading area.

Besides the growth in East-West merchandise trade described earlier these agreements have been accompanied, as would be expected, by increasing trade in licences, which is the major component of the technological balance of payments.

## V. SOME OPEN QUESTIONS

An argument is often put forward to the effect that, on account of technological lags and long years of relative austerity in the allocations made for consumers' durable goods, the Eastern European countries stand to gain more from research-intensive exchanges with the West than their partners, and consequently have a keener interest in opening up and developing the new forms of agreement outlined above. Although this may be true in terms of macro-economic reasoning, the big multi-national corporations can scarcely afford to neglect the

---

[1] Published information on the detailed contents and provisions of agreements is very fragmentary – though understandably so, since these are matters within the realm of business secrecy. Even governments (in the West) have not statutory access to such information.

[2] This thus represents a welcome advance on the type of straightforward barter earlier practised, where metal-working machine tools were exchanged – at a loss to both sides – against sandals or sunflower-seed.

opportunities held out by the potentially large Eastern European market to which technical co-operation agreements provide one path of access. The massive investments required in the research, development and manufacture of science-based products (such as computers) necessitate large markets both to amortise these expenditures and to harvest economies of scale. Consequently, while it is possible that the motives for expanding East-West enterprise-to-enterprise agreements may differ as between the partners, there is no necessary presumption that they differ appreciably in strength.

Besides its attractiveness as an increasingly technology-conscious, large-scale market, the Eastern European region holds out the additional opportunity to multi-national enterprises of access to cheaper sources of supply (on account of lower real earnings) of material-intensive or labour-intensive components. The 'technological gap' and 'product cycle' theories of international trade explain the dynamism of exports from high-cost sources of supply, such as the United States, in terms of the lag occurring between the commercialisation of an innovation in the technologically most advanced countries and their imitation in lower-cost producers. By the time the latter have entered production on a large enough scale to undermine the competitive advantage of the original commercial innovator it, in turn, has generated innovations and, by a process of technological parthogenesis, maintained its competitive leadership. The dynamics of international trade are then explained as much by 'competition *via* innovation' as by the comparative cost advantages of classical theory. Available evidence certainly indicates some such product-cycle influencing trade and investment flows between the United States and Western Europe. Some multi-national enterprises – Control Data Corporation, for example – have entered into agreements with Yugoslav enterprises which provide for the supply of equipment and know-how by the former in exchange for components manufactured by the latter at as much as 25 per cent below world market prices.

So far as United States-based multinational enterprises are concerned, however, the strategy for containing the text-book threat of only brief monopoloid profits before competitive low-cost imitators erode their market advantages has been to invest directly in manufacturing capacity in Western Europe. In this way, they have established a beachhead in the Western European market before competitors can appear on the scene in strength, thereby acquiring the double advantage of control over low-cost supplies to North America (e.g. in automobiles) and access (behind tariff walls) to Western European markets on as favourable terms as local suppliers.[1]

Text-book reasoning seldom matches the intricacies of reality, and as is well known the presumed attractiveness of locating production in countries with low-wage costs is often offset in practice by economic factors such as transport costs and tariff liabilities as well as by more political or institutional factors such as non-insurable risks and inhospitable legislation governing foreign investment. These factors, in various combinations, presumably account for the surprisingly few manufacturing facilities created by multi-national enterprises in developing countries. An additional factor which probably inhibits the economically rational location of technology-intensive production in low-wage countries, is the shortage of highly qualified scientific and engineering manpower in such countries. In the Yugoslav case already referred to, however, the lower price paid for Yugoslav components is stated to be due to the less reliable quality of goods produced in a developing country. In other words, lower prices may not be sufficient to outweigh the disadvantages, from the point of view of multi-national corporations, of the other factors mentioned unless they can establish a system of technical surveillance over their sub-contractors in lieu of acquiring direct control by direct investment.

A very important difference in the relative attractiveness of the Western and Eastern European markets for multi-national companies is the impossibility of direct investment in the latter due to the prohibition of private industrial ownership (let alone foreign ownership) in the socialist system.[2] This has been the practice preferred by multi-national corporations in Western Europe and North America to the alternative of non-organic, contractual arrangements.[3] To the extent that the rate of profit, rather than enlarging the market, is the principal motive in extending the operations of the multi-national corporation, this is a limiting factor. In the absence of direct investment, the only clear links between the operation of the multi-national company and evolution of industrial relations in the Eastern European

[1] The role of the multi-national enterprise in trans-Atlantic trade is the subject of a major study undertaken at the M.I.T. by a research team under the leadership of Professor Raymond Vernon.

[2] The legislation introduced in Yugoslavia on 1 July 1967 making provision for joint investment of foreign and domestic capital (with 49 per cent and 51 per cent shares, respectively) is not really an exception, in the sense that the resultant establishment does not acquire a separate legal personality. In short, there is no transfer of ownership between the two partners, only a pooling of investment and managerial resources.

[3] Except as regards straightforward sub-contracting, the volume of which has increased greatly over the past ten years.

countries become the related changes in management and personal earnings.

Most students of the development of Yugoslav economic institutions and policies over the past decade would agree that the point now reached constitutes a system *sui generis*. Consequently, Yugoslav experience in promoting enterprise-to-enterprise agreements – particularly since the enactment of the 'Decision on Production Co-operation Which is Considered Long-Term' (22 November 1967), following the Law on Foreign Exchange Transactions passed as part of the economic reform of the previous year – need not foreshadow the development of such agreements with Eastern European countries. Still, when this qualification has been made, it nonetheless seems likely that Yugoslav experience in according a much larger role to enterprise decision-making and to internal and external market forces in macro-economic policy will be closely studied by enterprises in the East as in the West, and some features of its practice in industrial co-operation emulated.

In all, Yugoslavia had by early 1969 concluded over one hundred enterprise-to-enterprise agreements for co-operation in production and technical assistance over a period of three years or more (about eighty with Western Europe, a few with the United States and nineteen with Eastern Europe).[1] Most of these belong to the categories already distinguished, only some sixteen taking the form of joint investment as permitted under the 1967 legislation. An economic analysis of the benefits obtained by both sides from the non-organic forms of co-operation shows some advantages in terms of scale and unit costs of production, the speed of acquisition of new technological knowledge and productivity gains. It is the last point, in conjunction with the provisions for joint management, research and training, which is probably most relevant for speculation about future developments.[2] If the economic

---

[1] Some of the agreements with Western Europe are with affiliates of United States-based multi-national enterprises.

[2] Joint investment projects, such as that between Printing Development International (New York), Centre for Europe, and the Belgrade Graphic Works (17 May 1968), also make provision for sharing of income and losses which could have far-reaching implications for labour earnings for employees of the Yugoslav partner. However, the detailed clauses governing such matters are contained in Annexes to the main agreement which have not been published. So far as managerial powers are concerned, the agreement lists the powers which the parent Yugoslav company *does not transfer* to the joint venture and states that employees of the latter retain all the rights and obligations prescribed by Yugoslav legislation. By implication, this suggests that the managing organs of the parent Yugoslav enterprise retain their right to hire and fix wage-rates for labour in the joint enterprise, the workers of which will continue to elect their own managing bodies, etc. This serves to underline the special characteristics of Yugoslav industrial relations legislation.

results obtained by enterprises participating in such agreements yield higher incomes and better training facilities than those obtained by comparable but non-co-operating enterprises, the incentive to enter into such arrangements could be generalised. In Yugoslav circumstances such pressure could probably be accommodated within existing wage regulations which are centred on enterprise performance. In Eastern European countries, however, the appearance of strong differentiation between earnings levels in co-operating and non-co-operating enterprises could seriously disturb the present highly schematic system of occupational, industrial and regional wage tariffs.

# REGIONAL ECONOMIC INTEGRATION AND INDUSTRIAL RELATIONS IN THE EUROPEAN COMMON MARKET

THE five chapters united in this section lead from different angles to the same conclusion: the impact on industrial relations of economic integration in the E.E.C., the most developed region[1] in this respect, has so far been astonishingly small. In particular, no supra-national collective bargaining has emerged, although trade unions paid lip service to this concept for years without concentrating their organisational power on the proclaimed goal.

The editor of the present book, attempting an overall appraisal of the E.E.C. experience in Chapter 15, therefore concludes that regional economic integration does not appear a sufficient condition for bringing about substantial changes in industrial relations pattern. These are found deeply rooted in the national historical, sociological, political and economic environment.

Saying that no substantial transnationalisation of industrial relations has occurred does not mean, however, that national patterns have remained fully unaffected. As a matter of fact, some transnational potentialities and tendencies have gradually emerged. The creation and functioning of the European Coal and Steel Community and the European Economic Community, their institutional set-up, permitting participation of the social partners at the supra-national level, and the social policies pursued by the Commission (issues treated in the chapter written by J. E. Van Dierendonck) have contributed towards an environment favourable to transnational interaction of industrial relations parties. In the advisory bodies and joint committees of the E.E.C., European trade unions and employers encounter each other continually and acquire co-operative habits which tend to spill over to their relations outside the formal Community framework; social programmes of either European unions or employers, plus the demonstration effect of social advances in member countries have resulted in a certain informal co-ordination of national bargaining objectives. Furthermore, tremendous efforts have been made, as the chapter

---

[1] As judged on attitudinal indicators of economic and social transactions as well as on the degree of centralised decision-making.

written by Roger Blanpain demonstrates, to organise trade union and employers adequately at an E.E.C. level.

Yet these organisational efforts were on the whole less intended to promote European bargaining relations between unions and employers and more to develop counterpart structures to the existing organisation of the supra-national authorities. In general, trade unions and employers prefer to use E.E.C. institutions instrumentally, that is to promote their own objectives, rather than to bargain with each other freely at Community level.

But all these efforts on the European scene are of marginal complementarity, judged on the whole industrial relations setting. The decisive factors for industrial relations – main decision-making locus, economic potentialities, practical trade union solidarity and, last but not least, the legal framework – are still found within the national boundaries.

Transnationalisation of industrial relations in the E.E.C. is therefore mostly thought of as a trend which needs to be helped along; and the harmonisation of economic and social conditions is proposed as an appropriate means to this end. Likewise, the importance of legal harmonisation, at times neglected, is highlighted in the chapter written by Michael Despax, which represents an investigation into possible legal and organisational approaches for transnational industrial relations. After discussion of the present legal basis, Despax considers the scope and objects of European collective bargaining, as well as the role which international organisations, especially the E.E.C., but also the I.L.O., could assume in promoting this goal. Yet it would appear that once a fair harmonisation of social legislation and economic conditions has been attained, union perception of the need for international collective bargaining would be decisive. Putting this as a goal on their priority list would presuppose a substantial change of attitudes towards concrete European solidarity.

Even within the integrated area of the European Common Market, unions' transnational concern is for the moment primarily with the challenge and the economic potential of multi-national firms; they are likely to become the prime poles of transnationalisation of industrial relations, and from the viewpoint of trade union strategy, this may well turn out to be a necessary pre-stage for regional industry-wide bargaining.

In the last chapter of the present section, Jacques Houssiaux attempts to respond to a number of questions related to these problems. One of his major assumptions is that the development of transnational industrial relations policies at company levels depends on the degree of environmental similarity (economic, social, administrative and political) in which the actors (primarily trade unions and multi-national management) find themselves. For multi-national firms of European origin, embodied in the continuum of the integrated area, this environmental similarity should be easier to achieve than for their great protagonists, the American-based firms working in Europe. Adoption of a uniform European Company Law, including provisions for workers' representation in its decision-making bodies, would add a further element of environmental compatibility to the European multi-national firm.

In the longer term Houssiaux sees a mixed system likely to emerge, in which local collective bargaining will remain the basic feature of industrial relations, but which will be complemented by agreements reached at the level of European companies. Influenced by this evolution, the multi-national corporation of American origin is expected to follow a more polycentric industrial relations policy on a European scale. This analysis seems to bring out the proposition, already apparent in the Canadian case study, that, although the multi-national corporation is a stronger structure of economic organisation than regional integration, both phenomena are intimately entangled with regard to the transnationalisation of industrial relations.

Chapter 12

# REGIONAL ECONOMIC INTEGRATION AS THE CREATION OF AN ENVIRONMENT FAVOURABLE TO TRANSNATIONAL INDUSTRIAL ORGANISATION IN THE E.E.C.

*by*

*J. E. van Dierendonck*

ONE of the Rome Treaty's[1] main objectives is social progress. In the Preamble of this Treaty, the signatories declare that they direct 'their efforts to the essential purpose of constantly improving the living and working conditions of their people'. According to Article 2 of the Treaty, the Community is to promote 'an accelerated raising of the standard of living'.

The fundamental bases of the Community are (1) the free movement of goods (the customs union), (2) the common agricultural policy, (3) the free movement of persons, services and capital, (4) the common transport policy. Two chapters appear under the Title 'Social Policy', the first of which is devoted to 'Social Provisions' and the second to the 'European Social Fund'.

According to Article 2 of the Paris Treaty,[2] the purpose of the European Coal and Steel Community (E.C.S.C.) is to contribute to the expansion of the economy, the development of employment and the improvement of the standard of living in the participating countries. Article 56 and Section 23 of the Convention, concerning the transitional provisions annexed to this Treaty, are devoted to re-adaptation programmes and Articles 68 and 69 to wages and movement of labour.

The aim of this chapter is to sketch the background for industrial relations. It therefore deals mainly with the measures to facilitate capital movements and to harmonise company law and labour conditions, the free movement of workers, the European Social Fund, E.C.S.C. re-adaptation programmes and industrial relations legislation.

[1] Establishing the European Economic Community.
[2] Establishing the European Coal and Steel Community.

263

## FREE MOVEMENT OF CAPITAL

All restrictions on capital movements from one member country to another are being gradually removed and, under Article 67 of the Treaty of Rome, are scheduled to disappear entirely at the end of the transition period.

A wide range of capital movements were unconditionally freed from control in May 1960, and other measures followed in December 1962 to speed up the elimination of such restrictions, especially those on the issue of securities in one Community country by companies incorporated in another.

Further measures are now being prepared for the liberalisation of exchange controls. Also, with a view to eliminating the fiscal obstacles to free capital movement, the Commission has submitted to the Council of Ministers a directive on the harmonisation of legislation on capital duty in connection with the stock participation of one company in another.

If capital movements disturb the economies òf member States however, governments may take defensive measures, subject to authorisation by the Commision and approval by the Council of Ministers (in an emergency these can be obtained *after* application of the measures the governments consider necessary).

As regards migrant workers' remittances, no restrictions exist.

## FREE MOVEMENT OF WORKERS

The arrangements made to liberalise the movement of workers between the six countries of the Community are based both on Articles 48 and 49 of the Rome Treaty, and Article 69 of the Paris Treaty, the latter concerning only workers of recognised qualifications in the coal and steel industries.

In virtue of the E.E.C. rules, the Council has so far adopted three regulations: Regulation No. 15, Regulation No. 38/64 and a Regulation of 29 July 1968. The first was effective between 1 September 1961 and 1 May 1964 and was replaced by Regulation 38/64, which abolished, in principle, priority of nationals in access to employment, containing, however, certain safeguard clauses enabling each member State to restore it temporarily in certain areas or trades with heavy manpower surpluses. The 1968 regulation provided for complete freedom of movement for workers. It rounds off the legal arrangements made by the preceding regulations by eliminating the remaining restrictions, thus fully realising the aims of the Treaty.

The main provision and the most important advances made by the new regulation concern the willingness to lay aside all practices granting 'national priority' for jobs. Nationals of the member States will henceforth have access to employment under the same conditions as nationals of a particular E.E.C.country, as work permits will be abolished. Equality of treatment with national workers is also to be granted as far as working conditions, especially wage and dismissal requirements, are concerned. Migrant workers will also be able to vote in the election of workers' representatives and members of works' committees, and stand for election themselves, without any discrimination whatsoever.

The whole system of regulation is essentially based on the principle of close co-operation with national government administrations and with the representatives of the employers' and workers' organisations. This principle is being realised in the form of two committees, namely the Consultative Committee (on a tripartite basis: equal representation of governments, workers and employers) and the Technical Committee (composed of government representatives and destined to assist the Commission in the solving of technical problems.) These committees will have a leading role to play and will assist the European Commission in its quest to solve the problems raised by freedom of movement. Finally, to improve and accelerate the co-operation between the Labour Exchanges of the six member States a co-ordinating office at the Community level has been set up to clear offers of and applications for employment. The yearly average (1961–67) of first permits issued to workers of the member States moving from one Community country to another, was 250,000 of which 200,000 concerned Italians.

## SOCIAL SECURITY FOR MIGRANT WORKERS

Article 51 of the Rome Treaty provided the legal basis for E.E.C. Regulations Nos. 3 and 4 in respect of social security for migrant workers which came into force on 1 January 1959 and have been amended and supplemented at various times since then. The basic principles underlying these regulations are:

(i) equality of rights as between nationals of the country concerned and nationals of other Community countries;

(ii) the adding together, for the right to benefits and their calculation, of all periods of employment and of insurance;

(iii) the export of benefits to any other member State.

The interpretation and practical application of the regulations are in the hands of the Administrative Committee, which has certain discretionary powers. Its members are the heads of social security departments in the six countries and representatives of the European Communities; meetings are also held periodically with workers', employers' and farmers' representatives.

It is estimated that there are about 2 million beneficiaries of these social security provisions; a sum equivalent to nearly U.S.$100 million is being transferred each year from member State to member State.

It should be noted that a preliminary decision of the Court of Justice, based on Article 177 of the Rome Treaty, in respect of the interpretation of the regulations may entail some harmonisation in the field of social security legislation.


## EUROPEAN SOCIAL FUND AND E.C.S.C. READAPTATION PROGRAMMES

### (a) European Social Fund

In order to improve employment opportunities in the E.E.C., a European Social Fund has been established on the basis of Articles 123–7 of the Treaty of Rome. In the social field it is the only financial instrument mentioned in this Treaty.

The Fund is administered by the Commission assisted by a consultative committee composed of representatives of governments, trade unions and employers' associations.

At present there are three cases in respect of which the Fund may make grants:

(a) in the retraining of unemployed workers or workers in a situation of prolonged under-employment;

(b) in resettling workers who must move to find new jobs;

(c) where a firm undergoing fundamental structural changes must retrain or suspend its workers, to ensure that workers receive 90 per cent of their previous wage during the period of conversion.

The Fund covers 50 per cent of the expenditure defrayed by a government or public body for the above-mentioned purpose. By the end of 1967 the Fund had contributed a sum total equivalent to U.S.$54 million to the retraining of more than 250,000 workers and the resettlement of nearly 300,000 workers. No payment had so far been made for structural changes in industry.

More recently the Commission submitted to the Council of Ministers a number of suggestions in order to bring about a reform of the Fund and thus to make it a more suitable instrument for the functioning of the E.E.C. and the implementation of common policies.

After pointing out that constant adaptation of manpower to the requirements of accelerated technological development will be one of the vital problems confronting the Community in the next decade, the Commission considered that the Fund should encourage this adaptation by concentrating on specific objectives in well-defined fields in accordance with the requirements and priorities of the Community and the E.E.C.'s medium-term economic policy.

On the basis of the Commission's proposals the Council would determine the fields qualifying for aid from the Fund (sectors of activity, regions, categories of manpower) and define the amount of aid which the Fund will be competent to grant and which should meet the basic requirement of protecting the employment and income of the worker, while facilitating his betterment. Programmes in these fields and qualifying for aid could be drawn up by public or private bodies and would be presented by member States to the Commission. The Commission would give its approval after confirming that the respective programmes were eligible for aid from the Fund and, in particular, that the measures proposed did not clash with Community policies. The Fund could then help to finance these programmes as they are implemented; in this way, it would play a truly stimulating part such as is not possible in its present legal framework, which prevents it from offering anything but belated compensation for financial efforts made several years earlier.

### (b) The E.C.S.C. Readaptation Programmes

Under Article 23 of the Convention concerning the transitional provisions annexed to the Paris Treaty and (since 10 February 1960) under the new Article 56.2 of the Treaty (aid in case of radical changes in the coal and steel markets not directly connected with the establishment of the Common Market) the High Authority (now the Commission) may assist the financing of approved programmes submitted by governments for the readaptation of enterprises or for the creation of new, economically sound activities capable of assuring productive employment for redundant workers.

Outright grants may be made as a contribution: (a) to the payment of compensation to tide the workers over until they can obtain new employment (in case of the complete or partial closing of enterprises); (b) to enterprises in order to ensure payment of their personnel (in case of temporary redundancy due to a change in the firm's activities); (c) to the payment of re-settlement allowances to the workers; (d) to the financing of technical retraining for workers who need to change jobs. E.C.S.C. grants have to be matched by equal contributions by the governments concerned.

Up to 1967, the E.C.S.C. had provided nearly $94 million to help finance readaptation schemes for about 333,000 Community coal- and steelworkers. Most of them (83 per cent) were coalminers whose jobs have disappeared as reorganisation of the coal industry progresses.

In addition, up to the end of 1967 the E.C.S.C. had lent $74 million to help introduce new industries in areas affected by closures in iron and coalmining or where the steel industry had run into difficulties.

## LABOUR AND INDUSTRIAL RELATIONS LEGISLATION

### (a) Equal Pay

According to Article 119 of the Rome Treaty, each member State was, in the course of the first stage, to ensure and subsequently maintain the application of the principle of equal remuneration for equal work as between men and women workers. In 1958 there were great disparities, the gap in some industries being as wide as 30 per cent.

At the end of 1961, however, the member States found that it had been impossible to comply with the time-limit and they agreed on progressive equalisation measures in three stages.

In 1967 the Commission submitted to the Council of Ministers its latest report on the state of application of Article 119 in the six member States. In essence, its findings were that progress had been made, but that disparities had not yet been completely eliminated. The disparities were less pronounced in jobs done by both sexes than in industries, such as textiles, where more women than men are employed. Even if the principle of equal pay was being followed theoretically, discrimination still existed in practice, mainly due to inadequate job descriptions which were taken as criteria for collective bargaining agreements.

*(b) Paid Holidays*

Another rule laid down in the Treaty concerns holidays with pay. Article 120 says with forceful brevity: 'Member States shall endeavour to maintain the existing equivalence of paid holiday schemes.'

A Commission survey confirmed in 1960 that, while annual holidays were longer in some countries, the total of national holidays spread out through the year was greater in other countries, and together they came to about twenty to thirty working days a year. Since 1958, the law, or collective agreements, have generally made progress; the number of annual holidays – including the national holidays – has now reached or is very close to the average of thirty days in all Community countries.

*(c) Overtime*

With regard to the payment of overtime, the authors of the Treaty had provided for some degree of alignment during the first stage, which ended in 1961. There has been no real difficulty on this point.

*(d) European Company Law*

In the field of company law, representatives of the six member States signed on 29 February 1968 the first European Convention on the Mutual Recognition of Companies and Legal Persons. One of the principles laid down in the Treaty of Rome is that companies and legal persons shall be treated in the same way as natural persons for the purpose of freedom of establishment and freedom to supply services (Articles 58 and 66). In accordance with Article 220, it is the objective of the Convention to unify and consolidate the rules on recognition of companies, and thus give full effect to this principle.

On 9 March 1968, the Council adopted the first directive on coordination of company law in the E.E.C. The directive concerns the guarantees required in member States of firms or companies in order to protect the interests both of company members and of outsiders. It deals mainly with disclosure requirements, validity of company commitments and grounds for nullity.

Convention and directive constitute a first step towards the harmonisation of company law in the Community and the creation of a 'European' company.

As it has become apparent that harmonisation of company law is not sufficient to satisfy the needs of firms extending their activity to other member States, the Commission has accepted the French Government's suggestion that European industry should be given the opportunity of forming 'European joint-stock companies'. It has submitted a memorandum on the subject to the Council of Ministers and submitted the preliminary draft of a 'Statute' for a European-type joint-stock company (published in 1967).

Chapter V of this preliminary draft deals with workers' representation in the bodies of the proposed European-type company. There are different proposals based on the situation in the most advanced countries (right to appoint representatives to boards of directors and co-determination) and the least advanced countries (joint consultative committees). For the time being, a group of experts is examining them with the aim of arriving at a proposal applicable in all member States that may satisfy both trade unions and employers' associations.

## (e) Rapprochement of Conditions of Work in Certain Sectors

There has been a particular evolution in two sectors in respect of which the Treaty of Rome contains special provisions aimed at implementing 'common policy', namely, agriculture and transport. Since the removal of any form of distortion affecting conditions of competition is one of the principal aims of these common policies, constant pressure towards a rapprochement of conditions of work has been brought to bear both by the employers and by the workers.

In 1968 a contractual framework concerning harmonisation of hours of work for regular agricultural wage-earners engaged in cultivation was signed by the representatives of the employers and workers at Community level. It recommends to national member organisations to ensure that the standards it lays down are respected when collective agreements within the respective countries are signed. A second contractual framework is to cover wage-earners engaged in animal husbandry.

Regarding transport, the Council of Ministers, acting on a proposal by the Commission, adopted in 1969 a first set of regulations concerning the harmonisation of certain social provisions relating to road transport. This first set of regulations, which includes provisions regarding maximum driving periods and minimum rest periods, will be followed by a second set stipulating standards with regard to daily and annual hours of work and overtime arrangements. It is intended to issue parallel regulations for water-way and railway transport.

All of these agreements and regulations are drafted at Community level by joint advisory committees, composed of equal numbers of representatives of the employers' and workers' organisations of the six member States, the Commission supplying the secretariat facilities.

## HARMONISATION OF SOCIAL SYSTEMS

Article 117 of the Rome Treaty specifies that the harmonisation of social systems is to be promoted not only through the functioning of the Common Market, but also through procedures provided for in the Treaty and of the harmonisation of laws and regulations.

It cannot be said that substantial progress has been made as regards harmonisation of laws and regulations, though there have been noteworthy advances in the fields of social security for migrant workers and of equal pay for men and women. In this connection a distinction has to be made between the fields in which the Commission has a function defined by the Treaty – for instance, with regard to free movement of labour, social security for migrant workers and the European Social Fund – and those fields covered by Article 118, where its task is restricted to promoting collaboration between member States.

The progress made in social security for migrant workers has already been mentioned. At the same time, however, the Commission has encouraged the harmonisation of social security systems in the Community, thereby insisting on the fulfilment of the provisions of the Treaty which call for harmonisation 'in an upward direction'.

Recommendations on occupational diseases, on industrial medical services, on the conditions for the payment of indemnities to victims of occupational diseases, and others, have been addressed to the member States by the European Commission (see below).

In accordance with the objective of long-term harmonisation of social security provisions in the member States, the Commission has drawn up comparative studies of the schemes applied in the six countries and undertaken studies of specific problems, such as the financial and economic impact of social security arrangements.

Notwithstanding the variety of schemes and the differences in the relative value of benefits, there is already one common element in the financing structure of the E.E.C. countries: social security in the E.E.C. has always been tied closely to the insurance principle, its financing depending more on specific social security contributions than on appropriations from general taxation.

On the other hand, the levelling-up effect resulting from the operation of the Common Market has been important as demonstrated in a survey of social developments in the E.E.C. during 1958–65 (see introduction to the Ninth Report on the Social Situation in the Community). The numerous actions taken at the initiative of the Commission have certainly not been in vain.

In this context mention should be made of the symposia and seminars; the lectures on technical progress, on social policy in agriculture and in transport, on the social services, on housing, on vocational training and on industrial health and safety; the wage surveys and the many reports and studies which have contributed in an important way to the dissemination and exchange of ideas in all social fields. In its concern to align conditions throughout the Community, the Commission has kept in touch with governments, trade unions and employers' associations; and this has encouraged and speeded up simultaneous approaches to problems and the search for solutions that would achieve parallel results. Examples of progress in this field are provided by the Community-wide programmes of the trade unions and by the efforts of unions and employers to set up central offices which can co-ordinate activities and policies at Community level.

*Vocational Training*

It goes without saying that vocational training and guidance should be constantly adapted to technical advances and the changing needs of the economy. It has been found that similar needs are felt in all six countries, despite the diversity of structure and of methods.

According to Article 128 of the Treaty of Rome, the Council, on the basis of a proposal by the Commission and after consulting the European Parliament and the Economic and Social Committee, adopted in 1963 'General Principles' for the implementation of a common vocational training policy. In its approach to a common training policy, the Commission does not intend to create a uniform system of training in the member countries.

It aims at making vocational training broad enough to encourage a harmonious development of the individual and to meet the requirements of rapid progress both of national economies and of the E.E.C.

Taking the 'General Principles' as a basis, the Commission has worked out a general action programme (and also a special programme for agriculture), including the establishment of an inventory of training facilities, the search for ways and means of improving the training of teachers and instructors, and the examination of the scope for multi-craft training.

Closer alignment of levels of training, which requires the definition of necessary qualifications, is another field in which work is under way. The tripartite Consultative Committee for Vocational Training has already approved common lists of minimum qualifications and skill required for turners, milling – and grinding – machine operators, and in the metal-working trade. Lists for other trades are being established.

In July 1966, the Commission sent to the member States a recommendation concerning the improvement of vocational guidance, urging co-operation between national services. Another aspect of training policy at Community level is the exchange of young workers provided for in Article 50 of the Rome Treaty. A first programme, approved in 1964 by the representatives of the member States, aims at increasing the number of exchanges already organised under bilateral and multi-lateral agreement

## HARMONISATION OF LABOUR RELATIONS

In the field of labour relations, the Commission sees its role as that of a stimulating force by acting as a co-ordinator for the collection of information. It has commissioned studies by experts to obtain comparisons of labour law and of collective bargaining agreements.

Certain aspects of labour relations have already been or will be dealt with in separate studies. They include procedural rules for the settlement of industrial disputes, the participation of workers in management decisions, legal and practical arrangements for collective bargaining in the member States, legal problems posed by the territorial scope of collective agreements, exercise of the right to strike, and the various measures taken in the case of men being laid off. The Commission has since 1969 maintained a central collection of material for the metal-working trades, where the key clauses in collective agreements are collated.

The Commission hopes that by providing the necessary information it will promote a development which ultimately may lead to some form of collective bargaining at the European level. It is quite clear that the initiatives for this have to be taken by the employers' organisations and trade unions themselves; their autonomy has also to be strictly respected at the Community level.

## ANNEX

### *Recommendations Concerning Social Matters*

which have been addressed to member States by the E.E.C. Commission

1. Equal Pay for Men and Women (20 July 1960) (not published in the *Official Gazette* of the European Communities).
2. Activities of Social Services in respect of Migrant Workers (20 July 1962) (*Official Gazette*, No. 75, 16 August 1962).
3. Adoption of a List of Occupational Diseases (23 July 1926) (*Official Gazette*, No. 80, 31 August 1962).
4. Industrial Medical Services (20 July 1962) (*Official Gazette*, No. 80, 31 August 1962).
5. Housing of Migrant Workers and their Families (7 July 1965) (*Official Gazette*, No. 137, 27 July 1965).
6. Development of Vocational Guidance (18 July 1966) (*Official Gazette*, No. 154, 24 August 1966).
7. Conditions for the Payment of Indemnities to Victims of Occupational Diseases (20 July 1966) (*Official Gazette*, No. 147, 9 August 1966).
8. Medical Supervision of Workers Exposed to Special Hazards (27 July 1966) (*Official Gazette*, No. 151, 17 August 1966).
9. Protection of Young Workers (31 January 1967) (*Official Gazette*, No. 25, 13 February 1967).

Chapter 13

# EFFORTS TO BRING ABOUT COMMUNITY-LEVEL COLLECTIVE BARGAINING IN THE COAL AND STEEL COMMUNITY AND THE E.E.C.

*by*

*Roger Blanpain*

## INTRODUCTION

ON the European level, within the countries belonging to the European Economic Community (E.E.C.) and the European Coal and Steel Community (E.C.S.C.), extensive collective bargaining is widely considered to be urgently necessary in order to achieve harmonisation of working conditions as a tool for social progress; but there are also those for whom this is still a merely academic subject which does not offer any real prospects of success in the near future.

Although only the future will show who was right, developments in the past fifteen years within the European Communities, especially as regards labour relations, make it worthwhile exploring the possibilities of collective agreements concluded between employers' associations and trade unions in different European countries.

In the E.E.C. countries trade union action is generally conducted with two partners: private employers and public authorities. The trade unions also exert influence on the policy-making bodies of the European Communities; and, as integration increases, they will have to develop this Community-directed action. Moreover, there is no doubt that, as a *common labour market* comes into being, trade union solidarity will have increasingly to transcend national frontiers in order to defend successfully the workers' interests in bargaining with employers on a European scale.[1] Many trade union leaders have

[1] See Levi Sandri: Statement made on 17 April 1964 at the Third European Conference of the International Federation of Christian Trade Unions (I.F.C.T.U.), now the World Confederation of Labour (W.C.L.).

275

grasped this necessity and are advocating a comprehensive European trade union approach. European collective bargaining thus becomes increasingly plausible as the European Communities become a more and more integrated reality and carry out an effective European social policy.

Whatever the outcome of these speculations may be, collective bargaining in the full sense of the word presupposes the conclusion of agreements between partners; and to a certain extent collective bargaining also remains a power relationship. The first important question to be asked, therefore, when examining the possibilities of European collective bargaining is: have national trade unions developed (power) structures with a European dimension and have they a counterpart on the employers' side (employers' association or European companies) competent and willing to bargain on a European level?

Moreover, employers' representatives and trade union leaders have, in fact, opportunities for meeting on the European level, mostly within the framework of the E.E.C. and the E.C.S.C. What are the results of these meetings and do they provide possible structures within which collective bargaining could be developed?

Up to now collective bargaining in the E.E.C. countries has taken place at the national level.[1] The main question is whether the trade unions are really convinced of the need for collective bargaining at a European level. Their attitudes towards collective bargaining require examination – especially the different ways and means through which they feel it can be achieved.

This chapter is limited to the following three major problems:

(1) The structure of trade unions and employers' associations within the European Economic Community. Since trade unions usually are the motivating force of collective bargaining, more attention will be paid to trade unions than to employers' associations.[2]

(2) The attitudes of trade unions and employers' associations toward the need for collective bargaining.

(3) The practical results of efforts to bring about collective bargaining in E.E.C. countries.

[1] For an exception in the field of agriculture see pp. 298–9.

[2] It is significant that it was decided in February 1968 to set up in Brussels a Trade Union Committee for the European Free Trade Area (EFTA – T.U.C.). Its initial purpose is to develop co-operation and the exchange of information amongst EFTA unions; but an equally important part of its task is to maintain close contact with the European Confederation of Free Trade Unions in the Community (E.C.T.U.C.) and to keep informed about what is going on generally in the European Economic Community.

Undoubtedly there are many other questions arising in the context of European collective bargaining, including the legal implications of European collective agreements. These will not be examined in this chapter since they have already been treated in previous studies.[1]

## A. THE SOCIAL PARTNERS IN THE EUROPEAN COMMUNITY

### *I. TRADE UNION DIVERSITY: WEAKNESS AND POWER*

Even a short description of trade unions in the member States of the E.E.C. shows up the great diversity, not to say the division, among them. Labour relations in Europe are indeed still marked by ideological differences. Moreover, the degree of unionisation and consequently of union strength also differs in the six member States.

In *Belgium*, it is claimed that more than 60 per cent of the workers are organised in the Belgian Confederation of Christian Trade Unions (A.C.V.–C.S.C.) and the (socialist) Belgian General Federation of Labour (A.B.V.V.–F.G.T.B.). The Belgian General Federation of Liberal Trade Unions (A.C.L.V.B.–C.G.S.L.B.) covers only a small percentage of workers.

In the *Federal Republic of Germany*, the German Confederation of Trade Unions (D.G.B.), which includes workers regardless of their ideology, religion or party allegiance, has a total membership of over 6·5 million (about 80 per cent of the organised workers). Less important are the German Union of Salaried Employees (D.A.G.), the German Civil Service Federation (D.B.B.) which affiliate white-collar and clerical workers, the Christian Trade Union Movement of Germany (C.G.D.), and the German Commercial Employees' Union (D.H.V.).

The degree of unionisation in *France* is rather low. Only 22 per cent of the workers seem to be organised in trade unions, which are extremely politically minded. About half of the organised workers belong to the communist-led General Confederation of Labour (C.G.T.). The

[1] Michel Despax: 'Les conventions collectives de travail européennes', *Droit social*, 1965, No. 12, pp. 616–26; Georges Spyropoulos: 'Le rôle de la négociation collective dans l'harmonisation des systèmes sociaux européens', *Revue internationale de droit comparé*, 1966, p. 65; G. Schnorr: 'Rechtsfragen europäischer Tarifverträge', *Sozialer Fortschritt*, 1963, No. 7–8, pp. 155–62.

majority of the other half are affiliated with the French Democratic Confederation of Labour (C.F.D.T.), the (socialist) General Confederation of Labour – *Force ouvrière* (F.O.), the General Confederation of Executive Staffs (C.G.C.) and the French Confederation of Christian Workers (C.F.T.C.).

In *Italy*, the majority of the 43 per cent of workers who are organised belong to the (communist/socialist) General Confederation of Italian Workers (C.G.I.L.), while the others are mostly affiliated with the Italian Confederation of Workers' Unions (C.I.S.L.), and the Italian Workers' Union (U.I.L.). The C.I.S.L. and the U.I.L. are affiliated with the International Confederation of Free Trade Unions (I.C.F.T.U.).

*Luxembourg* also has pluralistic trade unions: the Luxembourg General Confederation of Labour (C.G.T.L.) and the Confederation of Luxembourg Christian Unions (L.C.G.). A minority of workers belong to the Free Luxembourg Workers' Federation (F.L.A.) and to the Federation of Private Employees of Luxembourg (F.E.P.).

In the *Netherlands*, the trade unions are generally organised according to ideological orientations or creeds. The 34 per cent of workers who are organised belong to the (socialist) Netherlands Federation of Trade Unions (N.V.V.), the Netherlands Catholic Federation of Trade Unions (N.K.V.), the Netherlands Federation of Protestant Christian Trade Unions (C.N.V.) and the Unity Trade Union Central (E.V.C.) respectively.

The Christian trade unions are affiliated with the World Confederation of Labour (W.C.L.), formerly the International Federation of Christian Trade Unions (I.F.C.T.U.)[1]; the Socialist and Free trade unions with the International Confederation of Free Trade Unions (I.C.F.T.U.); and the communist trade unions with the World Federation of Trade Unions (W.F.T.U.).

About 37 per cent of the total labour force in the six E.C.C. countries are organised, or about 19 million workers out of a total of about 56 million. Fifteen per cent, or about 2·8 million, belong to the W.C.L.; 56 per cent, or about 11 million, to the I.C.F.T.U. and 24 per cent, or about 4·5 million, to the W.F.T.U.[2]

The communist-led trade unions have a rather dominant position in France and Italy; the I.C.F.T.U. has a strong position in the Federal

---

[1] 'In line with policy in recent years of de-emphasising the Christian aspects in order to maintain a wider appeal to workers of all beliefs'. See R. C. Beever: *Trade Unions and Free Labour Movement in the E.E.C.* (P.E.P., European Series, 1969), p. 6.

[2] See J. P. Windmuller: *Labor Internationals. A Survey of Contemporary International Trade Union Organisations* (New York, 1969).

Republic of Germany, the Netherlands and Belgium, while the W.C.L. has influence especially in Belgium, the Netherlands and France. The diversity of the labour movement in the E.E.C. countries, shown by the fact that it splits into three main tendencies, clearly weakens the effectiveness and strength of organised labour – particularly since these three tendencies are not equally supported in the different countries. Until recently, the I.C.F.T.U., perhaps because of the influence of the American Federation of Labor – Congress of Industrial Organisations (A.F.L.–C.I.O.), has been outspoken in its refusal to collaborate in any way with the French and Italian communist-led trade unions affiliated with the W.F.T.U., while the stated view of the W.C.L. is that normally the Christian trade unions cannot visualise concerted action with the communist unions.

The question of contacts and collaboration with the French and Italian communist-led unions was widely discussed at the General Assembly of the European affiliates of the I.C.F.T.U. held at The Hague on 23–25 April 1969, where the European Confederation of Free Trade Unions in the Community (E.C.T.U.C.) was set up. The resolution in which the General Assembly asked the Executive Committee to follow developments in this area and to take the proper action did not reflect the divergence amongst the members of E.C.T.U.C. on this important point; the Belgian, Italian and some Federal German representatives seemed to favour collaboration with the C.G.T. and the C.G.I.L. A similar resolution was passed at the first congress of the European organisation of the W.C.L.[1] The fact that the Commission of the European Economic Communities has recognised these communist-led unions will certainly favour collaboration between labour movements of differing tendencies.[2]

[1] 7–9 May 1969.
[2] It is worthwhile noting that recently the Italian unions – the C.I.S.L., the U.I.L. and the C.G.I.L. – decided to consult each other on 'European problems'. They made the following statement on the manner in which the three confederations would be represented in the E.E.C. and the E.C.S.C.: 'As regards Italian trade union presence in the E.E.C. and the E.C.S.C. the three confederations agreed that, from the next nominations onwards, the C.G.I.L. will participate in these bodies to represent, together with the C.I.S.L. and the U.I.L., the Italian workers and to fulfil a common commitment to strengthen the European Community institutions' (see *Informations syndicales et ouvrières – Notes rapides*, No. 6, 1969). Another example of collaboration is the recent meeting of five federations of Italian and French metalworkers held on 27–28 May 1969 in Paris. The discussions focused on the automobile industry and particularly on 'Fiat–Citroën–Berliet'. The following federations participated: the Italian Metal Mechanics' Federation (C.I.S.L. affiliate), the Italian Metalworkers' Union (U.I.L. affiliate), the Federation of Metal Workers and Employees (C.G.I.L. affiliate), the General Federation of Metal Trades' Workers (C.F.D.T. affiliate), the Federation of Metal Trades' Workers (C.G.T. affiliate) (see *ibid.*, No. 8, 1969).

The relationship between the I.C.F.T.U. and the W.C.L. is of a different nature and is characterised by regular contacts and even joint statements.

The following table gives a picture of the relative strengths and weaknesses of the main national trade unions within the six E.E.C. countries and their international affiliations.

## II. ADAPTATION OF TRADE UNION STRUCTURES TO THE REQUIREMENTS OF EUROPEAN INTEGRATION

Since the creation of the European Economic Community, the I.C.F.T.U. and the W.C.L. have been adapting their international structures to the requirements of European integration. And the communist-led trade unions that did not favour European integration, especially the French C.G.T., recently opened a special office in Brussels.

(1) *Structure and Activities within the I.C.F.T.U.*

(*a*) '*The Committee of 21*' – '*E.C.S.C. Inter-Union*'. With the establishment of the E.C.S.C. in 1952, a Liaison Department was set up under

---

(*Footnotes to table on page 281*)

[1] Belgian Confederation of Christian Trade Unions.
[2] Belgian General Federation of Labour.
[3] Belgian General Federation of Liberal Trade Unions.
[4] German Confederation of Trade Unions.
[5] German Union of Salaried Employees
[6] Christian Trade Union Movement of Germany.
[7] General Confederation of Labour.
[8] French Democratic Confederation of Labour.
[9] General Confederation of Labour – *Force ouvrière.*
[10] General Confederation of Executive Staffs.
[11] French Confederation of Christian Workers.
[12] General Confederation of Italian Workers.
[13] Italian Confederation of Workers' Unions.
[14] Italian Workers' Union.
[15] Italian Confederation of Workers' National Unions.
[16] Italian Christian Workers' Association.
[17] Luxembourg General Confederation of Labour.
[18] Confederation of Luxembourg Christian Unions.
[19] Federation of Private Employees of Luxembourg.
[20] Free Luxembourg Workers' Federation.
[21] Netherlands Federation of Trade Unions.
[22] Netherlands Catholic Federation of Trade Unions.
[23] Netherlands Federation of Protestant Christian Trade Unions.
[24] Unity Trade Union Central.

MEMBERSHIP OF NATIONAL TRADE UNIONS
IN THE E.E.C.*

| Country | Trade Unions | Membership |
|---|---|---|
| Belgium | A.C.V.-C.S.C.[1] | 810,000 |
| | A.B.V.V.-F.G.T.B.[2] | 700,000 |
| | A.C.L.V.-C.G.S.L.B.[3] | 80,000 |
| Federal Republic of | D.G.B.[4] | 6,500,000 |
| Germany | D.A.G.[5] | 650,000 |
| | C.G.D.[6] | 270,000 |
| France | C.G.T.[7] | 1,700,000 |
| | C.F.D.T.[8] | 1,000,000 |
| | C.G.T.-F.O.[9] | 800,000 |
| | C.G.C.[10] | 300,000 |
| | C.F.T.C.[11] | 80,000 |
| Italy | C.G.I.L.[12] | 2,900,000 |
| | C.I.S.L.[13] | 1,800,000 |
| | U.I.L.[14] | 300,000 |
| | C.I.S.N.A.L.[15] | 100,000 |
| | A.C.L.I.[16] | 100,000 |
| Luxembourg | C.G.T.L.[17] | 22,000 |
| | L.C.G.[18] | 11,000 |
| | F.E.P.[19] | 7,000 |
| | F.L.A.[20] | 3,000 |
| Netherlands | N.V.V.[21] | 520,000 |
| | N.K.V.[22] | 420,000 |
| | C.N.V.[23] | 230,000 |
| | E.V.C.[24] | 10,000 |
| Totals according to | I.C.F.T.U. | 10,642,000 |
| international | W.F.T.U. | 4,713,000 |
| affiliations: | W.C.L. | 2,881,000 |
| | Others | 1,077,000 |
| Total membership in the E.E.C. | | 19,313,000 |

\* Based on D. Sauer: *Europa en de vakbeweging* (Leuven, 1966), p. 16.

the direction of the 'Committee of 21'.[1] Its objectives were mainly concerned with the co-ordination of trade union activities in the six member countries and the representation of the workers within the Community. Decisions within the Committee were taken by unanimous vote. The 'Committee of 21' did not really dispose of any supra-national power. The different component organisations remained completely independent; and the Committee had no competence at all to bargain about labour or working conditions on the European level.

With the establishment of the European Trade Union Secretariat in 1958, a new organisation was created in Luxembourg, namely the 'E.C.S.C. Inter-Union'. This inter-union committee is composed exclusively of twenty-five representatives of the national trade unions of mine and metal workers and of their international trade secretariats.

Its sole objectives are information, co-ordination and representation in the E.C.S.C. The committee has not been an executive organ of international trade union policy. Its merits lie in its effectiveness as a co-ordinating body rather than as a powerful organ for policy mplementation.[2]

(*b*) *The European Trade Union Secretariat.* As soon as the European Economic Community was brought into being in 1958, the trade union federations of the six countries set up a European Trade Union Secretariat in Brussels in order to facilitate the representation of workers' organisations within the European Communities and to protect trade union interests. The broad lines of the Secretariat's policy are determined by the General Assembly and by the Executive Committee.

The *General Assembly*, which meets every other year, brings together representatives of the trade union federations in the Common Market countries, observers from trade union organisations[3] and observers from the international trade secretariats of the I.C.F.T.U. This Assembly decides the main lines of policy to be followed within the framework of the Common Market by the Executive Committee and the Secretariat.

---

[1] The Committee was composed of representatives of the International Trade Secretariats of metal and mine workers and the I.C.F.T.U., one member per national inter-occupational trade union congress, and one member per national trade union of miners and metalworkers affiliated with the national trade union congresses.
[2] R. C. Beever: *European Unity and the Trade Union Movements* (Leiden, A. W. Sythoff, 1960), p. 108.
[3] Mostly affiliated with the European regional organisations of the I.C.F.T.U.

The *Executive Committee* acts as a management committee and supervises the work carried out between meetings of the Assembly.

The *Trade Union Secretariat* assumes the functions of a permanent secretariat for the General Assembly, for the Executive Committee and several industrial trade union committees. The Secretariat is responsible for carrying out the decisions of the Executive Committee, for co-ordinating trade union action and for the development of a common viewpoint towards political, economic and social problems which come within the scope of the E.E.C. and the European Atomic Energy Community (Euratom).

A number of subsidiary bodies have been set up. There are major sub-committees for each of the integration projects: the social commission, the economic commission and the nuclear energy commission. There are also *industrial trade union committees*, guaranteeing adequate representation of the trade union federations of interested industrial branches.[1]

The Executive Committee, the Secretariat and the different committees and subsidiary bodies have acted as a medium through which the trade unions of the Common Market countries pass information to each other and have assured their representation in the E.E.C. Commission and Councils. They have had no real competence as far as negotiations with employers are concerned.[2]

*(c) The European Confederation of Free Trade Unions in the Community (E.C.T.U.C.), April 1969.* The E.C.T.U.C. was created on the occasion of the VIth General Assembly of Free Trade Unions in the Common Market held at the Hague from 23 to 25 April 1969. Its statute was prepared by a working group consisting of members of both national centres and trade union committees, set up in pursuance of a resolution of the General Assembly adopted in Rome in November

[1] The following industrial trade union committees exist: the Working Party of the European Landworkers' Federation; the Transport Trade Union Committee of the Community; the Group of E.E.C. Trade Unions affiliated with the International Union of Food and Allied Workers' Associations; the Committee of Trade Unions for the Metallurgical Industry; the E.E.C. Co-ordination Commission for the International Federation of Chemical and General Workers' Unions; the Joint Commission of Building and Woodworkers in the European Communities.

[2] Since July 1967 the EFTA–T.U.C. has been represented in the Executive Committee. The Secretary-General and another member of the General Council now regularly attend the meetings. Danish and Norwegian trade unions have also been invited; but only the Norwegians participate though not on a regular basis. See I.C.F.T.U., European Trade Union Secretariat, VIth General Assembly: *Progress Report 1966–8*, The Hague, 23–5 April 1969, I, 3.

1966.[1] The working group prepared its report between February and September 1968. This report was discussed by the Executive Committee at its meeting on 9 and 10 October 1968 and at its meeting on 21 February 1969. The draft statute of the E.C.T.U.C. is reproduced in the annex to this chapter.

A. Kloos (Netherlands Federation of Trade Unions (N.V.V.)) was elected President of the E.C.T.U.C. and B. Storti (Italian Confederation of Workers' Unions (C.I.S.L.)) and H. Vetter (German Confederation of Trade Unions (D.G.B.)) became Vice-Presidents. T. Rasschaert was confirmed as General Secretary.

With the setting up of the E.C.T.U.C. a further step has no doubt been taken towards trade union integration at the European level. However, it would be going too far to claim that the E.C.T.U.C. is a genuine international body serving as a central locus of decision-making. The stated aims of the E.C.T.U.C. are to be achieved through 'a declaration of principles' and co-ordination of the activities of the affiliated organisations. It was also pointed out by the Executive Committee when it submitted the E.C.T.U.C. statute adopted at the General Assembly in The Hague that 'it would be premature to seek a final form regarding the international relations of our E.C.T.U.C. organisations with each other'. This clearly indicates that the main thrust of trade union action still remains in national trade union centres.

(d) *The International Trade Secretariats* (I.T.S.s). The I.T.S.s are *autonomous* federations of national unions, operating in specific or related trades or industries, and as such associated with the I.C.F.T.U.

At present there are seventeen I.T.S.s with a total of over 33 million members[2]. As autonomous organisations, the I.T.S.s have their own governing bodies, such as their congresses and executive committees,

---

[1] This resolution reads as follows: 'The General Assembly requests the Executive Committee, supported by a working group consisting of the responsible representatives of the affiliated trade union national centres, the trade union committees and the European Trade Union Secretariat, to prepare proposals for strengthening co-operation among the affiliated organisations. Proposals in this field will concern, among other things, the passing of resolutions, the procedure for executive power of the Executive Committee, the General Assembly and the Trade Union Secretariat, as well as relations between these bodies. The Executive Committee will present the relevant proposals to the VIth General Assembly.'

[2] The 17 I.T.S.s are:
 – International Federation of Building and Woodworkers;
 – International Federation of Commercial, Clerical and Technical Employees;
 – Universal Alliance of Diamond Workers;

(*Footnote continued on page 285*)

and receive their own affiliation fees from member unions.[1] The I.T.S.s serve mainly as centres of information and co-ordination of representation in international organisations. They have no competence to bargain as regards wages and working conditions. Their role may be enlarged in the future, but up to now their scope has been restricted.

*(2) Structure and Activities Within the W.C.L. (formerly I.F.C.T.U.)*

*(a) The Federation of Christian Trade Unions in the E.C.S.C.* The Christian trade unions also decided to have specific representation in Luxembourg. They first set up a Co-ordination Committee – E.C.S.C., and then in 1955 the Federation of Christian Trade Unions in the E.C.S.C. This Federation was described as an *independent* Christian trade union of blue- and white-collar workers in the member countries of the E.C.S.C. Its objectives were: co-ordination, information, and the study and defence of the interests of the workers in the Community.

Individual trade unions of metalworkers and miners as well as national centres were represented within the Federation, which had the following organs: General Assembly,[2] Committee of the Federation,[3] the Executive Board, and the Secretariat.

The Committee was the main guiding organ of the Federation and its decisions were binding if a two-thirds majority was obtained.[4] Generally, the Federation performed the same function as the Committee of 21. It did not develop into a bargaining agency replacing national unions.[5]

---

– European Union of Film and Television Technicians;
– International Union of Food and Allied Workers' Associations;
– International Graphical Federation;
– International Federation of Chemical and General Workers' Unions;
– International Metalworkers' Federation;
– Miners' International Federation;
– International Federation of Petroleum and Chemical Workers;
– International Federation of Plantation, Agricultural and Allied Workers;
– Postal, Telegraph and Telephone International;
– Public Services International;
– International Shoe and Leather Workers' Federation;
– International Federation of Free Teachers' Unions;
– International Textile and Garment Workers' Federation;
– International Transport Workers' Federation.

[1] I.C.F.T.U.: *International Trade Secretariats* (Brussels, 1962).
[2] Meeting every two years.
[3] Meeting every three months.
[4] Except in the case of religious matters, which required a unanimous vote.
[5] See Beever, *op. cit.*, p. 111.

In 1959, after the establishment of the European Organisation of the I.F.C.T.U. in Brussels, the Federation was dissolved. The International Federation of Christian Metalworkers' Unions and the International Federation of Christian Miners' Unions set up a joint secretariat under the supervision of a board, composed of eight members representing the two I.T.S.s. The Secretariat consists at present of two full-time officers and one part-time secretary. Its function also is only to inform, co-ordinate and represent; and neither by statute, nor in practice[1] has it the capability of being a bargaining agency.

*(b) The European Organisation of the W.C.L. (formerly I.F.C.T.U.).* The European Organisation of the I.F.C.T.U. was established officially on 27 May 1958. Its membership consists of national trade union federations and of the international trade secretariats. Its structure consists of the European Congress (formerly Conference), the Committee, the Executive Committee and the Secretariat.

The European Conference was composed on representatives of all the members of the Organisation, and met every two years. Its function was purely consultative in relation to the activities of the Organisation. In 1967 it was decided to change the Conference into a *Congress* and grant it powers of decision.[2]

The *Committee*, which is composed of thirty-five members, is the main policy-making body; it also supervises the work of the Executive Committee. The Committee meets twice a year.

The *Executive Committee* meets at least once every three months and supervises the activities of the *Secretariat*.

In principle, decisions within the different organs are taken by majority vote. The European Organisation of the W.C.L. has the same general aims as the European Trade Union Secretariat of the I.C.F.T.U.: co-ordination of trade union activities and working out common viewpoints on problems coming within the scope of the E.E.C. The European Organisation of the W.C.L. lacks, supra-national competence as far as the setting of working and wage conditions is concerned.

Although Mr Auguste Cool pleaded at the Congress of Amsterdam (1966) for stronger trade union powers on the European level, the

[1] The annual budget of the International Christian Federation of Metalworkers' Unions, grouping about 330,000 members, is only about 1,250,000 Belgian francs – and there are no other financial resources.
[2] The Congress consists of twenty-four representatives of national trade union centres and of 11 representatives of the I.T.S.s.

present situation is unchanged: the European Organisation of the W.C.L. is understaffed and does not have the financial means needed to carry out a real trade union policy.

In accordance with the resolution of the Amsterdam Congress of 1966, a working party was set up by the Executive Committee. The working party was composed of five representatives of national federations, two representatives of the I.T.S.s and of the General Secretary of the European Organisation. The working party, which started its activities on 21 December 1966, finished its work on 20 December 1968, when it adopted a report on 'The orientation of the structures and the action of the trade union movement at the European level'. The proposals in this report are less far-reaching than the resolutions of the 1966 Amsterdam Congress. As regards the structure of the European Organisation the working party proposed:

1. the setting up of joint action programmes for co-ordinated efforts at the national level as well as within sectors;
2. the transformation of the Conference into a Congress;
3. the establishment of a system of qualified majority voting in the governing organs;
4. a yearly debate within the European Organisation on the policy of member organisations;
5. the regrouping of the international federations (I.T.S.s) in conjunction with the Secretariat of the European Organisation;
6. the improvement of financial and secretarial resources.

Points 2 and 3 have already been implemented. The implementation of the other points depends largely on point 6; and it is known that this point will not be given effect to in the near future.[1]

The working party report proved disappointing for those who had expected a genuine European trade union structure. It was discussed at the First Congress of the European Organisation of the W.C.L., held in Brussels from 7 to 9 May 1969.

It was decided at this Congress to revise radically the statutes of the W.C.L. European Organisation on the basis of the conclusions reached by the W.C.L. World Congress (Geneva, 28–31 May 1969)[2] and some important features can already be noted. First, the change of title to the European Organisation of the W.C.L.; and secondly, the transfor-

---

[1] A proposal to double the financial contribution over a period of five years was not approved and was referred back for further study.
[2] Final decisions were due to be taken by the Executive Committee at its meeting scheduled for 9–10 October 1969.

mation of the Conference into a Congress with decision-making powers and a system of qualified majority voting. Now a unanimous vote is required for questions of principle of concerning action by national federations or by European regional organisations of the international federations (I.T.S.s); a two-thirds majority is sufficient as regards public statements; and a simple majority applies in respect of all other matters. A. Cool has been appointed President and J. Kulakowski General Secretary of the European Organisation of the W.C.L.

## (c) International Federations

The different international federations[1] of the Christian trade unions perform the same functions as the I.T.S.s of the I.C.F.T.U. They are essentially centres for the exchange of information and for co-ordination of viewpoints.

## 4. Conclusions

The above description of trade union structures in the E.E.C. countries and their European organisations leads to the following conclusions:

The diversity of the labour movement, split up into three main tendencies (social-democrat, Christian and communist) weakens considerably the effectiveness of organised labour within the E.E.C. Contacts between the social-democratic and the Christian unions seem to be quite satisfactory. On a number of occasions the I.C.F.T.U. and the W.C.L. have, in fact, expressed a desire to collaborate.[2] Up until recently there were no contacts (and even a stated refusal[3] to collaborate on the part of the I.C.F.T.U.) with the communist labour movement. Latterly, however, a move has been made towards co-operation with communist-led unions on the European level as well; and the fact that the Commission of the European Communities has recently recognised these unions will certainly facilitate this potential collaboration.

Although the I.C.F.T.U. as well as the W.C.L. have adapted their

---

[1] Eleven in number.

[2] See Joint motion of 27 January 1966, *Vakbondsvoorlichting*, No. 1, p. 1; joint memorandum of the mineworkers' unions of the I.C.F.T.U. and I.F.C.T.U. of 10 February 1966 *ibid.*, 1966, No. 2, p. 30; joint memorandum concerning social policy of the E.E.C. of 20 December 1966; joint meeting with the Commission on 11 December 1967, etc. Declarations towards this end were also made at the Congress of the E.C.T.U.C. at The Hague, 1969, and at the Congress of the European Organisation of the W.C.L. at Brussels, 1969.

[3] I.C.F.T.U. declarations Paris, 1964 and 17 March 1966, *Vakbondsvoorlichting*, 1966, No. 2, pp. 24–5; Congress, Rome, November 1966, *ibid.*, 1966, No. 8, p. 30. See also R. Clain and R. Guilbert: *La vie ouvrière*, No. 1061.

structures to meet the requirements of European integration, the main trade union activities are still carried on at the national level. The different European organisations are merely liaison departments and centres for information and the co-ordination of trade union viewpoints at the European level. They have neither the competence, nor the staff, nor the finances to play an important and decisive role at the European level. They are not at present equipped – and presumably will not be in the near future – to be the bargaining agent within Europe,[1] even though trade union leaders have often stressed the need for a more effective European trade union structure.

## III. EUROPEAN ORGANISATIONS OF EMPLOYERS WITHIN THE E.E.C. COUNTRIES

*(1.) Union of Industries of the European Community (U.N.I.C.E.)*

The Union of Industries of the European Community (U.N.I.C.E.) was founded on 1 March 1958. It groups the following employers' organisations:

- German Confederation of Industry ⎫
- Confederation of German Employers' ⎬ (Federal Republic
  Associations ⎭ of Germany)
- Federation of Belgian Industries (Belgium),
- National Council of French Employers (France).
- General Confederation of Italian Industry (Italy),
- Federation of Luxembourg Manufacturers (Luxembourg),
- Federation of Netherlands Industry ⎫
- Central Social Federation of Employers ⎪ The
- Catholic Federation of Agricultural Entrepreneurs ⎬ Netherlands
- Federation in the Netherlands of Christian ⎪
  Employers ⎭

---

[1] This is also the viewpoint of L. Levi-Sandri, Vice-President of the European Commission: 'It is about time, in my opinion, that the trade union movement (I am thinking equally of employers' associations and workers' organisations) advanced beyond the stage of being a mere liaison mechanism, a mere secretariat, and that it tackled courageously and decisively the problem of a European trade union organisation, setting an example by transferring to such an organisation part of the powers of the national organisations and making a real effort towards trade union integration. Its powers and role in the Community would then be altogether different, and no one would think of raising the question whether the social partners should be consulted or not. Because in such circumstances these social partners would no longer have merely a consultative function but would play an active part in the promotion and achievement of a European social policy.' (Statement of 17 April 1964, *op. cit.*)

289

The main aims of U.N.I.C.E. are to develop an industrial policy in a spirit of solidarity on the European level, and to represent the industries of the six countries in E.E.C. bodies. These objectives are pursued through studies and the exchange and co-ordination of viewpoints.

As regards its structure U.N.I.C.E. consists of a Council of Presidents, a Secretariat-General, a Committee of Permanent Delegates and special study commissions.

The *Council of Presidents* is the policy-making organ of the organisation. It meets every two months. Decisions are taken unanimously. The *Secretary General* carries out the decisions of the Council. He presides over the Committee of Permanent Delegates, which meets weekly and assures the representation of U.N.I.C.E. in E.E.C. organs.

U.N.I.C.E. has no supra-national bargaining competence at the European level as regards wages and labour conditions.

*(2) European federations of employers' associations by branch of industry*

Different autonomous federations by branch of industry, grouping national associations of employers of the six countries, have been set up. In addition to their representative function they act mainly as study committees, reviewing the social situation and developments in the E.E.C. Up to now, they have never been called upon to act as bargaining agents on the European level.[1]

There are organisations similar to U.N.I.C.E. for the agricultural and the commercial sectors. They are C.O.P.A. (Committee of Agricultural Employers' Organisations) and C.O.C.C.E. (Committee of Commercial Organisations of the E.E.C.).

## B. ATTITUDES TOWARDS THE NECESSITY FOR EUROPEAN COLLECTIVE BARGAINING

### I. TRADE UNION VIEWS

The trade unions have indicated on different occasions the necessity for European collective agreements, or at least national collective bargaining inspired by a 'common' programme.

---

[1] ORGALIME, for instance, the liaison body of the metal industries, has a social commission, which meets three or four times a year to review the social situation in the E.E.C. countries. Up to now it has made no contact with European trade unions. Likewise, the fields of action of the Western European Coal Producers' Study Committee does not exceed its title.

The first move in this direction was made at the IVth General Assembly of the I.C.F.T.U. European organisation on 11–13 March 1964. It aimed at the formulation of a common programme to be implemented through *national collective agreements*. This programme called for:

– a 40-hour, 5-day week,
– an improvement in the annual holidays system,
– the same rules for blue- and white-collar workers,
– equal pay for male and female workers.

This approach was endorsed in May 1965 and at the Luxembourg Congress in June 1967. The common programme then adopted called for:

– a 40-hour working week;
– an extension of annual holidays;
– guaranteed income in case of incapacity.

The I.C.F.T.U. timber and building trade unions conference held in Milan in December 1966 moved in the same direction and proposed a reduction in hours of work, an extension of holidays with pay and a guaranteed annual income.

The trade unions have also pressed repeatedly for direct negotiations at the European level.

The I.C.F.T.U. re-emphasised this point at the above-mentioned Luxembourg Congress, drawing particular attention to the need both for *general collective bargaining* as well as *bargaining per branch of industry* keeping European standards in mind.

This attitude was supported by the W.C.L. According to A. Cool,[1] the W.C.L. had proposed in vain to the employers the following procedure which would have led ultimately to collective bargaining at the European level:

1. First, the establishment of an inventory of social regulations affecting labour costs in the different countries;
2. A subsequent attempt at harmonisation of such regulations; and
3. Finally, the conclusion of general collective agreements fixing specific labour conditions.

The European organisations of the I.C.F.T.U. and of the I.F.C.T.U., as well as many European I.T.S.s, also urged the setting up of *joint*

---

[1] See his speech of 17 May 1967, *Vakbondsvoorlichting*, 1967, No. 4, p. 13.

*committees* per branch of industry composed of an equal number of trade union and of employer representatives.[1] While according to the I.C.F.T.U. and the I.F.C.T.U. representatives at the 1964 Stresa Conference, the undertaking of studies was intended to be the main task of such joint committees, their functioning could ultimately lead to the conclusion of European collective agreements.[2]

The European Commission has likewise recommended the creation of joint or mixed committees, with a view to the conclusion of European agreements.[3]

The *joint committees* proposed by trade unions were to cover the following industries: building,[4] textiles,[5] food and agriculture,[6] metal and transport.[7] Moreover the Christian I.T.S. for the food, tobacco and related industries proposed a European collective agreement including provisions for hours of work, holidays, guaranteed annual income and similar matters.

A further possibility of European collective bargaining is the conclusion of agreements covering multi-national corporations. There have already been initial contacts between trade unions and such corporations which might ultimately lead to collective bargaining of this type in the metal industry.[8]

## II. EMPLOYER ORGANISATION VIEWS

As indicated in its Memorandum on Social Policy within the E.E.C. (1966), U.N.I.C.E. believes that social policy is above all a *national problem* and should be determined by the political authorities and the social partners at the national level. According to U.N.I.C.E., European collective bargaining therefore does not make much practical sense.

---

[1] See *Round Table Conference*, Stresa, May 1964; see *Vakbondsvoorlichting*, 1964, No. 5, and also Proceedings of the Congress of Advisory Committees within the E.E.C. of the French C.F.T.C., 17–19 November 1967.

[2] Action programme of the European Organisation of I.F.C.T.U. 1965; see *Vakbondslichting*, 1965, No. 8 bis.

[3] Social memorandum of the Commission, December 1966, *ibid.*, 1967, No. 1, p. 10.

[4] Congress of the International Federation of Christian Trade Unions of Building and Wood Workers, Spa, 7–9 September 1964. The Congress rejected, however, the idea of a European collective agreement fixing wages and harmonising other labour conditions.

[5] Congress of Christian I.T.S.s, Scheveningen, 15–17 June 1965; see *Vakbondsvoorlichting*, 1965, No. 6–7.

[6] Congress of Christian I.T.S.s, Koblenz, 26–7 September 1967; see *ibid.*, 1967, No. 8, p. 15.

[7] Congress of Christian I.T.S.s, Brussels, 25–6 October 1967; see *ibid.*, p. 5.

[8] See Chapter 16.

## C. EFFORTS AND RESULTS

As stated above, numerous contacts have developed at the European level between trade unions and employers as a result of initiatives by the European Communities. For the most part, however, the aim of these contacts is not collective bargaining.

### 1. EFFORTS AND RESULTS WITHIN THE E.C.S.C.

*(1) Consultative Committee of the E.C.S.C.*

The Consultative Committee of the E.C.S.C., provided for in articles 18[1] and 19[2] of the Paris Treaty, was intended to be, and is, an organisation representing the viewpoints of parties interested in the working of the Community: producers, workers, consumers and dealers.

Out of a possible number of 51 members, 17 represent producers, 17 workers[3] and 17 consumers and dealers. According to Article 19, the High Authority may consult the Consultative Committee on all matters it deems proper. The High Authority is required to do this whenever such consultation is prescribed by the Treaty.

As its name suggests the Committee has a purely *consultative function*.

[1] Article 18 reads: 'There shall be created a Consultative Committee, attached to the High Authority. It shall consist of not less than thirty and not more than fifty-one members, and shall include an equal number of producers, workers, and consumers and dealers.

'The members of the Consultative Committee shall be appointed by the Council. As concerns producers and workers, the Council shall appoint the representative organisations among which it shall allocate the seats to be filled. Each organisation shall be asked to draw up a list comprising twice the number of seats allocated to it. Appointments shall be made from this list.

'The members of the Consultative Committee shall be appointed in their individual capacity for a period of two years. They shall not be bound by any mandate or instruction from the organisations which proposed them as candidates.

'A president and officers shall be elected for periods of one year by the Consultative Committee from among its own members. The Committee shall make its own rules of procedure.

'The allowances of members of the Consultative Committee shall be determined by the Council on the proposal of the High Authority.'

[2] Article 19 reads: 'The High Authority may consult the Consultative Committee on all matters it deems proper. It shall be required to do so whenever such consultation is prescribed by the present Treaty.

'The High Authority shall submit to the Consultative Committee the general objectives and programmes established under the terms of article 46, and shall keep the Committee informed of the broad lines of its action under the terms of articles 54, 65 and 66.'

[3] There are eleven to twelve seats for I.C.F.T.U. representatives and five to six seats for W.C.L. representatives.

*(2) Joint Committees*

In 1955, the High Authority, in accordance with a resolution adopted by the Consultative Committee, created two joint committees for the harmonisation of labour conditions, one for the steel industry and one for the coalmining industry.

The committees are composed of representatives of trade unions and of employers' associations; government representatives are also invited to the meetings of the committee for the coalmining industry.

The task of the two committees is to:

– collect information on working conditions in the industries of the E.C.S.C.;
– review the differences in the systems of the member countries; and
– study ways and means of facilitating an upward harmonisation of working conditions.

Both committees meet every six months under the presidency of the executive head of the E.C.S.C.

The steel committee has carried out studies on different issues – e.g. hours of work, the form and content of individual labour contracts and the workers' representation at the undertaking and industry level.

These studies have been published after endorsement by the Consultative Committee. They merely reflect the existing situation in the E.C.S.C. countries.

The same type of work has been done in the coal committee, which from 1961 to 1964 passed through a very difficult period. Different trade unions proposed the drawing up of a 'European Miners' Charter'[1] which they considered would be an ideal way of harmonising working conditions. This Charter would have provided for various benefits to be granted equally by governments and employers to miners in all the Community countries. Subsequently the trade unions, supported by resolutions of the European Parliament[2] as well as by the E.C.S.C. High Authority, called for the opening of discussions concerning the European Miners' Charter.

The employers refused, however, to discuss the Charter on the grounds that:

---

[1] Sponsored by the late Paul Finet, High Authority member, who first suggested such a Charter.
[2] Resolutions of 27 June 1962 and 27 June 1963.

1. the matters proposed to be dealt with in the Charter fell within the competence of *national* authorities (legislatures, governments, and social partners);
2. the economic conditions necessary to permit an upward harmonisation of working conditions as required by the proposed Charter were lacking.

Some governments questioned the competence not only of the coal committee but also of the E.C.S.C. High Authority to deal with a project such as the Charter. At a meeting of the workers' representatives on the joint committee convened by the High Authority on 18 December 1964, the representatives of the workers affiliated with the International Confederation of Free Trade Unions (I.C.F.T.U.) and those of the workers affiliated with the International Federation of Christian Trade Unions (I.F.C.T.U.) adopted a common position. After first pointing out that they still regarded a European Miners' Charter economically as well as socially indispensable, and that they were in no way withdrawing their demand for its introduction, the union representatives stated that, in a spirit of conciliation and having regard to the need for a speedy solution of the labour problems of the coal industry, they were prepared to consider the introduction of the Charter in stages. They then stated that the first stage should comprise the extension to all Community miners of the shift bonus paid to miners in the Federal Republic of Germany, and the introduction of a long-service bonus. The combination of these two measures would, in the unions' view, give a new impulse to the drive for the Community-wide alignment of living and working conditions and would result in a substantial upgrading of the occupation of coal miner. This would help the coal industry to overcome the difficulties created by the dislike of mining and the instability of the labour force, which resulted in heavy financial burdens for the industry (e.g. as regards the cost of recruitment, training and adaptation of a large number of workers, many of them from non-Community countries) and had serious adverse effects both on work safety and on profitability. The unions expressed the belief that if the occupation of coal miner were adequately upgraded, the coal mines would be able to attract and retain a labour force capable of meeting modern technological requirements.

The High Authority decided to submit the workers' proposals to the member governments and the employers' organisations. In

January 1965, it submitted to them the document which the unions had drawn up in the light of the meeting of 18 December 1964, and invited the government and employer representatives on the joint committee to meet separately with the High Authority for a preliminary study of this document. The separate meetings with the employer and government representatives took place in February 1965.

After another exchange of views, the High Authority in March 1966 put the issue to the Council of Ministers but so far there have been no further developments.

Since 1965, other *joint committees* have been set up – for example for white-collar workers in the coal and steel sectors. Their aim is to study questions of remuneration, conditions of work and social security within the six E.C.S.C. countries and the possibilities for upward harmonisation of standards in these fields.

This short description of activities within the E.C.S.C. clearly indicates that despite great efforts by the competent E.C.S.C. organs the trade unions have been unable to exercise pressure on the employers or even to enter into discussions with them about the principle of European bargaining. Regardless of the reasons advanced by the employers and even by some of the governments, it has emerged quite clearly that the trade unions lack effectiveness and power at the European level. Nevertheless, the proposed European Miners' Charter represents the first large-scale attempt at industry-wide collective bargaining at the European level.

## II. EFFORTS AND RESULTS WITHIN THE E.E.C.

### (1) The Economic and Social Committee (E.S.C.) and other Advisory Committees

The Rome Treaty of 1957 provided for the creation of the Economic and Social Committee (E.S.C.) as a purely consultative body, despite union demands that it should have broader powers, especially the right of initiative. The main task of the E.S.C. is to give advice in respect of proposals which are made by the Commission and are referred to the E.S.C. either by the Commission itself or by the E.E.C. Council of Ministers.

The E.S.C. is composed of 101 members, including 24 each from the Federal Republic of Germany, France and Italy, 12 each from Belgium and the Netherlands, and 5 from Luxembourg. According to

Article 193 of the Rome Treaty these members represent the various categories of economic and social life, especially producers, agriculturists, transport operators, workers, merchants, artisans, the liberal professions and the general interest.[1]

The trade unions hold at present thirty-four seats in the E.S.C., which is somewhat more than one-third of the total membership.

They have been complaining that with their thirty-four seats they are not adequately represented in view of the fact that forty-nine seats are occupied by categories representing directly or indirectly employers interests. They argue that this does not correspond to 'adequate' representation of the different social and economic groups as stipluated by Article 193. According to the I.C.F.T.U.[2] co-operation in the E.S.C. between trade unions and employers has produced only poor results. In the unions' opinion the main reason is that employer representatives do not want, or do not have the competence, to be considered as bargaining partners; and there is also the negative attitude of some governments towards any progressive social policy at the Community level.

Other meeting places of trade unions and employers within the E.E.C. are the Consultative Committee of the European Social Fund, the Committee for Free Movement of Labour and the Committee for Vocational Training. Their activities are marked by characteristics similar to those of the Economic and Social Committee; and this is true also of the activities of the Central Committee of Social Partners set up in 1961 by the European Commission under Articles 117 and 118 of the Rome Treaty to give advice on how to achieve social harmonisation. However, just like the joint committees of the E.S.S.C. the E.E.C. Central Committee of Social Partners has been unable to go beyond the stage of study and survey of such problems as remuneration, hours of work and safety regulations. There has been no agreement to follow up and implement these studies through recommendations, as suggested by the Commission.[3]

[1] The distribution of seats among these groups is as follows:
Producers: 16.
Agriculturists: 14.
Transport operators: 6.
Trade unionists: 34.
Merchants: 6.
Artisans: 7.
[2] See Luxembourg Congress, 1–2 June 1967, *Les relations, au niveau Européen, entre les organisations des employeurs et des travailleurs*, pp. 7–12.
[3] A recent exception is the agreement of principle in respect of the guidelines of the Commission in the social field.

## (2) U.N.I.C.E. – Trade Union Contacts

The E.C.T.U.C. and the W.C.L. have had contacts with U.N.I.C.E.: two in 1967 and two in 1968. The discussions covered social activities in the E.E.C. The parties agreed on the role trade unions and employers' associations should play in social harmonisation within the Community and on the need for co-ordination at the Community level of national employment policies; on the organisation of a tripartite conference on employment problems; on matters arising from the U.N.I.C.E. Memorandum on Social Policy of 1966; and on questions concerning vocational training. These talks led to the setting up of three joint working parties: the first on vocational training, the second on the European Social Fund and the third on free movement of labour. However, the meetings of these working parties have not yet led to concrete results. Contact is also maintained with the European Centre for Public Enterprise (C.E.E.P.), which groups government undertakings.

## (3) Relations by sector

(a) *Agriculture.* It is not by chance that a European collective agreement concerning the harmonisation of hours of work of agricultural workers was concluded on 6 June 1968 between C.O.P.A. and representatives of the I.C.F.T.U. and the I.F.C.T.U. Indeed from the very outset the European Economic Community has pursued a very active common agricultural policy; and social problems constitute a specific part of this policy.[1]

The agreement was concluded within the framework of an *ad hoc* committee created in 1967 on the initiative of Levi Sandri.[2] The *ad hoc* committee was composed of nine representatives of C.O.P.A., six representatives of the I.C.F.T.U. (agricultural organisations) and three representatives of the I.F.C.T.U.

[1] As early as July 1958, the Stresa conference was convened to work out basic guidelines for a common agricultural policy. At this conference special attention was paid to social problems, and the need for achieving equality of the social conditions of farmers and farm-workers with those of persons employed in industry was stressed. When in 1960 and 1962 the Commission worked out its proposals for implementing a common agricultural policy, considerable attention was devoted to social considerations. In 1961, a conference on social aspects of agriculture was organised by the Commission. In 1963, on the occasion of the formulation of the Commission's action programme, the importance of achieving equality of social conditions in the agricultural sector with those in other sectors was again stressed. (See J. D. Neirinck: *Social Policy of the E.E.C. Commission – A General Survey: Achievements and Trends at the End of 1967* (Leuven), p. 38.)

[2] The agreement had been prepared by the joint committee for social problems of agricultural workers, created on 17 May 1963.

The agreement covers in particular annual hours of work,[1] maximum weekly and daily hours, overtime, night work, holidays, etc. The following points are important in the present context:

(i) The agreement is not a legally binding instrument directly enforceable in the E.E.C. member States. The parties merely agreed to recommend the text of the agreement to their member associations for implementation when national collective agreements are being modified or renewed.

(ii) More generous national provisions remain in force.

The advisory joint committee for social problems of agricultural workers has been operating since 1963 as a result of decisions taken by the 1961 conference on social aspects of the common agricultural policy. Various suggestions have already been formulated by this committee on vocational training, hours of work, wages, protection of young agricultural workers, job security, protection of working mothers, social security, etc.

(b) *Transport.* Since 1958 there have been an impressive number of institutionalised as well as *ad hoc* contacts between employer groups and trade unions within the framework of E.E.C. activities aiming at a common transport policy.[2] In addition to the *Advisory Transport Committee* established in accordance with Article 83 of the Rome Treaty, *a joint advisory committee for social problems of transport by road* was created by the European Commission on 5 July 1965.

(c) *Other sectors.* In other sectors, most contacts between employers and trade unions are arranged through institutionalised organs created within the E.E.C. framework for advisory purposes.

It is undoubtedly true that there are numerous contacts on the European level between trade unions and employers and that an

---

[1] 2,348 (45 by 52 plus 8) hours.

[2] *Ad hoc* contacts organised as a result of E.E.C. initiatives include the conference on technical progress in the Common Market (1960); the European social security conference (1962); and the round table conference on social policy in the transport sector (1963). In accordance with the decision of 13 May 1965 of the Council of Ministers of the E.E.C., the E.E.C. Commission proposed on 22 July 1966 regulations harmonising certain social standards in road transport. The proposed regulation contains provisions concerning the minimum age of drivers, the composition of crews, driving time, daily rest periods, etc. (See J. D. Neirinck, *op. cit.*, p. 38.)

impressive number of topics are debated in an equally impressive number of committees within the framework of the E.E.C. So far, however, these contacts have only exceptionally opened the way to direct negotiations and collective bargaining.

## III. CONTACTS WITH MULTI-NATIONAL CORPORATIONS

An initial contact between Philips and representatives of the two trade secretariats of metalworkers (linked to the I.C.F.T.U. and the W.C.L. respectively) and of the International Federation of Christian Trade Unions of Salaried Employees, Technicians, Managerial Staff and Commercial Travellers took place in Eindhoven (Netherlands) on 14 September 1967. Philips has 252,000 employees, of whom 80,000 are in the Netherlands and 134,000 in other European, especially E.E.C., countries. This first talk, described as 'informative, informal and constructive', concerned mainly production problems within the E.E.C. and their consequences on manpower policy and job security within the Philips undertakings.[1]

## CONCLUSIONS

No doubt one of the key issues determining the possibility of collective bargaining on a European scale is whether the power and structure of trade unions are adequate to cope with bargaining problems on that level. For the E.E.C. countries the answer tends to be negative.

[1] See *Vakbondsvoorlichting*, 1967, No. 6, pp. 20-2. Another meeting was held in June 1969.

A Fiat–Citroën co-ordination committee was set up under I.C.F.T.U. auspices in 1968, but there have been no contacts between the multi-national corporations and the committee. The following goals, to be achieved through a European collective agreement, were given as the first target:

1. a common minimum wage;
2. protection against the repercussions of rationalisation and economic concentration;
3. equal status for white- and blue-collar workers; and
4. guaranteed trade union rights at the plant level (see I.C.P.T.U. European Trade Union Secretariat VIth General Assembly: Progress Report 1966–8, *op. cit.*, p. 21). See also C. Levinson: 'International Collective Bargaining – Historic I. M. F. Action on Saint-Gobain', *I.M.F. Bulletin*, June–July 1969, pp. 9–18.

*Diversity*, not to say *weakness*, characterises the labour movement in Europe. With this movement split up into three main tendencies, one can question seriously the effectiveness of organised labour within the E.E.C. countries. Social democratic and Christian unions tend to collaborate. However, communist-led unions, apparently the most powerful in France and Italy, have been, until recently, completely isolated from the I.C.F.T.U. as well as from the W.C.L. by being kept out of the E.E.C. framework. This lack of collaboration and the fact that trade union strength is not equally spread in the various E.E.C. countries cast heavy doubt on any possibility of continued serious trade union action in an environment where decisions affecting labour conditions are being gradually removed from the national to an international level. This applies to decisions taken by supra-national public authorities as well as to those taken by supra-national private corporations. However, the extension of co-operation with communist-led trade unions to the European level might be envisaged as an improvement of trade union possibilities.

However, the trade unions still remain much too 'nationally involved'. The newly created structures on the European level within the I.C.F.T.U. and the W.C.L. (formerly I.F.C.T.U.) and the I.T.S.s have not yet advanced beyond the stage of *liaison departments*; *and they have neither the competence, nor the staff, nor the finance to play an important bargaining role within Europe.* The statements of various trade union leaders about the need for a more effective trade union structure have not amounted to more than mere lip-service. *Diversity, lack of general co-operation* and the absence of adequate supra-national *structures* appear as the main drawbacks of the European trade union movement; and unless there are drastic changes these features will determine the outlook for future European labour relations.

Other difficulties clearly influencing the scope of collective bargaining at the European level are of the same nature as those accounting for the lack of a real common European social policy. There are still vast differences in the social situation of each of the six countries of the European Community. It suffices to recall that the gross national product per inhabitant varies from a maximum of $2,063 in France to a minimum of $1,184 in Italy; that the European labour market still has regional pockets of unemployment as well as regions with full and over-full employment; and that the social security systems, although involving comparable percentages of national income, still differ largely as to risks covered and needs met. For instance, in the

Federal Republic of Germany 56 per cent of the resources devoted to social security are spent on old age and invalidity pensions and only 5·3 per cent on family allowances; in France, on the contrary, 31·4 per cent are spent on pensions and 28·3 per cent on family allowances; in Belgium the respective figures are 31·4 and 21·4 per cent, while in Italy 46·7 per cent are spent on pensions and 15·7 per cent on family allowances. Health insurance is the only branch to which the different member States devote the same amount of money (about 30 per cent). In the different countries different problems arise and different priorities are fixed in response to the political, social and economic forces at work.

A second point to be considered when examining the possibilities of European bargaining is the very nature of the Treaty of Rome. The European Community was essentially conceived in a liberal economic perspective. The weak legislative provisions and machinery designed to achieve ambitious social objectives clearly show that, according to the E.E.C. founding fathers, economic progress should by itself engender social progress.

Under article 118, the European Commission is required to maintain close contact with member States by means of studies, advice and consultation. This is tantamount to saying that European social policy is the exclusive responsibility of national governments. What is missing in fact is not only effective legislative machinery, but also the political will on the part of some of the national governments to evolve a common social policy. So far social policy has remained a privileged area of national governments, conceived and applied on a national scale.

Yet it would be unfair to say that no work has been done: the basic features of the social and economic situation in the member States have been revealed as a result of studies, surveys and statistics. This objective knowledge is of the first importance 'in order to be able to make a comparative examination of conditions and to establish where and when harmonisation should eventually be carried through'.[1] Since the setting up of the Common Market, differences in social conditions and remuneration have been considerably reduced.

Moreover, what has been stated above should not be taken to mean that there are no useful contacts between trade unions and employers on the European level. On the contrary, within the framework of the E.C.S.C. and the E.E.C. an impressive number of valuable meeting

[1] J. D. Neirinck, *op. cit.*, p. 5.

opportunities have been created and they are also some contacts between the I.T.S.s and multi-national corporations.

But, by and large, these contacts have not led to direct negotiations and international collective bargaining. Even with the help of the High Authority of the E.C.S.C. and the European Parliament, mineworkers' trade unions were not able to succeed in making the employers bargain about a European Miners' Charter, or even to discuss the principle of such bargaining. The recent European collective agreement on hours of work in the agricultural sector by no means typifies present European labour relations; on the contrary, many governments and employers' associations, and even some trade unions, do not want collective bargaining at a European level.

Unless there are drastic changes, particularly in trade union structures, in attitudes as regards the convergence of trade union forces and in the provision of adequate staff and finances for international trade union entities, there is only meagre hope of achieving collective bargaining at the European level.

# ANNEX

## *Draft Statute of the E.C.T.U.C.*[1]

The Executive Committee presented to the VIth General Assembly a draft statute with the following comment:

'Under the present conditions it would be premature to seek a final form regarding the international relations of our organisations with each other. It is best to lay down some general rules for working methods so that by this means flexibility in the light of circumstances can be achieved.

'For this reason the working group set up by the General Assembly will continue its activities after the VIth General Assembly.

'As to the name of the organisation, the working group and the Executive Committee had a long discussion. During its meeting on 21 February 1969 the Executive Committee decided by a majority to suggest the title, "European Confederation of Free Trade Unions in the Community".

---

[1] Authors' translation from French original.

'In the text of the Draft Statute which is reproduced below only the abbreviation, "European Confederation" is used.'

### (i) *Aims and composition*

'The purpose of the European Confederation shall be to represent and defend the economic, social and cultural interests of the workers at the level of the Community. Its aim shall be to promote economic and social progress and to strengthen democracy in Europe. In order to achieve this aim, the European Confederation shall establish a declaration of principles and co-ordinate the activities of the affiliated organisations.

'The European Confederation shall consist of trade union committees and of the following trade union confederations:

| | |
|---|---|
| Federal Republic of Germany | German Confederation of Trade Unions (D.G.B.) |
| France | French Democratic Confederation of Labour (C.F.D.T.) |
| Italy | Italian Confederation of Workers' Unions (C.I.S.L.) Italian Workers' Union (U.I.L.) |
| Netherlands | Netherlands Federation of Trade Unions (N.V.V.) |
| Belgium | Belgian General Federation of Labour (F.G.T.B.) |
| Luxembourg | Luxembourg General Confederation of Labour (C.G.T.L.) |

'Groups of democratic trade unions covering economic sectors at the Community level may form trade union committees on their own initiative and establish their own 'standing orders'. The Executive Committee shall decide about the participation of such trade union committees in the activities of the European Confederation within the framework of the statute. The European Confederation shall promote the setting up of trade union committees in all economic sectors of the Community.

(ii) *Organs*

'The Organs of the European Confederation shall be:

- the Congress,
- the Executive Committee,
- the Secretariat, and
- the Annual Assembly

'*The Congress.* The Congress shall consist of representatives of the national confederations which have been allocated a fixed number of seats plus an additional seat for each million of affiliated workers, as indicated below:

| | | |
|---|---|---|
| Federal Republic of Germany | D.G.B. | 12 |
| France | C.F.D.T. | 12 |
| Italy | C.I.S.L. ⎱ U.I.L. ⎰ | 12 |
| Netherlands | N.V.V. | 8 |
| Belgium | F.G.T.B. | 8 |
| Luxembourg | C.G.T.L. | 4 |

and of the trade union committees, each of which shall send three delegates plus one for each additional 500,000 members.

'The Executive Committee may invite to the Congress representatives and observers of the I.C.F.T.U., of sister organisations in other countries and of Community institutions and organisations.

'The Congress shall meet at least once every *three years.* It shall be prepared and convened by the Secretariat acting under the supervision of the Executive Committee.

'The Secretariat shall submit to the Congress a report on activities. On the basis of this report, the Congress shall evaluate past performance and determine the work programme for the future.

'The Congress shall elect the members of the Executive Committee on the basis of proposals made by the affiliated confederations, and it shall elect the President and the General Secretary on the basis of proposals made by the Executive Committee.

'The Congress shall endeavour to achieve unanimity as far as possible. Should a vote be necessary, the Congress shall decide by a two-thirds majority of those representatives present and entitled to vote. Amendments and proposals which fail to receive the required two-thirds majority, but which receive more than half of the votes, shall be referred to the Executive Committee for further examination.

'*The Executive Committee.* The Executive Committee shall be composed as follows:

|  | Full members | Deputy members |
|---|---|---|
| D.G.B. | 2 | 2 |
| C.F.D.T. | 2 | 2 |
| C.I.S.L. | 1 | 1 |
| U.I.L. | 1 | 1 |
| N.V.V. | 1 | 1 |
| F.G.T.B. | 1 | 1 |
| C.G.T.L. | 1 | 1 |
| Inter-union (E.C.S.C.)[1] | 1 | 1 |

[1] The E.C.S.C. shall be represented on the Executive Committee until the merger of the Treaties of the European Communities.

'One representative of each trade union committee shall attend the meetings of the Executive Committee on a consultative basis. Full members of the Executive Committee may be accompanied by advisers from their organisation; and the Executive Committee may invite to its meetings representatives of the I.C.F.T.U. and of sister organisations in other countries.

'The Executive Committee shall elect from amongst its own members two vice-presidents and it shall make proposals concerning the General Secretary of the European Confederation. It shall meet at least six times a year; and at least once a year it shall review the trade union position in the various countries as well as future prospects. The meetings shall be convened by the General Secretary on the basis of an agenda approved by the President.

'The Executive Committee shall determine the measures to be taken in pursuance of resolutions and action programmes adopted by the Congress. It shall represent the European Confederation in the institutions of the Community and in relation to employers. It can delegate its powers to one or more of its members or to the Secretarait.

'To facilitate the preparation of its work, the Executive Committee shall set up sub-committees with specified terms of reference. If the work of the European Communities calls for comment by a subcommittee the Secretariat shall inform the Executive Committee about it and submit the respective conclusions to the subsequent meeting of the Executive Committee.

'The Executive Committee shall endeavour to reach unanimous agreement as far as possible. In case of a vote, resolutions shall be adopted by a two-thirds majority of the Executive Committee members present. Amendments and proposals which fail to receive the required two-thirds majority but obtain more than half of the votes shall be retained on the agenda and referred to the Secretariat for further examination.

'*The Secretariat.* The Secretariat shall consist of the General Secretary and of Secretaries whose number is determined by the Executive Committee. The Secretariat shall submit proposals to the Executive Committee: it shall carry out all the tasks assigned to it by the Congress and the Executive Committee; and it shall ensure contact between the Executive Committee and the trade union committees by arranging regular meetings between the secretaries of the European Confederation and the trade union committees.

'The General Secretary shall propose to the Executive Committee candidatures for the post of secretaries and shall be responsible for the internal organisation of the Secretariat.

'With the agreement of the Executive Committee, the General Secretary can submit to the affiliated confederations proposals for the co-ordination of important questions of European trade union policy.

'*The Annual Assembly.* The Annual Assembly shall consist of the full members and deputy members of the Executive Committee, and their advisers, together with five representatives from each trade union committee and their advisers. It shall be convened by the Secretariat acting in liaison with the Executive Committee and the trade union committees during those years when the Congress does not meet.

'The Annual Assembly shall be required to:

- examine specific questions which are broad enough to be of interest to all participants;
- give advice and guidance to the Executive Committee in the execution of its tasks between meetings of the Congress; and
- maintain contact amongst trade union committees and facilitate their activities.

### (iii) *Financing*

'The activities of the European Confederation shall be financed by subscriptions from the affiliated confederations. The level of subscriptions shall be determined by the Executive Committee, on the basis of proposals made by the Finance Committee, which shall be composed of one full member and one deputy member from each affiliated confederation.

'The Finance Committee's budget proposals shall be as a rule cover a three-year period.

'The expenses arising from participation in meetings of the European Confederation shall be debited to the participating organisations.

### (iv) *Common Fund*

'In order to carry out its task the European Confederation shall have a common fund. This fund shall also be used to strengthen the organisation of the affiliated confederations and other federations within the E.E.C. countries and to back activities of common interest.

'The resources of the fund shall be derived from subscriptions paid by confederations and federations; from interest payments on invested capital; and from other sources.

'The fund shall grant interest-free loans.

'The Executive Committee shall determine the use of the common fund on the basis of proposals submitted by the Administrative Committee, which shall be composed of a full member and a deputy member of each affiliated confederation.'

Chapter 14

# EUROPEAN REGIONAL ECONOMIC INTEGRATION AND COLLECTIVE BARGAINING

*by*

*Michel Despax*

## I. THE PROBLEM

THE prior existence of an intergovernmental institutional framework apt to reinforce the economic solidarity already in being among the member States is itself a factor likely to encourage the development of relations between employers' and workers' organisations.

With regard particularly to the effects of European regional economic integration in this field, it may be remarked that such integration could well have certain social consequences quite apart from any specific action undertaken. There is indeed no absolute correlation between economic progress and social advance, but the links between the two are obvious enough. So much so that the authors of the Rome Treaty setting up the European Economic Community (E.E.C.) started from the premise that 'improvement of the living and working conditions of labour so as to permit the equalisation of such conditions in an upward direction' (Article 117, para 1) will result '*not only from the functioning of the Common Market which will favour the harmonisation of social systems* but also from the procedures provided under this Treaty and from the approximation of legislative and administrative provisions'[1] (Article 117, para 2).

The 'social fallout' from a common economic policy will certainly not be negligible, but it would be a dangerous illusion to expect more than lies within its possibilities. A completely *laissez-faire* social policy leads at best only to stagnation and very likely regression.

In this context an active social policy should not neglect, at the international level, so effective a technique as collective bargaining,

[1] Author's italics.

309

which has already long since proved its worth in the national setting. Two encouraging factors may be noted with regard to the use of this machinery in the European framework: first, the international aspect set forth in Section 118 of the Rome Treaty: 'Without prejudice to these provisions of the Treaty and pursuant to its general objectives, the Commission shall have the function of promoting close collaboration between the States Members in social matters and in particular the following: employment, labour law and working conditions, industrial training; accident protection; industrial health; *the law relating to trade unions and collective bargaining between Employers and Workers.*'[1] The rules of the Community thus provide a favourable basis for the development of collective bargaining at the international level. With regard to the national systems of law, it has been correctly observed that 'in spite of the differences revealed in the national systems concerned, the general principles followed by the laws of the Members of the Community are reasonably compatible. If we inquire into the concept of "collective agreement" in the various legal systems, we find everywhere the same considerations and similar general trends.'[2]

Recourse to collective bargaining thus appears generally desirable on a European scale, and juridically feasible. Nevertheless, several years have passed since Community legislation came into operation and the spontaneous germination of agreements on this apparently favourable ground has internationally speaking, with a few striking exceptions, produced no very great result.

A brief summary of the reasons for this slow start is required before we embark in Section 2 (Solutions) on consideration of the right techniques for overcoming the obstacles thus identified:

(a) While the laws governing all collective bargaining in the E.E.C. countries are fairly uniform in their fundamentals, they differ in a series of important national peculiarities[3] and this makes harmonisation of European social systems by way of collective bargaining difficult. For example, the capacity to engage in collective agreements is regulated differently among the different member States. There are differences, sometimes considerable, in the legal effect of collective agreements under the various national systems. There are similar divergences in the opportunities and methods for

---

[1] Author's italics.
[2] Georges Spyropoulos: 'Le rôle de la négociation collective dans l'harmonisation des systèmes sociaux européens', *Revue Internationale de Droit Comparé*, 1966, p. 29.
[3] See Georges Spyropoulos, *op. cit.*, p. 35.

extending collective agreements. While these 'asperities' of the national laws may very likely be reduced in time to come – though this will not be an easy task – it remains a fact that in the present state of affairs these differences are an obstacle to the development of collective bargaining on a European scale.

(b) The lack of information at the disposal of workers' and employers' groups that might be interested in European collective bargaining. It certainly seems that the need for collective bargaining no longer restricted to the national scene is beginning to make itself felt in some industrial and trade union circles.[1] The lack of concrete information on the actual possibilities open in the present state of the law, however, means that this remains rather a vague and even merely a pious aspiration, not very easily converted into meaningful negotiations. The uncertainty as to the ways and means whereby national organisations might establish 'trans-national' industrial relations (which could be dissipated by appropriate informative action taken by the international institutions, the I.L.O. or the Commission of the European Communities, see below II, E) is itself a consequence of industrial and trade union structures still poorly adapted to this kind of relationship.

(c) The unsuitability of trade union structures. Here it has been justly observed that 'although they represent a considerable force, with almost 20,000,000 members and speaking for 50,000,000 workers, the employees' unions in the European Economic Community do not yet really constitute a European trade union entity. The reasons are to be found primarily in their ideological divisions, the inadequacy of their European Secretariats vis-à-vis the national offices, the weakness of the European spirit among the mass of the members and the quite marked national feeling of the leaders.'[2] Certainly European groupings and structures have been set up, such as the regional offices of the International Confederation of Free Trade Unions and of the World Federation of Labour (W.F.L.) (formerly the International Federation of Christian Trade Unions (I.F.C.T.U.)). But the trade unions' structures are still in embryo, whereas the remodelling of the employers' associations has been carried much further, and supposing that collective bargaining

---

[1] See the resolution of the Book Trade Union (Syndicat du Livre) Congress at Toulouse, May 1967, calling for the negotiation of a European collective agreement for the industry.

[2] J. M. Verdier: 'Syndicats', Tome V, *Traité du Droit de Travail*, edited by G. H. Camerlynck, Dalloz, 1966.

could be embarked on in the circumstances, the lack of balance between the two sides entails the risk of failure.

(d) 'Regional' arrangements and European collective bargaining. The regional pattern looks at first sight promising for collective bargaining. It is a well-known fact that the higher the negotiating level, the greater the risk of losing contact with reality and of the talks leading nowhere. Recently there has been a tendency to decentralisation in bargaining, and the increasing number of plant collective agreements in the various countries of the E.E.C. is an indication of this. In this context the choice of a 'regional' setting for bargaining looks attractive; in so far as this offers an intermediate stage, collective bargaining would have a fairly good prospect of getting down to concrete problems. It is no use being satisfied with a mere form of words, however, and the vagueness of the concept of 'regionalisation' must be emphasised. 'Region' is not an unambiguous term: a 'region' may be taken to mean a part of a national unit. Certainly this is an intermediate level that may usefully be considered in the framework of collective bargaining; but the 'region' may also be defined in terms of a grouping within the whole international community. In this second meaning – the usual meaning in the terminology of worldwide international institutions – the region, a mere fraction of an immense whole, nevertheless covers a vast extent of territory under different sovereign states, with many differences in local law and local conditions. The expression 'European regional economic integration' is very currently employed in this sense; but it must not be forgotten that as far as collective bargaining is concerned, the region, far from being an intermediate stage is a very high level. Avoiding failure in any discussions at this level – obviously, too remote to remain in touch with many concrete problems – means developing machinery to facilitate collective agreements limited in the geographical scope of their application, i.e. to certain specified countries within the Community, or certain portions of the territory under their sovereignty. Certainly if collective agreements are to be concluded at the highest European level, provision must be made to allow for adaptation, as within the national legal systems, to local district or plant circumstances.

This brief review of the difficulties in the way of fruitful collective bargaining on a European scale leads to the conclusion that unless the competent international institutions (the Commission of the European Communities, or the I.L.O.) help the leaders of the industrial organisations over the obstacles, such collective bargaining will not take place. There is nothing improper about such an external push being given by existing organisations, in the light of current practice, where the governments of the various countries of the European Economic Community, without being party to collective bargaining, are always present, either setting the negotiations on foot, supervising their progress or guiding them towards their conclusions.

## II. SOLUTIONS

The following will be considered in turn: the legal basis for collective bargaining on a European scale; negotiating procedures that might be adopted; the scope of the negotiations; the object of European collective bargaining; and the international institutions' role of promotion.

### (1) The Legal Bases of European Collective Bargaining

There is at present no uniform legal basis governing the conclusion, effect and implementation of collective bargaining within the E.E.C. with obligatory force over-riding the member States' domestic law. European collective agreements are therefore possible, at present, only outside the existing legal structure. This gap in the law is explained by the slowness in the development of collective bargaining. But of course there is no doubt that a mere contract can be a source of rights, quite apart from any legislative provisions. The I.L.O. Collective Agreements Recommendation (No. 91), 1951, recognises that the legal basis of a collective agreement may be contractual and not necessarily a statutory provision. The legal basis of contractual agreements that might be concluded within the E.E.C. has been affirmed by two I.L.O. Conventions. Regarding the matter of freedom of association the International Labour Conference has adopted two instruments: the Freedom of Association and Protection of the Right to Organise Convention, 1948, and the Right to Organise and Bargain Collectively Convention, 1949, numbered 87 and and 98 respectively. Under Article 5 of Convention No. 87, it is expressly recognised that national workers' and employers' organisations shall have the right to affiliate with international organisations of workers and employees. Article 8 (2) provides that the law of States that have ratified the Convention shall not be such, and shall not be applied in such a way, as to impair this right. Article 3 guarantees the right of workers' and employers' organisations to organise their own administration and activities.

Convention No. 87 has been ratified by all member States of the European Economic Community and Convention No. 98 by all except the Netherlands. In so far as these Conventions have become binding under international law, they constitute the legal basis on which European collective agreements may be concluded to govern working conditions within the Common Market.

### (2) Bargaining Procedures

The practice of collective bargaining in the countries of the E.E.C. preceded the elaboration of a law on the subject. Difficulties peculiar to bargaining internationally have so far prevented a similar spontaneous growth at the E.E.C. level. There is no point in drawing up over-elaborate procedures because the organisations would hesitate to use them if the formulae were too restrictive. Here the best arrangements are the most flexible; though this should not discourage the competent international organisations from their useful role of prompting and encouragement (see (5) below).

Two possible techniques are open. Paul Durand, in his preface to George Spyropoulos's work *Le droit des conventions collectives de travail dans les pays de la C.E.C.A.*[1] cleverly suggested turning the difficulty inherent in supra-national agreements by reducing the European agreements to a series of national agreements. According to this scheme, the national workers' and employers' organisations would set up a European Committee of delegates with equal representation for each side. The function of the Committee would be to come to an agreement on each proposed European collective agreement and recommend its adoption to the national associations of workers and employers. It would then be incumbent on these associations to conclude a collective agreement based on the draft, adjusting it to the requirements of the national law. Under this scheme, the collective agreements would carry authority at national level not under any

---

[1] Spyropoulos, Georges: *Le droit des conventions collectives de travail dans les pays de la Communauté européenne du charbon et de l'acier* (Paris, Les Ed. de l'Epargne, 1959), p. xi–xv.

314

binding agreement of the European Committee but by virtue of a national agreement. 'There would not as a result be uniform working conditions imposed by European collective agreements, but closely similar working conditions imposed by national collective agreements.'[1]

The advantage of such a procedure is obviously its flexibility, and its drawback the absence of real compelling authority. It may be feared that the 'model agreement' drawn up for Europe by the joint Committee would not in practice be the wished-for instrument of harmonisation, in so far as in one country or another, for reasons connected with the national legislation or with trade union, political or economic difficulties, a part or the whole of the agreement would not be applied or enforced. It could happen that for one reason or another some trade union or employers' organisation might not think it possible to sustain the common front worked out for Europe in collective bargaining at the national level. National workers' or employers' organisations in other countries would be helpless to take action against such a defection. A similar situation might arise with some entrepreneur refusing to recognise a national collective agreement based on the European agreement, which in the present state of the law could only be impugned by the unions and legal processes in the country concerned, without any opportunity for organisations outside the countries where the business was carried on being able to bring any pressure to bear.

In spite of its disadvantages this procedure respecting national differences seems to be favoured by the leaders of the labour interests directly concerned, and it was followed by the European organisations of agricultural employers and workers and the European Secretariats of the I.C.F.T.U. and the I.F.C.T.U. (now W.F.L.) in negotiating the signature on 6 June 1968 of 'an agreement for harmonising the hours of work of farm workers permanently employed in agriculture'.

It would be appropriate for research on the ways and means to facilitate or reinforce international – and especially European – collective bargaining to concentrate on the methods whereby the flexibility of this procedure could be preserved and its binding force increased. Perhaps arrangements could be made for the signatory organisations to undertake mutual exchange of information on the effect given to European recommendations in their respective coun-

---

[1] G. Schnorr: *Les possibilités d'une convention collective sur le plan européen*, 1961 Report to the E.E.C., p. 35.

tries. Some provision might be made for financial contributions towards the operation of a joint body set up specially to survey the implementation of the agreement to be charged to any national organisations that did not, after signing a European agreement, sufficiently support it to achieve any result at national level.

A variant of the scheme proposed by Paul Durand is suggested by G. Schnorr in his Report to the E.E.C. Commission. As in the original proposal, national workers' and employers' organisations would together set up a Joint Committee to conclude European collective agreements in each branch of industry. It would not in this case simply be a matter of negotiating a European agreement to be acted upon in each country separately: the Joint Committee would be mandated by the national organisations to negotiate with full powers to conclude European collective agreements binding upon the members of the national organisations concerned.

This type of procedure is by no means unknown in the countries of the E.E.C., where it is usual for joint committees to be entrusted with the negotiation of collective agreements. In setting up European Joint Committees the various national workers' and employers' organisations would not feel they were giving up their independence, as they are not dependencies of the European organisation, structurally their superior. In merely delegating representatives to the European Joint Committees, they would not incur the impression that they were sacrificing themselves on the altar of European social harmonisation. The European Committees would be acting only within the terms of their mandate, as extensions of the national organisations, so that to validate the agreement signed it would only be necessary for each organisation to have regard to the strict requirements of the national laws in virtue of which they have their being. The collective agreement signed under this prodecure would be binding on the organisations concerned and their members under the terms of reference.

This formula, attractive in that it would seem more firmly binding on the national organisations, might have some disappointments in store as regards its practical application. For it to correspond effectively to the need now felt for the standardisation of European law on collective agreements, it would be necessary for each workers' and employers' organisation party to the agreement to give its representative a legally valid mandate to contract on its behalf; and for the European agreement to be applicable in each country represented it would have to comply with the more or less specific requirements of

French, German, Belgian or Netherlands law. If this requirement were not met, the effects of the European agreement would be different in each of these countries. These difficulties are readily foreseeable and should not deter recourse to a formula of this kind if the legal jungle can be cleared up a little in advance by the specialist international institutions and the work already done at various meetings and symposia.

In any event, whatever the formula selected (the first would appear, at the moment, the easiest to set European collective bargaining in motion), the establishment of joint committees in the industries where the need is apparent should be preceded by the conclusion of an agreement between the organisations concerned on the procedure to be followed in negotiating European agreements. The role of the Commission of the European Communities or the I.L.O. might be to facilitate the task of the parties by laying down guidelines on the rules to be followed in drawing up mandates by the groups concerned, on the lines of procedure and on the form of collective agreements (see Schnorr Report, *op. cit.*, pp. 39 *et seq.*).

### (3) Scope of the Negotiations

It goes without saying that this cannot be pre-determined but will be whatever the parties to the discussion decide upon. There can be no question here of going beyond advising potential bargainers against excessively ambitious projects. In geographical terms, a European collective agreement need not necessarily aim at imposing uniform working conditions throughout the six countries of the E.E.C. Genuine 'regionalisation' of international collective bargaining implies only that it will be undertaken to solve specific difficulties in an area extending beyond the boundaries of a single State and constituting an economic, social or even cultural entity. The most useful field for international collective bargaining will be the frontier regions. It is certainly to be hoped that as large a territory as possible will be subject to a single collectively agreed regime, but experience shows that the greater the territory, the greater the problems in devising an agreement. Without, therefore abandoning in any way the hope of one day arriving at a collective agreement covering the whole of the E.E.C., it would not be prudent to exclude the possibility of negotiating a European agreement applicable in the first place only to two or three member States, or even only to particular regions of such countries.

All *a priori* conceptions should be set aside in regard to defining the industrial scope of a European collective agreement. However desirable it may be for a branch of industry to be covered by the same legal regime throughout the Six, there is no reason for rejecting less ambitious aims at the outset. For an agreement to be reached covering a whole branch, there must be a sufficient degree of organisation and concentration among both employers and workers. This prior condition cannot always be fulfilled, and the first steps towards the conclusion of collective agreements might take the form of collective agreements for international industrial groups. It may be hoped that collective agreements regulating a single industrial group internationally would meet with the same success as that already obtained in plant agreements nationally. Agreements covering undertakings in different branches of activity could perhaps be concluded in the border regions and wherever else the need for harmonisation is felt.

*(4) The Object of a European Collective Agreement*

Collective bargaining can be effectively engaged and brought to a successful conclusion only if it it corresponds to some real need. In this context an inventory of matters to be dealt with in the agenda for such negotiations drawn up in abstract terms would be a futile and risky enterprise. It may simply be observed that recourse to an international collective agreement would be particularly opportune to give concrete expression to the social provisions of the Treaty of Rome. It has been justly observed that some aspects of working conditions could not appropriately be settled by governmental regulation and a European collective agreement would perhaps be the only way to realise the objectives of the Treaty.[1] The problems of paid annual holidays (Section 120), equal pay for men and women workers (Section 119), shorter hours of work and training policy (Section 128), would seem to be the first matters to merit attention in such negotiations. It may also be thought that a European collective agreement could be used to settle the problems of workers who go from one country in the Community to another and find conditions under the rules of the territory where they are working relatively disadvantageous. Protection against the social effects of industrial concentrations and take-overs could also usefully be the subject of bargaining. The matter of wages, though basic, hardly seems ripe for fruitful bargaining internationally. When embarked upon at some unforeseeable time in the future, would it be possible to avoid, at the

---

[1] Spyropoulos, *op. cit.*, p. 26.

international level, the unfortunate divergences often to be found in individual countries between agreed rates and actual wages?

In any event, international bargaining should not be allowed to lead in any of the E.E.C. countries to a deterioration in the standards already won by the national organisations.

*(5) The International Institutions' Role of Information and Promotion*

In view of the many difficulties to be expected in the endeavour to negotiate a European agreement, the role of the existing international institutions may be important. The I.L.O. or the Commission of the European Communities could take some useful short- or long-term initiatives.

*Short-term:* (a) Publication of a Recommendation on international collective bargaining might have the effect of stimulating public opinion and attracting the attention of the industrial circles directly concerned. Publication should if possible be accompanied by a draft of a model agreement of general application and suggestions for the procedure to be followed in seeking such an agreement.

While publication of a Recommendation would only have the effect of a declaration of principle, without giving ground for hope of any immediate change in the attitude of the industrial interests concerned, the dissemination of information on the steps to be taken to initiate international collective bargaining might greatly facilitate the task of potential negotiators.

(b) The competent international institutions could also undertake extremely valuable practical action by preparing a systematic inventory of the economic branches where international collective bargaining might provide a solution for particular difficulties. There can be no question of drawing up an *a priori* list of these branches, which should include not only those where official representatives of the interests concerned have already demanded international bargaining, but also those where recourse to the procedure could be of present use. Associated undertakings, frontier industries and industries that already owing to their nature are subject to international regulations would presumably appear in this list.

(c) When the appropriate sectors have been pin-pointed the specialised institutions could usefully initiate promotional activity in favour of international collective bargaining. This might take the form of a series of study and information meetings on the possibility of collective bargaining at the European level, for each branch indicated as favourable ground, bringing together not only employers' and workers' organisations in the industries concerned, but also representatives of the national labour departments and experts from European organisations.

*Long-term.* The specialised international institutions should:

(a) Carry out a systematic study of workers' and employers' organisations already existing on a European basis and try to encourage reorganisation of the structure where this might help towards European collective bargaining.

(b) Encourage the harmonisation of national laws in regard to collective agreements.

Studies on the harmonisation of laws regarding collective agreements might usefully be coupled with a special project on the elaboration of a uniform law on collective bargaining which might later be taken up in the various countries of the Community.

Chapter 15

INTERNATIONAL COLLECTIVE
BARGAINING AND REGIONAL ECONOMIC
INTEGRATION:
SOME REFLECTIONS ON EXPERIENCE
IN THE E.E.C.

*by*

*Hans Günter*

## INTRODUCTION

SURPRISINGLY enough, for some observers of the European industrial
relations scene, economic integration through the creation and operation of the European Coal and Steel Community (E.C.S.C.) and the
European Economic Community (E.E.C.) has apparently had a relatively small impact on the relations between trade unions and employers. In particular there has so far[1] been no collective bargaining at the
Community level, even though the similarity of organisational
structures and of the roles of the social partners in the E.E.C. member
countries, as well as the Community's basic supra-national legal
framework,[2] would have seemed propitious for such negotiations.
Furthermore, the diversity in national labour legislation cannot be
regarded as an insurmountable obstacle.[3]

This chapter tries to review, in a tentative way, the main areas in
which factors might be located for an attempt to explain why there have
not been more substantial changes in industrial relations and why
international collective bargaining has failed to develop.

---

[1] Except for the 'Agreement on the harmonisation of working hours of agricultural
wager earners working full-time in farming', which in fact is no more than a frame
recommendation to national organisations of employers and of workers.

[2] Article 118 of the Treaty of Rome stipulates: '. . . it shall be the aim of the Commission to promote close collaboration between member States in the social field, particularly
in matters relating to . . . collective bargaining between employers and workers'.

[3] See Michel Despax: *Traité de Droit du Travail, Conventions Collectives* (Paris, Librairie
Dalloz, 1966), pp. 135–64.

It will only be possible to suggest certain tentative inferences from a quick review of the evidence. Fuller research will be required to confirm or refute these inferences.

It can reasonably be assumed that the factors making for changes in industrial relations in the E.E.C., and possibly for collective bargaining at the Community level, can be mainly identified in the following areas:

   (i) the growth of European attitudes and shared values, both amongst trade unionists and employers;

  (ii) union representation in E.E.C. institutions and the disparity in the power of trade unions;

 (iii) the organisational structures of the respective social partners at the Community level;

 (iv) supra-national social policy-making and industrial relations;

  (v) changes in the locus of industrial relations decision-making power as a result of the creation of E.E.C. institutions;

 (vi) the level of social and economic integration and harmonisation reached in the E.E.C.; and

(vii) the role of collective bargaining in establishing work rules in the European Community.

## THE GROWTH OF EUROPEAN ATTITUDES AND SHARED VALUES BOTH AMONGST TRADE UNIONISTS AND EMPLOYERS

With their three major groupings respectively of socialist, Christian and communist orientation, European trade unions are fairly diversified as regards their ideologies. The conception of Europe thus differs among them. The socialist[1] and Christian[2] unions have committed themselves, at least in broad terms, to European unification and economic integration 'accompanied by full employment and general social progress, including the harmonisation of living conditions in an upward direction'. Haas describes the evolution of a European regional labour ideology in these unions at an early stage of European integration as responding to a mixture of internal and external stimuli

---

[1] Affiliated to the International Confederation of Free Trade Unions (I.C.F.T.U.).

[2] Affiliated to the World Confederation of Labour (W.C.L.) (formerly the International Federation of Christian Trade Unions (I.F.C.T.U.)).

'. . . including internationally shared values of welfare planning, disappointment with the possibilities of purely national reforms and the conviction that only united action can result in bending the policy inclination of supra-national agencies in a pro-labour direction'.[1] It would seem, however, that the sharing of common values has not yet reached the level of international solidarity in practice vis-à-vis European employers that would be required to make the creation of European unions[2] – or, at least, joint negotiations over labour conditions – a psychological necessity.

A prominent earlier effort (1955) for common action by European trade unions, linked with the name of André Rénard and the move by the Christian Confederation to equalise fringe benefits in the E.E.C., proved unsuccessful on account of employers' resistance and the absence of support on the part of several national unions. Another outstanding attempt to achieve collective bargaining at the Community level is the European Miners' Charter. Its promoter was Paul Finet, of the E.C.S.C., and it was discussed in 1964–66 in the joint committee on mining, but was blocked both by the employers and by several governments.[3]

Fears of prejudicing national strength by too much concentration on European solidarity and concern about national economic problems affecting employment, including external competitiveness, may be among the factors causing the prevailing reserve among trade unions towards common action at the European level. In addition there is evidence of an increasingly analytical (rather than emotional) approach to labour problems within a given economic framework. This was stressed by Ludwig Rosenberg,[4] President of the German Confederation of Trade Unions (D.G.B.) with the words '. . . whatever our intentions and our claims might be, we must consider the necessities and facts in an over-all economic manner'.

One other major reason for the preoccupation with national affairs would seem to be that the main locus of decision-making power regarding industrial relations issues remains inside the nation State (as will be examined further below). It has also been argued that the speci-

[1] Ernst Haas: *The Uniting of Europe* (London, 1968), p. 388.
[2] Adherence to a common international trade union (U.A.W.) has no doubt fostered considerably common action by American and Canadian automobile workers, culminating in international collective bargaining with Chrysler on labour conditions for workers in both countries, particularly as regards wage parity.
[3] See Chapter 13.
[4] At the First World Congress of the International Federation of Chemical and General Worker's Unions (I.C.F.) on Industrial Democracy, Frankfurt-am-Main, 1968.

fic economic provisions of the Rome Treaty do not provide occasion or subject matter requiring trade union organisation at the Community level,[1] but this may be too sweeping a statement. At any rate, in the E.E.C. consultative bodies, trade unionists have rarely acted as a class-conscious entity on subjects of immediate practical interest. They have rather tended to enter into a coalition with their national employer counterparts, giving first priority to domestic economic considerations. French trade unionists have been highly interested in defending French industry against competition by working for an equalisation of social security contributions throughout the community. Belgian trade unionists, together with Belgian employers, opposed the closing of unprofitable coal mines; Italian trade unionists were likewise determined to protect marginal firms against external competition; Dutch unions were more concerned with the stability of internal prices and costs, and with peaceful labour relations and productivity, than with the class struggle at the European level; and Federal German trade unionists have been more concerned about the competitiveness of Federal German industry in the world market than about using supra-nationalism for improving labour conditions even, it would seem, to the detriment of greater militancy on the domestic wage front.[2]

In line with European tradition of relying much more on government action than on direct comprehensive negotiations with employers trade unions have used supra-national authority as a tool for fostering their own objectives through a Community social policy. Access to supra-national decision-making units has been obtained through lobbying, representation in consultative bodies[3] and a certain 'penetration' of Community organs by trade unionists.

No marked ideological coherence or solidarity can be observed among employers in the E.E.C. countries. The pattern of their co-operation is essentially of a more tactical nature; and thus '. . . no sharing of fundamental values is implied . . . French, German and Dutch managerial ideologies, for instance, remain far apart'.[4] Nevertheless,

---

[1] Pierre Traimond: 'Le syndicalisme ouvrier face à la Communauté économique européenne', *Droit Social*, No. 6, June 1966, pp. 354–9.

[2] This paragraph follows, to a large extent, the analysis of Haas, *op. cit.*, p. 355.

[3] For instance, in the Economic and Social Committee of the E.E.C., made up of representatives of employers' organisations, trade unions and members of various liberal professions. Although the Treaty of Rome (Article 179) mentions only agriculture and transport as special areas of concern to the Committee, consultations extend to policy issues regarding employment, social security, working conditions, vocational training, labour protection and legislation.

[4] Haas, *op. cit.*, p. 387.

the concept of European economic integration is widely accepted by employers. In business terms, it means bigger markets and higher specialisation, for which the price of increased competition within the community has to be paid – though sometimes it is attenuated by economic concentrations. Action by supra-national authority resulting, for instance, in the E.E.C. common outer tariff and the harmonisation of certain taxes and social security regulations, equalises certain economic conditions. Such developments put employers increasingly in a similar European economic environment. Nevertheless, employers still have greater difficulty in reaching common European positions on specific matters than their trade union counterparts.

The employers also tend to use the Community as a tool for promoting their interests. They have been very reluctant to engage in conversations with trade unions on industrial relations matters at the Community level. Their refusal to engage in collective bargaining at the Community level is sometimes attributed to the absence of a large representative trade union coalition determined to press for such bargaining by all possible means.[1]

## UNION REPRESENTATION IN E.E.C. INSTITUTIONS AND THE DISPARITY IN THE POWER OF TRADE UNIONS

So far there has been no communist-led union representation in E.E.C. consultative organs; and this has left French and Italian organised workers particularly under-represented. The French and Italian Governments have so far not proposed communist trade union leaders for membership in these organs.[2] Furthermore, the non-communist unions have always refused working contacts with the communist-oriented unions at the Community level, although the Christian Confederation appears to have been less categoric in this respect. Members of the Association of Industries of the European Communities (U.N.I.C.E.) secretariat tend to think that the question of the C.G.T and C.G.I.L. representation is primarily an internal trade union affair.

---

[1] *Ibid.*, p. 388.
[2] The C.G.I.L. also contains some socialist union leaders. On the proposal of the Italian Government two of them were appointed by the E.E.C. Council of Ministers to the Consultative E.E.C. Committees for the 1966–70 term.

The General Confederation of Italian Workers (C.G.I.L.) and the French Confederation of Labour (C.G.T.) have adopted an attitude of opposition towards the European institutions, which, in earlier years, were qualified by the communists as a tool of Western imperialism and monopolies. Nevertheless, the C.G.I.L. has already at an early stage recognised the need for contact with the European Communities. By 1962, the E.E.C. had become generally accepted as 'an objective reality' and since 1966 these trade unions have even been striving for representation in the Economic and Social Committee, the European Parliament, and other consultative bodies,[1] claiming that their present exclusion . . . 'is not only inconsistent with the legitimate rights of the C.G.I.L. and C.G.T. to assume their rightful place in the institution of the Common Market; it is also prejudicial to the interests of the workers in France, Italy and the other E.E.C. States in that it vitiates the over-all representation of the working man'.[2] At the same time at least some of their representatives stress the utility of a universal trade union coalition outside E.E.C. organs and hold that, irrespective of international affiliation, European trade unionists could unite their forces in order to achieve collective bargaining at the Community level, provided they aimed at common objectives without an ideological content, such as the forty-hour week, paid leave, retirement benefits, etc.[3]

In the opinion of Pierre Traimond[4] the exclusion from the Community scene of the communist-led trade unions, representing in France and Italy a substantial part of the organised workers '. . . deprives the labour movement of an essential force'. At the same time Traimond holds that this causes an imbalance of power inside the E.E.C. institutions between the French and Italian socialist and Christian trade unionists, each speaking for a minority of organised workers, and their counterparts in the Federal Republic of Germany, Belgium and the Netherlands, representing the great majority of union members in these countries.

On the other hand, several members of the European Christian and

[1] On the question of communist-led trade union representation in the E.E.C., see 'The French and Italian Communists and the Common Market: The Request for Representation in the Community Institutions', by Werner Feld, *Journal of Common Market Studies*, Oxford, 6 March 1968, pp. 250–66.

[2] European Parliament: *European Documentation*, Vol. 8, No. 5, May 1966, pp. 9 and 10.

[3] See statement of Mr Pascre of the French C.G.T. at the Second International Symposium on European Labour Law, Nice, 1965 (organised by the Association pour la comparaison et l'étude des droits européens du travail) published in *Les conventions collectives européennes*, Nice, 1965–6, pp. 105–6.

[4] Pierre Traimond, *op. cit.*, p. 358.

free trade union central offices do not feel that this situation has adverseley affected trade union co-operation and consider that the access of communist trade unionists to the E.E.C. institutions, which may come one day, would not have much effect on the power relationships amongst unions within the E.E.C. framework.

If power is approximately proportionate to membership, there might also be a case for claiming that there is a disparity of power among national European trade unions themselves, quite apart from the question of their representation in E.E.C. institutions. On the one hand, there are unions with 3,000 to 10,000 members, like the *Freie Letzeburger Arbrechtsverbund* (in Luxembourg) or the Dutch *Eenheidsvakcentrale*, while, on the other, there are unions with a membership of nearly 2 million, such as the French C.G.T. and the Italian Confederation of Workers' Unions (C.I.S.L.), or even of well over 6 million, such as the Federal German D.G.B., which is also the biggest union in the E.E.C. This means that a single large national trade union organisation could in practice block any European initiative.

## ORGANISATIONAL STRUCTURES OF TRADE UNIONS AND EMPLOYERS AT THE E.E.C. LEVEL

It is therefore not really surprising that the organisational structures of trade unions and of employers at the E.E.C. level are not very strong. The European offices of trade union organisations and of employers' associations have no real executive power.[1] Their tasks are mainly information, co-ordination and liaison (lobbying) with the E.E.C.; they lack the power and competence to conclude industrial relations agreements.[2] Trade unionists as well as employers are thus at present fairly unprepared, from an organisational point of view, for any collective bargaining at the European level.

It is possible that the failure to evolve a centralised European bargaining structure may not be unconnected with the recent marked

---

[1] For a detailed review of the organisation of trade unions and employers at the E.E.C. level, see Chapter 13.

[2] Therefore, for the treatment of substantive matters, the E.E.C. seems to prefer discussion with national trade unions and employers' representatives, who have decision-making power.

trend in several European countries towards decentralisation of national collective bargaining and increasingly frequent plant-level agreements, which could even weaken the position of the existing national organisations. However, organisational inadequacies are not the main explanation for the absence of international collective bargaining; they are rather a reflection of the present lack of interest in it. One might expect, on the contrary, the organisational prerequisites to develop spontaneously once a real need for such bargaining is felt both by trade unionists[1] and employers. This is not likely to happen rapidly; but it may be worth noting that, particularly inside the European central trade union offices, there have been certain signs in recent years of greater (informal) authority vis-à-vis affiliated members.

In the last few years there have been regular direct contacts between the European social partners in the form of meetings between representatives of the U.N.I.C.E. and the I.C.F.T.U. as well as the W.C.L., and at these meetings there have emerged certain common viewpoints on problems of employment, freedom of movement and vocational training[2] – all of them subjects covered by E.E.C. social policy. This has not been the case so far as regards the industrial relations field proper, concerning which employers have expressed the view that '. . . after an exchange of information on the principles laid down in the U.N.I.C.E. Memorandum on European social policy,[3] it had to be noted that the trade unions are not inclined to abandon their abstract theory of social harmonisation'.[4]

In the employers' view, such harmonisation, as indeed all social policy, 'has to fit in with the evolution of over-all economic productivity so as to avoid endangering price and monetary stability, the productive capacity of undertakings and their competitiveness both inside and outside the Community'.[5]

---

[1] In Solomon Barkin's opinion 'unions would have to surmount many ideological differences and structural problems to create an aggressive agency with supra-national power' (*Trade Unions Face a New Western Capitalist Society*, unpublished manuscript submitted to the 1968 Chicago Meetings of the Social Science Societies).

[2] See *Arbeitgeber*, Annual Report (for 1968) of the Confederation of German Employers' Associations, p. 139.

[3] U.N.I.C.E.: *Memorandum concernant la politique sociale dans la C.E.E.*, December 1966.

[4] *Arbeitgeber, op. cit.*, p. 139, referring to the meeting on 28 October 1968.

[5] U.N.I.C.E.: *L'industrie européenne face à l'intégration économique et sociale* (Brussels, November 1966), p. 10.

## SUPRA-NATIONAL SOCIAL POLICY-
## MAKING AND INDUSTRIAL RELATIONS

Social harmonisation, as provided for in the Rome Treaty setting up the E.E.C., has been fostered by a number of statutory regulations emanating from the E.E.C. These cover, for instance, freedom of movement, social security rights of migrant workers, conditions in road transport, uniform vocational training and the principle of equal pay for equal work (laid down in Article 119 of the Treaty). A direct impact on social affairs has also been obtained through the operation of the European Social Fund, which assists in ensuring the re-employment of displaced workers by means of vocational retraining, the granting of resettlement allowances and other appropriate measures. The E.E.C., and particularly the Commission, has limited competence, however, in the social policy field, which is, furthermore, the subject of controversy.[1] In addition to setting common norms and formulating recommendations the E.E.C. carries out comparative studies on pertinent subjects and compiles uniform social statistics with a view to promoting indirectly, through the diffusion of knowledge concerning important economic and social conditions, a gradual harmonisation in member States. The E.E.C. has viewed the harmonisation of social conditions largely as an automatic process[2] following economic integration. This is close to the employers' concept of the primary importance of the economic situation. The trade unions, however, generally maintain that mere knowledge of economic and social factors does not by itself lead to social harmonisation and that it would be wrong, therefore, to rely entirely on the functioning of an economically integrated area in order to get all possible social advantages in any given set of circumstances.[3] More recently the E.E.C. seems to have moved towards a middle position, stressing that '. . . the link between general economic policy and social policy is the basic theme of the medium-term economic programme approved in 1967 by the Council of Ministers and the Governments of the member States . . .'.[4]

[1] Partly due to controversial interpretations of certain Articles of the Treaty (e.g. Articles 117 and 118).
[2] See Commission of the European Communities: *Exposé sur l'évolution de la situation sociale dans la Communauté en 1967* (Brussels, Luxembourg, February 1968), p. 15.
[3] See preamble of the *European Social Plan* of the Free Metal Workers' Trade Unions in the E.C.S.C. sector (Luxembourg, 1960).
[4] Commission of the European Communities: *Exposé sur l'évolution de la situation sociale dans la Communaué en 1968* (Brussels, Luxembourg, February 1969), p. 249.

A certain degree of harmonisation can also be observed in the field of collective bargaining. The Commission of the European Communities has noted the development of this trend[1] in such respects as the continuous evolution of the status of the wage-earner, the efforts being made towards guaranteed income and employment, the improvement of specific trade union rights and arrangements for profit-sharing by workers. It may be that E.E.C. regulations have had little to do with this. Often similar tendencies may result from similar preoccupations in response to similar problems arising in various industrial societies. However, to some extent at least they result from an imitation of solutions adopted in neighbouring countries; and sometimes they are also the outcome of a co-ordination of national collective bargaining efforts.

In formulating their claims for longer annual holidays Federal German trade unionists have no doubt been inspired by the achievements of their French colleagues. Dutch trade unionists seem to have developed the habit of following very closely Federal German wage negotiations so as not to endanger the competitive position of Dutch industry through their own demands. Similarly Italian trade union efforts to improve domestic labour conditions may well have been influenced by statistical knowledge of differentials separating Italian workers from those in other E.E.C. countries. Co-ordinated or *ad hoc* statistics issued by the Statistical Office of the Communities have advanced the knowledge of significant social and economic yardsticks in the E.E.C. countries; and they are regarded by both trade unions and employers as a useful guide worthy of further development.

In addition to the 'demonstration effect' of the conditions in other member countries, certain conscious efforts towards co-ordination have been made by means of recommendations. For instance, on May Day 1965, the European Secretariat of the I.C.F.T.U. launched an action programme urging national affiliates to strive jointly for (1) a reduction of the working week to forty hours, (2) an extension of annual holidays to four weeks, (3) an increase in special holiday pay, and (4) a guaranteed income in case of incapacity for work.

Members of the European Secretariat of the I.C.F.T.U. believe that this programme had a definite influence on the choice of priorities in

[1] Commission of the European Communities: *Exposé sur l'évolution de la situation sociale dans la Communauté en 1967, op. cit.,* p. 14.

national union claims and was responsible for strengthening European solidarity in practice. Thus, Belgian trade unions, for instance, campaigned with the slogan 'Together with the workers of Europe for a 40-hour week'. Recently the Executive Committee of the I.C.F.T.U. discussed new recommendations for a joint policy on the need, conditions and possibilities for a common trade union policy regarding collective bargaining in Europe.[1]

There is not much evidence of conscious co-ordination of action among the national employers' organisations affiliated to the U.N.I.C.E The U.N.I.C.E. secretariat has issued no equivalent to the 1965 action programme of the I.C.F.T.U. but appears to be limiting itself, at least for the time being, to exerting an influence on an informal basis. This includes issuing warnings to employers not to yield to certain national trade union pressures for fear of contagion in other industries and countries.

The trade unions, however, although their expectations have not always been fulfilled, appear to have come to the conclusion that the supra-national social policy of the E.E.C.[2] despite its limitations, its heavy reliance on indirect approaches and its belief in a somewhat automatic harmonisation of labour conditions, is likely to be more effective and rapid in its achievements for the time being than direct negotiations with employers, especially in the form of international collective bargaining. This does not mean that they have definitely renounced a direct confrontation with European employers. Their approach is typical, however, of the pragmatic attitude that all possible means should be used for achieving the end of social harmonisation.

The trade unions have also realised that their participation in E.E.C. advisory organs mainly concerned with economic matters, such as the joint committee on transport, has important social repercussions. Thus E.E.C. regulations on hours of work in road transport, aimed at a standardisation of European competitive conditions, also standardise work rules.

With several potential subjects for international collective bargaining having been yielded, so to speak, to supra-national authority, it

[1] Meeting of the enlarged Executive Committee, Brussels, 21 February 1969, fifth item on the agenda: 'Basic principles for the collective bargaining policy of the Free Trade Unions in the European Community.'
[2] The trade unions have in particular tended to feel that the recommendations of the Economic and Social Committee, in which they are represented, have not always been sufficiently taken into account by the Council of Ministers of the E.E.C.

might be argued that the remaining areas are unlikely to stimulate unduly direct negotiations with employers. However, this assessment needs some qualification. In many European countries the range of subjects that may be dealt with by collective bargaining has been widened in recent years[1] so as to include matters for which (more general) statutory regulations often exist, such as vocational training and retraining, health and welfare measures, early retirement, holiday pay and, occasionally, participation in management. Hence there may still be room for special treatment in international collective agreements of subjects which may already be covered in some way or another by the E.E.C.

The above-mentioned broadening of the scope of collective bargaining to include subjects already covered by national law also tends to weaken the argument of Despax that the existence of well-developed labour legislation in the countries of the E.E.C., ensuring the necessary protection of the workers, has relieved the social partners from themselves establishing provisions at an international level.[2] At any rate the trade unions maintain that '. . . the thesis according to which trade union pressure can be replaced by action by Community organs is untenable. Trade union pressure is irreplaceable. The institutions can create the framework within which contacts and negotiations are possible; however, the results of these negotiations depend exclusively upon the power of trade union action.'[3] The trade unions have thus found that there is also, therefore, a need to continue to press for direct negotiations with employers on industrial relations issues and that 'finally, one has to study . . . the means of arriving at the conclusion of European collective agreements'.[4]

Quite a number of trade unionists and employers' representatives hold that, through their work in the advisory bodies of the E.E.C. (particularly on matters for which Community regulation had to be introduced, as in the case of transport and freedom of movement), the social partners have developed certain co-operative habits which also have a 'spill-over' as regards their mutual relations outside the Common Market institutions. The above-mentioned direct contacts

---

[1] See I.L.O.: *Technological Change and Social Progress: Some Problems and Perspectives.* Report of the Director-General, prepared for Second European Regional Conference of the International Labour Organisation (Geneva, 1968), p. 92.

[2] Michel Despax: *Traité du Travail, op. cit.,* p. 151.

[3] European Secretariat of the I.C.F.T.U.: *Les relations, au niveau européen, entre les organisations des employeurs et des travailleurs* (Luxembourg, June 1967), p. 4.

[4] European Organisation of the W.C.L.: *Programme d'action pour une politique sociale au sein de la C.E.E.* (Brussels, Nov. 1965), p. 6.

between the European offices of trade unions and employers' organisations, as well as the fact that, at the request of the Commission, both parties are now preparing a joint report on their ideas about future European economic and social policy and the fusion of the different European bodies, may be mentioned as examples in this respect.

Regarding the June 1968 Agreement between representatives of employers' and workers' organisations at the European level on the harmonisation of hours of work in agriculture, the E.E.C. even claims to have acted directly as a catalyst stating that '. . . it is gratifying to note that the Commission was able to play an important role in its conclusion[1] . . . the conversations which preceded this agreement started in December 1966 at the request of the Commission, which for its part, had been inspired by a motion drafted in December 1964 by the joint consultative committee on social problems of agricultural workers'.[2]

## THE LOCUS OF DECISION-MAKING POWER ON INDUSTRIAL RELATIONS

Despite transfers of authority to supra-national institutions, the main decision-making units in the economic and especially social fields still remain within the boundaries of the nation State. Power relationships concerning these issues involve, above all, national governments, national trade unions and national employers' organisations. And this pattern appears to have gained strength as the integrative thrust of the European institutions has tended to slow down in recent years. Moreover, somewhat in contrast to the E.C.S.C., E.E.C. decisions flow more from government consensus than from any display of supra-national authority.

Pressures of trade unions and employers are brought to bear at the 'real seats of power'[3], i.e. mainly on the above-mentioned national units. The different power relationships in each national setting require specific responses by the social partners. The handling of industrial

[1] Commission of the European Communities, *Exposé sur l'évolution de la situation sociale dans la Communauté en 1968, op. cit.,* p. 100.
[2] *Ibid.,* p. 102.
[3] See R. Colin Beever: *European Unity and the Trade Union Movements* (Leyden, A. W Sythoff, 1966), p. 285.

333

relations and especially collective bargaining therefore develop a tendency to stay within the national social and economic sphere.

As regards wages for instance – a priority item on the list of industrial relations issues – the usual criteria for accepting or refusing wage claims are clearly national: the industry's or firm's productivity, capacity to pay, profit and wage evolution, competitive situation, etc. Economic frame programmes for wages and incomes policies are likewise presented in purely national terms, such as the 'concerted action' or the 'social symmetry' in the Federal Republic of Germany, the 'social programming' in Belgium or the 'democratic planning' sought by some French trade unions.

Furthermore, while in the E.E.C. setting employers and trade unions play only a consultative role, they usually participate directly – and sometimes even with a defined institutional status[1] – in economic and social decision-making at the national level.

This approach is borne out by the fact that a prominent specialist, Jean-Daniel Reynaud, in an I.I.L.S. public lecture on the future of industrial relations in Western Europe, did not even refer to any possible changing impact of supra-national authority, but instead stressed the increasingly positive and co-ordinated role in the future of the nation State.[2] In any event, any growth in the impact and authority in the industrial relations field of the E.E.C. institutions as well as of the European organisations of employers and workers would appear to be at best a slow and gradual process.


## THE ATTAINED LEVEL OF ECONOMIC
## AND SOCIAL INTEGRATION

Unquestionably progress has been made since the establishment of the E.E.C. in the field of economic and social integration, if this term is taken to mean the existence of important economic and social links between a group of countries,[3] or a high level of economic and social

[1] See Ellen M. Bussey, 'Organised Labour and the E.E.C.', *Industrial Relations*, Vol. No. 2, February 1968.

[2] See Jean-Daniel Reynaud, 'The Future of Industrial Relations in Western Europe: Approaches and Perspectives', *I.I.L.S. Bulletin*, No. 4, February 1968, pp. 86–115.

[3] Paraphrasing the definition of 'economic integration' given by Franz Gehrels and Bruce F. Johnstone in 'The Economic Gains of European Integration', *Journal of Political Economy*, August 1955, pp. 275–92.

exchange.[1] However, if the usual definition of political integration, i.e. increased power of the central decision-making unit, is applied to the economic and social scene, it is doubtful whether one can speak of much progress in integration. Economic integration has been accompanied by a certain harmonisation, i.e. a narrowing of national differences.

Statistical indicators for measuring economic integration include figures on inter-Community trade and the movement of labour and capital. In the case of the E.E.C. they all show a rising trend. It is particularly striking that intra-Community exports between 1958 and 1967 increased by 257 per cent, while during the same period E.E.C. exports to third countries moved up by only 99 per cent.[2] The main indicators for economic and social harmonisation would have to cover productivity, wages and hours actually worked and social security,[3] as well as the legal and organisational structures of economic and social life and labour conditions and relations. Changes in the latter cannot be assessed on the basis of simple statistical measures and would have to be subjected to a comprehensive country by country analysis, which is not feasible in this chapter.[4]

One can conclude even from a brief statistical analysis limited to the more easily accessible statistical indicators for industrial relations that

---

[1] Economic exchanges include the exchange of products and of production factors (labour and capital). Social exchanges are more difficult to describe. They might be loosely defined as mutual penetration through social policy concepts and approaches.

[2] Cf. European Communities: *Selected Figures, The Common Market: Ten Years On* (Brussels, 1968), pp. 58–9.

[3] Social security charges in the E.E.C. have levelled off considerably for the whole of the economy, as the following figures indicate:

SOCIAL SECURITY EXPENDITURE (EXCLUDING TRANSFERS)
EXPRESSED AS A PERCENTAGE OF G.N.P. AT MARKET PRICES

| Year | Belgium | Germany (F.R.) | France | Italy | Luxembourg | Netherlands |
|------|---------|----------------|--------|-------|------------|-------------|
| 1960 | 12·3 | 13·5 | 12·5 (1962) | 10·6 | 13·1 | 11·3 |
| 1966 | 14·8 | 15·1 | 14·0 | 15·1 | 16·0 | 16·3 |

Source: Commission of the European Communities: *Exposé sur l'evolution de la situation sociale dans la Communauté en 1968, op. cit.*, p. 290.

The share of social security charges in hourly labour cost in industry still varies considerably from country to country. (See 'Wages E.E.C.', *Social Statistics*, different volumes.)

[4] A number of such comparative studies have been published by the E.E.C. in its *Série politique sociale*, including:

'Le droit et la pratique des conventions collectives dans les six pays de la C.E.E. (No. 6)';

'Critères à la base de la fixation des salaires et problèmes qui y sont liés pour une politique des salaires et des revenus (No. 19)';

'Etudes sur la physionomie actuelle de la sécurité sociale dans les pays de la C.E.E. (No. 3).'

differentials in real wages, labour cost and labour productivity amongst the E.E.C. countries have narrowed over the years. However, they still remain considerable for the economy as a whole[1] or, in the case of specific industries, between the Federal Republic of Germany and Italy for instance. These differentials, therefore, are not conducive to the inclusion of wage rates in collective bargaining negotiations at the Community level if more than a fixing of standards at the level of the lowest common denominator is intended. Considerable differences in productivity, in the supply of and demand for labour and in other relevant factors between different regions of a single country frequently even require the conclusion of special regional collective agreements within such a country.[2]

The only partial harmonisation of policies and parameters within the E.E.C. policy framework results in national leads and lags in the business cycle. Particular national monetary, price and employment problems also contribute to a situation in which trade unions and employers still have to face a widely different data constellation for collective bargaining in the different countries. All this, just as the essentially national locus of decision-making referred to in the previous section, tends to restrict collective bargaining, at least regarding major labour issues, such as wages, to the national level.

---

[1] The following table is significant in this respect. It includes internal estimates by the Commission of hourly labour cost for the last ten years, based on the result of uniform labour cost inquiries and other pertinent statistics:

ESTIMATED HOURLY LABOUR COST (WAGES AND FRINGE BENEFITS) FOR
WAGE EARNERS IN INDUSTRY (a), INCLUDING MINING AND CONSTRUCTION
(in Belg. Frs.)

| Year | Belgium | Germany (F.R.) | France | Italy | Luxembourg | Netherlands |
|------|---------|----------------|--------|-------|------------|-------------|
| 1959 | 43 | 40 | 40 | 32 | 60 | 34 |
| 1960 | 45 | 45 | 43 | 34 | 62 | 38 |
| 1961 | 47 | 51 | 47 | 37 | 65 | 43 |
| 1962 | 51 | 57 | 51 | 42 | 69 | 48 |
| 1963 | 56 | 62 | 56 | 51 | 74 | 52 |
| 1964 | 63 | 68 | 60 | 57 | 78 | 61 |
| 1965 | 70 | 75 | 64 | 61 | 82 | 66 |
| 1966 | 76 | 80 | 68 | 63 | 88 | 74 |
| 1967 | 82 | 83 | 72 | 69 | 90 | 80 |
| 1968 | 88 | 88 | 82 | 73 | 97 | 87 |

(a) Establishments with 50 and more employees (Luxembourg: 20 and more).

[2] Consequently, per industry labour cost for various regions of a country frequently tends to differ more than national industry averages between the E.E.C. countries. *See* Statistical Office of the European Communities: 'Wages E.E.C., 1964', *Social Statistics*, 1966, Vol. 5.

## THE ROLE OF COLLECTIVE BARGAINING IN THE ESTABLISHMENT OF WORK RULES IN THE EUROPEAN COMMUNITY

In complete contrast to the situation in North America – where, under the influence of a deep-rooted philosophy of liberal democracy, the technique of collective bargaining is looked upon as *the* instrument for regulating industrial relations '. . . capable of progressively embracing all labour/management problems as they arise'[1] – in Europe other instruments also play an important role, in particular and by tradition, statutory regulations.[2] This is also increasingly true for the different, mostly still emerging, forms of workers' participation in management decisions (generally at the plant level), for which specific national solutions are again sought, mostly on a statutory basis.

A paragraph in the resolution adopted by the First I.C.F. Conference on Industrial Democracy is symptomatic of the resulting relative depreciation of the role of collective bargaining in establishing work rules in Europe. It specifies that 'traditional bargaining procedures constitute a basic democratic right of workers. Yet they are not sufficient by themselves alone to prevent detrimental consequences for the workers arising from arbitrary decisions by management at the planning stage and in matters of investment.'

It is possible that the growing emphasis on workers' participation in management has tended to push somewhat into the background of trade union concern the issue of international collective bargaining in the E.E.C.

### PRELIMINARY FINDINGS ON INTERNATIONAL COLLECTIVE BARGAINING IN EUROPE

From the above outline of E.E.C. experience, a number of tentative inferences may be drawn which, in most cases, are in effect a summary of points already raised.

---

[1] Charles Levinson, Secretary General of the International Federation of Chemical and General Workers' Unions at the First I.C.F. World Congress on Industrial Democracy held in Frankfurt-am-Main on 28 and 29 November 1968.

[2] In the different E.E.C. countries the balance varies between collective agreements and statutory regulations, the latter being, for instance, more important in France than in the other countries. However, with the agreement on employment signed in France on 17 February 1968, between the trade unions and the National Council of French Employers, the position of collective bargaining has been advanced.

(1) Solidarity of the trade unions in the E.E.C. countries has not yet reached a level where common European action, in particular international collective bargaining with employers, might become a psychological necessity.

(2) The absence of communist-led trade unions from the European scene, on the one hand, and the power disparity between the different national unions, on the other, may account in part for the absence of a comprehensive trade union coalition, which could have exerted effective pressure on European employers to accept the idea of collective bargaining at the Community level.

(3) The main decision-making locus regarding industrial relations issues is still to be found inside the national boundaries; trade unions and employers are thus obliged to give domestic issues priority over action at the E.E.C. level.

(4) Consequently the Community-level organisations of trade unions and employers, which lack both organisational attributes and decision-making power, remain unequipped to enter into meaningful bargaining in the industrial relations field.

(5) However, there is some evidence of a gradual increase in the competence and authority of these organisations in relation to their national affiliates.

(6) In accordance with the European tradition of relying very much on the State, trade unions and employers prefer to use E.E.C. institutions as a tool for having their own views reflected in E.E.C. social policy rather than to bargain with each other at the Community level.

(7) In taking this attitude they have conceded to supra-national authority matters which thus tend to disappear from the range of possible subjects for international collective bargaining.

(8) The co-operation of trade unions and employers in the E.E.C. institutions has a 'spill-over' effect as regards their relations outside these institutions. With encouragement from supra-national authority, they have been entering into a dialogue at the European level. As a result, standpoints have been clarified and common positions have developed regarding the E.E.C.; and eventually negotiations on industrial relations issues may emerge from this process.

(9) A fair amount of harmonisation of major economic parameters (in particular a substantial narrowing down of existing productivity differentials) is a prerequisite for successful international

bargaining regarding major aspects of labour conditions affecting production costs, and especially wages. This substantial narrowing down of differentials has so far not occurred in the E.E.C. countries.

(10) As long as this situation prevails, international collective bargaining in the E.E.C. may have to be limited to labour conditions less affected by productivity differentials, such as hours of work and fringe benefits.

(11) Possibly as a preliminary stage on the way to fully-fledged international collective bargaining, a certain co-ordination of national collective bargaining is gradually developing through the 'demonstration effect', through European trade union programmes and through European agreements in the form of recommendations agreed between the social partners, such as the agreement on hours of work in agriculture.

(12) Other methods of shaping worker/employer relations, e.g. the fixing of work rules by law and the various forms of participation, tend to reduce the importance of the techniques of collective bargaining both at the national and international levels, and to divert the attention of the social partners from the question of international collective bargaining.


## CONCLUSIONS

The E.E.C. experience tends to show that regional economic integration is not by itself a sufficient condition to bring about substantial changes in industrial relations. Whether or not it is a necessary condition remains to be established. Industrial relations seem to be very much rooted in the national historical, sociological, political and economic environment. Fairly radical changes in the values and attitudes of the social partners in the locus of decision-making regarding economic and social policy and in economic differentials amongst E.E.C. member countries seem to be required before industrial relations can acquire an effective international dimension.

If international collective bargaining is to occur, a suitable set of conditions, which might evolve only slowly, seems to be needed. These conditions would have to include a high level of European solidarity in practice; a representative coalition of trade unions; some shifts in the locus of decision-making towards the European central organisations; and a fair amount of harmonisation of economic parameters, especially a substantial narrowing down of productivity differentials.

It can reasonably be assumed that the trend towards economic harmonisation will continue, so that the material basis for international collective bargaining over major work rules in Europe should be attained in a few years' time. Whether such bargaining will then spread entirely depends upon the attitudes of the social partners, and in particular on their preference as regards the choice of instruments for setting standards in the E.E.C.

For the time being only frame recommendations on those labour conditions which are least dependent on national levels of productivity (such as the recent agreement on hours of work in agriculture) would seem to stand a chance of coming into being.

Chapter 16

# TOWARDS AN EXTENSION OF MULTI-NATIONAL CORPORATIONS OF EUROPEAN ORIGIN: IMPLICATIONS FOR INDUSTRIAL RELATIONS

*by*

*Jacques Houssiaux*

EXPERTS in international economics often emphasise the asymmetrical nature of trade between industrial countries.[1] The explanation involving the role of the product cycle in international trade stresses the time lag in demand for new products according to the country as a reason for changes in trade patterns from the point of view of time.[2] This theory is generally supported by an explanation based on an examination of technological gaps between countries[3]: at a given time in their historical and technological developments, some countries are unable to turn out goods for which advanced technology is required.

These asymmetrical theories, based on gaps between countries as regards supply and demand, are dynamic and involve two aspects: (1) an examination of the comparative processes whereby innovations come into being in the various developed countries; (2) an examination of the process whereby demand is created or innovations spread among the developed countries.

[1] See Charles Kindleberger: *American Business Abroad* (Yale University Press, 1969) and *International Economics* (Irvin, Homewood 1968).

[2] See Raymond Vernon: 'International Investment and International Trade in the Product Cycle', *The Quarterly Journal of Economics*, May 1966, p. 190; L. T. Wells: 'Test of a Product Cycle Model of International Trade', *The Quarterly Journal of Economics*, February 1969, p. 152.

[3] See O.E.C.D.: *Gaps in Technology: an Analytical Report*, 1969; William Gruber, Dileep Mehta and Raymond Vernon: 'The Research and Development Factor in International Trade and Investment of the United States Industries', *The Journal of Political Economy*, February 1967, p. 20.

341

Among the factors involved in this pattern of change, multi-national corporations certainly play a decisive part, as do human migration and mass communication media.[1] They constitute a suitable means of transferring new techniques, spreading 'know-how', stimulating demand in countries which are behind in this respect, and increasing competitive power in relation to the country of origin. In some cases, on the other hand, multi-national corporations can delay the process whereby non-leading industrial countries might catch up with the more advanced countries as regards science and technology by maintaining a retarding international division of labour between the industrial countries. The influence of multi-national firms in filling or maintaining the technological gap within the industrialised world will depend on the balance of motives resulting, in a complex manner, from the large international firms' objectives of a social function. If one accepts this asymmetrical concept of international trade, the motivating force behind the dynamic historical evolution it implies may come not only from nation States and local firms acting within the framework of national industrial policies but also from multi-national corporations.

Is it possible, moreover, not to make a distinction between the latter? In the past the appearance of multi-national firms has always been the result of three trends:[2]

- a tendency for the environments of companies to become more international in character, so that the conditions in which the firms operate in all countries come to resemble each other more closely;
- a tendency towards the internationalisation of markets: elimination of protectionism and freeing of trade, free circulation of capital, and freedom to set up firms throughout the industrialised world;
- the development of large-scale production economies and particularly the improvement of management techniques for a scattered group of industrial firms.

It is obvious that between 1958 and 1968 circumstances were favourable to the development of multi-national corporations. A distinction

[1] See Sidney Rolfe: *Les sociétés internationales – leur droits et responsabilités*, XXII Congress of the International Chamber of Commerce, Istanbul, 31 May–7 June 1969.
[2] See Jacques Houssiaux: 'La Grande entreprise plurinationale', in *Economie appliquée*, April–September 1964, p. 403.

should nevertheless be made between multi-national firms of American origin and those of European origin, for the diversity of culture and methods of business organisation on this side of the Atlantic calls for rules to be drawn up on the constitution of multi-national European companies – which is not so essential in the case of multi-national firms of American origin. The latter may adopt the 'geocentric method'[1] with its corresponding decentralised management, after a temporary stage of intensive Americanisation ('ethnocentrism') or even of 'anarchical' local independence ('polycentrism'). On the other hand the establishment of multi-national European companies involves stages which cannot be eliminated and which take time. The development of interpenetration between countries of the European Economic Community,[2] the increasing similarity between modern techniques of management in Europe, the progress of community institutions (European standards of law, taxation system applicable to inter-community mergers, etc.) will facilitate the slow process of constituting multi-national European corporations.

The distinctions between multi-national corporations of European and of American origin is, of course, in some respects largely artificial. During the setting-up period, decision-making centres remain national in the case of European firms; they are American, national or even European – when European headquarters are being set up – in the case of multi-national corporations of American origin. The inter-nationalisation of markets has influenced the setting up of multi-national firms; but frequently the first and third conditions indicated above – internationalisation of environments and greater similarity of management methods – are not sufficiently met to enable the respective functions of national and multi-national decision-making centres to be definitively established.

This situation will have repercussions on every aspect of relations between multi-national corporations and their environment. This of course calls to mind, firstly, relations with States, which raise the delicate problem of legitimacy and divided loyalties.[3] It also calls to mind relations with firms, competitors, suppliers, clients, which raises the difficult question of discrimination and respect for local

---

[1] See Howard Perlmutter: 'L'entreprise internationale: trois conceptions', *Revue économique et sociale*, May 1965, p. 151.
[2] See A. P. Weber: 'L'interpénétration des entreprises en Europe', *Direction*, April 1969.
[3] See Raymond Vernon, 'Multi-National Enterprise and National Sovereignties', *The Harvard Business Review*, March–April 1967, p. 156.

professional rules.[1] Lastly, one thinks of the industrial relations of multi-national firms which are obviously conditioned by their majority[2] environment and by their habits in the context of the labour world. In this respect is there a great difference between multi-national firms of American and European origin?

In the field of industrial relations, multi-national corporations of American origin have always hesitated between two fundamental attitudes. The first consists in disregarding differences in environment encountered around their main industrial installations. The second attitude consists in leaving responsibility for industrial relations entirely in the hands of local managers, such relations being considered as an unavoidable constraint. The central head office merely draws conclusions from these constraints when developing its various international establishments.

The first attitude generally prevails in relations with higher grade staff in the firm. Conditions of employment for executives of foreign origin are determined by United States labour market practices. The reaction of foreign governments to the internationalisation of the managerial staff of local subsidiary companies may, however, delay the application of this policy which will then be accompanied by a policy of standardising the education of foreign executives as well as a policy of grooming these executives to assume positions of responsibility on an international scale. It is the internal and external resistance to the consequences of the first attitude – the adaptation in foreign countries of systems of relations applied in the majority environment – which will lead to methods being adjusted on the basis of American traditions.

The second attitude, acceptance of foreign environments as a constraint to industrial relations, is the only conceivable one in initial relations with local trade unions, staff delegates, social administrations and local employer associations. It involves responsibility for industrial relations as a whole being entrusted to the local management of multi-national firms for geographical areas corresponding to a given socio-economic environment. From the point of view of collective bargaining, local units are thus able to take part in regional agreements; this system is generally preferred by the public authorities and em-

---

[1] For example, the policies of computer makers with regard to the joint or separate sale or leasing of hardware and software are relevant here. These policies differ according to the country and according to the period of observation.

[2] i.e. the environment from which the majority of decision-makers and stockholders come.

ployer associations. Gradually, however, those responsible for staff policy at head office may seek to complement the industrial relations activities carried out in accordance with local traditions by co-ordinated intervention in fields of activity hitherto little explored. These would take the form, for instance, of continuous staff training, the management of social activities, keeping the staff informed as to the development of the group's industrial activities, participation in the fruits of expansion, etc. The large international corporations then tend to entrust the head office with the task of standardisation and of stimulating the realisation of new aspects in the group's industrial relations. The head office thus takes part in constituting a different environment for the various industrial establishments of the group in different parts of the world; the head office may even go so far as to promote the setting up of an international discussion group made up of workers' representatives in order to consider with the management of the multi-national group the industrial problems which the different national subsidiaries of the group have in common: conditions of work, remuneration techniques, conditions of promotion, workers' information, etc.

The development of these two approaches towards a coherent industrial relations policy for the entire group – at least as regards the main lines of action and sometimes as regards systems of relations with the labour world and bargaining practices – will depend on the degree of similarity between national environments which are decisive for industrial relations, that is to say on the attitudes of national social administrations and of national trade union organisations. In present-day Europe fundamental differences still exist between national social administrations; the same applies to the trade union world, despite the development of certain international trade union organisations whose sphere of activities still remains very marginal – the existence of 'supra-national' trade unionism has not yet resulted in any real change in the responsibilities of local trade unions in industrial relations practices.[1]

Is the situation any different in the multi-national European firms? It would not seem so. A study on the behaviour of firms and trade unions in the groups affected by the phenomenon of inter-penetration should be carried out in order to reply more accurately to this question. An analysis based on some of the experiences of European corporations reveals that they have not given up methods of decentralised collective

[1] Pierre Traimond: 'Le syndicalisme ouvrier face à la Communauté économique européenne', *Droit Social*, June 1966, p. 354.

bargaining applied on a regional basis. Nor do they appear so far to have decided on the doctrine which should serve as a basis for the gradual extension of an over-all industrial policy covering their establishments in various countries. Unlike the big American corporations, the European undertakings do not generally have a majority environment whose reactions might help in the adoption of a uniform approach to industrial relations. The stimulus for a coherent industrial policy within the European groups will therefore have to come from outside. European trade unions will agree more readily to apply a converging policy to European than to American firms; and the trade unions from both sides of the Atlantic have to be induced to co-operate. Governments, particularly within more or less integrated regional groupings (E.F.T.A., E.E.C.) will be able to reconcile their attitudes in respect of social policy (wage agreements, staff training and promotion, conditions of work, information, participation in management and sharing out the fruits of expansion). It is thus by increasing the degree of environmental similarity within Europe that the multi-national European corporation may gradually be encouraged to prepare an over-all industrial relations policy applicable without too many differences to all their European establishments. In this way increased environmental similarity within Europe should also lead to a harmonisation of bargaining procedures between representatives of employers and workers within Europe, applying not only to international but also to national and local firms.

The situation is thus more or less identical, regardless of whether multi-national firms of American origin or big European firms are involved. The development of coherent industrial relations policies at group level, to be introduced gradually into new fields of social action and then into the traditional sectors of collective bargaining, depends on the degree of political, administrative and social environmental similarities. Which factors are propitious to and which likely to impede the increase in environmental similarity in Europe on the one hand, and between Europe and the United States on the other?

There are considerable obstacles within Europe, for although progress has been achieved in the field of economic integration since 1958, it has not yet been possible to set up a coherent economic and social policy at Community level, whether in the monetary or social fields or as regards the business cycle, the development of infra-structures or employment policies. Consolidation of legislation, the freeing of trade, freedom to set up businesses and greater labour mobility were the only factors that contributed to a reconciling of national attitudes in the fields affecting industrial relations. Nor should one overlook the role played by better informed economic and trade union circles, or the habit acquired of establishing relations at the European level, particularly within the framework of the consultative institutions of the European Communities.

As regards the fundamental problems with which industrial relations are concerned (employment, wages, productivity, conditions of work, job security and stability, vocational training, the employment of women and young persons, retirement age, etc), the trade union organisations of the six countries continue to study the repercussions of the business cycle and of deep structural changes with the national authorities and national or regional employer organisations. Consultation cannot take place at the international level so long as the essential decisions are taken and applied at national level. Up to this stage of integration the international trade union organisations can do no more than exchange information on the respective problems encountered by their members at the level of their specific environment. Assistance proffered by the organisations at the international level can only be occasional and limited: at times certain local trade unions may justify particular claims by invoking solutions found in other countries, as when the outcome of the June 1968 negotiations in France were cited at collective discussions in the Netherlands and even in the Federal Republic of Germany. When general situations have little in common and economic and social policies diverge, unity of action appears impossible to achieve beyond the broad principles of solidarity among European workers. Representation of a larger proportion of trade unionists at all levels on the consultative bodies of Community institutions is unlikely to change this situation very much.

The only way in which national environments within Europe might now be brought closer together is to increase information on the industrial relations policy and techniques of the more advanced States. Thus information disseminated by the International Labour Office, by the Organisation for Economic Co-operation and Development and by the European Communities has led some States to adapt certain techniques of social policy used abroad: examples of this are the methods of vocational training applied by the Industrial Training Boards in Great Britain, procedures used in the Scandinavian countries for collective bargaining on wages, the techniques of workers' participation in management used in Federal German firms, and the system of information on employment recently tried out in France (national and regional employment agencies). Thus unobtrusively but probably effectively, concepts and administrative techniques are coming closer together. Leaving aside the traditional political involvement of trade union circles in Southern Europe, it is even conceivable that conceptions of the role of trade union organisations may reach a greater degree of similarity within Europe: certainly current consideration of possible combinations of claims and participation in industrial relations still runs into opposition within industrial circles, but this opposition is no longer uncompromising.

Such a development can be seen particularly in sectors covered by multi-national European corporations. The trade unions which are more or less representative of the basic sectors have already set up permanent action committees corresponding to the European or even international activities of certain large firms in the Common Market. These are concerned with developing international bargaining cells involving the entire activities of the firm. Of course many questions may be raised about the setting up of the permanent action committees: are we heading towards a new form of collusion between the top European employers and the more privileged workers to establish the comparative advantages these workers will obtain in relation to those who do not share with them the privilege of working in a leading multi-national group? Or, conversely, are we heading towards supervision by national trade unions to prevent multi-national firms from overpowering the isolated local trade union sections and thus ensure that workers' solidarity on a European scale becomes more effective? With the gradual abandoning of regional collective bargaining methods, which imply active participation by specialised employer associations, are we heading towards vast company agreements, 'frame agreements' between plant unions, federated at the European level, and the representatives of national subsidiaries of multi-national European firms?

At the moment it would seem that a mixed system is likely to emerge in which local collective bargaining will remain the basic system, complemented, in areas that are related by agreements reached at the level of the firm, with the participation of a permanent action committee, grouping representatives of the firm's European employees. Over time these two bargaining systems will change, as will the procedures of the second system. When national administrations and occupational organisations have recognised the complementary character of bargaining in the firms it will become possible to extend this new bargaining system to the European firm. This, however, will take time.

As regards multi-national groups of American origin, on the other hand, it would seem more difficult to achieve an environmental change by reconciling customs and improving information. Here the setting up by trade unions of company liaison committees on an international scale will certainly aim at improving the trade unions' knowledge on the manner in which the various cells of the multi-national firm apply their industrial relations policy; but this will also make it possible to step up the fight against the establishing of these vast international monopolies which evade the control of the authorities in the countries of their parent companies. Moreover such politically-tinged activities may not be supported by certain sections of the international trade union movement, nor by workers of all nationalities. Thus, during the recent strikes in North America which paralysed the output of non-ferrous metals and of their manufactured products, the solidarity of workers in the foreign subsidiaries of the group concerned failed to manifest itself in any active form. To a certain degree over-all industrial relations policies may perhaps develop more rapidly in the case of European firms than in that of multi-national corporations of American origin. This will be achieved despite the difficulties of harmonising national environments in Europe and despite the quality of the industrial relations policy characterising firms of American origin.

In the long run it is possible that multi-national European corporations will stand a better chance to develop than multi-national corporations of American origin, which are likely to be increasingly obliged to follow a 'polycentric' policy at the European level.[1]

In both cases the type of industrial relations that will be applied in Europe by both categories of firms – those of European origin, and those which became European through gradual separation from their American head office – will differ both from the methods now being used in collective bargaining in Western Europe and from the concepts resulting from the socio-political and socio-cultural environment of the North American continent. It is too early to venture to describe the principal lines, the methods, the historical accidents of this develop-

---

[1] See Jacques Houssiaux: 'Le facteur américain dans l'apparition et l'orientation des politiques industrielles en Europe occidentale depuis la seconde guerre mondiale', *Conference of the International Economic Association* (Portugal, September 1969).

ment of types of relations between large European firms, trade unions and public authorities. It will be necessary to await the appearance of specific cases and to follow their development patiently, whilst at the same time seeing to it that a crystallisation of trade union rights in Europe does not prevent the setting up of systems of consultation and bargaining that would be more efficient for both European firms and their workers.

# SUMMARY OF THE SYMPOSIUM DISCUSSIONS

*by*
*Hans Günter*

## MAJOR THEMES

As suggested in a discussion outline prepared by the Institute, the purpose of the proceedings was to consider prospectively the impact of the multi-national corporation and of regional economic integration upon the future of industrial relations and, conversely, how the pattern and trends in industrial relations might influence the growth of the multi-national corporation or regional integration. In both cases the particular focus was to be on the prospects for transnational industrial relations.

Expanding on these ideas, *Mr Kahn-Freund* proposed that in proceeding with the discussions, an attempt might be made to separate the diagnostic and the prescriptive considerations. As regards the diagnostic or fact-finding part, one had first to turn to the *basic trends affecting the location of decision-making powers in industrial relations* which arise from the growth of the multi-national corporation and economic regionalism. This might lead to an *assessment of the evidence to date of transnational industrial relations*, both in the developed and in the developing world. It could also include a tentative review of the possible implications of East-West industrial co-operation for industrial relations.

As regards the *implications of these developments for the future of industrial relations*, it was essential to consider in prescriptive terms what was necessary to promote transnational industrial relations. Were there certain prerequisite conditions (economic, organisational, ideological, technological, articulation of interests) for the development of such industrial relations? What adjustments were needed by management, unions and governments in collective bargaining or related processes, in order to obtain transnational industrial relations and international collective bargaining?

Finally, attention might be given to the problem of how far this development might give rise to future international institution-building. Discussions on this point would, among others, have to investigate: (1) possible coalitions and lines of cleavages among corporations, unions and States which would underline any future institutional arrangements; (2) the problems of the accountability of transnational private power to international public authority; (3) the problem of participation in decision-making in industrial relations by multi-national corporations and international trade union, and (4) the role of regional and international organisations, such as the E.E.C. and the I.L.O., in the development of transnational processes or of new international structures relevant to industrial relations.

Mr Kahn-Freund continued his introduction by recalling that the three phenomena in the present world which made transnational industrial relations a timely subject for discussion were obviously: (a) the growth of multi-national business units; (b) the growth of regional political bodies, and (c) the penetration into the developing countries of the multi-national companies. The latter was one of the most fundamental political processes of our time and therefore, owing to the possible clash of interest between multi-national management and national aspirations, had to be treated with particular urgency. However, after reading – for instance – Mr Perlmutter's and Mr Roberts's papers, the question might be asked: what was really so new in the multi-national form of business enterprises? Why had problems connected with these enterprises leapt into prominence since the Second World War, although an appreciable number of multi-national corporations had been operating and had been growing for some decades? Was it because the older type of multi-national enterprises appeared to aim more at a financial co-ordination of a number of units which, from the managerial point of view, operated independently, whereas the modern multi-national enterprise appeared to co-ordinate management and, to some extent at least, gave the impression of one unit vis-à-vis its environment, especially when compared with labour? Mr Blake's paper had dealt with an extreme case of managerial unification (that of the Chrysler Company on both sides of the U.S.–Canadian border) which had resulted in the creation of a single international collective bargaining unit on wages, despite allegedly different levels of labour productivity in both countries.

Compared with international collective bargaining arising from the powerful structure of the multi-national corporation, that arising from economic integration appeared (as the papers of Messrs Günter, Dierendonck, Blanpain and Despax had brought out for the E.E.C.) to be little more than an aspiration. This was even more true (looking

354

at Mr Kaplan's paper) as regards the Latin American common market. Turning to the role of the supra-national authorities in the development of transnational industrial relations, Mr Kahn-Freund felt that their role was that of a midwife while the major efforts had to be made by the social partners themselves.

The special problems of the developing countries were referred to in part in Mr Casserini's paper. Furthermore, Mr Harrod's paper on the situation in Jamaica gave, so to speak, a specimen of possible clashes of interest between multi-national corporations and the requirements of local conditions.

Commenting now on the prescriptive side, Mr Kahn-Freund stressed that a prime requirement seemed to be the adjustment of the managerial decision-making process to the needs of an international collective bargaining apparatus. Mr Perlmutter had dealt in his paper with the problems of the decision-making level by defining his concepts of ethnocentric, polycentric and geocentric management, which were eminently important for the present discussions. The question of adjustments on the trade union side was likewise closely linked to shifts in the decision-making locus.

Observing actual developments, one could discern a continuing tendency, at least in Europe, for centralisation in collective bargaining culminating in industry-wide and district bargaining, but also a recent counter-tendency for the shifting of bargaining power back to the periphery and, in extreme cases, to the work group in the plant. As the British example had illustrated, the latter tendency was a handicap, however, for the collective bargaining processes at the national level. The question was therefore pertinent whether, at the international level, problems were not similar, with the added difficulty that the task of grouping international or supra-national bargaining units, especially in the face of a politically divided trade union movement, looked sometimes almost desperate. Hence, which form of bargaining could realistically be envisaged on an international level: a joint bargaining unit both on the workers' and the employers' side (as in the United States and Canadian automobile industry) or merely a co-ordination of bargaining over the frontiers? Connected to this was the question of which topics lent themselves to international collective bargaining? This would probably mean in practice the choice of topics which could be isolated from the nexus of productivity levels and of the rates of exchange. Misgivings were justified in respect of wage levels, as appeared from Mr Blake's paper, although the alleged discrepancies in the productivity of labour sometimes seemed to be exaggerated – as the agreement with Chrysler had shown. Maybe hours of work, holidays and similar subjects were more easily accessible to international collective bargaining.

Mr Kahn-Freund believed that of prime importance for all the issues under discussion was the relationship of multi-national companies to the State, more particularly in the case of developing countries. There were perhaps limits to what national governments could do in the direction of promoting international collective bargaining. This problem was connected with the politically hot issue of the status of multi-national corporations in developing countries and with the application to them of the law governing economic and social conditions, including, for instance, taxation, social security, and safety legislation. In the same vein, one had to look closely into the question of which role international and supra-national bodies might play in helping to bring transnational industrial relations and international collective bargaining into existence.


## TRENDS AFFECTING THE LOCATION OF DECISION-MAKING POWER

Mr Cox opened up this part of the discussion by presenting his paper. He stated that he had attempted to make a kind of inventory of the external forces which might be expected to influence development either towards or against transnational industrial relations in the years to come. One of Mr Cox's assumptions about transnational industrial relations was that processes for making decisions about work rules, incomes and other subject matters of industrial relations would increasingly flow across the national boundaries and would therefore go beyond the competence of the national institutions which had been dealing with them, until such time as they became restructured in an international way. Another assumption was that there was no dynamic native to industrial relations which would tend to transform them from a national into an international process; it could rather be expected therefore that such a transformation would be subordinated to influences from other systems, e.g. economic and technological.

However, industrial relations systems in the more industrialised countries would themselves affect the basic trends in the world economic structures. Five critical factors which might influence the locus of decision-making about work rules and unions were, in Mr Cox's opinion, significant in this respect, viz: (1) the growing differentiation in the labour force and the accompanying differentiation of occupational interest expressed through new occupational associations, side by side with the older trade unions of manual workers; (2) the increasing importance of plant-level agreements in European countries, resulting in more local autonomy; (3) the seemingly contrary tendency towards enhancement of the authority of central organs of social partners over their members, attributable mainly to the State calling in these bodies as consultants, and possibly partners, in economic policy; (4) the demand for employee participation in management, enhancing local plant autonomy, and (5) changing attitudes of wage-earners, embracing middle-class values and personal adaptations to the large organisations, lessening the tendency to identify with class. Yet, just as the end of ideology had been proclaimed, an anti-organisational revolt, asserting personal freedom against the claims of organisational conformity, appeared to be spreading.

In purely abstract terms, three possible types of reaction by trade unions and employers were conceivable: disappearance, opposition and symbiosis. Opposition to multi-national companies, perhaps in alliance with the State, was a more likely possibility than disappearance. Symbiosis was the reaction most likely to lead towards transnational industrial relations; it implied a sharing of values. Concretely, it meant for unions the objective of building security systems for employees around the corporation, rather than the State, and for employers that national industries would play a complementary role to the multi-national giants. One might extrapolate from the multi-national corporation a vision of a functionally organised world in which control lay with technocrats and rational organisation. Alternatively, one might think of a world organised in larger regional groupings, although this alternative seemed to carry less conviction today than in the early 1960s. Hence, the State remained as the major territorially-based force to be reconciled with multi-national corporations.

Mr Cox concluded by saying that in his paper he had attempted to work towards some kind of research model which might help us to understand a little better how the dynamics of the developments under consideration might occur in the future. He had intended to identify the variables and try to find out what might be the relationship among them. It was hoped that the Symposium discussion would contribute towards clarification of ideas about research possibilities. For its part the Institute would be prepared to carry forward the enquiry opened up by the Symposium.

### Prospects for the Growth of the Multi-National Corporation

The propositions contained in Mr Perlmutter's paper that the multinational firm was to gain in economic strength because of its international resources and external opportunities, was accepted by most of the participants.[1] Increasing concern of governments was recognised as a major factor that could counteract growth of multi-national corporations deemed excessive. However, this problem received fuller attention only later in the discussion when the relationship between the multi-national corporation and the State was considered (see page 404 onwards). At this stage interest focused mainly on the factors responsible for growth and the historic perspective of growth of the multi-national corporation.

*Mr Houssiaux* held that the multi-national corporation was a management system with specific features which had emerged out of the profound evolution in the operations of enterprises on a world-wide scale most noticeably in the course of the last twenty years. However, this system was not a completely uniform one nor a definite phenomenon.

While the subsidiaries of multi-national firms might for a long while continue to bear the stamp of the national environment in which they were situated and were mainly operative, as had been suggested in Mr Nye's paper, it was likely that, in the long run, new socio-economic or socio-political entities would appear, created by an aggregation of the national subsidiaries. This form of multi-national corporation would add a new dimension to the relations which existed at the present time between countries and States in their capacity as national protectors and controllers of the activities of the enterprises.

As to the advent of the present multi-national corporations, Mr Houssiaux suggested that these were the inevitable consequences of the convergence of three, not entirely independent, evolutions. Firstly, the enlargement of markets since the Second World War. Against this assumption it could be pointed out that multi-national

---

[1] Mr Perlmutter expects to see, by 1985, around 300 supergiant multi-national firms in all key sectors, in addition to a very large number of middle-sized or small regional or global multi-national firms.

corporations had been able to live before this period mainly by virtue of a segmentation of markets; it also remained to be seen whether multi-national enterprises would not resort, in the future, to other segments of the markets, replacing the old geographical barriers created by the history of the nation States. It was revealing in this context that the policy of intensified competition adopted by the European Common Market was not so much geared to achieving a satisfactory functioning of markets as to avoiding the establishment of segmented markets within the Community.

The second evolution was connected with the cultural aspect of the enlargement and internationalisation of the environment of enterprises, which meant that they simultaneously encountered in all countries largely the same types of constraints to their action. For technical reasons and for reasons of communications, the internationalisation of the environment was very pronounced in industrial countries. This permitted the survival of enterprises in environments which in earlier times had been considered hostile to their existence. However, the inverse phenomena was also true, in that multi-national corporations were singularly apt to benefit from the specific cultural aspects of one society and to transmit them inside their worldwide network. In this way, the particular qualification of the Anglo-Saxon world in the management of enterprises had, for instance, been transmitted to other parts of the world.

The third evolution favouring the growth of multi-national firms was the progress made in management techniques during the last decade, first of all thanks to the techniques of 'corporate planning' and to strategic decision-making in a planned universe. It was somewhat surprising to see that many decisions of great multi-national enterprises were, nevertheless, still taken without full prior consideration of all intervening factors. Not surprising, on the other hand, were the different weights which the various national subsidiaries of a multi-national corporation attributed to these factors. Where these weighting coefficients were particularly different among subsidiaries, the internal solidarity would of course be substantially affected, thus diminishing the possibilities of a common strategy by the whole of the corporation. For these reasons, and despite the internationalisation of the environment and the enlargement of markets, there existed in international corporations considerable areas of decision-making which remained in the dark; this situation impeded the enlargement of common strategies (the proper objectives of multi-national enterprises) and transformed the co-ordination centre of the corporation often into a place of doubtful arbitration. Hence, the need for decentralisation of decision-making, making subsidiaries responsible for an important part of the activity of the whole corporation.

*Mr Haenni* viewed the growth of the multi-national corporation as the most recent element in the historic chain of internationalisation. Before the industrial era, internationalisation had extended itself mainly to armies and to banking. Four phenomena (in part already touched upon by Mr Houssiaux) had, in Mr Haenni's opinion, contributed to the growth of multi-national companies, namely (i) technological innovation (which, for the chemical industry, had found its apogee before the war in the form of patents held by European firms, like I. G. Farben and Solvay); (ii) strategic possession-taking of raw materials (locations of oil, bauxite, iron ore, etc.), and (iii) imperialistic occupation of markets and ports in which both European and American firms had joined. The dominance of American multi-national corporations on the markets of products of affluence was a well-known contemporary concern to many people. Apart from other reasons, these firms possibly captured public imagination as their production related to fields about which there was some mysticism, such as outer space, nuclear energy and computers. (iv) The last phenomenon was the growth of the international service industry (hotels, car renting, etc.).

There was not much uniformity in these phenomena, except that an element of dimension appeared to be involved. Enterprises with more than 100,000 employees had increased in industrialised countries at a ratio of 1 : 3 over the last ten years. This growth appeared to be an irreversible trend which was bound to spill over the boundaries of countries, with or without formal mergers of firms. The industrial internationalisation did not embrace, however, all sectors of the economy; usually mining and the steel industry were excluded, which might have significance for a gradual emergence of countervailing forces other than the State, as precisely in heavy industry trade union strength was greatest. Sedentary industries, like printing, furniture, construction, brewing and insurance, were also largely unaffected by internationalisation and the same was true, for more obvious reasons, of armaments, nuclear energy, space, aircraft and shipyards. It added to the complexity of the phenomena that the situation was heterogenous, even within industrial branches; in the electrical industry, for instance, General Electric had become very greatly internationalised, while Westinghouse much less so.

Expanding broadly on Mr Haenni's ideas, *Mr Conlon* thought that the great post-War II thrust in the continuing growth of American-based multi-national corporations was connected with the emergence of the wide range of electronic industries. A characteristic of these new successful industries was that they were not only highly technical-oriented but also highly service-oriented (as opposed to product-oriented). It was a known fact that a number of American companies with more traditional production, operating largely locally before the Second World War – like Heinz, Singer and Union Carbide – had to face a difficult time when jumping from virtually nothing into wholly-owned production subsidiaries around the world. The situation changed for the better as soon as these firms had taken over modern management techniques from the upstart new industries.

*Prospects for Growth of Economic Regionalism*

Evidence on this issue appeared to be mixed. *Mr Nye* thought that the obvious numerical increase in new regional inter-governmental organisations, which accounted for about 60 per cent of all inter-governmental organisations founded between 1956/65, was no real proof of growth of regional political integration. To understand this apparent contradiction one had to recall that regional organisations were not only instruments of co-operation but also served very important diplomatic functions in the modern international system where power was often more closely geared to less tangible goals, like prestige.

This view was supported by Bruce Russets's findings[1] that numerical growth was not paralleled to the same extent by the emergence of regional voting pattern in the U.N. or regional trade pattern. The frequently quoted enormous increase in intra-E.E.C. trade could not be considered a specific feature of regional proximity as, for instance, trade between the U.S. and Japan which were very separate in geographical space, had increased to much the same extent. Similarly, the argument that the worldwide type organisations, such as the British Commonwealth, tended to be superseded by regional organisations was countervailed by the evidence that the O.E.C.D. (which, in its origin appeared to be an Atlantic organisation) had included since 1964 also Japan.

A number of scholars had tried to predict future world organisation, more or less convincingly, on the basis of technological trends. This

---

[1] Cf. Bruce Russets: *International Regions and the International System* (Chicago, Rand McNally, 1967) p. 213.

type of prediction also cast some doubts on the statement of Jean Rey, President of the Commission of the European Communities, that the world was becoming increasingly organised at the level of continents. Finally, while there was mixed evidence for the argument that the nation State was obsolete, there was little evidence that the next step in world co-operation must therefore be regional. If technological arguments were probably too mechanical, this argument was too teleological.

As no clear trend regarding the growth of regionalism in the current period was therefore perceptible, it was necessary to conjecture about alternative possibilities. It could, for instance, be assumed that future growth of regionalism might occur as a result of growing regional loyalties. Possibly this transfer of loyalties might be dependent on a generational change. Another possibility was that multi-national corporations might indirectly help to strengthen regionalism as national governments might opt for regionalism as a co-operative device for meeting the challenge of multi-national corporations. The most likely future, in Mr Nye's opinion, was that the three structures of the nation State, the multi-national corporation and the regional organisation, would continue to exist and that the regional organisation would remain the weakest of the three.

While in agreement with Mr Nye's general analysis, *Mr Odhner* questioned Mr Nye's assertion on the continuing importance of the nation State. The nation State was perhaps not to be superseded by regionalism. However, there was a clear tendency for districts (i.e. regions within a country) to become units with economic and political competence. For psychological reasons, loyalty was much more easily transferred from the nation State to such districts (including historical units like Scotland, Wales and Brittany) than to regional groupings. This evolution was, at the same time, under-pinned by municipal amalgamations, enabling local authorities to better fulfil their functions. This was a particular aspect of the centripetal and centrifugal tendencies mentioned by Mr Cox, which eventually might have implications on the organisation of industrial relations.

## TRANSNATIONAL INDUSTRIAL RELATIONS: ASSESSMENT OF THE EVIDENCE TO DATE

The discussion confirmed that transnational industrial relations were, for the moment, mostly only emerging. They appeared a near possibility in response to the worldwide operations of multi-national corporations. In respect to regional economic integration, little evidence was found so far on transnational approaches; the participants focused on the reasons for this state of affairs, coupled with the intent to detect prerequisite conditions for transnational industrial relations. The subsequent exchange of opinion on the possible effects of East-West economic co-operation on industrial relations ended, much as expected, in a completely speculative mood.

In addition to assessing the evidence of transnational industrial relations, the discussion contributed towards a clarification of the main underlying phenomena, i.e. the character of multi-national corporations, in particular their decision-making locus as regards industrial relations and their industrial relations approaches in developed and developing countries; trends in bargaining pattern and trade union organisation and strategy. General aspects of regional economic integration and of East-West industrial exchanges were likewise further highlighted.

*Transnational Bargaining with Multi-national Corporations*

*Mr Casserini* looked at the issue from the angle of practical experience gained within the International Metal Workers Federation. He pointed out that no fully-fledged transnational agreements had so far been concluded in Europe but that preliminary contacts had shown some of the problem areas. Trade unions had, for instance, noticed in their daily relations with multi-national corporations that, in spite of a certain diversification and decentralisation of business policy (of which the recent reorganisation of Westinghouse was an example), the main personnel policy decisions were still made at the top by central headquarters management.

Even where industrial relations decisions might also be made at the level of the local subsidiary of a multi-national corporation, headquarters always had a strong say in the matter; firstly, because there were constant contacts between local management and headquarters and secondly, because there existed common principles of personnel policy to which all subsidiaries had to subscribe. Therefore, in the last instance, industrial relations issues were always settled at headquarters, and frequently attempts were made to increase the competence of central personnel management and to influence even the wage policy in subsidiaries. An illustration of this latter fact had been provided by the interference of central management in a wage dispute at the

General Motors (Holding) Company in Australia which, according to the country's practice, had been put before a Labour Court which had tried to keep a certain national pattern of wages. Obviously, such procedures did not now fit in with the dynamism of multi-national corporations and the dynamic bargaining which they required.

The type of problems to be encountered and the possible scope of transnational bargaining were particularly highlighted by the contacts which the International Metal Workers Federation Metal Committee of the Six Common Market countries had recently made with the Philips Company. Shop stewards and local trade union representatives had been called together by the Committee to design a common action programme which had been subsequently discussed with the top management of Philips. The immediate cause of this programme had been dismissals in connection with a certain recession in the electrotechnical industry.

The discussion with the management of Philips had taken place in a good atmosphere and could be classified as a general exchange of views. In preparation for further developments, the trade unions had then elaborated special points which they now wished to discuss with Philips. They might be mentioned as an illustration of possible topics which might be subjected to transnational bargaining: (i) timely information of trade unions as regards production transfers and cut-downs in subsidiaries; (ii) training and retraining policy; (iii) social protection of workers hit by rationalisation; (iv) profit transfer from subsidiaries back to the mother company (in connection with profit-sharing schemes in subsidiaries); (v) competence of local management (which trade unions regarded as a crucial point); (vi) a survey of social conditions in all Philips subsidiaries, and (vii) regular consultations between the European trade union committee and the top management of Philips.

The Philips Company had replied that they were ready for a second general exchange of views with the unions but that they were doubtful whether the stage was already reached at which specific points could usefully be taken up. Mr Casserini added that he was convinced, in spite of this reluctant reply, that if bargaining was to be advanced in Europe, contacts between international trade unions and top management of international corporations were a first step to be undertaken. Although corporate reticence had to be overcome by trade unions, European collective agreements with multi-national firms were a much more likely possibility than general industry-wide European agreements. In evaluating the present situation, it could not be over-looked that a major factor accounting for the slowness of the develop-ment of transnational industrial relations was the refusal of a number of multi-national firms to deal with unions internationally and face their attempts to bring up local problems in an over-all context.

Mr *Weil* felt that the dominance of central headquarter decisions on industrial relations issues was a typical characteristic of American multi-national corporations in Europe. On the other hand, European corporations operating abroad adopted more easily the local or regional industrial relations pattern. Where, however, American-based multi-national firms had integrated themselves in the national industrial relations system (as General Motors, International Harvester and I.B.M. had done in Germany), they had reinforced the trend towards a unification of general conditions of work (i.e. hours of work and holidays) in an industry or even on a national basis. At the same time, there was a tendency for bargaining on actual wages to shift from the industry or district level to the enterprise or plant which, as Mr Kahn-Freund added, appeared to be a prominent general feature in the development of industrial relations of our time.

Mr *Parion* said that in developed countries (particularly in France) multi-national corporations tended to integrate themselves in the national industrial relations system and in the existing local or industry-wide structure of collective agreements. Multi-national corporations faced, in these countries, problems analogous to those of nation-wide firms, and to judge from the example of the French building industry (of which Mr Parion knew most) had usually to adhere to the local employers' associations and the existing local collective agreements.

Mr *Roberts* wondered whether a distinction between the industrial relations behaviour of American multi-national corporations and the behaviour of European corporations was analytically useful. The most fundamental question to be answered was whether the behaviour of American firms was a case of what might be called American cul-tural imperialism or whether it was rather a product of more basic functional factors which one had to discover. Such factors might, for instance, include the nature of technology applied; obviously most of the multi-national corporations were, generally speaking, using more advanced technologies than any competitive firm in the host country, a fact which induced the need for a high degree of headquarters' management and control. Secondly, there was the element of belief that the multi-national corporation, coming from a highly advanced economy, had the know-how which did not exist in the host country. This was a universal phenomenon which one could find with American companies in Europe as well as with British or German companies in less-developed regions of the world.

Consequently, the phenomena of multi-national corporations was not entirely an American challenge. It was of interest to note, in this context, that, according to well-informed sources, around 1950 the amount of foreign capital invested in the U.S. exceeded by ten times the amount of American capital overseas. Today the American overseas investments had just surpassed the amount of foreign capital invested in the U.S. by the rest of the world. This certainly pointed to the dramatic increase of American foreign investment but it also revealed that one could not discuss the multi-national corporation exclusively in American cultural terms. It could not be doubted, for instance, that the British-based multi-national corporations operating in formerly British overseas territories had made a tremendous impact on the local pattern of industrial relations.

In conclusion, Mr Roberts felt that the multi-national corporation was a species with many different varieties. To obtain a comprehensive picture of the reality, one had to examine differences in technology, size of the organisational units and differences in the capital structure of the corporations, as well as the influence of cultural factors (including political systems and socio-economic situations) that emanated from the headquarters of the corporation and were mitigated by the cultural environment of the host country. Yet having found out the dominant element, one was still left with the value question: how to judge the developments from the different angles of interest and the different levels of economic development.

The remarks of the previous speakers had shown, *Mr Kahn-Freund* suggested, that one of the most crucial issues in the development of transnational industrial relations was the locus of decision on industrial relations. More detailed evidence on this matter and on the factors underlying it would certainly advance the discussion.

In response, and wishing to provide more factual evidence on these issues, *Mr Lee* pointed out that, in his experience, the decisions in regard to industrial relations were made at the level of the operating subsidiary. Headquarters were obviously informed but they were occasionally worried about the lack of direct information and it sometimes happened that they learned about a strike or a new collective agreement in subsidiaries from the newspapers only. Personnel managers and industrial relations chiefs of subsidiaries were mainly nationals of the host country all over the world, assisted by a few expatriates who trained them. Referring to Mr Casserini's statement, Mr Lee stressed that he and many managers wished to work with trade unions. This was one of the reasons for a company's success. Close working contacts, for instance, existed between some oil companies and the International Federation of Petroleum and Chemical Workers, a situation which had helped to conclude first-class collective contracts in different countries of operations. In principle, multinational companies were often prepared to accept improvements in labour conditions and even to harmonise parts of their collective agreements; but it should be recalled that they had frequently to oblige local government policy, such as the decisions of the Prices and Incomes Board in the U.K.

*Mr O'Leary* thought that it was dangerous to generalise from a few specific examples of decision-making in multi-national corporations. However, even without knowing the complete picture, it was probably safe to say that multi-national corporations were unable to rigidly centralise their industrial relations decisions for long because of both the particularities of the local situations and the technical impossibility of keeping track of all the various labour provisions existing in the different countries, and making adequate decisions of a worldwide scope. This seemed to be at least the upshot of the experience of his own organisation. The policy of his corporation was therefore that industrial relations decisions, including those on wages, had to be taken at local levels, head offices being kept advised on the issues. Hence this firm did not spread North American industrial relations approaches. In line with this policy, European subsidiaries, for instance, were covered by the general metal agreements in the various countries.

On the other hand, there existed certainly cases where a multinational firm could not simply follow national patterns if these were counter-productive. One could not condemn, therefore, an American firm trying to introduce, in such cases, American methods in order to solve the problem of raising productivity, called for by a productivity agreement. Although there might perhaps be other ways of dealing with such types of problems, resorting to methods which had proved useful in the mother country certainly was a first remedy which management would see. As to relations with trade unions, his company's philosophy was to deal with them wherever they existed. On the other hand, the establishment of trade unions and their organising in the company's plants were considered a trade union business. Mr O'Leary felt that it was essential that this be known, as some of the discussion had inferred that multi-national firms usually refused to deal with unions.

Finally, Mr O'Leary thought that the existence of adequate legal provisions, setting the frame for collectively agreed rules, was essential for good industrial relations. Of great importance, in this respect were, for instance, legally required 'cooling-off periods' before a strike could be called.

Pursuing this point in a more general vein, *Mr Kahn-Freund* expressed his conviction that if international collective bargaining was to develop, unification of the law would have to be set in motion in order to make the process work; unions had to exert pressure on governments to bring this modification about.

*Mr Blanpain* wished to agree that a less absolute view was needed on the decision-making level in multi-national corporations. Detailed case studies were required to bring about all necessary evidence and they were often likely to produce unexpected results. His own studies on the operation of multi-national corporations in Belgium (focusing in particular on the Ford Motor Company) had revealed that basic responsibility for personnel matters was in the hands of local management. However, local management tended to hide itself behind alleged headquarters jurisdiction when assaulted by trade union claims.

*Mr Schregle* felt that there was not just one locus of decision for personnel questions, but a multitude of levels where such decisions were made, depending on the type of decision and the subject matter concerned. At each level the question arose of associating workers and their representatives with the decision. His visits to headquarters of multi-national corporations had convinced him that not all decisions concerning labour matters could be centralised in one particular spot. However, a multi-national corporation, irrespective of all differences in national labour legislations and customs, might wish to define general principles of labour relations and personnel policy which should be applied in all its subsidiaries. This was an important task for the personnel manager or industrial relations adviser at the top and might contribute to the positive image of the company. Undoubtedly, quite a number of multi-national corporations possessed such an internal industrial relations code.

Common industrial relations principles might, for instance, cover the following issues: (1) objective criteria for the determination of a representative trade union with which the subsidiaries would negotiate; (2) a statement that representation of its employees by a trade union was in the interest of the company; (3) maximum promotion of consultation with local trade unions; (4) common policies on providing employees with full and objective information and an opportunity for them to voice their views on this information; (5) objective, expeditious grievances procedures supplemented by clear-cut disciplinary measures; (6) training policies for staff and supervisors, and (7) promotion procedures and similar matters.

In this connection, the question arose whether it was not in the interest of top management to have such policy guidelines drawn up not only by top personnel managers at headquarters but also discussed, at an early stage, with trade unions where they were internationally organised. It was quite conceivable that an international industrial relations policy of a worldwide company set up along these lines might form the first step towards collective bargaining at an international level.

## Special Problems in Developing Countries

Mr Schregle held that the possibility of a conflict between multi-national corporations and the local system of industrial relations was particularly acute in the case of developing countries. As an example, he took the local enterprise, in a developing country, of an American company which, according to the American pattern, did not encourage its local plants to join the local employers' organisation, but favoured the existence of shop stewards and direct bargaining between them and local management. The labour code of the country in question was conceived, however, after the French model, according to which bargaining was done between employers' and workers' organisations. The introduction of plant-level bargaining by the American company was naturally hailed by the local trade unions but was looked at with less joy by local employers' organisations.

Naturally, a multi-national corporation could also use its power to exert a beneficial influence on the industrial relations pattern in developing countries. As the management of foreign companies was often more progressive than local enterprises and its attitude was often more pro-union, modern industrial relations practices might find their way into a developing country.

*Mr Kahn-Freund* wondered whether, under the favourable circumstances referred to by Mr Schregle, multi-national corporations did not appear, in a way, as the heirs of the colonial powers in that their presence may result in developing the existing industrial relations. At least as regards the promotion of the instrument of collective bargaining, this had also been the concern of most colonial powers.

Drawing on his own experience, *Mr Lee* wished to confirm that multi-national corporations operating in developing countries had often made a good pattern of industrial relations. Against the advice of local employer organisations, his organisation had, for instance, concluded plant agreements in certain parts of the then French Equatorial Africa, which had subsequently been extended to other establishments, by law.

In this context, it had to be added that multi-national corporations did not boycott local employer organisations as a matter of principle; they tended to use the anti-trust argument only where it suited them. Otherwise, quite a number of firms were members of local employers' organisations in developed as well as developing countries.

*Mr Casserini* admitted that the experience with multi-national corporations in developing countries was manifold. The more frequent experience made by the Metal Workers International was, however, that the corporations did not want any unions. In a number of cases, attempts were being made to create unions at the plant level with no relationship to the existing national trade union movement. In view of this state of affairs, a particular task for the international unions was the amalgamation of national groupings to arrive at strong national unions, capable of self-defence. A corollary task was the education of trade unionists who had to face plant-level top management of multi-national corporations.

Focusing on the same problems, *Mr Maier* said that the operations of multi-national corporations had, on the whole, brought with them anti-trade union consequences although the situation might have somewhat changed after the Second World War. However, multi-national corporations had usually negotiated with trade unions only where, by imposing their organisational strength, the unions had forced them to negotiate. This was illustrated by two examples found in Liberia and in Peru. In Liberia the influence of Firestone had prevented the creation of proper trade unions. But only three years ago, as a result of strike movements, the international trade unions were approached to organise workers appropriately, as this had proved to be a pre-condition for the good functioning of the company. The outstanding feature of the Peruvian case was that in this country very favourable legislation for multi-national corporations existed, especially as regards taxation. Furthermore, certain government provisions made it very difficult for trade unions to organise employees in these firms. Occasionally this situation had almost been presented as an additional incentive for the settlement of international corporations in Peru. Taking all known cases together, the evidence of the impact of multi-national corporations on industrial relations in developing countries was quite mixed.

*Mr Harrod* thought that in many developing countries governments and trade unions were in such a weak position that multi-national corporations could often impose their own pattern, while in developed countries they had to respect the local patterns.

Mr Roberts was certainly right, he continued, in highlighting that cultural imperialism of corporations was independent of their nationality. For a number of reasons the usual attempt of multi-national firms of all origins was to duplicate their own environment within the cultural, economic and social framework of the developing country. Of course, the same applied to the trade unions; national unions working alone or through international confederations would likewise attempt to duplicate the environment and organisations they had at home. This had been a typical feature of his own case study on Jamaica as well as, it might be added, that foreign unions attempted to support national foreign policy. In this latter respect both British and American unions had tried to follow the policy laid down by Sidney Webb, in 1930, then Secretary of State for the Colonies, that colonial trade unions should not be allowed to 'fall into the hands of disaffected persons'. The foreign unions had thus tried, unsuccessfully, to prevent the champion of national independence from retaining union leadership.

The evidence in Jamaica was also a case in point for Mr Casserini's assertion that multi-national corporations often did not want to deal with the existing national unions. In such cases it was common for alternative unions to be created, usually with the heavy involvement of foreign national organisations. It was reported recently by the press, for example, that a project in Trinidad, financed by a U.S. Government Aid grant of $1·2 million to the A.F.L.-C.I.O. and channeled through the International Federation of Petroleum and Chemical Workers, was to somehow correct a situation in which one of the latter's affiliates was claimed to have come under communist influence. In such a case a new and rival union would be created or current leadership replaced, both of which would no doubt be very competent in international collective bargaining but the side effects could be serious as, in the case of Trinidad, upsetting the delicate balance of economic and race relations.

Thus, Mr Harrod added, he would be rather reluctant to call bargaining involving multi-national corporations and such newly created unions, or unions absorbed by foreign unions from developed countries, 'international collective bargaining'. In his opinion these were merely devices for the extension of national collective bargaining on foreign territory.

### The Impact of Regional Economic Integration on Industrial Relations

This theme was discussed nearly exclusively in the light of the E.E.C. experience. Most participants recognised that the impact of the creation and operation of the E.E.C. on industrial relations had not only been small but was also difficult to separate from the stronger phenomenon of multi-national corporations operating in the Community. A number of hypotheses were advanced on why international collective bargaining had not come into existence so far, and inferences were drawn on its likely prerequisites, including adjustments in the behaviour and organisational structures of employers and trade unions.

Mr Grandjeat suggested that a starting point for the discussion of regional collective agreements might be to review what was really negotiable and at which level. As regards the content of negotiations, a distinction might usefully be made between the legal and the economic aspects. Legal aspects were taken care of mainly by the Commission of the European Communities and related to such questions as, for instance, the free movement of labour. The economic aspects were more the concern of the firms, including international firms. Four elements were important in this respect: (1) the identification of a discussion partner from within the firm; (2) the provision of correct information on the economic situation of firms and their subsidiaries, on which trade unions could safely base their claims; (3) the equalisation of labour conditions and wages, and (4) the form of the agreement, which could take various expressions. One could, for example conceive of a certain harmonisation of national collective agreements, which might result in a harmonisation of European labour conditions, without the need for formal international contracts.

As to the content of international agreements, one could ask the question whether negotiations on legal aspects, involving principally the States, or negotiations on economic aspects, involving the firms, were of prime interest to trade unions. The upshot of a recent meeting of trade unionists in Strasbourg, which Mr Grandjeat[1] had attended, appeared to be that negotiations and decisions on legal aspects taken care of by a multiplicity of legal bodies which had been created, were not thought of as major achievements by trade unionists. The decisions by which trade union interests were really affected were those on economic matters, i.e. decisions in the realm of the multi-national firm.

Finally, the question of international collective agreements seemed to be intimately linked to the question of the limits of workers' solidarity. Had collective agreements been an expression of solidarity, i.e. an instrument of upward modification of labour conditions? A seminar on the future of industrial relations in Europe, held two years ago at the Institute, has concluded in the negative.[2] Evidence showed that economic conditions and the fragmentation of the labour markets had led to considerable wage drifts, amounting, in countries like Italy, France and Germany, to 25 to 40 per cent, jeopardising all efforts of unification. Could one expect an international collective agreement to represent, under these circumstances, more than a sort of minimum standard invalidated by widely differing actual labour conditions; and was it therefore worthwhile to aim at the conclusion of such agreements?

*Mr Houssiaux* found that employer and worker organisations in the E.E.C. had oriented themselves towards the supra-national authority, expecting a substantial transfer of power from the nation States to the community. To the impartial observer, the European organisations of workers and employers remained weak and lacked cohesion. The European employers' organisation (U.N.I.C.E.) had to reconcile a fair amount of internal opposition, making the political rapprochement of its members a very delicate process.

Judging the weakness of the decision-making structure of the European organisation (Community, trade unions, employers and, to a certain extent, European multi-national corporations), one was

---

[1] International Symposium on the Labour Law in Western European Countries, organised by the Universities of Strasbourg and Paris, Strasbourg 18–20 October 1968.
[2] See 'The Future of Industrial Relations in Europe: Approaches and Perspectives', Pub. lecture by J. D. Reynaud and Seminar Discussion in *Bulletin* No. 4 of the International Institute for Labour Studies, pp. 86–146.

entitled to infer that supra-nationality was still a myth. Only very gradually these organisations seemed to take cognisance of the fact that they might act as poles of co-ordination, and this evolution was governed by similar fundamental conditions to which the evolution of European political organisation was subjected.

Mr *Roberts* recalled that when the Rome Treaty was signed, the Common Market was one of the most fascinating ideas in the evolution of international relations, opening up visions of tremendous development of economic and social welfare. Associated with this were, of course, ideas of harmonisation of economic and welfare policies. Whatever changes might have occurred in these fields, several authors of papers had concluded with justification that the European Common Market and its pale reflection, EFTA, had in fact exercised little effect on the national patterns of industrial relations. Mr Despax had quoted a number of reasons for this state of affairs, to which one could add a number of further factors – in particular, the absence of a common labour market in Europe. Furthermore, the large companies that were the main sources of development in Europe, were either national entities or really multi-national in that they had their interests spread over a much wider area than the European regional organisation.

As Mr Blanpain had mentioned in his paper, unions and employers had responded to some degree to the creation of the Common Market and EFTA by setting up corresponding regional organisations; but they had no real authority. In other words, neither side was really prepared to develop a Common Market system of collective bargaining because neither side was under pressure to do this or saw much objective advantage in negotiating European regional agreements.

As in other areas of the world, unions in Europe had realised that there was considerable advantage in supplementing national industry-wide bargaining by company bargaining. The question still remained, however, to ask whether it was desirable to stimulate, in spite of these developments, a European pattern of collective bargaining, which appeared to be the view expressed in Mr Despax's paper. Mr Roberts himself saw little value in such an evolution as there was no virtue in uniformity itself. However, it could be argued that a European regional industrial relations system would become a powerful force in consolidating and strengthening economic integration within the European Common Market, at a time when it appeared to be weakening. The issues to be concentrated on could therefore be put into the questions: was there a possible future development of regional industrial relations systems and would such a development be desirable?

*Mr Günter* thought that before an attempt was made to answer Mr Roberts's questions, it might be useful to try to shed light on the essential reasons accounting for the low impact of regional economic integration on industrial relations. The E.E.C. was a good example for finding out about these reasons because economic integration had indeed happened within its frontiers, for which he considered the enormous increase of intra-community trade and the movements of capital and labour clear proof.

Undoubtedly, Mr Blanpain and Mr Despax were right in stressing in their papers the absence of the organisational and legal prerequisites for international collective bargaining. However, there was reason to believe that these prerequisities would evolve as soon as a real interest was perceived in the development of international collective bargaining in the E.E.C. One had, therefore, first of all to find out why this interest was missing.

In Mr Günter's opinion, the explanation for this might be twofold: (1) no major shifts in the locus of decision-making in industrial relations had occurred, and (2) economic integration had offered no new community-wide economic possibilities for bargaining. Conversely, one was tempted to generalise in saying that as soon as there was a change in the shift of the locus of decision-making, and as soon as there was a new economic potential, a challenge was given to trade unions to modify the structure of industrial relations. Using these two criteria, it appeared possible to answer the question why trade unions (the only social partner from whom an initiative could be expected) had 'gone international' in the case of multi-national corporations and why not in the case of the European Economic Community.

In the first case there was a shift in the locus of decision-making from national enterprises towards headquarters of multi-national corporations, if not for industrial relations matters (which might remain the province of subsidiaries) then in respect of investment and employment policy, equally relevant to labour. In addition, because of their real or alleged possibilities of profit-pooling, multi-national companies appeared to trade unions as a single economic unit, i.e. a unit offering new bargaining possibilities. International collective bargaining, in the form of bargaining with multi-national and European companies, was therefore the most likely possibility for the moment and the contacts with Philips, to which Mr Casserini had referred, were undoubtedly a step in this direction.

Mr Kahn-Freund had said, the first day of the symposium, that international organisations might be the midwives in the process of the development of transnational industrial relations. The E.E.C. had widely assumed that role. As members of the consultation bodies of the Common Market, the social partners had learned co-operative habits which had tended to spill over to their mutual relations outside the E.E.C. institutions, and the recent contacts between trade unions and U.N.I.C.E. were a clear case in point. Eventually, when the material basis might have been achieved through a further narrowing down of economic differentials, negotiations over work rules in Europe might emerge from such contacts.

On the other hand, action by the supra-national authorities had probably not always had beneficial effects. The E.E.C. had involved itself in quite a number of issues which the social partners alone would perhaps have dealt with differently. The E.E.C. had also been very anxious to insert itself in all negotiations between social partners at the European level, which might not always have helped trade unions and employers to develop self-reliant links.

*Mr van Dierendonck* stressed that one could no longer speak of a lack of information as a major reason for the absence of collective bargaining at the Community level. Enquiries and publications by the European Commission furnished ample information on the labour and business conditions in the E.E.C. Mr Roberts's assertion that no common labour market existed in the E.E.C. was true as a factual statement, but legally speaking there was free movement of labour although, for the moment, only Italian workers found it attractive to move in larger numbers to other E.E.C. countries.

As regards the reason why international collective bargaining had not come into existence so far in the E.E.C., Mr van Dierendonck wished to agree with the speakers who had held that there was hitherto no need for it. In two sectors, however, viz: agriculture and transport, such a need might soon be perceived as a reflection of the common policy which the Rome Treaty provided for these sectors. In particular, the common price policy in agriculture had given rise to pressures for harmonising labour conditions, both on the workers' and the employers' side. Subsequent to the adoption of the frame agreement on working hours in agriculture, trade unions had strived for the introduction of minimum agricultural wages throughout the Community.

Outside these two sectors the role of the E.E.C. in the promotion of transnational industrial relations was a rather limited one, as social policy in general was a field which the member States had wished to keep under their own authority. Another reason why governments were not too desirous to see such relations and European collective bargaining develop was the fear of inflationary dangers, a point also mentioned by Mr Blake in his report on the negotiations with the Chrysler Company, operating in the United States and Canada.

As regards the future prospects for the growth of transnational industrial relations, Mr van Dierendonck was more optimistic than other participants. His optimism was based on a recent agreement reached in the Economic and Social Committee of the E.E.C. to establish joint commissions for all the more important industries. Following the example of agriculture and transport, the new joint commissions were likely to become the places from which common European conditions of work (excluding wages) might emerge.

Economic differentials existing amongst E.E.C. countries had, most probably, less importance for the absence of common agreements on labour conditions, than Mr Günter had thought. These differences were already now becoming very small and in many cases economically insignificant.

Finally Mr van Dierendonck added that he saw no evidence for Mr Günter's assertions that the supra-national authority had regulated European labour conditions otherwise than the social partners might have independently done. Certainly, the E.E.C. had taken the initiative in the case of agriculture and transport and had made a number of proposals, but these proposals were subsequently discussed by trade unions and employers in the joint committees. The social partners could freely defend their mutual interest in these committees and arrive at a draft agreement which the committee, acting as a secretariat, had to then bring in shape, and which was ultimately endorsed by the Council of Ministers.

Commenting on the latter point, *Mr Günter* said that, in spite of the co-operation of the social partners in the joint committees, the statutory regulations on labour conditions in agriculture and transport, emanating from the E.E.C., had the likely effect of excluding these sectors from the scope of direct negotiations between trade unions and employers. Mr van Dierendonck had rightly stressed the wealth of information now available, thanks to the work of the Commission. Major information was still missing, however, on levels of productivity in the different industries and countries. One could have a long argument on the significance or insignificance of existing economic differentials within the E.E.C. However, the fact that trade unions had not engaged in common action at a European level and that employers had stressed on all occasions that productivity differentials were considerable, could be taken as an indication that economic differentials were probably still far from being negligible.

*Mr Despax* first wished to give an answer to Mr Roberts's question whether European collective bargaining should be encouraged. In his opinion, the workers' and employers' organisations – the main interested parties – had the prime role to play. The mere fact that European collective bargaining had not come into existence so far proved that the social partners had not perceived of this instrument as being within their sphere of interest.

One main lesson to be drawn from the history of the E.E.C. was that there was a need for pragmatic approaches, for which the national experience might serve as a model.

As to the legal form of European agreements, Mr Despax felt that it was not essential that a formal instrument was signed. European negotiation could take a multiplicity of forms, including contacts and discussions between social partners, participation of employers and trade unions in the elaboration of statutory regulations, etc., in short negotiations on all possible occasions.

Mr Roberts had discarded regional collective agreements because he did not appreciate their unifying effect. However, the main result of such agreements was to guarantee minimum conditions, favouring the most needy social groups. It would therefore be regrettable, in Mr Despax's opinion, if the technique of collective bargaining, which at a national level had enhanced social progress, were to be discarded for the international level.

In conclusion, Mr Despax recalled that the present difficulties for concluding European collective agreements were not only economic but also of a sociological and legal nature. Although the legal problems were certainly not the most important, they could not be lost sight of.

Continuing on the prescriptive side, *Mr Parillon* wondered whether the conscious harmonisation of national economic and social conditions could perhaps pave the way for European collective bargaining. A step forward might be reached by the extension of the harmonisation efforts by the E.E.C. Secondly, it might be useful to harmonise gradually the national legislation on collective agreements, which was one major aspect of the legal problems to which Mr Despax and Mr Kahn-Freund had referred. Thirdly, attempts could be made to obtain the same occupational coverage of national industry agreements; this coverage still differed very widely from country to country.

Fourthly, national collective agreements should consciously take into account European imperatives. Not infrequently, national agreements still tended to aggravate existing differences (which was for instance the case with the introduction of a fourth week of vacation in France). Obviously, a European orientation of national collective bargaining presupposed a European state of mind which did not yet exist and which the European organisations would be called upon to promote.

Referring to the same problems, *Mr Weil* added that three factors were contributing towards a gradual automatic harmonisation: (1) the enlargement of markets over the national borders; (2) mergers of national firms and growth of multi-national firms, entailing a certain unification of labour conditions; (3) the movement of labour, allowing millions of workers to enjoy more favourable conditions of labour than at home. When returned to their home countries, these workers would then press for similar labour conditions.

Somewhat in contrast to Mr Parillon's opinion, Mr Weil felt that already now national collective bargaining took account of labour conditions prevailing in other E.E.C. countries. In this way, a pre-stage to international collective bargaining had virtually been reached, although an impressive number of hurdles in the field of labour law and industrial relations practices had still to be taken, and the diversity of languages in Europe was a further handicap to harmonisation.

Listening to the last speakers, *Mr Kahn-Freund* suggested that Mr Despax was probably right in stressing that interest should not be restricted to formal international collective bargaining but should extend to all forms of suitable co-operation. If one considered, for instance, co-operation of the social partners in the various E.E.C. Committees, then, as Mr van Dierendonck had intimated, the potentialities of regional industrial relations development in Europe appeared to be greater. On the other hand, certain doubts might be allowed as regards the influence of supra-national policies on industrial relations, if one took the case of the E.C.S.C.; in spite of the pronounced common policy to which the E.C.S.C. was committed over quite some time, Community-wide collective bargaining had not been forthcoming in the coal and steel industry.

Speaking as a lawyer, Mr Kahn-Freund wished to underline that if the members of a federation enacted the same law, then there was no longer a need for federal legislation. Maybe something of that nature was gradually appearing in the area of labour conditions in the European Community.

Commenting upon the lessons furnished by the earlier attempts to introduce international collective bargaining for the E.E.C. countries, *Mr Schregle* recalled that the concept of European collective agreement was in the first instance discovered by lawyers in the early 1950s as a possible instrument of harmonisation. As the fate of the proposed European Miners' Charter had shown, attempts to conclude such agreements had failed, chiefly because trade unions had tried to incorporate in them the best prevailing labour conditions of all countries in the Common Market. Collective bargaining was, by its very nature, however, a package deal. Employers might accept as European standards certain favourable labour conditions prevailing in some countries if trade unions were prepared to drop claims about other labour conditions. Naturally, it was almost inconceivable that trade unions could forego something at the European level that they already had at home. These problems of upward harmonisation furnished also an explanation to Mr Kahn-Freund's statement on the missing common agreements for the coal and steel industry.

Turning to conceptual issues, Mr Schregle said that the conclusion of European instruments (of the kind mentioned by Mr van Dierendonck for agriculture and transport) was completely different from traditional collective bargaining between social partners in a given country. As regards European instruments, the supra-national authority could undoubtedly act as a midwife, as Mr Kahn-Freund had suggested. As a matter of fact, the I.L.O. had been assuming this role all the time in Industrial Committees or at the International Labour Conference. In these meetings, the final text was often the result of some sort of negotiation between the employers' and workers' groups. An example of this practice, in the I.L.O. context, was the recent adoption of a new recommendation on grievance procedures. A few representatives of the employers' and the workers' groups had formed a small working party to negotiate a draft text which was later accepted also by the government delegates without any discussion. However, referring to these procedures as collective bargaining would mean stretching the term very considerably.

*Mr Blanpain* thought that despite the abortive attempts of collective bargaining within the E.E.C. framework, for which Mr Schregle had given one of the most valid reasons, it had to be recalled that the existence of the European Common Market had changed industrial relations in many ways. True, this had happened by statutory regulations emanating from the supra-national authority, but the element of collaboration of social partners was important. This collaboration reflected the fact that in Europe industrial relations involved not merely a confrontation of social partners but that trade union and employer action was also directed against the public authorities.

Discussing the issue of international collective bargaining, one had to remember that the instrument of collective bargaining was of less importance in Europe than, for instance, in the United States; it covered, in the main, wage provisions. Maybe under the influence of the writing of American scholars and the American industrial relations philosophy, the unifying effect of collective agreements in Europe was frequently over-rated. Bargaining existed in Europe at different complementary levels. Inter-industrial national agreements were complemented by industry-wide, plant-level, and even informal agreements with individual workers. National and industry-wide agreements did not usually have the function of setting, by means of central decisions, the actual general standards for labour conditions, but were nevertheless, comparable in their effect to the American statutory minimum wage.

Bearing this situation in mind, Mr Tacke of the German D.G.B., had stressed in his report to the April 1969 Congress of E.E.C. Trade Unions affiliated to I.C.F.T.U. in the Hague that European collective agreements would not take the place of national industry or plant agreements but would first of all set European minimum standards. Secondly, they would include provisions for problems which could only be solved at a European level, for instance, rationalisation agreements with multi-national corporations.

As to the steps to be taken to promote European collective agreements, Mr Tacke had advocated that at a first stage comparative studies had to be favoured with a view to harmonising labour conditions; at a second stage frame agreements, like the agreements for agricultural workers, would be envisaged and only at a much later stage could there be a conclusion of full-fledged collective agreements. Mr Tacke had also emphasised that European negotiations about wages and salaries were premature.

*Mr Lee* wished to agree with those speakers who had stressed that the main locus of decision-making in collective bargaining was situated in the national environment. For this reason, he believed that the development of regional collective bargaining was a doubtful matter for the next ten or twenty years. In the local subsidiaries of a company of Mr Lee's experience, each national union laid emphasis on particular types of claims which were often incompatible with the claims of unions in other countries.

It should also be considered that employers had, anyway, not much interest in regional collective bargaining, which could run contrary to prime employer concerns, such as the increase of productivity level.

To the extent that, according to Mr van Dierendonck's and Mr Weil's suggestions, harmonisation of labour conditions was keeping pace with economic integration, trade unions likewise might not find much incentive to press for formal international bargaining; but if moves for such bargaining were coming at all they had to come from the trade unions, as Mr Günter had rightly emphasised.

*Mr Maier* said that there was a fundamental difference between collective bargaining in the usual sense of the word, which yielded binding work rules, and informal arrangements, such as the European agreements on hours of work in agriculture. The only obligation for the contracting parties stemming from the agricultural agreement was the obligation to recommend its content to the national member federation which remained completely free in their decisions.

As regards the role of a midwife, which some speakers had attributed to the E.E.C., Mr Maier thought that in the interest of free bargaining neither unions nor employers desired too great an involvement with the E.E.C. He would therefore support what had been said on this issue by Messrs Despax and Günter.

Referring to Mr Blanpain's statement, Mr Maier wished to add that the European trade union secretariats had been established not so much to pursue negotiations with the weak top organisation of the European employers, but to act as a counterpart to the E.E.C. Secretariat. For the moment the only other adequate counterpart with which trade unions could effectively negotiate at the European and international level were multi-national corporations.

*Mr Kahn-Freund* wondered whether, despite the terminological problems referred to by several speakers, it was not useful for the present discussions to stick to a fairly wide and flexible concept of collective bargaining. Progress in the transnationalisation of industrial relations appeared to be possible precisely through informal instruments. National industrial relations experience seemed to confirm this view. In some of the Scandanavian countries, Sweden in particular, the adoption of central and inter-industry model agreements which implied no formal legal obligations was one of the most important aspects of collective bargaining.

Expanding on this point, *Mr Odhner* explained that probably one essential reason for a general adoption, at the local level, of the Swedish model agreements was that they were freely negotiated between the central trade union and the central employers, organisation. This was in line with the guiding principle in Sweden of negotiation without government intervention. As a result, both sides felt responsible for the actual application of the agreements. Moreover, a number of them had afterwards been taken over by State legislation.

*Possible Implications of East–West Industrial Co-operation*

*Mr Conlon* recommended that East–West economic relations should be considered in their broadest perspective. For many multi-national corporations, socialist countries were now the fastest growing market area in the world, with average annual growth rates of 10 to 12 per cent. A very interesting coincidence in timing was the present trend in Eastern Europe away, from overall centralised national management.

*Mr Scott* had feared, in his paper, that the increase of East–West co-operation had perhaps been to the disadvantage of North–South co-operation. Bearing this possibility in mind, *Mr Conlon* submitted that East–West co-operation, aimed at solving the North–South problems, was probably one of the few solutions open to the present world, and this involved of course the multi-national corporation, the nation State and the trade union.

Expanding on his paper, *Mr Mošna* made some observations on the present situation of economic organisation and co-operation in the Eastern European countries. For the moment there existed no mutual economic relations amongst COMECON countries, based on 'market relations', i.e. there existed nothing similar to a common labour market or a common capital market. Free movement of labour and capital were a basic prerequisite, however, for the creation of a multi-national economic organisation. On the other hand, there existed in most Eastern European countries, far-reaching tendencies and plans connected with economic reforms which were apt to create favourable conditions for the emergence of international commodity, capital and labour markets, not only for co-operation within the COMECON, but also between East and West.

As Mr Conlon had mentioned, most East European countries were in a period of transition from old, strictly centralised and bureaucratic systems of management, to a model of management according to which enterprises became real business units with freedom of action, influenced from above only indirectly, for instance, through taxation. This shift to a completely new economic and social position of enterprises was already very noticeable in Czechoslovakia, to a lesser extent also in Hungary and in Poland. In Czechoslovakia, a Bill was just now being discussed conferring on enterprises the possibility to enter into direct economic and commercial contacts with foreign partners all over the world. Under the old economic system, all basic arrangements in the field of foreign trade and international economic operations had been the monopoly of the State.

The new role of the enterprise in the Czechoslovak example implied also a change in the role of trade unions, which were starting to become independent in their relationships with the State, and were gradually assuming the representation of interest of employees and thus substantially changing the present pattern of industrial relations.

Another favourable trend for more intensified East–West co-operation was the need of East European countries to modernise equipment in the course of the projected structural changes in industry. Equipment incorporating modern technology was frequently found on the Western markets. In addition, some of the East European countries, like Czechoslovakia or Hungary, considered the development of East–West trade as a factor enhancing domestic co-operation which might assist, in turn, in achieving market equilibrium. On the other other side, competitive markets in the West might force some Western countries, including the U.S., to offer goods and capital increasingly to Eastern countries. In this way, the stage was gradually being set for the possibility of East–West industrial co-operation which would also include implications for industrial relations.

*Mr Scott* stressed that the subject under review was still a very speculative one, where the dearth of factual information did not permit firm conclusions to be reached. Recalling briefly some points made in his paper, Mr Scott referred to the growing interest taken by students of economic systems in the growth, over the last two or three years, of trade flows in research-intensive products between subsidiaries of multi-national corporations and Eastern European countries where reforms of economic planning and enterprise management were taking place. These flows were very dynamic and due to the accelerated rate of technical progress in all industrial economies.

As far as Western countries were concerned, research-oriented exports were concentrated in multi-national corporations, as only the biggest companies could readily finance the expenses incurred in connection with investment in research facilities or research manpower, and their multi-national character provided a marketing network big enough to amortise fairly quickly these expenditures. In short, the joint effects of accelerated technical progress, concentration in industrial organisation and the drive to achieve economies of scale (productive, commercial and financial) accounted for the boom in the growth of multi-national corporations and their restless search for expanding markets.

As far as Eastern European countries were concerned, two main points explaining their new attractiveness as a market for sophisticated products should be noted: first, the recognition that beyond a certain degree of development of industrial complexity, the traditional highly centralised administrative forms of economic management tended to yield diminishing returns to investment in physical and human capital. The second was that accelerated technical progress – in conjunction with economic reforms which gave enterprises greater scope for initiative and more incentives to rationalise and innovate – was now believed to be essential for attaining satisfactory growth rates of national income. In short, economic policy was now opting for intensive rather than extensive paths of development. This shift in emphasis had important implications for the future of East–West trade, in which multi-national corporations would probably play a major role.

Decentralisation of decision-making gave the labour force a greater direct participation in the economic results of their employment. Given existing levels of applied technology in East and West, technical progress was in the former likely to be fostered – in the next few years, at least – through flows principally from West to East. There was thus an incentive to develop East–West trade beyond its present abnormally low level and asymmetrical composition because both the innovating performance and the cost-consciousness of the Eastern countries was increased, as Mr Mošna had pointed out. Industrial co-operation, by means of enterprise-to-enterprise agreements between East and West, was proving to be a very convenient channel for the expansion of such trade because it offered marketing and payments advantages within the framework of long-term (5–8 years) contracts. Moreover, industrial co-operation seemed to be a means of creating, in East–West dealings, forms of industrial ties resembling those which had grown up *within* each group of countries, in response to the imperatives of modern technology and marketing.

The link between these developments and the multi-national corporation was particularly important an account of the highly professional management, advanced market techniques and highly developed information techniques, as well as the considerable financial resources which could be regarded as important sources of the growth of these companies. Consequently, there was a willingness amongst the Eastern European countries to enter into industrial co-operation arrangements with the suppliers of research-intensive manufactures in the West. However, the question arose whether there was a corresponding interest amongst multi-national enterprises to engage in operations in Eastern Europe. In his paper, Mr. Scott had tried to sketch an answer to this question with reference to the current 'technological gap theory' of trade which held that leading trading countries were obliged, in order to maintain their market shares, continuously to pursue commercial innovations to keep an edge on imitators with lower labour costs. Multi-national corporations tried to reduce this threat by acquiring direct control over enterprises in their main markets. The anxiety about losses of control over economic decision-making, which these direct investments had given to governments and unions in Western Europe, was of course also present in Eastern Europe, although the impossibility of acquiring direct investment rights in these countries meant that it took a different form.

In this connection, the experience of industrial co-operation between Western enterprises and Yugoslav enterprises was particularly interesting. Yugoslavia had been the most innovating of all the Eastern European countries in terms of the developments under review. In earlier years, Western companies were not allowed to acquire ownership over assets in Yugoslavia; but since 1967 new legislation had given Western enterprises and multi-national corporations the right directly to invest in joint enterprises in Yugoslavia to a limit of 49 per cent of fixed assets, the Yugoslav enterprise retaining 51 per cent. There was reason to believe that the Yugoslav Government would revise the present regulations in order to attract more foreign direct investment within the framework of industrial co-operation, in spite of the possible disruptive implications for national wage and productivity differentials, and over-all employment policy.

Commenting on Mr Conlon's observation, Mr Scott felt that the southern hemisphere would have great difficulty in deriving any benefit from the present closed circuit of research-intensive exchange of products in the northern hemisphere unless they were granted much better access – and hence incentives – for their exports of technologically simpler manufactures. At present, for example, the O.E.C.D. countries (Western Europe, North America and Japan) satisfied all but 2 per cent of their requirements of machinery and equipment from their own intra-trade. In addition, probably because of their fiscal and balance-of-payments policies, only a few developing countries were able to attract the direct investments of multi-national corporations on an important scale. There was therefore a risk that intensified East–West exchange might enlarge the closed circuit within the northern hemisphere. On the other hand, joint East–West ventures in developing countries – of which there was already a number of cases – might open up new possibilities for a wider international division of labour.

To go beyond this rather vague conclusion, careful study of the points of tangency between economic nationalism and the means of accommodating multi-national companies was required. As this was still relatively unexplored research terrain, Mr Scott thought that he could not go beyond the speculative approach to the question of the possible impact of East–West industrial co-operation on industrial relations contained in his paper.

*Mr Levinson* felt that the integration of investment between East and West raised ideologically very interesting questions. In the co-production arrangements, Eastern countries, still ideologically committed to the extermination of capitalism, accepted a capitalist minority participation in investment. On the other hand, first stages of Eastern investment in the West clashed with Western ideology, especially the emphasised menace of Marxism to private property. The intensification of East–West industrial co-operation created for the trade unions a new dimension. Trade unions were confronted with a worldwide institutional split which had to be overcome but which was a greater obstacle to co-operation than in the case of management. Plant-level management contacts between East and West had undoubtedly been eased by the increasing divorce in the West of management from ownership, leaving management a free hand in its dealings as long as it was successful.

*Mr Perlmutter* pointed out that there was already a large spate of East–West relationships which were trans-ideological in character, such as relations in the fields of art, music, sport, medical science or transport. Although we were living in politically sensitive times, there was no other way for a multi-national firm to continue growing without developing a zone which was trans-ideological in character and worldwide in its views, involving resources and men in East and West. Trade could not be considered as a form of East–West exchange to bring about increased economic efficiency in Eastern countries; efficiency had to be promoted in a perpetual way through the slow development of the few demonstration projects of co-operation that Mr Scott had referred to.

The mere fact that a variety of practical arrangements existed already between Eastern and Western enterprises (the legal form of which had still to be determined, but was of second priority) proved that functional requirements were met. To bring about permanent links for collaboration, new kinds of trans-ideological multi-national firms were needed. The resulting expansion of the trans-ideological zone of East–West relations might eventually reduce a good deal of the political tension.

Like Mr Scott, Mr Perlmutter felt unable to fit international collective bargaining precisely into this picture. One could, however, wonder what might happen if, as it appeared, management did understand the logic of the construction of the project while, to their own disadvantage, some rather large ideological gaps seemed to continue to exist between the labour unions.

## IMPLICATIONS FOR THE FUTURE OF INDUSTRIAL RELATIONS

This part of the discussion centred around the problems of the pre-requisite conditions necessary for the development of transnational industrial relations and, eventually, formal international collective bargaining with the multi-national corporation. How were interests perceived in this process? Who would support and who oppose the development of transnational forms of industrial relations? What adjustments were required on the part of trade unions and of employers as well as in collective bargaining and related processes?

*Adjustments of Trade Unions*

Mr *Casserini* believed that the rise of big corporations had challenged traditional industry-wide or district bargaining. A first trade union reaction was the move in Europe towards more plant bargaining, which would set the stage for dynamic transnational bargaining with multi-national companies. One could not expect, however, that formal agreements with such companies could be obtained immediately. A step in the right direction was discussions and informal negotiations between unions and management over the most pressing issues. Of main concern to unions were the employment implications of shifts by multi-national corporations of production capacities from one country to another. Provisions were required for obligatory negotiations with the unions in case of such production and employment transfers. Asked by Mr Roberts whether such clauses, which might prevent production transfers to low-wage countries, would maximise the welfare of organised labour all over the world or only protect already privileged workers, Mr Casserini replied that what trade unions wanted, above all, was the right of discussion. No doctrinaire trade union policy could be fixed beforehand on these issues but policies would have to be gradually conceived bearing all relevant factors in mind. It added to the complexity of the problems that wage differentials were only one element of consideration for management in planning investments. Other, more important elements were, e.g., tax differentials, transport cost and market positions. As a consequence, production and employment policies of multi-national corporations were extremely unpredictable. In their constant attempt to maximise returns, it was not rare to see companies shifting capacities back to the old location. All these factors meant that trade unions had a difficult task in reconciling the issues of solidarity and protection of jobs in negotiations with multi-national corporations.

Mr *Despax* said the well-known fact that, in the national context, decentralised enterprises found it profitable to maintain a disparity of labour conditions, was a relevant parallel to the refusal of multi-national corporations to bargain internationally. The methods by which trade unions had been able to eliminate local differentials might provide certain lessons for developing a valid, international strategy.

Mr Casserini had referred in his paper to some elements of such strategy which, initially, might include, at first sight, some seemingly minor matters. For example, the attempt of the unions to align the dates of negotiation for all subsidiaries of a company might appear as minor but could certainly be a very favourable device for common bargaining. Secondly, one could try to equalise labour conditions for the small group of employees who frequently had to switch from one subsidiary of a multi-national company to another, an idea which had also been taken up at trade union meetings of the St Gobain group. Furthermore, trade unions might strive to obtain guarantees from management against compensatory overtime work in subsidiaries not affected by strikes.

In *Mr Levinson*'s opinion, trade unions could not passively adjust to the new situation created by the multi-national corporation, but had to develop an efficient strategy, focusing on the points of the greatest vulnerability of multi-national corporations in order to become their valid bargaining partner. The new dimension of internationalisation of companies had increased the power differential to the detriment of unions, bearing in mind Mr Despax's reference to the flexibility of multi-national corporations in compensating the effectiveness of trade union action by shifting production to plants not on strike. Trade union response to the new situation would probably have to be pragmatic as the institutional set-up existing in the trade union movement excluded theoretical or idealistic approaches; generally speaking, it would be conditioned by the recognition that more and more economic consequences were going to be determined by the national and international corporate entity while problems of the national economy would lose importance.

One adjustment which unions increasingly had to undergo was, in Mr Levinson's opinion, the shift of bargaining power from national organisations to lower levels of the union structure, in particular, to the company level. In Europe, this implied a major change in bargaining pattern which, traditionally influenced by the close link between unions and the political socialist movement, remained basically regional. District-wide (regional) agreements on an industry basis produced minimum standards determined largely by the pay capacity of the marginal firms. This state of affairs suited multi-national corporations as they were able to create an enterprise consciousness by granting labour conditions well above the average.

Even in the United States, where plant-level bargaining existed to a much greater extent than in Europe, it was necessary to arrive at enterprise or company-wide bargaining in order to confront management at its prime decision-making level. As management was fighting desperately to stop the unions' move towards corporate bargaining, this issue was likely to overshadow the industrial relations scene in the next years ahead.

As trade union reaction was pragmatic, there was already much more going on in terms of adjustments to the multi-national corporation than was generally appreciated. A regular occurrence was, for instance, that the International Chemical Workers' Federation gave the unions in subsidiaries of multi-national corporations information on actual labour conditions at company headquarters, to be used in negotiations as an orientation on wages and working conditions already set by the employer. Another example was the intervention of the International Federation at the parent headquarters in favour of bargaining problems which may have arisen at a distant subsidiary. This type of action might be related, in a way, to the ethnocentric phase of transnational industrial relations according to Mr Perlmutter's definition.

A second phase, loosely corresponding to Mr Perlmutter's polycentric situation, was direct assistance by the International Federation to the local union in form of monetary support, training of people, provision of specialists to help in case of important disputes and other kinds of involvements. It also included studies of the possibilities of the companies to locate end profits in 'tax havens' allowing subsidiaries to produce evidence to unions that no profits had been made.

Another aspect of the multi-national corporation of importance to bargaining was that it would borrow money anywhere in the world at the lowest rate and safeguard itself against currency risks. This possibility put in question, for instance, the common character of the European Common Market.

Therefore, Mr Levinson stressed, trade unions could no longer be saddled with considerations of the national economy, whether developed or developing. In particular, they could no longer accept the argument that wage increases buttressed inflation. An audible breakthrough had been achieved with the recent U.S.–Canadian automobile workers' agreement with Chrysler. Generally speaking, productivity agreements had become less important as technology was now quite similar, even in developing countries. As regards developing countries in particular, the argument that wage increases in line with plant-level productivity endangered their competitiveness, had not much significance since evidence proved that their economies grew by domestic developments rather than by exports. Concomitant development of domestic consumption and of local markets, even if limited, provided a basis for investment that could support real development. This was the reason why multi-national companies should be asked to pay higher wages more consistent with their financial capacities. One should not merely accept the argument that these wages (perhaps higher than in other sectors) would produce inflation, dislocation and discourage investment.

The next phase into which the International Chemical Workers' Federation was pushing included, first, co-ordination, and, second, integration of bargaining with multi-national corporations. By co-ordination, Mr Levinson understood an aligning of bargaining of a number of unions in the same corporation regarding the time of negotiations. The most far-reaching present attempt in this direction was being made in connection with St Gobain. The decision had been endorsed that no union would settle without the agreement of a permanent action committee. Furthermore, in case of a strike in any one country the other unions, by the intermediary of the International Federation would, if necessary, provide financial support. Thirdly, serious efforts would be made to impede shifts of production from one St Gobain plant on strike to a company plant in another country. Finally, it had been decided to stop all overtime in every St Gobain plant around the world in support of any plant on strike.

This was an innovation more efficient than to count on sympathy strikes in the different subsidiaries of the companies for which psychological, and also (foremost in Europe) legal, handicaps existed. On the other hand, no restrictive clauses existed in collective agreements as regards overtime.

Applying the new strategies, the unions in the United States subsidiaries of St Gobain had not accepted that the absence of company profits in America in 1968 was a reason for refusing a 9 per cent wage claim. As, according to management, total earnings of the corporation had risen by 35 per cent in 1968, and were expected to go up 200 per cent by 1971, the American unions held that the company was in a position to grant a total wage increase of 28 per cent for the period 1969-71. This was the first example of worldwide argumentation and represented a decisive step in the direction of integrated bargaining and Mr Perlmutter's geocentric situation.

Another important question was whether the traditionally retro-active bargaining pattern of the unions included enough dynamic elements to meet with projective dynamic top management. To reverse the situation, the right of participation of trade unions in the decision-making process of management (beyond the consultative relationships through plant committees as in France, Germany and Italy) was a clear necessity. As long as the worker at his place of work was affected, unions now claimed active participation in decision-making spheres which, in the past, had been the hallowed prerogative of management.

Mr Levinson stressed that essentially the challenge to the union was to find pragmatic ways and means to force the multi-national corporation into new relationships and interaction corresponding to the complex new economic realities. To arrive at this, trade union power had to be exerted as multi-national corporations did not freely accept trade unions as collaborators or social partners, which were conno-tations from the past.

In considering the adjustments of trade unions, *Mr Maier* suggested a careful review of the list of negotiable subjects as regards their impor-tance and timeliness, a point which Mr Grandjeat had earlier touched upon. Mr Levinson had set out the policy of his International mainly in terms of wage problems. Other important subjects, perhaps easier to cope with at the moment, were conditions of work such as holidays and hours of work on which the International Metal-workers Federation was mainly concentrating.

As regards the structural changes implied in the adjustment process, a certain division of labour among the different organisational levels was indispensable. Trade union confederations, like the European Trade Union Secretariat, could not, themselves, engage in international collective bargaining; this was rather the province of the industrial trade union federation. What confederations could provide, however, was the political climate conducive to negotiations by exerting pressure on governments and multi-national firms to ensure the acceptance of such fundamental principles as freedom of association, free collective bargaining and the right to strike.

*Mr Blake* suggested that, in line with Mr Perlmutter's distinctions on the types of international management, one might also speak about three types of international collective bargaining situations. The first type was bargaining with ethnocentric corporations. This could be called an ethnocentric bargaining situation and would require the major effort to be made by the union in the country where the multinational corporation had its headquarters. The unions around the world had to co-operate actively with the (hopefully) strong union located in the headquarters' country. An example of this approach was the recent Chrysler–United Automobile Workers agreement, the subject of his paper. In this case, Mr Blake said, it had been necessary for the Canadian branch of the United Automobile Workers' Union to work through the U.S. branch so that the main strength of the multi-national corporation was met by the stronger union at headquarters.

In the polycentric bargaining situation, negotiations were done with a corporation which was essentially a conglomeration of national, quite independent, subsidiaries. The appropriate type of bargaining which might exist at this level was the traditional form of national bargaining between the subsidiary and the domestic union.

Finally, a geocentric bargaining situation could develop where the corporation was worldwide in its approaches, without particular national ties or ideologies, a rare case in present circumstances. Here, the unions could act along similar lines, and international collective bargaining in the full sense of the word could develop. Certainly, unions had a long way to go to arrive at such a true international status propitious for geocentric negotiations.

*Mr Odhner* said Mr Casserini's and Mr Levinson's statements had made it abundantly clear that trade unions had to develop a countervailing power against the multi-national company at its top level. Corresponding adjustments of trade unions were only slowly coming forward, however, because trade unions were democratic organisations. Leadership had to take into account the most pressing interests of members and had, therefore, formidable problems of getting long-term strategies endorsed. The importance of workers' job security had been insufficiently stressed by the Symposium; the insecurity of workers forced unions to apply restrictive practices, thus enlarging the area of conflict with the corporations. The decision-making structure working up from below, put trade unions, *Mr Kahn-Freund* added, in quite a different position from the multi-national companies where managerial decisions came directly from the top.

*Adjustments of Multi-national Corporations*

As a background to these problems, *Mr Biart* gave an account of the national economic and social constraints which forced a substantial decentralisation of decision-making upon his company (which had subsidiaries in nine European countries and in Brazil and Algeria). These constraints were the framework for any adjustment processes towards transnational forms of industrial relations.

On the economic side, in spite of the disappearance of certain customs barriers in Europe, a multiplicity of legal, financial, fiscal and technical obstacles existed, which hindered a uniform development of the company. Regarding envisaged European mergers, the company had to fight protectionist reflexes, a manifest symptom of which was the anti-trust legislation in the E.E.C. countries.

On the social side, despite the economic constraints, the company had been able to develop a general frame policy for employment and industrial relations of the kind Mr Schregle had recommended. It was based on the following principles: (1) personnel was only recruited if life-time employment was guaranteed; (2) negotiations with trade unions were the basis of labour/management relations; (3) local management had to pay attention to the cultural differences amongst countries; (4) as far as possible, regarding essential needs, the workers had to be assured the same level of living irrespective of country of operations. Obviously, the management of subsidiaries had to reconcile these principles with the exigencies of the national environment determined for and by local enterprises of the chemical industry. As the subsidiaries of the company Mr Biart came from normally employed between 100 to 4,000 persons, and amounted to a maximum of 10,000 persons in certain countries (while national chemical plants had sometimes over 100,000 employees), they could not make a new pattern for industrial relations but had to adhere to the existing national legal and conventional standards.

The picture in the European countries was very varied. In Belgium, for instance, there existed a number of provisions at the national, the inter-industrial and the sectoral level, both for wage-earners and salaried employees. The majority of work conditions were determined, however, by enterprise agreements. A further factor was the trade union diversity with which local management had to cope. In France, the company was faced with a national collective agreement for all chemical workers, which also contained some special provisions for the different categories of workers. Additionally, certain labour conditions could be negotiated at an enterprise level. According to French law, domestic incorporated enterprises had to establish a central enterprise council of workers composed of representatives of the 'comités d'entreprise' of the different plants. Although not covered by these provisions, the company in which Mr Biart worked had offered to establish such a central committee. To give a further example, in Portugal and in Greece, different agreements had to be concluded with the various occupational groupings of workers represented at the plant.

Like St Gobain, Solvay had been the object of inter-plant level meetings of trade unionists. Negotiations for the whole multi-national company were extremely difficult, however, because trade unions were unable, as Mr Blanpain and Mr Schregle had said, to sacrifice national achievements in favour of acceptable uniform international standards.

As regards the transfer of profits to headquarters, mentioned by Mr Levinson and others, it had to be recalled that these funds were not simply available for distribution to labour as they had to serve mainly two important functions: (1) the payment of dividends to share-holders, and (2) the financing of centralised research, benefiting all national subsidiaries. Furthermore, transfers of profits were checked by different national legal provisions, such as the French law on profit-sharing.

In *Mr Casserini*'s mind, the majority of multi-national companies had still to undergo drastic adjustments of management practices before the ideal picture which Mr Schregle had painted became true, namely companies with established general personnel principles, communications throughout the company and consultations with trade unions. Unions welcomed worldwide principles of management policy of which Mr Lee and Mr Biart had given examples, but they wished to co-operate in their establishment. Such co-operation would avoid the disrupting separation between an independently established consultation machinery inside a company and wage negotiations to which trade unions obviously had to be admitted. A further step in the direction of transnational industrial relations could be seen in the establishment of a central works council[1] with multi-national corporations, corresponding to the structure of management.

*Mr Lee* thought that the existing adjustments of multi-national companies to social realities were responsible for a lot of progress in labour–management relations, without the need for the instrument of international collective bargaining. Some oil companies, for instance, had introduced retirement benefits for all employees, a company staff

[1] Where trade unionists from individual plants are represented.

policy and quite a number of other things that Mr Levinson and Mr Casserini had urgently claimed.

It was therefore relevant to ask whether trade unions and multi-national companies could get anything out of international collective bargaining in the circumstances which they had to operate. In many countries, where oil companies operated, for example, especially in the Middle East, there were not even any trade unions, let alone collective agreements. Governments in some Middle East and Latin American countries had reserved attitudes against unions. Although the multi-national oil company believed in good relations with trade unions it had to respect the national unions and policies of the countries in which its subsidiaries were located.

It was, undoubtedly, hypothetic to try to establish worldwide parity in labour conditions if one remembered that the prime need of workers in large parts of the world was employment. Consequently, worldwide strikes and boycotts, the envisaged weapons of trade unions to promote super transnational industrial relations, were to be qualified as utopic. However, there were a number of goals multi-national companies could already now strive towards in order to increase productivity and the living conditions throughout the world, as suggested by Mr Biart's statement. As an industrial relations practitioner, Mr Lee thought especially of the following two goals: (1) plant bargaining in the form of long-term agreements, and (2) continuing change of management attitudes throughout the world in order to assure real participation of people as modern social science suggested. This was part of the attitudinal change necessary for all parties concerned.

Change of attitudes included not only the adoption of personnel management guides in multi-national corporations; it also reflected upon the important role employers' associations had to play in raising standards of management, in particular in developing countries, as Mr Roberts had stressed in his paper. The institute of which Mr Lee was President as well as thirty other professional associations united in the European Association of Personnel Management had to contribute vitally towards the moulding of a better future in industrial relations.

In the same vein, *Mr Roberts* added that the multi-national corporation had also played a major part in stimulating the growth of the modern business school. From this, and from the training Mr Lee had referred to, the interesting question arose whether or not a uniform type of manager was being formed, spreading out into industry generally.

Turning to the monolithic power structure which Mr Casserini, Mr Levinson and others seemed to confer on the multi-national corporation, Mr Roberts cautioned against too general a view. The high degree of independence in terms of location of activities and production transfers existed only in the case of the large manufacturing type of multi-national corporations, partly checked, however, by such factors as transportation, marketability of products and the emergence of trade barriers. Multi-national companies with fixed location, such as oil companies, had a much smaller range of manœuvre.

Following Mr Roberts's argument, *Mr Conlon* wished to quote a statement by Professor Erich Jans (MIT, formerly O.E.C.D.) saying that modern management of multi-national firms was the international development of the national trend towards gradually vanishing dictation by top management. In Professor Jans's opinion, the root of this development was the increasing recognition that the maximum creative response of corporations to environmental conditions was elicited in a non-authoritarian form of organisation based on decentralised initiative and centralised synthesis. This conclusion had also been brought out by studies undertaken by the management consultant firm MacKinsey.

The stage had been reached where it became evident that while the corporations created environmental conditions, they also reacted to environmental conditions (as Mr Perlmutter had noted in his paper) in a set of internal driving and restraining forces to which their centres were exposed. This corrected substantially the impression gained by a lot of oversimplifying literature on central headquarters, ruling, dictating and controlling without any interaction, with repercussions on the adjustments expected from multi-national firms.

*Mr O'Leary* pointed out that even good employers in terms of industrial relations, of which Mr Biart and Mr Lee had given examples, were bound to be reluctant partners in international collective bargaining. While the discussion had shown the desire of trade unions and of academics to have international bargaining, one had to ask the question: what possible advantage or incentive was there for employers to have it?

International collective bargaining meant trade union interference in headquarters' decisions of multi-national companies on such economic issues as location of plant, its design and equipment (including labour-saving devices) production expansion or curtailment. Such interference made negative effects inevitable on management adjustments to market changes and to varying economic situations which, to be efficient, had to be made with maximum possible discretion. However, if international collective bargaining was, despite these factors, evolving, multinational companies would certainly try to adjust to it in a way to avoid excessive disruptions. Mr O'Leary concluded that, as a matter of precaution, management should participate in discussions of the present type to make its voice heard, especially if something new was to be designed affecting its interests.

*Some Conclusions on the Adjustment Problems*

*Mr Perlmutter* was certain that the power for the moment lay in the hands of the organised worldwide corporation, which, although it might have some difficulties with the managing directors of its subsidiaries, had power over the whole entity of the firm. People who were in the international trade union movement, like Mr Maier and Mr Levinson, knew that essentially their position was not a powerful one. This insecure position of the international trade union movement seemed to require a strategy of militancy. In this vein, Mr Levinson had made a strong case for getting the multi-national company to know that unions could have parity of power, realising, as Mr O'Leary's statement confirmed, that one could not expect the multi-national company to give some of its influence freely away to trade unions.

It followed that one had to hope for some kind of legitimation process by virtue of which companies and unions could talk together without creating the kind of defensiveness in respect to the multinational union leaders and aggressiveness in respect to multi-national management. Such legitimation of the multi-national company might flow out of its distinctive competence of providing products at competitive prices on a worldwide scale, which at least justified its existence in the eyes of the consumers. Looking at multi-national corporations from this angle meant that fighting it on every front by pressing, for instance, for wage increases, even if this resulted in the loss of worldwide markets for a country or a plant, had to be qualified as a dysfunctional policy.

On the other hand, one had to move to the stage of studying under what conditions would members of a worldwide firm consider the existence of a world-wide trade union indispensable. The dialogue on these issues involved, foremost, firms and unions, while not much place was left for the nation State as the stakes were international in character. Mr Perlmutter was not sure whether one could bypass the militant phase in moving to post-militant relations between multi-national firms and unions, but he at least believed that there was a stage beyond the kind of dialogue which Mr O'Leary and Mr Levinson had held.

*Mr Levinson* described the concepts put forward by Mr O'Leary and Mr Perlmutter as a suitable framework for future discussion. Mr Perlmutter was perfectly right in stressing that multi-national management had to be convinced of the advantage of discussions with international unions. To make this point evident, unions had now to develop the type of organisational power structure required. Top priority had to be given to establishing a bargaining pattern at the level of the company, embracing all relationships with its various plants in a given geographical area. Unless this adjustment was made, it was extremely difficult to arrive at any formal negotiations with companies.

*Mr Maier* added that in view of the present attitude of management he wished to differ from Mr Cox's view that symbiosis in form of free co-operation between multi-national companies and unions was the relationship most likely to lead to transnational industrial relations. Relations were still determined by the phase of strong opposition by multi-national companies, and transnational bargaining was only to emerge, as it had been made abundantly clear by numerous speakers, as a result of the trade unions' own organisational power.

*Mr Odhner* wished to agree with Mr O'Leary that management was hostile to the concept of worldwide bargaining because it feared that unions would introduce some kinds of restrictive practices which might impede the company's technical and economic development. But unions were not using such practices to condemn firms to in-efficiency; they intended, with these measures, to enhance workers' job security. Except for having been mentioned in the beginning by Mr Cox, this point had not received sufficient attention in the present discussion. Looking at the Swedish experience, it was probably safe to say that job security depended, first of all, on a public policy aiming at full employment, and secondly, an extensive labour market policy including retraining of redundant workers. Such a public policy of job security promotion would efface the need for restrictive trade union practices and consequently favourably influence managements' propensity for international collective bargaining.

*Mr Roberts* suggested that, at this stage of discussion, more clarification was required regarding the three following points: (1) the welfare issue raised by contemporary developments in collective bargaining between multi-national corporations and unions: (2) the role of governments and the State regarding the growth of multi-national corporations and their relations with the unions, and (3) the possibility and desirability of developing some kind of international supervision or regulatory code that would cover the relations between multi-national corporations and unions.

If the concern was maximising the welfare of all, one had to study whether this goal could be obtained by allowing multi-national corporations to find an equilibrium simply through the collective bargaining process, despite the fear, expressed particularly by Mr Blanpain, that trade unions might be unable to counter effectively the power of the supergiants. If it was likely, however, that multi-national companies and unions achieved a symbiosis (as Mr Cox called it) to their benefit and at the expense of the rest, one had to look for institutions to prevent this abuse of monopoly power.

The difficult problem arising from this situation was to whom were the multi-national corporations (and international trade union organisations) accountable, if the power of the nation State in which they operated and to whom they were legally responsible was insufficient. In these cases, some sort of international regulation was required which went beyond the more passive role of the international labour code, developed by the I.L.O. since 1919. The notion of international regulations was already actively discussed in various fields and was slowly emerging as a reality as regards a worldwide monetary order under the auspices of the I.M.F. and the World Bank. Multi-national corporations being a major instrument in regulating the world economy, it seemed clear to Mr Roberts that sooner or later their economic activities would be regulated in a similar way.

*Welfare Considerations*

Mr Roberts said the question of how to divide the benefits of international collective bargaining also affected the separate parts of the entities which were bargaining. In a big multi-national corporation, like General Motors, Ford or I.B.M., there was a tremendous struggle going on within that corporation itself as to where the specific activities should be carried out, where there should be greatest growth, whether the British subsidiary should export to the United States or whether the market should be entirely supplied by the

American company and other such questions. The managers for different countries or subsidiaries spent a great deal of their time fighting within the corporation for their special interests.

Again, if one looked at unions in this respect one found the same kind of internal conflict going on. If the Chemical Workers' Federation was, for instance, going to prevent I.C.I. from locating a plant in Southern Italy by insisting that I.C.I. paid the same level of wages as it did in the United Kingdom, this was depriving Southern Italy of economic growth to the disadvantage of local work people. Wage differentials had been prime factors in stimulating economic growth and the concept of uniformity behind the strategies of Mr Casserini and Mr Levinson might well have the consequence of keeping down the standards of living of the weakest workers. In fact, if one looked at the pattern of collective bargaining as a means of protecting the interests of workers, then one could categorically conclude that it had never protected the weak workers; collective bargaining was an instrument for workers in strong bargaining positions.

The real danger in terms of welfare which might develop from international collective bargaining was a cosy collusion between powerful multi-national corporations and strong unions at the expense of the developing countries and the weakest workers. In devising a policy on this issue, one had to reconcile conflicting interests. How much freedom and how much regulation in collective bargaining seemed very essential questions in this area.

*Mr Kahn-Freund* wondered whether Mr Roberts's assertion that collective bargaining did not protect the weak was not open to discussion. At any rate, in the national context, the political power usually intervened in collective bargaining to make it effective also for the weak, with legal instruments such as that providing for extension of collective bargaining in continental Europe, or the minimum wage legislation which was in force in the United Kingdom. Could similar devices be conceived as regards international collective bargaining?

*Mr Odhner* agreed with Mr Kahn-Freund and noted that the Swedish centralised bargaining system was so conceived that the strong unions backed the weak workers. One proof of the success of the system was the low skill differentials in Sweden. Protection of the weak by collective bargaining was certainly more difficult at the international level. The Swedish approach of negotiations on only wage increases, not wage levels, with over-proportional increases for the lower paid, was perhaps appropriate also at an international level. Admittedly, conflicting situations of the type referred to by Mr Roberts might arise. In order to solve them, one first had to identify the nature and magnitude of conflict.

Mr Nye emphasised that many developing countries had reached the point in import substitution where there was no further alternative to expansion than by high-cost production, which was a tremendous burden for consumers in these countries. Increasing production cost by wage claims would amplify these problems. They would also have adverse effects on the competitiveness on export markets, which UNCTAD still regarded as a major factor for growth, despite Mr Levinson's assertion that growth came mainly from the development of domestic consumption and local markets.

There was not just the danger of a collusion between strong multi-national corporations and strong international trade unions; there was also the fact that employees in multi-national corporations would become a small privileged group participating in the new developments at the cost of the general consumer and the general welfare in the less-developed countries. The case of the Jamaican aluminium workers, the subject of Mr Harrod's paper, was a striking example of this point; it presented itself as a coalition between two developed groups on the back of the poor, with a few co-opted into this coalition, which would make the bargain look somewhat more legitimate but which created tremendous long-run problems in growth. Mr Nye hoped that this type of problem would be further pursued in the I.L.O.'s future work.

Concluding the welfare discussion, Mr Roberts felt that the large variety of possible permutations in the relationships between multi-national corporations, unions and the State, made it difficult to formulate a general recommendation. There were, however, several negative indications for Mr Levinson's belief that an optimum solution was likely to be found by the pursuit of unbridled collective bargaining and wage claims. Undoubtedly, there were quite respectable economic arguments to back up the proposition of Mr Levinson. The recent growth model of Professor Kaldor would suggest, for instance, that such a policy could maximise the rate of economic growth in the countries concerned.

Applying this kind of model in practice, it would, however, tend to break down because it was impossible to sustain a corresponding policy in the face of the social and political tension it would create, and this would persuade the State to prevent its successful implementation.

## The Multi-national Corporation and the State

Mr Houssiaux introduced this topic with a review of the recent economic policy of national and E.E.C. authorities as regards the creation, functioning and growth of multi-national firms. There was an increasing preoccupation with the phenomenon of international concentration, especially by the Anti-Trust Commission of the U.S. Senate and, in response to the mergers with American firms, by the national governments in Europe. As the notion of public interest was conceived differently in each case and in each country, the approaches to this problem varied to a certain degree. However, it was striking that action of the different authorities concerned with these problems became more and more similar because they had the prevention of future difficulties in mind. The thorough investigation by the Commission of the European Communities of the consequences of multi-national companies in the field of social, sectoral, financial, foreign investment and monetary policies, as well as on the policy of competition, would undoubtedly promote understanding of the phenomenon and help to improve the co-ordination of measures taken by the member States.

Government measures directed at the multi-national corporation had the objectives of controlling their main decisions, of retarding their creation, and of concluding agreements ensuring their loyalty to the political and economic orientations adopted by the State. These measures pushed multi-national companies in a polycentric direction (to use Mr. Perlmutter's term) and conferred upon them a certain legitimacy.

The nation State used several techniques of intervention to enforce its policy of control. The first technique was nationalisation which was more often not a simple take-over of capital but also a means of monopolisation of transnational activities by the State. The second technique was the drawing up of guidelines, of varying values, to which multi-national firms, concerned about their legitimacy, usually adhered more strictly than national firms. A third policy consisted of an attempt to create some sort of 'countervailing power' (in Galbraith's sense), in most cases, however, without much success. Theoretically, there was a control of powerful firms by powerful unions, and vice versa, but in practice there existed certain areas of collusion. As all these techniques had considerable drawbacks, the general policy of competition was also put in the service of control of multi-national companies with three objectives: (1) to ensure workable competition in the principal sectors of the economy often endangered by international oligopolies; (2) to avoid the emergence of supergiant firms harmful for the maintenance of a competitive structure, and (3) to ensure the compatibility of actual economic development with the welfare objectives chosen by the government.

The approach of the American Government towards multi-national companies was an example of the use of the policy for competition. There was not much intervention in the actions of American-based multi-national firms in foreign markets and territories, apart from considerations regarding its side effects on the functioning of American domestic competition. Since 1951, the United States had a policy of restricting horizontal and vertical mergers which, according to recent announcements by the Anti-Trust authorities, was likely to be reinforced. It appeared that the American Anti-Trust policy was carried out without much consideration as to its implications on foreign countries. It was likely for, instance, that big American firms, hindered by restrictive policies on conglomerate mergers, might seek overseas expansion. This obviously raised the question of concerting national policies. For the Western hemisphere, the O.E.C.D. commission on restrictive practices had, from 1966 onwards, served as a meeting place for economic policy-makers concerned with the problems of concentration. Although no common policy had been formulated, the exchange of information was extremely important.

In order to conceive a valid international policy on the issue, it was important to know whether multi-national companies were really to be regarded as the main vehicles of international exchange in the years to come. Without wishing to venture into prophecies on future policies, there were indications that trends, perceptible in the United States, tended to be followed in other countries and regions as soon as these attained the same level of integration of markets. It was, therefore, very likely that the control adopted in the United States would one day also be applied in Europe.

This was not true, so far, regarding the policy led by the Commission of the European Committees which, in Mr Houssiaux's opinion, differing from Mr Biart's assertions, had been much in favour of international concentrations (at least for those in which European countries had the majority). Furthermore, in spite of provisions intending to prevent the abuse of dominant positions by firms, like Article 86 of the Treaty, the Commission did not dispose of sufficient jurisdiction for an efficient control of international enterprises.

Mr Houssiaux concluded that as the States were, more or less consciously, about to deal with the problem of multi-national corporations, was it then desirable that other forms of countervailing power develop, such as international entities of organised labour, corresponding to big multi-national business?

*Mr Blake* attempted to view the relations between multi-national companies and the State within the analytical concepts used by Mr Perlmutter. In the ethnocentric bargaining situation, the consequences were quite horrifying for the State. This could lead to considerable problems where States with pronounced nationalistic reactions were involved, especially in many under-developed regions.

In the polycentric case, the State had a greater role to play. In the geocentric case the State was ignored and was merely a competitor along with everybody else. As evidence suggested that the State might continue to be the most important aspect of international relations, and as nationalism, far from being dead, was going to remain very active in many parts of the world, prescriptions were required for accommodating multi-national companies, and also international unions, and the State. Perhaps the types of bargaining situations, which Mr Blake had earlier distinguished, might be of use in selecting proper prescriptions. Mr Blake expressed concern that the development of international collective bargaining might present a further threat to the sovereignty of the State. One major result of the Chrysler–U.A.W. agreement was that the Canadian Government retained little control over a critical sector of the economy. Therefore, while one had to be concerned with the challenge of the multi-national corporation to the State, one could not neglect the potential challenge fo the international union.

*Mr Blanpain* said that small developed countries were in a similarly weak position to developing countries when they attempted to defend their national interest and their own cultural system against multi-national companies. Frequently, they had to beg for employment opportunities offered by multi-national companies, sacrificing all other considerations. One case in point was the implantation, some years ago, of a Ford subsidiary in Genk, situated in the relatively under-developed Belgian province of Limburg. The government and the unions had done their utmost to secure its location in this area as it had meant the creation of some 7,000 new jobs. The otherwise strong Belgian unions had accepted a five years' collective agreement with substantially lower wages than in another Ford plant only fifty miles away. In autumn, 1968, a strike had broken out over wage differentials and both government and trade unions had to face the menace of a possible shift of production outside the Belgian borders. The problem for small countries, as for developing countries, was how to attract foreign capital and foreign investments to increase efficiency without losing their sovereignty.

The unchecked growth of multi-national companies posed, in Mr *Levinson*'s mind, a variety of problems also to major industrialised States. One issue, particularly, to be considered in this respect was their effect upon trade. The overseas growth of U.S.-based multinational companies had contributed to the transformation of the United States from a country with traditional balance of payments surpluses to one of permanent deficits. The ratio of sales of overseas plants to exports from the United States was already 5 or 6 to 1 and tended to increase further. The situation was particularly unbalanced for manufacturing goods which held a continuously declining share in exports. It was doubtful whether any fiscal or monetary measures taken by the U.S. Government could do anything substantial to modify this reality.

The emergence of the multi-national corporation called in question the traditional theories on national monetary equilibrium and trade balances. As long as national politicians had to find national solutions to international problems there was going to be growing dislocation and frustration.

*Regional Economic Groupings and Multi-national Corporations*

Would regionalism favour or obstruct multi-national corporations? In line with Mr Houssiaux's observations on the E.E.C. policy, participants tended to believe that regional groupings, an extension of the nation State, would reflect the attitudes of the individual members. How was the concern of the E.E.C. with the statute of a European company to be seen in this context, and what were the prospects of this company as compared with the American-based corporations, the latter having apparently benefited most from the existence of the Common Market?

*Mr van Dierendonck* confirmed that the E.E.C. Commission was not overly concerned about growth of multi-national corporations and that the active involvement of the E.E.C. in the formulation of the statute of a European company was, above all, part of harmonisation efforts.

An interesting aspect in the social sphere, impinging on industrial relations, was the participation of workers in the future European company. The Commission had asked for expert advice on this matter, in particular from Professor Sanders, and lately from Professor Lioncard. While the Sanders report had suggested that the European company should adopt the practice of each country in which it operated, Professor Lioncard had advocated a solution combining national and international elements. This was probably the orientation that the Commission would adopt. Could the European company, *Mr Blanpain* added, set an industrial relations pattern also for foreign-based multi-national companies operating in Europe?

*Mr Houssiaux* wondered whether it was possible to create a multi-national company of European origin simply by law, or whether, according to the American example, it was essential for there to be a pre-existing centre of co-ordination capable of defining a business strategy and of establishing contacts with employers' and workers' organisations. At any rate, evidence suggested that firms had to undergo a special process for acquiring a multi-national character.

In the United States, a process of concentration and of direct investment in other continents, which was part of a defined policy of penetration, had been the way companies had become international. It also appeared that a great amount of national concentration was the prerequisite of European multi-national business units. For quite some time there had been more national than international concentration in Europe, given that there were differences of degree in the various countries. For environmental reasons, production was more concentrated in the U.K., Germany and even Italy, but much less in France with its preference for cartels and corporatism.

In addition, the distribution between leading firms and firms of second order was different; in the U.K. and Germany, important leaders existed while these were practically non-existent in France where traditionally several major firms of similar size shared the market. It would, therefore, appear that one had first to encourage national concentration in the less-advanced European countries before European companies could be created.

These aspects resulted in a different structure of the European multi-national company, as compared to the American-based multi-national company operating in Europe and this had consequences for the shaping of industrial relations. Naturally, trade unions would try to act according to the same doctrine, vis-à-vis both types of corporations, but relatively quickly they might discover different approaches for the European multi-national corporations which were without a clearly defined central decision-making locus for industrial relations, and for corporations of the American type which usually had strong home-based decision centres.

*Mr Conlon* questioned the validity of Mr Houssiaux's assertion that national concentration was a necessary stage prior to the development of multi-national companies. It was true that one of the reasons that American firms were singled out as the 'greatest aggressors' was that they had the largest domestic market as a solid base with which to start.

However, the economics of geography did not appear valid as an explanatory factor if one considered, for instance, multi-national firms home-based in Switzerland or Sweden. On a per capita basis, both countries had more multi-national corporations than the United States. It followed that attempts to match multi-national corporations by increasing the size of national economic units were subject to failure. Mergers of companies within the national boundaries were an inadequate response to the challenge of American multi-national companies as well as a blow against European unification.

Why did not more across-the-border mergers happen in the E.E.C.? Perhaps the cultural aspects, to which Mr Houssiaux had referred, were responsible. It was, probably, harder for, say, a Dutch company to merge with a Belgian than an American firm, as it was harder for relatives to get together than for strangers. To use an analogy, European companies were probably in the same position as many U.S. companies were forty or fifty years ago. At that time, American companies were Eastern, Middle-West or Western companies, which suddenly found that they had to go national, learning through that process both organisation and management techniques which enabled them to go international more easily. The European companies, it seemed to Mr Conlon, had to do both things simultaneously; they had to go from a national to a European or a multi-national company at one stage.

Looking at the European situation, *Mr Nye* said, did not convey the whole picture, as multi-national corporations confronted quite different conditions in developing areas, like the East African Common

Market, the Central American Common Market, and the Latin American Free Trade Association. It was true that the multi-national companies tended to be the major engines of change in Europe as well as in these areas, but the response to them was different. To use Mr Perlmutter's terms, one might have a polycentric firm in a developing country, but it was practically certain that one tended to get a very ethnocentric response.

Many of the elites in developing countries viewed the nation State as the prime instrument for modernisation, and anything which might appear as a potential threat to its sovereignty was a real threat to their basic ideology. In his paper, Mr Kaplan had tried to reconcile the organisational form of the multi-national corporation with the market schemes in developing countries by suggesting the use of public multi-national corporations. Some of the problems which arose in this respect were touched upon by Mr Kaplan, e.g. distribution of benefits, provision of capital, employment policy and industrial relations, where different degrees of trade union freedom and bargaining capabilities existed. He had not brought out yet sufficiently one of the most crucial problems, that of inefficiency. Public corporations in many Latin American states tended to be highly politicised with a great deal of inefficiency in their management, and it was difficult to see how this could be avoided in the case of the public multi-national corporations.

Another problem was that of scale: would the public corporation have enough scale to be able to engage in research and development expenditure, essential to keep up with the outside competition? Partnership with the private multi-national corporation might be a solution to both problems (efficiency and scale), and international regulations (perhaps by UNCTAD, as Charles Kindleberger had recently suggested) might assist in this process of creating a situation of somewhat greater trust between private multi-national corporations and the seemingly threatened underdeveloped nation State (and its political extension, the regional groupings).

*International Supervision*

*Mr Maier* agreed that an international supervision of multi-national industrial relations, as requested by Mr Roberts, was an idea worth further exploration. How to lay down the rules, and which rules, and which institutions should be entrusted with this supervision, were major issues to be considered.

Certain basic standards for industrial relations had been incorporated in I.L.O. conventions. It would already mean a step forward if multinational firms, where necessary pushed by trade unions, would not just accept low-standard industrial relations as they found them in several countries, but would try to apply the standards set by the I.L.O., and in this way, convince national governments of the need for their acceptance.

As regards the institution which should exert supervision, Mr Maier thought that, because of their limited scope and their structural setting, regional organisations like the E.E.C. were not the organisations one had to choose. Supervision of industrial relations behaviour could be better entrusted to the I.L.O. which had the advantage of being a worldwide organisation in which, owing to its tripartite character, workers and employers were represented on an equal footing with governments. However, even within the propitious I.L.O. context, one could foresee a tremendous opposition to these plans on the part of the employers.

*Mr Kahn-Freund* added that the potentialities of international organisations for standard setting and supervision had been explored by Mr George Spyropoulos of the I.L.O. in an article written in 1966 on the possibilities of international collective bargaining from the lawyer's point of view.[1] The article ended with an analysis of the background which the existing body of the I.L.O. Conventions (most obviously Convention 98) could give to such an attempt.

In spite of Mr Maier's misgivings about regional organisations, one was also tempted to mention the activities of the Council of Europe, which, after all, had adopted a European Social Charter, ratified by eight member countries. It appeared to Mr Kahn-Freund that the role which regional organisations could play in respect of supervision of industrial relations behaviour might also be further explored.

## INSTITUTION-BUILDING

*Mr Perlmutter* asked himself whether, in the relations between nations, unions and multi-national firms, one was indeed coping with a process of institution building. By institution building, Mr Perlmutter understood, first of all, the design of viable organisations,

---

[1] George Spyropoulos: 'Le rôle de la négociation collective dans l'harmonisation des systèmes sociaux européens', *Revue internationale de droit comparé* (1966), No. 1, pp. 19–55.

which for a worldwide firm was equated with returning money on investment, making profits and creating wealth. Viability was one of two criteria for institutionality, the second being the perception by various claimants of the indispensability of an organisation. Applied to the multi-national firm, this latter criterion signified that the multi-national firm would have to be reintroduced if it disappeared, because it did something which no other institution could do.

If one was concerned with building a worldwide institution, one had to take into account the interest of other institutions and groupings, first of all the nation State and the trade unions. At the same time, however, the nation State and the trade unions would have to embark on a similar process.

To define the mission and the distinctive competence of a country, especially a small one, in the last third of the twentieth century was not an easy task. In particular the smaller countries had to specialise in some way in economic terms; they had to get resources from outside their borders, establish coalitions with other countries and multi-national firms.

The third unit seeking its worldwide mission was the international trade union. Its distinctive competence was not yet clearly perceptible, as Mr O'Leary had indicated. However, Mr Perlmutter was convinced that the future of the international trade union would finally be assured by defining such a distinctive mission; it had to stand for values and practices for which other institutions could not be directly responsible.

Three kinds of patterns or relationships could be seen between the three actors referred to: (1) the collision course; (2) the partnership course, and (3) the check and balance pattern.

Under the first pattern, the multi-national firm would ignore national boundaries, keep unions out of its activities and simply get on with the job of optimising the resources of a worldwide industrial system. The roots of such a course in the international trade union movement were perceptible; multi-national firms were conceived as a strong monolithic enemy which tended to enhance the kind of cohesiveness among unions upon which to build an institution. Similarly, the nation State was embarking, on the whole, on a defensive course when it realised the great flexibility of the multi-national firm.

The collision course was a likely scenario under the present circumstances. It seemed to make international collective bargaining a rather unattractive channel of communication for the international firm which, at the moment, had a good deal of influence in deciding whether such bargaining was necessary or not.

The partnership course left a place for international collective bargaining. It certainly had an idealistic connotation but it was not an unrealistic pattern in specific instances, as the Swedish domestic policy showed. In essence, it meant that one accepted a role for the worldwide trade union and for the nation State. The unions had to be recognised as the force or group aiming at the bettering of labour conditions and at the same time understanding the mission of the firm; firms themselves might aim at promoting labour conditions, but this was not their primary concern. Finally, the State, maybe less economically oriented in the future, served profound human needs of identification and loyalty. There were certain negative indications for a general realisation of the partnership course.

The check and balance relationship embraced the notion that, even though there were some similarities in missions, there was enough distinctiveness between the three institutions and that in having different points of view they in effect helped each other. In their attempt to check the other institutions, the parties had to be subjected to some international code which could intervene. Considering that this code had to incorporate world economic interest, national interest, interest of the workers and management, Mr Perlmutter was reluctant to designate which existing institution could be responsible for it.

Rather than to conclude with definite, but premature proposals, Mr Perlmutter intended to conclude by raising some further questions. How could one proceed to understand the kinds of relationships which the three institutions under consideration could evolve as they strived for the legitimate mission of expanding to the world's scale? Research had a prime role to play in examining options involved in these jelationships; but it was already possible to plot the course of the rustification of worldwide companies, worldwide unions and world-oriented nation States in terms of the kinds of values they hoped to create (beyond separating ideologies) for larger numbers of people. International collective bargaining should be defined in these terms, for it was a tool, and a tool was an instrument to higher goals. Considering the issues involved, one had to take the mood of the social architect, the architect who, according to the original Greek meaning of the word, was concerned with building sound structures, keeping human values in mind.

*Mr Harrod* said he would like to discuss the issue of international institution-building from the standpoint of his two basic interests, the relations between developed and developing countries and the behaviour of people in cross-cultural circumstances.

First, it had to be recognised that to create international institutions from the existing corporate base the cultural and adjustment problems related in the main to the Anglo-Saxon culture. This was because out of eighty-seven corporations operating internationally which had over $1 billion in turnover, sixty were from the United States. Thus when talking of the international spread of business organisation one was basically talking of the spread of an American-conceived and structured organisation; likewise when one talked of changes necessary for the creation of a worldwide organisation one was talking of changes which had to come from the U.S.A. In the same manner Mr Harrod objected to the loose use of the term 'international union' as in many cases these international federations of unions acquired most of their membership and much of their finance from the U.S.A. unions and decisions often had to be cleared in that country.

Considering institution-building from its basic behavioural standpoint, what was the behaviour of a corporate or union executive from a developed country working in a developing country? Entering a new culture, substantially different from his own, he would suffer from cultural shock and the usual escape hatch was a material and psychological attempt to re-create his home environment. In this respect his actions would not differ greatly from the colonial administrator of the past, except that his power was a purchased one rather than one of military enforcement. The obvious danger of duplicating the home environment was that it was basically dysfunctional to the setting in the host country and tended to create a dual society. The dysfunctional effects were amplified if major decisions were made at headquarters by persons who could not fully appreciate the results of their decisions or actions, especially when these tended to be more social than economic.

A meaningful solution to this problem, Mr Harrod thought, was the promotion of a greater degree of cultural relativity among field operators and headquarters staff. This, however, was not likely, as such changes would require changes in the orientation of some national education systems which had often been designed to wash out cultural differences or their appreciation.

The multi-national corporation's attempt to mitigate the dysfunctional nature of absentee control and home-environment duplication had been made on two levels – the managerial and the mass. At the managerial level corporate training was used to acculturalise the future managers, regardless of their nationality. Thus, for example, a Latin American manager for a U.S. company may defend American cultural values and at the same time soften the impact of absentee control. But this elite transformation was in itself socially disruptive and disintegrative. At the mass level the attempt was, through the commercial mass media, to establish an emulation of the specific material aspirations of the originating culture. Such attempts were often initially successful but in the long run the cultural, economic and physical boundaries to these aspirations would create severe frustrations. These attempts then, were counter-productive to the stability and accommodation necessary for international institutional building.

In what guise, asked Mr Harrod, were these changes and penetrations made? It was that the corporation was in the service of an apolitical managerial and economic rationalism, to which no rational person should object. The current force most subversive of this ideology was the emotional one of nationalism and this accounted for the rising attacks on nationalism. The ideology of rationalism asked one to ignore the nation as the human group of highest cohesion cemented by nationalism.

The denial that nationalism was relevant was as dangerous as its suppression, yet both were being attempted. Thus, Mr Harrod concluded, that while the multi-national corporation in many cases had, under the banner of equal access to markets and resources, assisted the anti-colonial revolution it was impeding the forthcoming nationalist revolution, if it could be so called. The conclusion was that rather than creating an international organisation, the current multi-national corporation was contributing to conditions unlikely to assist any true institutional building. It was also possible that it would not survive in anything like its current or predicted forms, therefore denying the possibility of international collective bargaining. Could then Mr Perlmutter's conceptual framework be considered as explanatory or predictive in the present circumstances?

In reply, *Mr Perlmutter* stressed that in order to find out about the nature of multi-national firms, one had to cover a representative number of cases, not only the single example on which Mr Harrod tended to generalise. It was also necessary to study people's cross-cultural behaviour in the context of long periods of time, not only the initial stages of cultural shock. Exposed to cultural inputs from all over the world for a long time, people in multi-national companies changed their perceptions and acquired the level of cultural relativity on which, as Mr Harrod had recognised, a really worldwide institution could be built. A case which came to mind was the Nestlé company which had functioned for about 100 years and had clearly developed beyond one nation's orientation. It proved that an orientation towards the task made in the long run differences of origin relatively unimportant.

The social psychologist's main task was to explain the advent of the institutions under consideration. This involved sampling well actual negotiation situations, drawing up of hypotheses and then testing them. Mr Perlmutter thought it quite possible that, in the course of further research, the categories which he had found useful might eventually be superseded by more adequate concepts. This was the usual process by which research grew. Although he had attributed some predictive capacity to his analysis, in the last resort only the future could show who was right or wrong about the outlook for multi-national companies and their effect on industrial relations.

## CONCLUSIONS

### Need for Future Research

Listening to the discussions, *Mr Walker* said he had gathered the impression that international collective bargaining, in the narrower sense, was, so to speak, really one small tip of the iceberg which appeared above the water. The much greater invisible part of the iceberg covered the broad field of transnationalisation of industrial relations, associated in particular with the activities of the multi-national corporation but also, here and there, with unions and also with regional trends and national institutions in various continents.

In the developing countries, a phenomenon which became more and more perceptible was the concern with the localisation of industrial relations, the need to develop an industrial relations system which was locally relevant and not merely patterned on some foreign model.

The International Institute for Labour Studies had been trying to help this process by providing, mainly through an international exchange of educational materials, information which could be used in training people and in making fruitful comparisons with other countries. Another effort to make problems and trends visible, and to promote recognition among acedamics that an ethnocentric view of industrial relations was out of date was being made by the International Industrial Relations Association.[1]

Looking into the broad field of transnationalisation of industrial relations (which, in the case of the multi-national corporation covered employment and other labour policy, not merely relations with trade unions) provided a focus by which not only prospective but also effective service-oriented research was possible – research which could indicate the major options open to persons concerned with the whole industrial relations system.

It was clear that one could not generalise about the multi-national corporations, nor about the situations which they confront, and it appeared necessary, either for purposes of policy or for purposes of academic understanding, that one developed some way of categorising these corporations, their policies and the situations in which they found themselves. Mr Roberts's paper had made a beginning in this direction and might perhaps provide the basis of more systematic empirical research.

It was also evident that there was, for the moment, an extreme shortage of systematic information on the labour problems arising in connection with the multi-national corporation. The papers furnished by Mr Harrod and Mr Blake were very interesting examples of what needed to be done on a much broader scale and what should, if possible, be illuminated by hypotheses fitting into a general conceptual approach.

For this reason, Mr Walker hoped that participants would offer opinions and ideas about the direction along which research might go. It seemed very likely, as Mr Cox had said in his opening remarks, that industrial relations, while of interest in themselves, might be of broader interest to the multi-national corporation because the developments in the industrial relations field might feed back into the corporation as a whole. It was also clear that, while Mr Perlmutter's classification was a stimulating approach, in practice it produced somewhat different results according to the particular managerial functions studied. As Mr Perlmutter himself had said, a company might be geocentric in one respect and ethnocentric in another.

[1] Founded by: The International Institute for Labour Studies, Geneva, The British Universities Industrial Relations Association, The Industrial Relations Research Association (United States) and The Japan Institute of Labour. The aims of the Association are of a purely scientific character and its general purpose is to promote the study of industrial relations throughout the world in the several relevant academic disciplines.

Mr Walker felt that, particularly in the last decade, there had been industrial relations problems which had sometimes pushed management of multi-national corporations into thinking in a less ethnocentric way, using polycentric and, here and there, geocentric approaches. Pursuing these issues, research might serve not only the immediate interest of illuminating the transnationalisation of industrial relations but also contribute to the knowledge of the future evolution of the multi-national corporation.

In addition to the conceptual problems, there was of course a variety of technical problems in getting information from corporations. Furthermore, if information was available on the principles of their policy, an example of which had been sketched in Mr Lee's paper, one was still left with the difference which always occurred between a policy and its implementation. There was practically no information as yet about the application of such policies in differing situations. One also had little systematic knowledge about the influences within the corporations, business schools and other institutions which were shaping the approaches of the men who would lead corporations in the future. As one could get hold of these future managers in the business schools, etc., where they were undergoing formative training, practical research appeared to be possible on the approaches which they brought to the labour problem in different countries and on influences which were brought to bear on them by these educational programmes.

Naturally, the same kind of research which Mr Walker had outlined for the future of multi-national corporations could be applied with appropriate modifications to trade unions and governments.

Closing, Mr Walker felt that all parties involved should welcome investigations of an objective kind in the broad field of research referred to and should support research by giving access to material, in the interest of finding appropriate solutions to the complex issues at stake.

*Summing-up by the Chairman*

Left with the task of summing up, *Mr Kahn-Freund* stressed that the main purpose of the discussions had not been to answer questions but to formulate the right questions. On the basis of the information available to the participants, a definite solution of the problems raised could, undoubtedly, not be expected. In view of this state of affairs, in a certain sense one of the most important contributions was the plea for further research made by Mr. Walker and others.

The subject of the meeting had been international collective bargaining, which had become an object of interest owing to the existence of the two factual phenomena: the multi-national corporation and the regional political enterprise. There appeared to have been agreement that the existence of the multi-national enterprise raised very different questions whether it operated in developed or developing countries. In this connection, disparities of cultures and the creation of new power relations were important issues to be looked into. The discussion had brought out that the multi-national corporation was not one and the same phenomenon everywhere; it actually showed very different aspects, depending on the type of its production, the location of power, and its managerial approaches.

Certain difficulties had been experienced during the discussion because the common factors relating to both regional political arrangements and to multi-national corporations were very few. As a matter of fact, Mr Kahn-Freund said, the only common factor was that both phenomena might provide certain opportunities or create certain needs for international collective bargaining. Consequently, looking at international collective bargaining, one had to speak about its possibility, utility and desirability.

One important aspect which had been touched upon but which certainly needed to be developed further was that, whatever one wanted to do by promoting international collective bargaining within regional groupings like E.E.C., EFTA or LAFTA, or with multi-national corporations, one had to reckon with the bare fact of the continuing existence of the nation State and its legal system. Connected with this was the question of what price democracy had to pay if supra-national enterprises encroached upon the exercise of national sovereignty or if such sovereignty was handed over to regional supra-national bodies. In other words, there arose the central question: to whom were both supra-national enterprises, and, in a different way, regional supra-national bodies to be made accountable?

Another factor linked to the nation State and its legal system was that (without wishing to exaggerate the importance of the law) international collective bargaining presupposed a degree of legal harmonisation nowhere achieved so far. The essential point here was the uneven distribution of regulatory power regarding the determination of the actual terms of employment between the collective partners and the law-making authorities in various countries. Therefore, while paying all possible attention in this discussion on international collective bargaining to the psychological and the human factors, the institutional factors, to which law belonged, had also to be closely considered and might justify the presence of lawyers in further discussions on the issues under review.

One result of the discussions had been the verification of the hypotheses, which most participants seemed to have shared, that collective bargaining at the level of regional political organisations was as yet no more than an aspiration. With the exception of the E.E.C. frame agreement for agriculture, there was no evidence of supra-national collective bargaining, either in Europe or elsewhere, although there was the hope to see it developed with a greater intensity of economic and social integration. A positive disposition towards this bargaining had yet to be shown by trade unions and employers.

On the other hand, international collective bargaining with multinational corporations had at least entered the stage where it was a controversy. The very pronounced tension created, for instance, by the statements of Mr Levinson and Mr Lee, not so much about the practicability as about the utility of international collective bargaining, made one feel that there must be something important in it. There had not been nearly the same excitement about the problems of regional collective bargaining.

Listening to the discussions, Mr Kahn-Freund said he had sometimes wondered whether the basic problems underlying the issues were all that new. The international enterprise as such was certainly nothing new, though, of course, the present type of international management was new. The cultural problems involved and the questions connected with the locus of power, the approaches of ethnocentric, polycentric and geocentric leadership, had already been experienced in other circumstances, as, for instance, in the administration of the medieval Catholic Church and, in part, by colonial administration. Similarly, the problems connected with the levels of bargaining, embracing the question of solidarity and the equalising function of unions, were, at the national level, found throughout the trade union history, anticipating the present dilemma of trade unionism as regards protection of workers in developed versus those in developing countries.

What had been discussed during the last three days was very much concerned with the question of whose welfare had priority: the shareholders, the consumers, or the workers (at headquarters or in the subsidiaries in the developing areas). But welfare seemed to have been a secondary concern; the primary concern had unquestionably been power, its location and the relations between the various actors. The area of the exercise of power was connected with the problems trade unions faced in the present situation which had come out especially in the dialogue between Mr Levinson and Mr Roberts.

What was the function of trade unionism? If a trade union saw itself as an organ of the solidarity of the workers of the world, everything had to be done to encourage multi-national enterprises to develop productivity and welfare in the areas where they were most needed. To trade unions this was a new formulation of the old question of either raising the level of the low-paid worker or maintaining differentials. Nothing had given him the impression, Mr Kahn-Freund added, that the trade union movement had as yet the clarity of purpose which it had to achieve to cope with this enormous problem. Another problem which had been highlighted, and which was impossible to answer right away, was the change in the locus of power in multi-national corporations. Was there a tendency for power to move from the centre to the periphery, or from the periphery to the centre, as regards labour relations? His own work in the British Donovan Commission[1] had convinced him of the extreme difficulty of obtaining unambiguous factual information in this matter. The inter-relation and interpenetration of power was a problem of highest importance in the relations between the multi-national corporation and the State, about which, for instance, Mr Blanpain had been very eloquent. On the one side there was a need for attracting investment which induced governments to grant all kinds of privileges to multi-national corporations; on the other, there was a need for protecting the democratic institutions of a country, as well as its culture. The seriousness of this political issue at stake, the encroachment upon the sovereignty of the nation State by multi-national institutions – which, in the long run, might be very beneficial to the area in which they operated – should not be forgotten in the midst of all sociological and economic problems.

The discussions had also borne out that it was nonsensical to view the issues under review in the simplistic confrontation of workers against employers. This was an inadequate approach because of the split of interest amongst the workers as well as the differentiation of attitudes amongst employers. Even in a country like the U.K., the attitudes of management of national firms differed widely from those of managers of international firms, for instance, as regards new forms of

[1] Royal Commission on Trade Unions and Employers Associations (1965–8).

collective bargaining (like productivity bargaining); how much more was this differentiation to be expected in a developing area.

Finally, Mr Kahn-Freund believed that the relationship between the multi-national corporation and the nation State had emerged from the discussion as the most important single issue: it raised the old problem of efficiency and democracy, not for the first time in history, and certainly not for the last.

# THE FUTURE OF TRANSNATIONAL INDUSTRIAL RELATIONS: A TENTATIVE FRAMEWORK FOR ANALYSIS

*by*

*Hans Günter*

As transnational industrial relations are a new field of study it has been thought useful in the first subsection of this concluding section to put forward some preliminary ideas concerning the analysis of this phenomenon. They are the basis on which several tentative hypotheses will be developed regarding the propensity of industrial relations to become transnational under the impact of multi-national corporations.[1]

In a second subsection, available evidence on transnational tendencies obtained from the 1969 Symposium on International Collective Bargaining and from other sources will be summarised and briefly compared with the proposed analytical concepts.[2]

Finally, the present section also offers an occasion to highlight information gaps and research requirements.

It should be stressed that the author is exclusively responsible for the ideas and conclusions offered in this section; it should therefore by no means be taken as a report of the 1969 Symposium or even as expressing a consensus of its participants.

## CONCEPTUAL TOOLS FOR ANALYSING AND FORECASTING TRANSNATIONAL INDUSTRIAL RELATIONS

One element of relevance for analysing and forecasting transnational industrial relations that emerged from the 1969 Symposium is

[1] The impact of regional economic integration is not considered separately as it had been the subject of the introduction to Section 7 and of the conclusions of Chapter 15. In the following, regional economic integration is treated as a possible environmental condition for the multi-national corporation.

[2] By and large David E. Apter's suggestions for forecasting in three levels are therefore followed in the present section, *viz*: (1) forecasting on the basis of hypotheses of the dynamics of industrial relations systems (tentatively applied in the first subsection); (2) gathering the opinion of practitioners about the present situation and its future evolution; and (3) the projection of trends as evaluated by independent observers with specialist knowledge (both types of information are used in the second section). See: 'Future Worlds and Present International Organisations: Some Dilemmas', seminar discussion following a public lecture by E. B. Haas, *I.I.L.S. Bulletin*, No. 6, June 1969, pp. 26–30.

Howard V. Perlmutter's typology of the behaviour of multi-national management (ethno-, poly-, and geocentric corporations). Perlmutter assumes that as a result of an adaptation process, required by the logic of optimum resource utilisation and allocation during the growth of operations, originally ethnocentric (home-base-oriented) management transmutes into geocentric (worldwide-oriented) management. Ethnocentric policies might not be compatible with environmental constraints in the host countries which may force the corporation to adjust towards a polycentric (host-country-oriented) direction. Polycentric adjustments are disfunctional to the operations of the multi-national corporation and a deviation from the evolution towards geocentrism. These adjustments reach a critical threshold when the single management decision-making system begins to break up as regards major issues. However, Sydney Rolfe's observation '. . . that the corporations cannot be aid programmes, and cannot for very long condone deficient investment decisions [taken in a subsidiary] where better alternatives exist . . .'[1] might suggest that the critical issues of multi-national management lie outside industrial relations proper, although not outside the interest of labour. Obviously, geocentric management behaviour is from a company's viewpoint the optimum situation.[2] But observed dynamics towards geocentric industrial relations policies are small and seem strongly counteracted by environmental forces. Recent research has yielded indications that factors external to management in the home and host environment of the corporation can considerably reduce the power of management to make adjustments. Constraints of this kind are, for instance, on the one hand pressures for the extraterritorial application of home country legislation and policies in subsidiaries,[3] and on the other the necessity of adjusting substantially to a strong host environment as a precondition to successful operations.[4]

As most multi-national corporations will probably continue to originate in the near future in the United States, which has an environment which largely demands home-country-oriented management, it

---

[1] Sydney Rolfe: *The International Corporation*, Background Report for the XXII Congress of the International Chamber of Commerce, Istanbul, 31 May to 7 June 1969, p. 143.

[2] In the industrial relations field, geocentric attitudes might possibly be equated with the adoption of an international labour code along the I.L.O. model.

[3] See for example I. A. Litvak and C. J. Maule: 'Conflict Resolution and Extra-territoriality', *The Journal of Conflict Resolution*, Vol. XIII, No. 3, September 1969, pp. 305–29.

[4] See for example Jean-Luc Rocour: 'Management of European Subsidiaries in the United States', *Management International Review*, 1966, No. 1, pp. 13–27.

seems likely that the ethnocentric component will keep a prominent place in managerial behaviour. Taking the areas of main interest to labour (industrial relations and certain economic policies affecting the job security of the workers) together, one might expect a mixture of ethno- and polycentric policies to prevail in the years to come, with the long-term prospect of a geo- and polycentric mix.

With the following box model an attempt is made to classify industrial relations situations and to explain tentatively the propensity

PROPENSITY OF INDUSTRIAL RELATIONS TO
TRANSNATIONALISE

| Behavioural pattern of multi-national corporations[2] | | Transnational power of unions[1] | | | |
|---|---|---|---|---|---|
| | | Small | | Great | |
| | Polycentric | unilateral low | bilateral low | unilateral low | bilateral low |
| | | (1) | | (2) | |
| | Ethno- and Geocentric | unilateral high | bilateral low | unilateral low | bilateral high |
| | | (3) | | (4) | |

[1] Exerted, e.g. through co-ordinated national strategies or the threat to use such strategies.
[2] Regarding decisions of prime interest to labour (work rules and economic issues affecting employment).

of industrial relations to transnationalise. Two variables have been selected as being relevant for this purpose: (1) behavioural pattern of multi-national management regarding labour relations and related issues, and (2) transnational power of unions. It assumes therefore certain internal dynamics in the industrial relations system.[1] Howard V. Perlmutter's distinctions are used for classifying behavioural patterns of management, but without implying assumptions about inherent

---

[1] This is a controversial issue. Usually industrial relations are supposed to have little native dynamics but rather an adaptive function towards influences from other systems. In the long run, however, internal dynamics are more readily accepted, for instance, by Friedrich Fürstenberg who notes that 'Major changes in industrial relations also may be caused by a dynamics of their own, leading to internal social innovations . . .' (See Friedrich Fürstenberg: 'Social Innovations in Industrial Relations', *Bulletin* of the International Institute for Labour Studies, No. 9 (1971).

behavioural dynamics of management. Ethno- and geocentric behaviour are lumped together as both emphasise central decision-making and should therefore have high potential for transnational industrial relations (although the value judgements which underlie decisions are entirely different in both cases). The criteria are classified according to ideal types which, as the preceding pages suggest, in reality are only approximated in that an ideal type may constitute a predominant component of real behaviour. Transnational union power is merely classified by degree. The entries 'unilateral' and 'bilateral' are shorthand for the two possible types of transnational industrial relations. 'Unilateral transnational relations' mean that the decisions of one party only (either management *or* unions) transcend national boundaries. 'Bilateral transnational relations' indicate that the decisions of both management and unions transcend national boundaries.

It should be stressed that the box model is used to derive hypothetical tendencies in industrial relations from supposed interrelationships between managerial behaviour and union reaction. These are not conclusions reached through the observation of real-life situations; the validity of the hypotheses needs therefore to be tested on actual observations.

Situation (1) does not show much propensity to transnationalise. Industrial relations are likely to remain within national boundaries as the multi-national corporation is for all practical union purposes a national firm. This does not necessarily imply a functional power balance between the corporation and the national union. It merely means that the locus of decisions for both industrial relations actors meet at the national level.

Situation (2) is somewhat atypical for the underlying assumptions which imply that union actions are a response to the behavioural pattern of multi-national management rather than its cause. Polycentric management should therefore not usually give rise to transnational union action. Possibly bargaining support from an international federation to a national union and other forms of strengthening the power of local unions might be assimilated to this situation. Generally, there should be a tendency for the situation to revert to the more stable situation (1) unless multi-national management modifies, under union pressure, its behavioural pattern in an ethno- or geocentric direction.

Obviously situations (3) and (4) are the most interesting ones. In situation (3) an appreciable number of decisions affecting labour in the subsidiaries of the corporation are taken in an ethno- or possibly geocentric headquarters. These may include company guidelines on personnel and industrial relations policies. Local unions may be accepted partners of management in the subsidiaries but are unable to influence directly headquarters decisions affecting labour. Situation (3) is therefore an asymmetrical industrial relations situation which tends to a new convergence of decision levels. In practical terms this may mean that unions are induced to apply countervailing strategies, such as co-ordinated bargaining and to press governments and international organisations to restrict the power of multi-national management so as to reach directly or indirectly the decision level of the company as a whole. Situation (3) represents a power vacuum on the side of the union which could constitute a 'passive provocation'[1] for foreign unions. They may, particularly in developing countries, be induced to sponsor the creation of outward-oriented enclave unions modelled on foreign patterns.

Through different means of union action, situation (3) should tend to develop into bilateral transnational industrial relations (situation (4)). Such relations would naturally not eliminate conflict but would provide a machinery to solve conflict which is compatible with the decision-making structure of the multi-national corporation. International collective bargaining with multi-national companies and related informal processes which are characteristic for situation (4) could therefore be seen as 'social innovations' in Fürstenberg's sense.

The box model – which isolates somewhat artificially labour relations from their broader context – needs to be supplemented by a review of environmental factors that may favour the development of transnational industrial relations. Jacques Houssiaux suggests[2] that environmental similarities in home and host countries of multi-national firms have the effect of promoting such relations. Expanding on this idea the following table lists tentatively a number of environmental factors which may be conducive to the development of bilateral transnational industrial relations. They are expected to either increase the capability of unions to develop their organisational power at the company level (i.e. throughout the whole of the company) or to increase the capability and willingness of management for negotiations at that level.

---

[1] Concept introduced by Inis L. Claude Jr. in 'Economic Development Aid and International Political Stability' published in *International Organisation: World Politics, Studies* in Economic and Social Agencies, Robert W. Cox (ed.) (London, Macmillan, 1969, pp. 49–58).

[2] See Chapter 16.

ENVIRONMENTAL FACTORS THAT MIGHT BE CONDUCIVE TO
TRANSNATIONAL INDUSTRIAL RELATIONS[1]

| | Affecting Multi-national management | Unions |
|---|:---:|:---:|
| Economic system | | |
| economic integration | x | |
| capital intensive production | x | |
| export orientation of multi-national firms | x | |
| type of their production | x | x |
| market economic features in host country's economy | x | |
| Political system | | |
| openness to foreign influences | x | x |
| liberalism | x | x |
| Social and cultural system | | |
| pluralist system | x | x |
| group-interest oriented unionism | | x |
| Western type oriented business culture | x | |
| Technological system | | |
| automation | x | |
| spread of production methods equalising productivity | x | |
| Legal system | | |
| international labour standards | x | x |
| international principles guiding behaviour of: | | |
| multi-national firms and State | | x |
| multi-national firms and labour | x | x |
| National industrial relations system[2] | | |
| workers' participation in management | x | x |
| free collective bargaining principle | x | x |

[1] For a complete analysis this list of favourable factors would have to be supplemented by a check list of possible adverse factors.
[2] The items listed are features of the 'specific environment' of transnational industrial relations. Industrial relations at other levels are counted here as environment.

The environmental compatibility with transnational labour relations increases with the number of marks which the valuation of a given present or future situation permits us to make in this list (leaving the relative weight of the different hypotheses aside for the moment).

Reasons for the inclusion of some of the less evident hypotheses are the following: capital intensive production and automation reduce the importance of labour cost in cost per unit of production and may there-

fore positively affect the capacity of multi-national firms to accommodate various union claims on a company level; export orientation of
firms may free them from constraints in the host or home country
thus improving their international bargaining capacity; prevalence of
market economic features correlates with management autonomy at
the plant level (the economic reforms in Eastern European countries are
a case in point); adoption of the principle of collective bargaining and
of workers' participation in management may increase the relevance of
transnational industrial relations for management and unions.[1]

## EVIDENCE OF TRANSNATIONAL TENDENCIES

This subsection reviews present positions and likely future attitudes
towards transnational industrial relations of the four actors of
importance in the circumstances: multi-national management, unions,
State and international organisations. Finally, the evidence is briefly
compared with the tentative analytical concepts suggested above.

*Multi-national Management*

Generally speaking, multi-national management conceives of
transnational industrial relations involving unions, and particularly of
formal international collective bargaining, as a misconception.
Bargaining internationally with unions necessarily means that some
sort of joint decision-making not only has to be applied for work
rules and their application but also for company decisions outside
the realm of a narrow concept of industrial relations, such as company
policies on investment, plant location, profits and applied technology.
The refusing of international bargaining by multi-national management is not merely a defence of traditional prerogatives but it is
seen as essentially safeguarding indispensable functional prerequisites
to worldwide operations.[2]

---

[1] Possibly, the existence of participation in management at the level of a subsidiary
might prevent unions from pressing for transnational labour relations. This should
not be expected to be the general feature, however, as many decisions of interest to labour,
especially on investment, will always be made ultimately at headquarters of the parent
company.

[2] It is mainly in this sense that former General Motors Chairman, Alfred P. Sloane
speaks proudly of his successful defence of management prerogatives (see: *My Years
with General Motors*, Pan Books, London, 1967, chapter 21: Personnel and Labour
Relations).

Management, perhaps under the influence of recent business literature and modern business school education, increasingly recognises the need for a certain standardisation of basic industrial relations principles which are usually unilaterally established by the company in the form of central personnel guidelines. They may cover, for instance, principles of co-operation with local unions, staff information, grievance procedures, career and training policies (especially for the internationally mobile upper white-collar level) and similar issues. Company guidelines may be made mainly in the interest of the operations and image of the company, but they also facilitate staff transfers and may contribute to a company-wide loyalty of employees. On the other hand, decisions on issues related to the labour market, such as wages and hours of work, are thought to have to be necessarily linked to prevailing local conditions, even though it is possible that similar productivity levels may prevail in all of the company's subsidiaries.

At the same time, the further development of national labour legislation and of local industrial relations systems (promoted in developing countries by the I.L.O.) should entail the growing application by the corporation of detailed local standards. However, both tendencies are probably more complementary than competitive. Their co-existence would mean a certain growth of transnational decisions by the corporation but also a reduction of the scope for individual policies and actual pattern-setting by multi-national management.[1]

The view is widespread among practitioners of multi-national management[2] that bargaining with unions for the whole company is not among the issues requiring particular attention in the years to come. The review of contemporary problems affecting the multi-national corporation at the XXII Congress of the International Chamber of Commerce[3] is significant for this state of affairs: relations with labour both at the national and international level were largely bypassed by the Congress.

Management views are the result of a seemingly clear assessment of cost and benefits: negotiations with unions for the whole company do not yield much benefit, if any; refusing the claims of unions for such

---

[1] Although this latter capacity may remain great for some time in the remoter parts of the Third World.

[2] This impression has been gained during the Symposium on International Collective Bargaining as well as from interviews which the author conducted with a number of employer delegates and observers at the 54th Session of the International Labour Conference.

[3] Istanbul, 31 May–7 June 1969. The theme of the Congress was 'World Economic Growth, the Role, Rights and Responsibilities of the International Corporation'.

negotiations does not entail much cost, as their means of international action are judged rather inefficient. Thus, enjoying on the whole a strong power position, multi-national management is determined to defend its positions. But this determination is not in reality as firm as dogmatic statements of principle may lead one to believe. Experience proves that, where the cost/benefit analysis favours them, concessions will be made in the future, even without an open struggle.

One case in point is the 1967 Chrysler/U.A.W. agreement. The high level of economic integration in North America and similar productivity levels in the United States and Canadian Chrysler plants accounted for a relatively low cost impact of concessions. The evasion of a likely harmful strike movement by the powerful bi-national U.A.W. in the case of a Chrysler refusal weighed much on the benefit side of management appraisal. Similarly, repeated talks between Philips and the International Metalworkers Federation which may result in an eventual agreement on some limited trade union participation in headquarters decisions, should not be too costly to a firm working in the fairly integrated European Common Market. In addition, the idea of workers' participation is a relevant concept to present-day European managerial ideology, both as reflection of national practices and of discussions on the statute of the European company.

The power and relevance constellation is completely different as soon as corporations with worldwide operations are involved. Obviously the cost to multi-national management of ceding to co-ordinated union pressure is here much higher in terms of impaired autonomy of resource allocation. At the same time, the resistance to pressures of unions, being apparently at pains to co-ordinate worldwide strategies, has high chances of success. The successful application of co-ordinated union strategies in the St Gobain case is usually viewed by management as an exceptional event and does not seem to put in question therefore the general validity of its position.

*Trade Unions*

The transnational decision-making power of multi-national corporations is decried by union spokesmen as an intolerable threat to labour. The Resolution on Multi-national Corporations and Conglomerates adopted by the Ninth World Congress of the I.C.F.T.U. (Brussels, July 1969) spells out this concern as follows: '. . . by concentrating vital economic and financial decisions at their international headquarters and establishing world-wide employment and industrial relations policies [multi-national corporations] may: undermine established industrial relations systems; restrict the right of the workers to organise in defence of their interests . . .; limit their right to enter into co-ordinated collective bargaining at whatever level is appropriate, exploit international labour cost differentials in order to boost profits'.[1]

The unions' target is limitation of the discretionary unilateral decision-making of central multi-national management on matters of prime interest to labour. Four main lines of strategy are applied towards this end: (1) direct use of unions' organisational power and related action co-ordinated by international federations; (2) instrumental use of the State or (3) of international organisations; and (4) influencing of public opinion by destroying a positive image of a corporation. Methods 2 through 4 reflect recognised limitations in unions' organisational power at the level of the whole corporation, but also historic alliances in Western industrialised countries with the public powers.

The main weakness of international unions is that they do not constitute a single worldwide decision system. They cannot command or co-ordinate action in the same integrated way as central headquarters of multi-national firms deals with its subsidiaries. National unions differ in strength and unity and play different roles in different societies. They therefore have different attitudes regarding international actions, national or sectoral priority concerns. Some unions may ally with multi-national corporations to the detriment of over-all international goals. In addition, national divergencies of labour law and practices are a considerable handicap to common strategies.

International unions therefore have the difficult task of inventing countervailing strategies within considerable constraints. Charles Levinson[2] sees two types of possible union action: (1) bargaining support of international federations to national unions mainly in the form of information and expert appraisal of a company's economic position, and (2) co-ordinated action, subdivided in (i) discussion by international unions with multi-national management on behalf of members employed in the corporation and (ii) co-ordination of claims addressed to the subsidiaries and co-ordinated direct action, including strikes. Bargaining support by international federations, already

---

[1] I.C.F.T.U.: *Economic and Social Bulletin,* Vol. XVII, 104, July–August, 1969, p. 16.
[2] See account of discussion (Section 8).

widely requested and supplied, is likely to increase in future in step with enhanced competence of the federations. It is not a strategy, however, which aims directly at bilaterial transnational relations.

The immobility of management positions makes, in Charles Levinson's opinion, co-ordinated direct action, focusing on well-identified points of vulnerability of multi-national corporations, the major breakthrough in union response. Protecting labour from unilateral company decisions confers, in his view, on the union movement a new legitimacy and the basis for a modern ideology.[1]

The successful co-ordination in 1969 of national union claims by the International Federation of Chemical and General Workers' Unions (I.C.F.) against the French-based multi-national glass manufacturer, St Gobain, is frequently considered a model for future action. Its main features may therefore be recalled. Under the auspices of I.C.F. a co-ordination committee was set up involving union leaders in the twelve countries in which St Gobain subsidiaries operate. The union representatives decided that no national union would sign an agreement with a subsidiary without permission of the Committee. Furthermore, they agreed upon mutual information and assistance in case of conflict with one of the subsidiaries in two ways: (1) through the support from a mutual strike fund, and (2) through the refusal to work overtime in subsidiaries not on strike to prevent the corporation from compensating production losses due to a labour conflict. Strikes were organised in the United States and Italian subsidiaries and with the threat of further co-ordinated action in mind, management accepted both union demands.[2]

How do unionists in general view needs, means and chances of different types of action against the multi-national firm? Incomplete evidence suggests that opinions are somewhat divided. By and large the following situation seems to emerge:

Not all international (let alone national) union organisations consider direct action against multi-national corporations their present priority concern or within their short-term capabilities. Some international trade secretariats (I.T.S.'s), especially those for the chemical and metal trades, lead the movement of direct action and consider themselves the natural counterpart to the multi-national corporation. The I.C.F.T.U.

---

[1] See 'L'une des plus puissantes fedérations internationales vise la conclusion des contrats collectifs mondiaux', Tribune-Travail, supplement to the *Tribune de Genève*, No. 98, 28 April 1969.
[2] Despite losses in the United States subsidiary in 1967 and 1968; the union argued that the corporation had the capacity to pay in view of its profits in the consolidated accounts.

secretariat, less equipped for direct action, sees its main task in mobilising international organisations and public opinion, and so does the European Federation of Free Trade Unions in the Community (E.C.F.T.U.C.) in the European Common Market. In many respects, unions are still in an evaluation phase regarding the exact impact of the multi-national corporation on labour conditions and relations. A comprehensive survey of industrial relations practices of multi-national firms carried out in 1970 by the I.C.F.T.U.[1] and the establishment of current data banks by several I.T.S.s supports this view. Their results would provide indications for conceiving appropriate union strategies. Many union practitioners seem prepared to explore action possibilities that avoid open confrontations, such as bargaining assistance to local unions and discussion with multi-national management especially on the scope of an economic integrated region.

Unionists should not expect internationally co-ordinated direct action against worldwide multi-national corporations to become soon the regular pattern of transnational industrial relations. The forging of a practical international solidarity of workers around a multi-national corporation is a far cry from the nineteenth-century class solidarity; it needs a gradual building up of positions and the education of workers to see their long-term rather than their short-term interests. For the immediate future large-scale strike action or overtime refusal by workers in developed countries in support of workers in developing countries is difficult to imagine, let alone the reverse situation. The St Gobain affair seems to be a special case for several reasons: (i) Direct action was carried through by two well-organised unions (United States, Italy) of the same group-interest orientated type more characteristic for developed societies. (ii) Strike action was related to direct short-term interests (wage increases) of both unions on strike. (iii) The practical solidarity of the unions in the remaining countries in which the corporation operates were not put to a test, as St Gobain gave in to the wage claims. (iv) The welfare issue inherent in a global strategy was not raised. (For example, should workers in developing countries use their organisational power to support wage increases of workers in developed countries and thereby widen the incomes gap and possibly endanger their employment prospects?)

Essentially, in view of their limited immediate possibilities to

[1] See: I.C.F.T.U.: *Economic and Social Bulletin*, Vol. XVIII, No. 3, May–June 1970, p. 16.

confront management directly, unions are for the moment likely to increase pressures on States, regional and international organisations to regulate the behaviour of multi-national corporations.

At the same time unions can be expected to continue to strive towards their basic, and possibly long-term, goal which is access to decision-making at the level of the entire corporation. Unions wish to confront the multi-national corporation as a whole because their main concern is job security and not claims for better wages or labour conditions which could be satisfied at the level of the subsidiaries. Trade unions are haunted by the seemingly discretionary power of multi-national headquarters to shift production facilities from one country to another under the pressure of union claims (but also for other reasons) and thereby endanger present employment. Trade union experts attending a 1969 O.E.C.D. meeting[1] had to admit that there was so far no evidence that corporations had actually closed down plants and transferred their activity to some other country as a reaction to trade union demand. Technological and geographical factors, but also government interference, appear to be the main constraints that reduce the international mobility of corporations, although social responsibility of management may be an additional reason. Nevertheless, international mobility of multi-national corporations as regards location of *new* investments remains a major preoccupation of unions. Workers' participation in the management of subsidiaries would not usually reduce this preoccupation as production shifts and new investments are generally decided at the company level. In the interest of over-all strategies, unions will, therefore, feel compelled to strive for a participation in central headquarters' decisions.

### The State

Growing involvement of the State in national industrial relations is a trend that has been forecast by experts, for developing as well as for industrial societies.[2] Will it be the same for the emerging transnational industrial relations? Goals and perspectives of development plans depend often on the performance of a small number of multi-national undertakings operating in key industries, particularly in the less-developed world. Transnational decisions by management on invest-

---

[1] See *Report on the Meeting of Trade Union Experts on Multi-national Companies*, Paris, 19–21 November 1969, O.E.C.D. Manpower and Social Affairs Directorate.

[2] For instance by Jean-Daniel Reynaud for Western Europe, see 'The Future of Industrial Relations in Western Europe: Approaches and Perspectives', *I.I.L.S. Bulletin* No. 4, February 1968, pp. 86–115.

ments, employment, profit transfers, as well as on industrial relations issues proper, should meet with State opposition where they run counter to the target of the plan. For the same reasons State interference is to be expected where, for instance, co-ordinated union action against a company tends to endanger incomes policy objectives. Generally speaking, therefore, the points of friction in transnational industrial relations are the same as with national industrial relations. With the spread of planning techniques and the goal consciousness of governments, these points of friction might possibly increase. Theoretically, the State should ally either with one side or the other depending on its overriding interest. In the past, priority given to economic objectives over social objectives may have favoured alliances with the corporation in a number of developing countries. Today the State is expected to safeguard against the multi-national corporation, all societal interests which are embraced in the complex and elusive concept of 'public interest'.[1] It is sometimes thought that small or developing countries may find it compelling to join together for imposing on the multi-national corporation the due observance of the public interest (whatever specific form this may take for them). However, it would seem that for the moment, primarily unions[2] and also multi-national business itself express interest in a demarcation of the rights and responsibilities of corporations and States.

Jeffrey Harrod argues in a recent article[3] that the activities of multi-national corporations will further increase the tensions and conflict of plural societies in developing countries mainly by enlarging the gap between the imitative culture in the modern sector and the dominant domestic culture. This could lead to popular opposition or organised opposition by local employers, and possibly parts of local labour with consequences for the attitude of the State. Ultimately, the growth prospects at least of the traditional (ethnocentric) multi-national corporation would be endangered. Higher cultural relativity on the part of multi-national management (which several participants in the

---

[1] The question of what fields the State should concretely defend held a prominent place in a round table discussion on the 'Future Relations between the Multi-national Corporation and the Nation State' organised by the Société d'études et de documentation économiques, industrielles et sociales, Paris, in May 1970. (See 'Les Sociétés Multi-nationales imposeront-elles leur volonté aux pouvoirs publiques?', *Le Monde*, 12 May 1970, supplement, page II.)

[2] The trade union experts of the O.E.C.D. meeting, *op. cit.*, thought that national unions would have to urge governments to request an international 'code of conduct' for multi-national corporations.

[3] Jeffrey Harrod, 'Non-governmental Organisations and the Third World', *The Year Book of World Affairs, 1970*, Vol. 24, pp. 171–85.

1969 Symposium seemed to consider as a contemporary trend) and the erosion of traditional values in the course of economic and social development, might reduce conflict potential. But there is little doubt that in several parts of the world (e.g. some Latin American countries) multi-national corporations, for reasons of politics and culture, operate on fragile foundations. The vision of a worldwide corporation which, by virtue of its competence and indispensability, transcends cultures and ideologies is unlikely to materialise in the foreseeable future. On the other hand, the strength of the forces of opposition might be easily overrated if the world as a whole is taken together. At any rate, opposition against the foreign-based corporation does not discredit the organisational form of the multi-national corporation. The proposals of Marcos Kaplan[1] for a public multi-national corporation for Latin America suggest a possible use of this organisational form in the interest of regional nationalism. In whatever form cultural relativity is expressed in the possible future types of multi-national corporations, these corporations should open avenues to a transnationalisation of industrial relations by virtue of the unavoidable creation of a central decision locus for issues of interest to labour.

*International Organisations*

Largely at the instigation of unions, international and regional organisations are becoming increasingly interested in the labour aspects of the operations of the multi-national corporation. The most concrete discussions are taking place within the E.E.C. regarding the participation of workers in the management of the European Company. The E.E.C. provides the platform on which the specified claims of unions[2] can be discussed with delegates of European management and acts as a catalyst in accommodation processes. Union demands on international organisations are usually less specific. For instance, the 1969 meeting of Trade Union Experts on Multi-national Companies, held under the auspices of the O.E.C.D., requested that multi-national

---

[1] See Chapter 9.

[2] In a consultation with the Commission of the Communities on 14 April 1970, the E.C.F.T.U.C. requested, for instance, provisions in the European Company Statute for a permanent representation of the interest of all workers through a central company council composed of worker representatives elected in all subsidiaries. The Federation claims for this council the right to discuss with management decisions on investments, changes in the production line, reorganisations, closing and removal of plants, mergers, distribution of profits and recruitment and dismissals of senior personnel. (E.C.F.T.U.C. Press Release No. 80, dated 15 April 1970.)

companies should be internationally obliged (through the medium of O.E.C.D., I.L.O. and World Bank) to observe certain minimum conditions as regards implications of their investment policies, applied technology and profit-transfers for welfare in the host countries. The I.C.F.T.U. Resolution already referred to above urges the International Labour Organisation '. . . to act swiftly on the request of the I.C.F.T.U. and the International Trade Secretariats to examine the social and economic problems engendered by the growing power of the multi-national corporations and the problems arising in international industrial relations'.[1] Several resolutions originating within the International Labour Organisation likewise request study of the problems raised by multi-national corporations.[2] While the Resolutions make no mention of international labour standards for multi-national corporations these are a possible ultimate goal of unions.

As any type of viable international agreement or model code depends upon co-operation of multi-national management, its future attitude is decisive. The basis for management co-operation is apparently getting stronger for a possible international regulation of relations between corporations and the State. Both parties have the power of countervailing each other in various respects and feel increasingly the need for mutual accommodation. The intent of the International Chamber of Commerce: '. . . to give continuing consideration to a possible formulation of agreed principles governing the conduct both of international corporations and of government'[3] illustrates the willingness of multi-national management to enter into a dialogue with the State. Trade unions would benefit indirectly from such regulations as companies would have to give more consideration to national investment, employment and incomes policies. Unions would be directly engaged in the formulation and application of such principles where they take a part in the preparation of national economic decisions.

Multi-national employers are not keen, however, to see special labour standards developed for them, basing their arguments on the grounds that uniform solutions are not appropriate for companies that have increasingly to reconcile functional requirements of worldwide profit-oriented operations with a variety of social and economic objectives

[1] *Op. cit.*, p. 17.
[2] e.g. Resolution No. 69 adopted by the Eighth Session of the Metal Trades Committee (December 1965), a resolution submitted by a number of workers' delegates to the 1968 International Labour Conference and a resolution adopted by that Conference in 1971.
[3] Statement of Conclusions of the Istanbul Meeting referred to earlier.

in the host countries. As trade unions have few concessions to offer on a world scale, a reconciliation of positions by 'splitting the difference' (as in the case of the corporation and the State) is not a present possibility. It remains to be seen whether international organisations can eventually promote accommodation through 'upgrading the common interest'.[1] The International Labour Organisation in view of its field of responsibility and tripartite structure appears destined to play a role in this area.[2] The further promotion by the I.L.O. of international labour standards, with the Freedom of Association Convention (No. 87) and the Right to Organise and Collective Bargaining Convention (No. 98) as centrepieces, may also help create environmental conditions conducive to a transnationalising of industrial relations.

## EVIDENCE AND PROPOSED ANALYTICAL CONCEPTS COMPARED

Unilateral transnational industrial relations corresponding to situation (3) of the box model proposed in the first subsection seem to be the most typical actual relationship between multi-national management and labour. In this situation, company headquarters take an appreciable number of decisions that affect labour in the subsidiaries in different countries. Unions, on the other hand, are nationally organised and their action can merely affect management in the subsidiaries. At least in the shorter run, multi-national management usually seems to be in a position to maintain this state of affairs. But in the longer run the evidence shows that there are forces at work which tend to push industrial relations of this type in the direction of the theoretically

---

[1] To use concepts proposed by Ernst B. Haas. Haas distinguishes three types of conflict resolution within the framework of international organisations: (1) accommodation at the level of a minimum common denominator (non-existent in the circumstances); (2) splitting the difference; and (3) upgrading the common interest of the parties, i.e. achieving an agreement in order to promote a goal of higher value. Such a goal of higher value could, for instance, be seen in the free collective bargaining principle. (See: *Beyond the Nation State*, Functionalism and International Organisation, Stanford, California, 1964, p. 111.)

[2] The I.L.O. long-term programme proposals 1972–7 include under its industrial activities (grouping the work of the Industrial Committees) studies impinging on these aspects. Especially mentioned are the automobile industry, the electric and electronic industry and the chemical industry, all characterised by high growth rates of multi-national business and many international mergers. Further attempts to influence within the I.L.O. context the behaviour of multi-national corporations might in part flow from the Industrial Committees' work.

more stable situation (4) of the box model which conforms with the earlier made hypotheses. In the international industrial relations system, the following observed trends may support such an evolution:

– Development of trade union structures (especially by the I.T.S.s) for negotiations with multi-national management both of a regional and an international scope (co-ordination committees, company councils, etc.).
– Development of countervailing strategies by unions, such as co-ordinated direct actions against a company.
– Action by regional and international organisations.
– Continuing institutionalisation of workers' and employers' co-operation and participation in regional economic and social policies.
– Creation of regional multi-national companies with region-wide union participation in industrial relations and selected managerial issues (e.g. through the European Company Statute).

Furthermore, a number of tendencies in the national industrial relations system and in the economic system should contribute to a gradual emergence of many of the environmental factors which were selected in subsection 1 as favouring transnational industrial relations. They include the following observed developments:

*National Industrial Relations System*

– Growth of group-interest oriented unionism in developing countries as a result of: (i) the process of role differentiation and value changes in the course of modernisation; (ii) creation of group-interest oriented unions under the influence of foreign-based unions; (iii) industrialisation.
– Trend towards greater authority of top national union organisations, and the corollary advance of plant bargaining, anticipating the concept of company-wide bargaining.
– Growing adoption of the idea of workers' participation in management for issues affecting labour (investment, employment, profit-sharing), formerly regarded as managerial prerogatives.
– Growing (possibly State imposed) stability in industrial relations in the interest of national planning goals.
– Informal co-ordination of national union demands by the 'demonstration effect'.

*Economic System*

– Trend towards productivity equalisation throughout the corporation as a result of a uniform application of modern production methods.
– Increasing interest in co-operation and stabilisation of labour employed in the multi-national corporation as a result of growing interdependence of subsidiaries and high investment in training.
– Equalisation of economic and social differentials in regionally integrated areas creating similar conditions of resource allocations to multi-national management.
– Adoption of principles regulating mutual behaviour of corporations and States reducing possibilities of production shifts by corporations and increasing thereby their willingness to accept accommodations with labour.[1]

These and concurrent trends in other systems should influence management behaviour by affecting either its willingness or its capacity to accommodate union demands for the whole corporation, and also increase the ability of unions for internationally co-ordinated action. Some of them are more relevant in the context of developed countries, others in that of developing countries. The strength and incidence of the individual trends and their exact inter-relationships need to be assessed by further study.

Taking the proposed concepts and the above list of trends as a tentative basis for prediction, it might be assumed that transnational industrial relations are likely to emerge and grow in future in developed Western societies, foremost in regions with a high level of economic integration. Conditions in certain developing countries, at least in some sectors of their economy, might likewise become propitious for the growth of transnational industrial relations especially where these countries evolve along models of Western developed societies. On the other hand, despite the recent economic reforms, it appears unlikely, because of constraints in the political environment in most socialist countries, that in the next years a trend towards industrial relations will develop that would bind together unions and management in East and West.

---

[1] Might also be classified under the legal system.

## FUTURE RESEARCH REQUIREMENTS

The preliminary analysis of the phenomenon of and the setting for transnational industrial relations presented in this section is in the author's opinion a step in a direction which has potential for more sophisticated future research. Future research would need to develop the rudimentary tools applied into a full analysis of the dynamics of the industrial relations system and of the influences from other systems which have a bearing on them. In essence, this would mean that the relationship between industrial relations actors, processes, results and the environmental factors of importance to them need to be systematically examined. Its main features would then need to be incorporated in explicative and predictive models suitable for various types of industrial relations situations. The diagram shown on page 445 is a schematic presentation of the relationships in questions.[1]

More precisely, the following stages of research appear to be required:[2] (1) data analysis to identify significant variables in the industrial relations system and in influencing systems;[3] (2) construction of typologies of industrial relations systems and situations (a device for classifying observed situations and for identifying types with transnationalisation potential); (3) linking of the various types of industrial relations situations with other relevant domestic and external situations (i.e. the detection of correlations and hopefully causal relationships, e.g. between bilateral transnational industrial relations and specific legal, economic, technological or political conditions); and finally (4) predictions of the future development of transnational industrial relations based upon several models of linked variables.

In order to broaden the basis for the identification of major relevant variables and their likely trends it would be highly desirable if more complete information on industrial relations practices of multinational firms in the different parts of the world could be obtained. The

[1] Adapted from a scheme of Canadian labour relations included in the Report of the Canadian Task Force on Labour Relations (*Canadian Industrial Relations*, Privy Council Office, Ottawa, December 1968, p. 10).

[2] Paraphrasing suggestions in an outline prepared by Robert W. Cox for future industrial relations research in the International Institute for Labour Studies.

[3] They may include in the industrial relations system such factors as size, structure and functions of national and international unions, strength and function of employers' organisations, type of industrial relations regulations by government, etc. Examples of possibly relevant variables in the influencing systems, such as regional economic integration or Western-type oriented business culture and others have been referred to as environmental factors or observed trends earlier in this section.

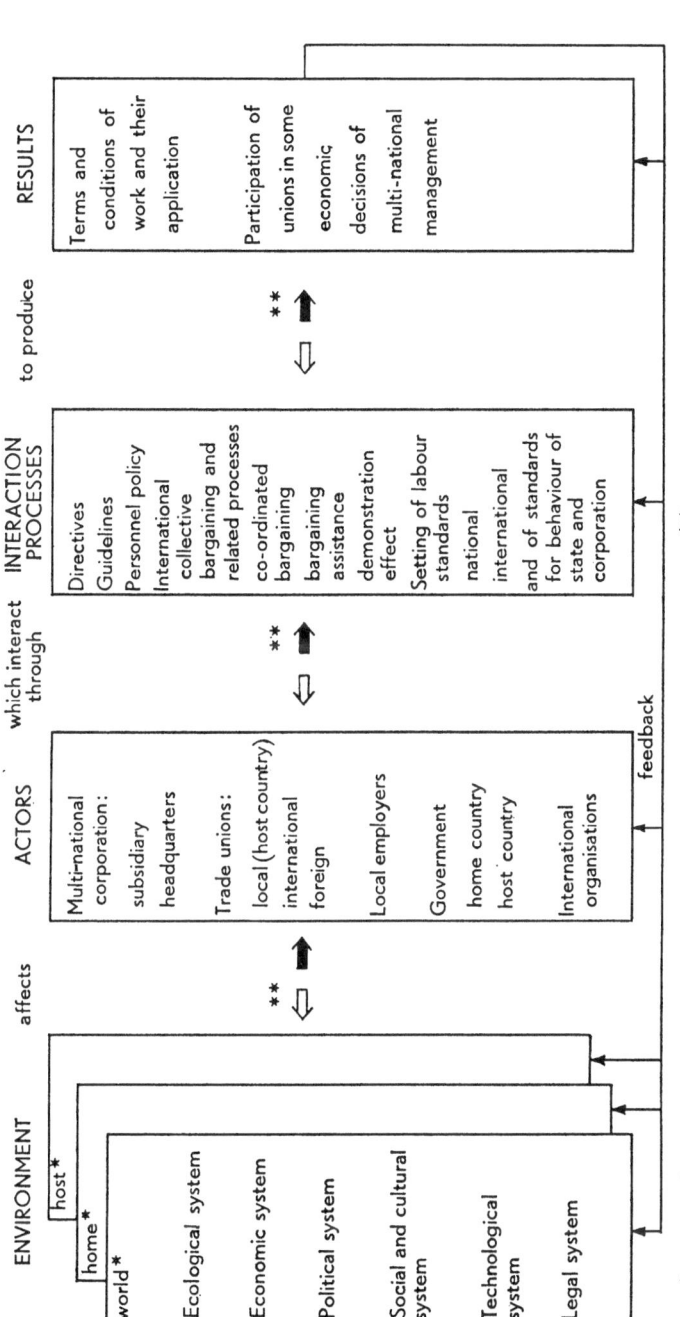

Transnational industrial relations: scheme of interactions

ENVIRONMENT    affects    ACTORS    which interact through    INTERACTION PROCESSES    to produce    RESULTS

ENVIRONMENT

host*
home*
world*

Ecological system

Economic system

Political system

Social and cultural system

Technological system

Legal system

ACTORS

Multi-national corporation:
subsidiary
headquarters

Trade unions:
local (host country)
international
foreign

Local employers

Government
home country
host country

International organisations

INTERACTION PROCESSES

Directives
Guidelines
Personnel policy
International collective bargaining and related processes
co-ordinated bargaining
bargaining assistance
demonstration effect
Setting of labour standards
national
international
and of standards for behaviour of state and corporation

RESULTS

Terms and conditions of work and their application

Participation of unions in some economic decisions of multi-national management

feedback

* As seen from the view of the multi-national corporation    ** Flow ⬆ and reverse flow ⬅ of influence

1969 Symposium on International Collective Bargaining has brought out the need for such information particularly with a view to the consequences which the operation of the multi-national corporation may entail for the orderly development of labour relations in less developed countries. A comprehensive worldwide survey drawing on the collaboration of multi-national management, unions and governments could help to gain a balanced view of such practices[1] and provide a body of comparable information of use for any further research.

[1] There are formidable problems of selecting both a representative and manageable sample of multi-national firms, unions and governments which are amplified by the problem of obtaining access to partly confidential information. Aspects to be covered in the survey would have to include: locus of decision-making in corporations regarding the whole range of issues affecting labour; existence, nature and application of company guidelines for personnel policy; relations between multi-national management and other industrial relations actors: unions (local and international), national employers associations, state; conditions of work in multi-national firms as compared to national firms, training facilities, dispute pattern, etc.

# Appendix

## MULTI-NATIONAL CORPORATIONS: A SELECTED AND ANNOTATED BIBLIOGRAPHY

AITKEN, THOMAS. *A foreign policy for American business.* New York, Harper and Row, 1962, 159 p.

Overseas business seen as an extension of American foreign policy. Treats the problems of operating a business in an industrialised country as well as in the developing, industrialising country.

BALASSA, BELA. 'American direct investments in the Common Market', *Banca Nazionale dell Lavoro. Quarterly review* (77), June 1966, pp. 121–146.

Although American subsidiaries will have a comparative advantage in manufacturing in the E.E.C. for some time, legal means for establishing a 'European-type' company and other legislative action can reduce this lead. Suggests some American methods which might profitably be employed by European firms.

BALL, GEORGE W. 'Cosmocorp: the importance of being stateless', *Atlantic Community quarterly*, 6(2), Summer 1968, pp. 163–170.

Poses the question of the 'legitimacy of power' raised by the *de facto* national identity of the multi-national corporation which renders host nations legally unable to influence corporate policy. Specific proposal for the establishment of a supranational regulatory body created by treaty is discussed.

BALL, GEORGE W. 'Multinational corporations and nation states', *Atlantic Community quarterly*, 5(2), Summer 1967, pp. 247–253.

Characterises the multi-national corporation as an advancement over the system of nation states which is out of step with modern needs and economic requirements. Corporations and nations will have to develop a system to resolve serious legal problems. Belief expressed that a danger exists in the inequity of development of North–South trade.

BAROVICK, RICHARD L. 'Labour reacts to multinationalism', *Columbia journal of world business,* 5(4), July–Aug. 1970, pp. 40–46.

Growing international structures will greatly increase the synchronisation of union policies and demands on a world scale. A critical factor is the problem of solidarity of national unions.

BEHRMAN, JACK N. *Some patterns in the rise of the multinational enterprise.* Chapel

Hill, 1969, xv, 180 p. (University of North Carolina. Graduate School of Business Administration. Research paper, 18.)

Basic data on investment and original research on the organisation of firms are used in an attempt to distinguish the characteristics that separate the multi-national enterprise from others.

BETTE, A. 'Possibilités d'avenir des entreprises communes', *Revue du Marché commun* (92), June 1966, pp. 587–596.

Defines the concept of an E.E.C. corporation and its possible role. Analyses the existing law of the E.E.C. in this respect and the possible results of its application.

BORRMANN, WERNER A. 'The problem of expatriate personnel and their selection in international enterprises', *Management international*, 8(45), 1968, pp. 37–48.

Studies expatriates in American and German corporations in order to determine what factors are utilised to define the optimum choice of employees to be sent abroad. Several factors are examined, employment requirements are indicated and examples are drawn from current practice.

BRANNEN, TED R.; HODGSON, F. X. *Overseas management.* New York, McGraw-Hill, 1965, 231 p.

Recognises the inconsistency between local custom and habits with those necessary for efficient industrial co-ordination. Examines the relationship between overseas managers from industrial nations who must work in harmony with people from developing countries. Discusses the necessity of industrial managers to adjust to cultural differences.

BROEHL, WAYNE G. *The international basic economy corporation.* Washington, National Planning Association, 1968, 314 p.

Description of a Rockefeller group enterprise which aims at improvement of economic standards in developing countries while achieving profits for the company; indicates that results have so far been limited in both areas. Suggested factors for this uneven performance are advanced, e.g., economic nationalism and resistance to American marketing methods.

BROES, ERNEST. 'La dimension des entreprises', *Revue du Marché commun* (99), Feb. 1967, pp. 85–91.

Discusses the formation of European corporations, their characteristics and possible problems that such enterprises will face.

BROOKS, T. R. 'Labor relations abroad', *Dun's review and modern industry*, 86, Nov. 1965, pp. 75–76.

Analyses conflicting points of view regarding methods of handling labour relations on international scale, e.g. centralisation of policy versus flexibility in local situations. Examples of strong and weak points of both positions are given, as well as specific discussion of varying labour practices in Europe.

BUGNION, JEAN ROBERT. *La politique d'investissement et de financement des entre-*

*prises internationales.* Genève, Ed. Médecine et Hygiène, 1967, 314 p. (University of Geneva – Thesis.)

The study is centred on the definition of a budgetary procedure which permits an international undertaking to obtain the maximum net profit. The general problems of management are also treated, particularly financial management.

BUTLER, W. J.; DEARDEN, J. 'Managing a world-wide business', *Harvard business review*, 43(3), May–June 1965, pp. 93–102.

Examination of principal managerial problems (and their significance) facing international companies in an effort to meet competition from overseas. Presents several hypotheses on the conditions in business not related to any particular industry or nationality which could be used as guidelines to increase returns or investment.

CASIMIR-LAMBERT, P. *The development of European enterprises.* Geneva, 1968. 101 1. (Graduate Institute of International Studies – Mémoire.)

Reviews current European situation for development of European corporations. Suggests improvements and developments in creating a common legal framework, harmonising tax laws and integrating capital markets.

CASSERINI, KARL. 'L'internationalisation de la production et les syndicats', *Revue économique et sociale*, 24(3), July 1967, pp. 189–202.

Describes the process of internationalisation of resources and the centralisation of decisions in the multi-national corporations. Suggests the actions and attitudes that should be taken by the unions in the face of this new development.

CHARTIER, FRÉDÉRIC. 'Vers la société de type européen', *Revue du Marché commun* (102), May 1967, pp. 310–316.

Summary of resolutions adopted by an international Congress in 1967 which studied European corporation. Describes legal conditions necessary for official designation of European corporation, the problems of European social law, legal personality and common interpretations of the relevant law.

CLEE, GILBERT H. 'Guidelines for global business', *Columbia journal of world business*, 1(1), Winter 1966, pp. 97–104.

Reviews the history and impact of the multi-national corporation and presents a three-stage plan for the development of a multi-corporation. Considers the problem of long-range versus short-range planning.

CLEE, GILBERT H.; SACHTJEN, WILBUR M. 'Organizing a world-wide business', *Harvard business review*, 42(6), Nov.–Dec. 1964, pp. 55–67.

Examines structural pattern of world-wide business as subject to variation and modification – international division, geographic and product structure – citing examples. Discusses the advantages and problems for management of these organisational patterns.

## Appendix

*Collective bargaining and the metal workers.* Geneva, International Metalworkers' Federation, 1964, 88 p.

Trade union manual on collective bargaining. It is recognised that multinational firms and the E.E.C. raise the possibility of regional and global units of employers. Trade unions, particularly automotive workers, are preparing for bargaining with these firms.

CORNUELLE, HERBERT C. 'Le défi du monde', *Industrie*, 22(11), Nov. 1968, pp. 678–685.

Describes through the example of the canning industry, the characteristics and activities of some of the multi-national corporations. Also the national, legal, political and commercial framework which enable these undertakings to operate successfully.

COX, ROBERT W. 'Labor and the transnational society', *International organization*, 25(4), Autumn 1971.

Regional economic organisation and the emergence of multi-national corporations have tended to change the pattern of labour relations. The nature of these changes has varied according to the national, social and political context. Union policies, business attitudes, psychological and ideological factors and government policies have interacted, but the role of the nation still remains the critical factor.

DEMONTS, ROGER. 'La recherche dans la firme plurinationale et la propagation des techniques'. *In*: PERROUX, FRANÇOIS (ed.). *Recherche et activité économique.* Paris, A. Colin, 1969, pp. 389–411.

A description of some of the institutional and economic characteristics of the multi-national firm. The costs of research and technical know-how in developed and developing countries are compared.

DESMAISON, JEAN. 'The automobile industry: giant trusts and European deception', *World trade union movement* (1), Jan. 1969, pp. 16–18, 24.

The Fiat–Citroën merger is part of a series of mergers in the European automobile industry which cross national boundaries and create monopolies. Urges auto workers to move toward joint activity in bargaining and other areas on an international level to meet this new challenge.

*Developing management for the world-wide enterprise.* New York, Business International Corporation, 1965, 66 p.

Discusses the problem of finding managers to run both domestic and international operations and describes innovations in selection and training processes as well as long-range planning and appraisal techniques.

'Developments in industrial relations', *Monthly labor review*, 91(2), Feb. 1968, pp. 69–72.

United Auto Workers' settlement with General Motors containing agreements on wage parity for its Canadian members.

450

## Appendix

DIXON, D. A. 'A neglected aspect of the foreign ownership of wealth', *Economic record*, 44, Sept. 1968, pp. 349–356.

Foreign-owned international corporations tend to accumulate funds that are relatively free from host government redistributive policies. They thus receive preferential tax treatment vis-à-vis resident-owned corporations.

DONNER, FREDERICK G. *The world-wide industrial enterprise.* New York, McGraw-Hill, 1967, 114 p.

The growth of General Motors Corporation as a multi-national operation is described by its president, with special detail on various policy decisions made by the company to facilitate its expansion. Proposed changes in geographical distribution of shareholders are indicated.

DOWD, LAURENCE P. *Principles of world business.* Boston, Allyn and Bacon, 1965, 573 p.

Establishment of a multi-national business enterprise, written in detail for the management. Covers practical matters, as well as the theoretical bases for setting up such a firm and the managerial attitudes necessary for successful operation.

DRANCOURT, MICHEL. 'Enterprises transnationales contre étatisme industriel', *Entreprise* (706), Mar. 1969, pp. 124–125, 127, 129, 131, 134–139.

Examines growth and position of multi-national corporation and includes charts and list of corporations. Suggests reforms in management and staffing before multi-national corporation can maximise world welfare.

DUERR, MICHAEL G.; GREENE, JAMES. *Foreign nationals in international management: a survey.* New York, 1968, 50 p. (National Industrial Conference Board. Managing international business, 2.)

A general examination of corporate staffing policies for international management and a specific review of corporate policy concerning use of foreign nationals. Notes lack of local talent and suggests means of developing foreign managerial expertise.

DUNNING, J. H. 'The multinational enterprise', *Lloyd's Bank review* (97), July 1970, pp. 19–36.

Describes the economic significance and impact of multi-national corporations, their growth and relations with domestic firms. Emphasises the differences in their behaviour and their effects on national economic welfare. Deals with the corresponding government policies and alternatives open to the companies.

ECONOMIST INTELLIGENCE UNIT, London. *The growth and spread of multinational companies.* London, 1969, 55 p.

Describes the responses to the multi-national corporation on national firms, developing countries and government policies. Includes some national case studies and sketches, some broad lines for future development.

EL SHERBINI, ABEL AZIZ. 'The quandry of foreign manufacturing affiliates in

Q                                        451

## Appendix

less-developed countries', *California management review*, 7(3), Spring 1965, pp. 7–14.

Foreign multi-national manufacturing affiliate faces problems such as profit sharing, selection of industrial site and fastening equities in utilisation of skilled local manpower from both the public and private sector of the host country.

EWING, JOHN S.; MEISSNER, FRANK. *International business management: readings and cases.* Belmont, Calif., Wadworth, 1964, 560 p.

Presents a broad background of international business, especially regional co-operation, economic development and international trade, as well as managerial and financial aspects.

FARMER, RICHARD N.; RICHMAN, B. M. *International business: an operational theory.* Homewood, Ill., R. Irwin, 1966, 314 p.

Sets forth a systematic basis for selection of sites for direct investment based on the various national and international constraints placed on a multi-national business. An evaluation scheme is proposed for studying the factors involved in the operation of a corporation.

FAYERWEATHER, JOHN. *The executive overseas: administrative attitudes and relationships in a foreign culture.* New York, Syracuse University Press, 1959, xi, 195 p.

Identifies the problem of the executive overseas as one of inherent cultural differences. Deals with the relationship between men in an organisation, the attitudes of the employee toward his job, and the motivation of the executive. Illustrates the points by an extensive study done on Mexican management.

FAYERWEATHER, JOHN. 'Long-range planning for international operations', *California management review*, 3(1), Fall 1960, pp. 23–35.

Advocates three ways by which international corporation can combat nationalism and competition, namely, utilising local managers, sharing financial benefits and internationalising top management.

FAYERWEATHER, JOHN. *Management of international operations.* New York, McGraw-Hill, 1960, 604 p.

Case studies illustrate problems faced by companies entering the field of international enterprise. Deals with human relations, marketing, community and labour relations, organisation, finance and operating policies.

FAYERWEATHER, JOHN. '19th century ideology and 20th century reality', *Columbia journal of world business*, 1(1), Winter 1966, pp. 77–84.

Examines the fundamental structure of multi-national corporation, the 'hard core' of conflict between the inherent concept of nationalism and the character of the multi-national corporation. Recognises the need for a 'political internationalism' which would reduce the tensions between the multi-national corporation and its base of operation.

## Appendix

FLIGER, CARLOS. *Multinational public enterprises.* Washington, International Bank for Reconstruction and Development, 1967, 145 p.

Reviews existing and proposed multi-national public enterprises. Indicates the role of the states in a joint action with regard to the establishment of the project, jurisdiction, nationality, organs, control, privileges and immunities, tax status, personnel, and special provisions. Discusses various methods for the settlement of disputes.

FOURAKER, L. E.; STOPFORD, J. M. 'Organizational structure and the multi-national strategy', *Administrative science quarterly*, 13, June 1968, pp. 47–64.

Studies the organisational structure of American-based foreign corporations, indicating that the most successful firms are those having previously developed general managers capable of handling diverse enterprises.

FOWLER, HENRY H. 'National interests and multinational business', *California management review*, 8, Fall 1965, pp. 3–12.

Views multi-national corporation as positive force with a strong role in building international interdependence but subject to increasing nationalism. Develops areas of potential conflict: balance of payments, conditions of entry and regulation, confiscation and state operation, transfers of production and employment.

GENEEN, HAROLD S. 'The human element in communications', *California management review*, 9(2), Winter 1966, pp. 3–8.

Presents the methods used at International Telephone and Telegraph Corporation to keep its management advised and involved in diverse operations.

'The Giant's Causeway', *The economist*, Dec. 27, 1969, pp. 10–11.

Suggests current economic trends point to increased manufacturing opportunities for developing countries via multi-national corporations.

GLOOR, MAX. 'Nestlé's multinational mode', *Management today*, Oct. 1968, pp. 82–93, 152–158.

Describes the main difference between Nestlé and the other international companies, i.e., that more than 97% of their turnover is achieved outside Switzerland.

HAIDER, MICHAEL L. 'Tomorrow's executive: a man for all countries', *Columbia journal of world business*, 1(1), Winter 1966, pp. 107–113.

With the increasing number of multi-national corporations, there is a need for international managers. Reviews the Standard Oil Company procedures with regard to its promotion policies.

HAIRE, MASON; GHISELLI, EDWIN E.; PORTER, LYMAN N. *Managerial thinking: an international study.* New York, J. Wiley, 1966, 298 p.

Survey of 3,641 managers in 14 countries reveals that managers tend to have similar orientations towards leadership and managerial motivation. The implications of these findings for the multi-national corporation on foreign

453

subsidiaries are discussed, particularly in the areas of management education and cultural bias.

'A hard-headed look at this European market place', *Business management*, 27 (1), Oct. 1964, pp. 58–61.

Suggests that American businessmen consider the joint venture with European firms as the most effective way to enter the European market.

HARROD, JEFFREY. 'Non-governmental organisations and the Third World'. *In: The year book of world affairs, 1970.* London, Stevens, 1970, pp. 170–181.

Critically examines claims that the multi-national corporations are international organisations and have a role to play in functional theory of international integration. Suggests their activities will further increase tensions and conflicts of plural societies in developing countries.

HAYDEN, SPENCER. 'Personnel problems in overseas operations', *Personnel*, 45 (3), May–June 1968, pp. 14–28.

Deals with the problems of multi-national corporations in recruiting foreign and local personnel. The issue of labour unions is raised with reference to labour mobility and its relevance to future collective bargaining especially in Europe.

HAYDEN, SPENCER. 'Problems of operating overseas: a survey of company experience', *Personnel*, 45 (1), Jan.-Feb. 1968, pp. 8–21.

Surveys leading multi-national companies on various aspects of a foreign-based corporation: personnel recruitment, finance, firm relations with parent, etc.

HELDRING, FREDERICK. 'Multinational banking strives for identity', *Columbia journal of world business*, 3 (6), Nov.-Dec. 1968, pp. 49–53.

Banking is one of the oldest multi-national institutions, and has lately experienced growth of a number of branches and affiliates all over the world. Discusses the problem the banks are facing, trying to serve the corporations and also maintaining their position in the host country.

HELLMANN, RAINER. *The challenge to U.S. dominance of the international corporation.* New York, Dunellen, 1970. xix, 348 p.

Analysis of American direct investment in 18 European countries and of the extent of European competition in the U.S.A. Examines these investments and their economic, financial and social implications. Presents the E.E.C.'s and governments' policy and their reactions to the growing influence of American multi-national corporations.

HOGHTON, CHARLES DE. *Cross-channel collaboration: a study of agreements between British and continental firms.* London, P.E.P., 1967, 63 p.

110 British firms with 'collaboration agreements' with one or more European firms were surveyed essentially on the 'organic, still evolving relationships between firms of different nationalities'. These joint arrangements of middle-sized firms which retained their basic character but co-operated on a tem-

## Appendix

porary or permanent basis, are seen as the forerunners of multi-national corporations which are yet to be viable, according to the author.

HOUSSIAUX, J. 'La grande entreprise plurinationale', *Economie appliquée*, 17(2–3), Apr.–Sept. 1964, pp. 403–440.

Defines the important traits of the large multi-national undertakings in order to emphasise the principles which regulate and govern their functioning and growth. Also considers the means by which these principles are effectively put into action. The International Telephone and Telegraph Corporation is used as an example.

HOWARD, C. G. 'The extent of nativization of management in overseas affiliates of multinational firms: a world-wide study', *Indian management* 10(1), Jan. 1971, pp. 11–20.

Results of a survey on employment and utilisation of local employees in managerial positions of multi-national corporations. Covers restrictive employment policy, legislation on immigrant managers and political implications.

HUNTER, A. 'The Indonesian oil industry', *Australian economic papers*, 5(1), June 1966, pp. 9–106.

An account of the development of the oil industry in Indonesia through the activities of major international oil corporations. Despite numerous concessions made by the companies, gradual takeover by the government appeared likely to end in nationalisation. Author suggests an intermediary plan which would ensure profit and development to both the companies and the nation.

HUYS, MARCEL. 'Vers la société européenne', *Industrie*, 21(12), Dec. 1967, pp. 707–717.

Describes the justification for the existence of a European corporation. Analyses their needs, the obstacles encountered, and the legal basis for such a corporation.

HYMER, STEPHEN. 'Direct foreign investment and the national economic interest.' *In:* RUSSELL, PETER (ed.). *Nationalism in Canada.* Toronto, McGraw-Hill, 1966, 11 p.

Argues against the presumption that direct investment is in the economic interest of Canada. The 'imperfect competition' of multi-national corporations tends to the self-sustaining. The companies do not decrease their share of the national market nor make the technological advances available to the host country. Advances policies to correct this situation.

HYMER, STEPHEN. 'La grande corporation multinationale', *Revue économique*, 19(6), Nov. 1968, pp. 949–973.

Examines the motives which impel an undertaking to become multi-national, together with the problems it encounters in the process.

INSTITUT DE SCIENCES ECONOMIQUES APPLIQUEES, Paris. 'Firmes plurinationales', *Economies et sociétés*, 2(9), Sept. 1968, pp. 1701–1867.

## Appendix

A collection of articles on the theme of 'large firms and small nations'. Includes political, financial and economic aspects of multi-national corporations in small countries, particularly small developing countries.

INTERNATIONAL CONFEDERATION OF FREE TRADE UNIONS. 'Multinational corporations and labour relations', *Economic and social bulletin*, 17(9), Mar.-Apr. 1969, pp. 1–8.
Examines the positive and negative aspects of the multi-national corporation. Specifies areas which need close observation or regulation and cites instances of international collective bargaining. Stresses the need for worldwide labour co-ordination in order to check possible abuse of power by the corporations.

'International direct investment by private enterprises in Western Europe and North America', *Economic bulletin for Europe*, 19, Nov. 1967, pp. 57–68.
Reports on the absolute and relative increase of direct investment, primarily American and British, during the period 1959 to 1966. Charts, graphs and comparative figures are included to indicate the size and proportion of this investment.

INTERNATIONAL METALWORKERS' FEDERATION. World Auto Conference, 6th, Turin, 1968. *Preparatory documents*. Geneva, 1968, 19 fasc.
Reports and papers on the world automobile industry. Includes general reports on growth of industry and wages, working conditions and trade union situation. Specific corporation reports covering history, expenditures, subsidiaries, sales and profits, etc., for G.M., Ford, Chrysler, Volkswagen, Daimler-Benz, Toyota, Nissan, Leyland, Fiat and Renault. Also regional reports on the industry in Western Europe, Eastern Europe, Latin America and the U.S.–Canadian Automotive Common Market.

JAGER, ELIZABETH. 'Multinationalism and labor: for whose benefit?' *Columbia journal of world business*, 5, Jan.-Feb. 1970, pp. 56–64.
Critically examines the economic theories underlying the justification of the multi-national corporation. Considers the phenomena in relation to labour and world welfare and especially position of labour in U.S.A. Suggests the overall benefit if the multi-national corporation is not proven.

JOHNSON, HARRY G. 'Directives à l'intention des gouvernements au sujet des sociétés multinationales', *Revue de la Société d'Etudes et d'Expansion*, (243), Nov.-Dec. 1970, pp. 888–894.
Governments are increasingly aware of the problems created by the growth of multi-national corporations, especially with regard to questions of their sovereignty, balance of payments and economic development in general. The author suggests a redefinition of the concept of sovereignty and codification of basic government policies towards multi-national corporations.

JOHNSON, SAMUEL C.; PARKS, NEWTON F.; RHODES, JOHN B. 'How common is the Common Market?', *Business horizons*, 6(4), Winter 1963, pp. 81–88.

Advances reasons for the retardation in the development of multi-national firms of European origin since the creation of the Common Market. Gives an example of the Johnson Wax Co.'s spread from England to the Continent as a successful multi-national undertaking.

JUDGE, ANTHONY. 'Multinational business enterprises as a new category of international organizations', *International associations*, 21(1), Jan. 1969, pp. 3–11.

Lists reasons why Union of International Associations now considers multi-national corporations as a category of international organisations although profit-making associations were previously excluded.

KAMIN, ALFRED (ed.). *Western European labor and the American corporation.* Washington, The Bureau of National Affairs, 1970, 574 p.

Collections of papers on labour problems in Europe resulting from American-based multi-national corporation. Descriptive sections on labour relations and law, social policy and collective bargaining and on American management and labour relations philosophy.

KINDLEBERGER, CHARLES P. *Business abroad: six lectures on direct investment.* New Haven, Yale University Press, 1969, vii, 225 p.

Multi-national corporations' structure and operations are described and explained. Attitudes of reactions of host countries, developed and developing are discussed. Regulatory, supervisory international institutions and policies are recommended as means of insuring effective and equable activities in the corporations.

KINDLEBERGER, CHARLES P. 'European integration and the international corporation', *Columbia journal of world business*, 1(1), Winter 1966, pp. 65–73.

Examines the question of European economic integration as limited by the E.E.C. and the cartels. Analyses European feelings against the U.S.-based international corporations' ability to cross their boundaries. Reviews the problems for U.S. industry competing in the European community.

KINDLEBERGER, CHARLES P. 'The international firm and the international capital market', *Southern economic journal*, 34, Oct. 1967, pp. 223–230.

Surveys the complex relationships of the international firms and the international capital market. Notes the advantages the American firm has over other national firms in regard to international expansion. Questions whether or not the international corporation and the capital market are of value in view of the effort necessary to form them. Develops an analogy between the adjustment mechanism in the United States and on international level.

KNOPPERS, A. T. 'The multinational corporation in the Third World', *Columbia journal of world business*, 5(4), July–Aug. 1970, pp. 33–39.

Activities of multi-national corporations often tend to clash with political realities of the host governments. At present the future relations between the corporations and developing nations is in doubt. Recommendations of the Pearson and Peterson Commissions especially with regard to incentives, co-operation with local firms, investments and financial assistance are also discussed.

KOLDE, ENDEL J. 'Business enterprise in a global context', *California management review*, 8(4), Summer 1966, pp. 31–48.
Highlights the advantages and challenges in the continuing shift from traditional foreign trade to multi-national industrial and marketing operations.

KOLDE, ENDEL J. *International business enterprise*. Englewood Cliffs, N.J., Prentice-Hall, 1968, viii, 679 p.
Basic text for broader aspects of international corporations includes chapters on general concepts, dynamics of international integration and the environment of developing countries.

KOLDE, ENDEL J.; HILL, R. 'Conceptual and normative aspects of international management', *Academy of Management journal*, 10(2), June 1967, pp. 119–128.
Indicates the administrative adaptations and innovations required by the change from international trade to multi-national operations.

LAZAR, ARPAD VON. 'Multinational enterprises and Latin American integration: a socio-political view', *Journal of inter-American studies*, 11(1), Jan. 1969, pp. 111–122.
Discusses different views held in Latin America concerning the positive and negative roles of multi-national corporation in economic integration. Also examines role and attitudes of the managers and technocrats in relation to economic integration.

LEE, JAMES A. 'Cultural analysis in overseas operations', *Harvard business review*, 44(2), Mar.-Apr. 1966, pp. 106–114.
Perceives the basic cause of international business problems overseas as the unconscious reference to cultural values held by managers working overseas.

LEE, JAMES A. 'Developing managers in developing countries', *Harvard business review*, 46(6), Nov.-Dec. 1968, pp. 55–65.
Problems basic to the foreign environment are reflected in recruitment of local managerial candidates to operate U.S.-owned corporations. Suggestions on how to improve this situation are included. Compares, on the basis of survey materials, attitudes of American and Ethiopian and Pakistani managers. Suggests training programmes should be tailored to meet local problems.

LEVINSON, CHARLES. *Towards industrial democracy – Vers la démocratie industrielle*; 1st International I.C.F. Conference on Industrial Democracy, Frankfurt am Main, 1968.
Growth of multi-national corporation and its role in international production

is examined. Author sees it as the first international institution with wide powers of action and authority. Suggests international trade unions should be increasingly active in promoting worker participation in management.

LITVAK, I. A.; MAULE, C. J. 'Guidelines for the multi-national corporation', *Columbia journal of world business*, July–Aug. 1968, pp. 35–42.

Reviews certain guidelines set up by the Canadian government with respect to multi-national corporations. Illustrates on the example of Canada and U.S. some problems experienced by the host nations especially in the fields of politics and economics.

LUETKENS, WOLF. 'The chemical pacemakers of Germany', *Management today*, Oct. 1968, pp. 102–105, 164–168.

Describes how Hoechst, Bayer and B.A.S.F. expanded into multi-national operations.

MADEHEIM, HUXLEY; MAZZE, EDWARD; STEIN, CHARLES. *International business: essays and articles*. New York, Holt, Rinehart, and Winston, 1963, ix, 228 p.

Presents readings and essays on various areas of international business, including methods of organisation as well as financial operations. Analyses the role of law and government in business enterprises.

MALLES, PAUL. 'The multinational corporation and industrial relations: the European approach', *Industrial relations,* 26(1), 1971, pp. 64–81.

Considers whether the multi-national corporation constitutes a challenge to the industrial relations systems as they have developed in Europe over the last quarter of a century and what response such a challenge found in the trade union movement.

MARSH, J. 'International man and management developments', *Advanced management journal*, 33, Jan. 1968, pp. 11–20.

Concerned with the problem of how to develop management methods in developing countries. Traces the growth of multi-national management and the national management movement. Reflects on upward mobility in management.

MARTYN, HOWE. *International business: principles and problems*. New York, Free Press, 1964, 288 p.

Examines history and growth of international companies and extent of their influence. Suggests methods to involve local persons and capital as necessary reform measures.

MENDERSHAUSEN, H. 'Transnational society versus state sovereignty', *Kyklos*, 22(2), 1969, pp. 251–275.

Discusses conflict between transnational society and nation state, examines multi-national corporation's role and concludes it will not be able to challenge nation state either politically or economically.

MILES, CAROLINE. 'The international corporation', *International affairs*, 45(2), Apr. 1969, pp. 259–268.

## Appendix

Examines nature and operations of multi-national corporations, particularly in U.K. and Europe. Notes that corporations from U.K. are likely to expand internationally especially if entry to the E.E.C. is not secured.

MILLEN, B. H. *The political role of labor in developing countries.* Washington, Brookings Institution, 1963, 148 p.

Presents a typology of trade unions in developing countries and their differences from industrial countries. Indicates that management of foreign-owned business needs to understand political importance of unions in developing countries and to adjust their policies accordingly.

MODEL, LEO. 'The politics of private foreign investment', *Foreign affairs*, 45(4), July 1967, pp. 639–651.

In view of the global character of many American-based corporations, fears and resentments of host country producers and politicians are aroused, particularly if the corporation dominates one of the basic industries of the country. Ways of improving relations are suggested and companies are urged to stimulate investments, technology, and competition.

MODELSKI, G. 'The corporation in world society'. *In: The year book of world affairs, 1968.* London, Stevens, 1968, pp. 64–79.

Compares modern multi-national corporation with earlier European chartered companies. Considers growth and international characteristics of existing corporations and suggests they have a positive role to play in functional international integration.

MOUSSIS, NICOLAS S. 'A propos de Fiat-Citroën: l'entreprise internationale européenne est-elle nécessaire et pourquoi?', *Revue du Marché commun* (117), Nov. 1968, pp. 950–954.

Examines to what extent international firms can accelerate the economic integration in general and more specifically the dynamic expansion of the Common Market. Analysis of the principal factors contributing to the economic growth of national economics, namely: technological progress, optimum allocation of investments and the rational planification of the production process.

*Multinational investment programs and Latin American integration*; a report prepared by Development and Resources Corporation. New York, Inter-American Bank, 1966. 173 p.

Considers Latin American economic integration as inevitable. Specific needs and projects recommended to the Inter-American Bank are discussed. Multinational private companies should provide research, development and incentives.

NEIRINCK, J. D. *The E.E.C. on the eve of the Customs Union*; for presentation at Chicago Loyola University's Business and Law Summer Institute on 'The supranational corporation and Western European labor: lessons for Americans'. Highland Park, Ill., 1968, 98 p.

Reviews structures of the E.E.C. with emphasis on those aspects which will harmonise social policy. Discusses proposals which have implications for labour.

*1985: Corporate planning today for tomorrow's markets.* New York, Business International Corporation, 1967.

Describes plans and policies which should be adopted by companies in order to explore the world markets. Includes practical guidelines covering population trends, possible size of tomorrow's markets, new technology and relations between the international corporation and national governments.

*Organizing for worldwide operations.* New York, Business International Corporation, 1967.

Description of 50 international firms; how they structure and implement organisation plans. Includes case studies and organisation charts.

PENROSE, E. T. (ed.). *The large international firm in developing countries: the international petroleum industry.* London, G. Allen and Unwin, 1968, 311 p.

The history, growth and current policies of international oil industries are presented. Special reference is made to the various governmental attitudes towards such firms, relating directly to their affluence and position in the distributive process. Future control of firms is related to the establishment of international regulations and an 'international income tax' is suggested. General nature and dynamics of the multi-national firm is discussed in detail.

PERLMUTTER, HOWARD V. 'L'entreprise internationale: trois conceptions', *Revue économique et sociale*, 23(2), May 1965, pp. 151–166.

Presents three conceptions of managerial attitudes and organisation of multi-national corporation, ethnocentric, geocentric and polycentric. Speculates on form most suited to possible future conditions.

PERLMUTTER, HOWARD V. 'Nations, syndicats et firmes multinationales', *Analyse et prévision*, 9(4), Apr. 1970, pp. 221–237.

The three key institutions of world society, the nation state, the unions and the firms are not organised yet to deal with the world as a whole. Questions are raised concerning the worldwide development of these institutions. Multi-national enterprises seem best equipped for such geocentric orientation.

PERLMUTTER, HOWARD V. 'Super-giant firms in the future', *Wharton quarterly*, Winter 1968, pp. 8–14.

Depicts 300 companies as industrial leaders by 1985 based on their truly international operations, personnel selection, resources and market. Factors to be considered in an evaluation of their readiness for multi-national expansion are discussed and a profile of the successful company, with its social, political moral and economic obligations, is drawn.

PICKERING, MURRAY. 'The European company', *The banker*, 113, June 1968, pp. 519–525.

A proposed creation of a 'European company' to be achieved by the agreement of E.E.C. countries is discussed. Co-ordination of national laws with

# Appendix

respect to the creation and regulation of corporations is necessary. Questions regarding the possibilities of realising such a plan and its potential usefulness are raised, especially in the light of growing U.S. corporate expansion.

PRINS, D. J. 'International business: a challenge to management and to education', *Management international review*, 8(1), 1968, pp. 123–127.
Summarises a conference on education for international business held at Tulane University in 1967. The need for more planning and co-ordination of individual efforts to train potential world businessmen was stressed. Reports of existing educational projects in this field, concrete proposals relative to course curricula, objectives and methods of presentation were offered.

QUINN, JAMES BRIAN. 'Technology transfer by multinational companies', *Harvard business review*, 47(6), Nov.–Dec. 1969, pp. 147–161.
Sees the multi-national corporation as an important means of transferring technologies. Notes that the Japan and Belgium positive programmes for importing technology can be taken as models. Suggests receiving countries ensure easier access to multi-national companies.

ROBINSON, RICHARD D. 'The global firm-to-be: who needs equity?', *Columbia journal of world business*, 3(1), Jan.–Feb. 1968, pp. 23–28.
Investigates sociological aspects of the multi-national corporation in developing nations. Recognises the need for the parent company to give adequate training of local personnel.

ROBINSON, RICHARD D. *International business policy*. New York, Holt, Rinehart and Winston, 1964, 224 p.
Presents several dimensions of the international firm: historical, legal, economic, political, and environmental. Sketches the historical growth of enterprise and its effect in the non-western societies. Suggests principles which management might use to estimate its impact and adaptations to be made when becoming multi-national.

ROBINSON, RICHARD D. *International management*. New York, Holt, Rinehart and Winston, 1967, 178 p.
Examines the marketing strategy of an international business and financial and legal procedures which can obtain the best results from the new operation. Considers the ownership question of the subsidiaries as well as the problem of labour and supply.

ROCOUR, JEAN-LUC. 'Management of European subsidiaries in the United States', *Management international* (1), 1966, pp. 13–17. (French, German versions in same issue.)
A study of 59 American subsidiaries of European firms reveals a shareholder–management relationship rather than centralised type practised by American companies abroad. The subsidiaries are independent except in financial matters. It is suggested that a truly multi-national approach would help to solve the inherent struggles and tensions.

## Appendix

ROLFE, SIDNEY E. *The international corporation, with an epilogue on rights and responsibilities*; background report presented at the 22nd Congress of the International Chamber of Commerce, Istanbul, 1969. Paris, 1969, 202 p.

Covers all aspects of the multi-national corporation but particularly the legal and financial considerations. Chapters on the multi-national corporation in developing countries and the transfer of technology.

ROSE, STANFORD. 'The rewarding strategies of multinationalism', *Fortune*, Sept. 15, 1968, pp. 100–105.

Surveys a wide range of aspects of a multi-national corporation. Recognises the economic difficulties resulting from devaluation and host government restrictions and discusses personnel policies.

A rougher road for multinationals; special report on multinational companies', *Business week*, Dec. 19, 1970, pp. 57–142.

Multi-national corporations reshape the patterns of production and marketing; they also clash with national interests. The problem for them is to adjust to local situations. The article deals also with trade unions' attitudes and recent trends for co-ordinated strategy in bargaining with the multi-national firms.

RUDLOF, MARCEL. 'La grande firme pluriterritoriale étrangère'. *In: Economie politique du Tiers Monde*. Paris, Cujas, 1967, pp. 252–256.

General description of how foreign firms operate in developing countries and to what extent they can accelerate the economic development of the host countries. Author analyses also the political difficulties which arise due to ideological concepts, using the case of the Universal Suez Canal Company as an example.

RYANS, JOHN K.; BAKER, JAMES C. *World marketing: a multinational approach.* New York, J. Wiley, 1967, 391 p.

A collection of 32 readings by different writers on the cultural, decision-making, financial and communication problems of international marketing.

SERVAN-SCHREIBER, JEAN-JACQUES. *The American challenge.* London, H. Hamilton, 1968, xiv, 210 p.

Examines the American expansion in Europe and envisages, in the technological development and in the important investment in education, the principal factors necessary for the success of European firms in competing with their American counterparts in the world market.

SHEARER, JOHN C. 'Industrial relations of American corporations abroad'. *In:* BARKIN, SOLOMON; DYMOND, WILLIAM; KASSALOW, EVERETT M.; MEYERS, FREDERIC and MYERS, CHARLES A. (eds.). *International labor.* New York, Harper and Row, 1967, pp. 109–131.

Major differences between the labour relations of the U.S. and other advanced countries are identified and discussed. Similar contrasts between U.S. practices and those expected in developing countries are indicated. The implications of these differences for the advancement of the firms' interests and those of the U.S. are considered and reform measures suggested.

## Appendix

SHEARER, JOHN C. *The manpower environments confronting firms in Western Europe*; paper presented on July 11, 1968, at Loyola University's Summer Institute on 'The supranational corporation and Western European labor'. 28 l. (Roneographed.)

Examination of national economic and social policies affecting manpower and also the role of industrial relations and foreign workers. Considers manpower policies within foreign firms in Europe. Suggests training future foreign managers at U.S. universities.

SHEARER, JOHN C. 'The underdeveloped industrial relations of U.S. corporations in underdeveloped countries'. *In:* INDUSTRIAL RELATIONS RESEARCH ASSOCIATION. *Proceedings of the 17th Annual Meeting*, Chicago, 1964. Madison, Wisc., 1965, pp. 56–66.

Argues that U.S. corporations do not apply the same industrial relations and management practices in developing countries as they do in U.S.A. Suggests that the interests of the corporation and host country would be served if best elements in U.S. practice were used in developing countries.

SIMMONDS, KENNETH. 'Multinational? Well, not quite', *Columbia journal of world business*, 1(4), Fall 1966, pp. 115–122.

Examines the position of the foreigner in the multi-national corporation. Contains several charts which serve to illustrate that a foreign manager does not get ahead in the hierarchy of an American firm. Examples of Ford Corporation and Ford U.K. illustrate this problem.

SKINNER, WICKHAM. *American industry in developing economies: the management of international manufacturing*. New York, J. Wiley, 1968, 278 p.

Based on a personal survey of corporations and managers in developing countries the book explores all facets of operations of multi-national companies with particular emphasis on the quality of American managers. Gives specific examples and makes recommendations.

STEINER, GEORGE A. 'La planification dans les sociétés multinationales.' *In: L'entreprise et l'économie du XXe siècle*; étude internationale à l'initiative de FRANÇOIS BLOCH-LAINÉ et FRANÇOIS PERROUX. Paris, Presses Universitaires de France, 1966, v. 2, pp. 417–442.

Comparative study on planning in multi-national corporations of Europe and U.S. Part I describes the nature and the future perspectives of multinational corporations. Part II examines the existing resemblances between European and American corporations in structure and organisation as well as the differences which are mainly conceptual ones.

STEINER, GEORGE A. 'La planification des grandes entreprises multinationales', *Economie appliquée*, 17(2–3), 1964, pp. 441–466.

Comparative study of planning within the large multi-national corporations from both sides of the Atlantic. Describes the nature and prospects of the multinational corporations and the common features and differences in their planning.

*Appendix*

STEINER, GEORGE A.; WARREN, M. CANNON (eds.). *Multinational corporate planning*. New York, MacMillan, 1966, 330 p.

The significance of the multi-national corporate plan was discussed at a meeting of scholars and businessmen. Major environmental forces and their relationship to corporate planning were identified. Includes comparison between American and European company planning.

STRANGE, SUSAN. 'International economics and international relations: a case of mutual neglect', *International affairs*, 46(2), Apr. 1970, pp. 304–315.

Argues that the disciplines of international relations and international economics are not sufficiently integrated. Notes that there is insufficient recent literature on the role of multi-national corporations and direct investment in international relations.

STRAUS, DONALD B. 'Arbitration of disputes between multinational corporations', *The arbitration journal*, 24(4), 1969, pp. 228–234.

Outlines three types of disputes involving multi-national companies which are likely to develop. Suggests the creation of an international arbitration system to deal with such disputes, whether between corporations or between corporations and nations.

TASK FORCE ON THE STRUCTURE OF CANADIAN INDUSTRY. *Foreign ownership and the structure of Canadian industry*. Ottawa, Queen's Printer, 1968, 427 p.

Examines the role of the multi-national corporation in Canada. Finds that extension of U.S. law, foreign policy and balance of payments considerations into Canada via subsidiaries is undesirable and should be controlled. Despite growing international interdependence, a healthy national independence is essential.

THOMPSON, DENNIS. *The proposal for a European company*. London, Chatham House, 1969, 73 p. (European series, No. 13.)

Basically a legal analysis of a draft Statute for a European Company. Examines the historical development of companies in the European Common Market and the legal position of companies under the Treaty of Rome.

'The trade union response to multinational enterprise', *Monthly labor review*, 90(12), Dec. 1967, pp. iii–iv.

Reports on moves to establish 'coordinated councils' of national trade unions to bargain with multi-national corporations. Cites examples of the International Transport Workers' Federation and International Metalworkers' Federation to indicate the trend toward collective bargaining with their common employers on a multi-national basis.

TRADES UNION CONGRESS. *Report of a Conference on International Companies, London, Oct. 1970*. London, 1970, 91 p.

Reports on the trade union response to the growing internationalisation of the enterprise. Discusses trade union experience in collective bargaining, labour management relations and employment questions and suggests possible lines of action.

## Appendix

TURNER, LOUIS. *Invisible empires; multinational companies and the modern world.* London, H. Hamilton, 1970. 228 p.

Offers factual information on growth and organisation of multi-national corporations and argues that despite their power they must change in order to survive. Relates trade union responses to the corporations and makes specific suggestions for international regulations.

UNITED NATIONS ECONOMIC AND SOCIAL COUNCIL. *La société multinationale en Afrique.* [N.p.], 1971. 45 p.

Foreign investments are an important factor in Africa's economic development and multi-national corporations can do much in this respect. The paper discusses the consequences of establishing such corporations in different sectors of African economies. Includes proposals on regional corporation, technical aspects, export, research and governments' attitudes. A thorough knowledge of the operation of multi-national corporations is a necessary pre-requisite for proper Government policy.

UNITED NATIONS CONFERENCE ON TRADE AND DEVELOPMENT. *Trade relations among countries having different economic and social systems.* Geneva, 1969, 26 p. (Roneographed.)

Outlines the principal forms, geographic distribution and recent developments in industrial co-operation between enterprises from socialist and market economies. Notes the possible impact for developing countries.

UNITED STATES. CONGRESS. JOINT ECONOMIC COMMITTEE. *A foreign economic policy for the 1970's; hearings . . . Pt. 4: The multinational corporation and international investment.* Washington, 1970. 213 p.

Congressional hearings on the implications of U.S. investment abroad. Investigates the impact of multi-national corporations on international balance of payments, productivity and technological development. Includes an I.C.F.T.U. statement on multi-national companies and its proposed code of behaviour in international labour relations.

UNITED STATES. DEPARTMENT OF STATE. *Conference on the multinational corporation,* Feb. 1969. Washington, 1969, 63 p.

Report of discussions of leading academic experts and corporate executives. Subjects include economic implications, governmental relations and policy issues concerning the multi-national corporation.

UNITED STATES. DEPARTMENT OF STATE. *The multinational corporation.* Conference held at the Department of State, Feb. 1969; highlights and background papers. Washington, 1969, 1v.

Background papers on predictions of multi-national corporation in the seventies; economic implications and relations with nation state.

VAN GORKUM, P. H. 'La participation des travailleurs dans une S.A. de droit européen', *Synopsis,* 11(117), Jan.-Feb. 1969, pp. 21-28.

Describes the difficulties of creating a European enterprise in the framework of the Common Market, due to different types of workers' participation in these countries. Comparative analysis of the different concepts, methods and objectives of workers' participation in management in the E.E.C. countries.

VERNON, RAYMOND. 'Economic sovereignty at bay', *Foreign affairs*, 47(1), Oct. 1968, pp. 110–122.

Argues that the quality of interpenetration and interdependence of advanced countries has changed with the recent growth of multi-national enterprise presenting challenges of a new order to the nation state. Foresees accommodation of the tensions as a painful and complex process.

VERNON, RAYMOND. *Manager in the international economy*. Englewood Cliffs, N.J., Prentice-Hall, 1968, 429 p.

Places the multi-national corporation and international manager in framework of technical aspects of international trade and finance. Includes information on international payments, inter-governmental agreements on trade and direct investment. Over half book extensive case studies.

VERNON, RAYMOND. 'Multinational enterprise and national sovereignities', *Harvard business review*, 45(2), Mar.-Apr. 1967, pp. 156–172.

Analyses the attitudes of the businessman and the host nation regarding past, present and future roles. Considers the future reactions of the regional groupings towards the multi-national corporate group.

VERNON, RAYMOND. 'The role of U.S. enterprise abroad', *Daedalus*, 98(1), Winter 1969, pp. 113–133.

Reviews the historic development of the modern corporation, with special reference to the multi-national company of American origin. Observes the negative reactions to these enterprises from both developing and advanced countries. Proposes a supranational regulatory agency as a possible aid in reducing tensions.

WATERMAN, MERWIN H. 'Capital sources for multinational companies', *Financial executive*, May 1968, pp. 25–42.

The question of growth of multi-national companies is examined and sources of capital for foreign operations indicated. Suggests that multi-national banks are the most adequate source to meet needs of multi-national companies.

WAYS, MAX. 'Tomorrow's management', *Fortune*, 74, July 1966, pp. 84–87, 148–150.

Sees future managers to be knowledgeable about problems on economic, cultural and political matters. Paternalistic-authoritarian managerial model to be replaced by co-operation: broadened responsibilities at lower levels, greater 'professionalism' in management.

WILKINS, MIRA; HIU, FRANK ERNEST. *American business abroad: Ford on six continents*. Detroit, Wayne State University Press, 1964, 541 p.

History of the Ford Motor Corporation's expansion into a multi-national operation. Of special interest are the shifts in managerial philosophy and policy with regard to foreign operations, as seen in the separate development of Ford-Canada in a loose 'management-shareholder' arrangement and in managerial changes in European countries during the 1930's and after the World War II.

WILLATT, N. 'The multinational unions', *Management today*, Feb. 1971, pp. 70–73, 122–124.

As a response to the growth of multi-national corporations, trade unions now start to organise themselves on multi-national basis. The article describes the research, strategy and tactics of some unions, especially the International Federation of Chemical and General Workers' Unions and the International Metalworkers' Federation.

WILSON, CHARLES. *The history of Unilever: a study in economic growth and social change.* London, F. Cassell, 1954, 2v.

An exhaustive description of the growth of the international operations of a large company, including biographies and management philosophies of founders. Many charts showing historical development of organisation and operations.

WILSON, CHARLES. *Unilever 1945–1965.* London, Cassell, 1968, 291 p.

Analysis of the forces of growth in Unilever. Considers the aspects of management, the men, research and technology, markets, capital and finance. Reviews the importance of each sector in the expansion of the Unilever complex. The second part develops the patterns of growth in the areas of concern: the United Kingdom, Western Europe, Africa and the overseas markets.

YOSHINO, M. Y. 'Administrative attitudes and relationships in a foreign culture', *MSU business topics*, 16, Winter 1968, pp. 59–66.

Emphasises the necessity of the overseas executive to understand the environment of the host country. Points out that many executives have an inadequate background of their own environment. Recognises the need for better home office support and illustrates this through a study of American resident executives in joint ventures in Japan.

ZEFF, S. A. *Business schools and the challenge of international business.* New Orleans, Graduate School of Business Administration, 1968, ix, 292 p.

A collection of papers, comments and panel discussions arising from a 1967 conference on Education for International Business Administration. Includes discussions of business school curriculum strategy and technical assistance in management studies.

ZINKIN, M. 'Multinational companies', *Moorgate and Wall Street*, 1968, 15 p.

The reasons for multi-national expansion are discussed, as well as the natural anxieties of governments about their control. Proper selection of staff is a way to reduce fears.

# INDEX

# Index

## Index

Fraser, Douglas, 160
Free trade areas, xii
*Freie Letzeburger Arbrechtsverbund* (Luxembourg), 327
French Democratic Confederation of Labour, 92
Functionalism, 13
Fürstenberg, Friedrich, 427 n., 429
Future of industrial relations, 388–411: adjustments of trade unions, 389–94; adjustments of multi-national corporations, 394–9; conclusions on adjustment problems, 399–401; management hostility to worldwide bargains, 398–400; unions' militant strategy, 399–400; unions' need to develop organisational structure, 400; welfare considerations, 401–4; multi-national corporations and the State, 404–7; regional economic groupings and multi-national corporations, 407–10; international supervision, 410–11, framework for analysis, 425–46
 conceptual tools, 425–31: propensity of industrial relations to transnationalise, 427–9; unilateral and bilateral transnational relations, 428; environmental factors conducive to transnational industrial relations, 430
 evidence of transnational tendencies, 431–41: multi-national management, 431–3; trade unions, 433–7; the State, 437–9; international organisations, 439–41
 evidence and proposed analytical concepts compared, 441–3: future research requirements, 444–6; scheme of interactions, 445

Galbraith, J. K., 9, 186, 198, 404
García, Antonia, 221
Gelsenkirchener Bergwerke, 53
General Agreement on Tariffs and Trade (GATT), xiii n., 76, 87
General Electric (U.S.A.), 81, 86, 360
General Motors (G.M.), 25–6, 74, 80, 83, 85, 128, 144, 147, 148, 155, 159, 170, 401: and Vauxhall Motor Company, 120; integration in Germany, 365
General Motors (Holding) Company (Australia), wage dispute, 363–4

Geocentrism, 8, 19, 43, 49, 50, 117–18, 129, 130, 132, 343, 406, 417, 426–8: development, 22–3, 28–9, 34–43, 123–6; tables, 36–41
German Democratic Republic: centrally fixed targets, 233; economic system, 229 n.; industrial development, 229 n.
German Confederation of Trade Unions (D.G.B.), 277, 323, 327, 381
Germany (Federal Republic), 127, 324, 326, 327, 330, 334, 337, 347: social security, 302; trade unions, 277–9; wage drift, 373; workers' participation in management, 347, 393
Gloor, Max, 123
Grandjeat, Pierre, 372–3
Group conferences of workers, 91
Group of Ten, 55
Günter, H., 354, 375–8, 382: Introduction, xi–xvi; 'International Collective Bargaining and Regional Economic Integration: Some Reflections on Experience in the E.E.C.', 321–40; 'Summary of Symposium Discussions', 351–422; 'The Future of Transnational Industrial Relations: A Tentative Framework for Analysis', 425–46

Haas, Ernst, 322–3, 441 n.
Haenni, Paul, 360–1
Harrod, Jeffrey, 136, 355, 371–2, 403, 413–17, 438: 'Multi-national Corporations, Trade Unions and Industries Relations: A Case Study of Jamaica', 173–94
Headquarters of worldwide firms, locations of, 27
Hedley (Thomas), 121
Heinz Company, 361
Hoffman, Stanley, 62
Houssiaux, Jacques, xv, 260–1, 358–60, 373–4, 404–9, 429: 'Towards an Extension of Multi-national Corporations of European Origin: Implications for Industrial Relations', 341–50
Hungary, 247: centrally fixed targets, 233; economic system, 229 n., 247–8, 384; fixed, limited and free prices, 234; industrial development, 229 n.;

473